# Charles Olson's Reading

*A Biography*

Ralph Maud

SOUTHERN ILLINOIS UNIVERSITY PRESS
*Carbondale and Edwardsville*

Printed in the United States of America
Edited by Tracey Moore
Designed by Natalia Nadraga


99  98  97  96    4  3  2  1

Library of Congress Cataloging-in-Publication Data
Maud, Ralph.
    Charles Olson's reading : a biography / Ralph Maud.
        p.   cm.
    Includes bibliographical references and index.
    1. Olson, Charles, 1910–1970—Books and reading.   2. Books and
reading—United States—History—20th century.   3. Poets,
American—20th century—Biography.   I. Title.
PS3529.L655Z482   1996
811'.54—dc20                                              94-44403
ISBN 0-8093-1995-0                                       CIP

The paper used in this publication meets the minimum requirements
of American National Standard for Information Sciences—Permanence
of Paper for Printed Library Materials, ANSI Z39.48-1984. ∞

# Contents

# *Abbreviations*

Additional Prose
:   Charles Olson, *Additional Prose*, ed. George F. Butterick (Bolinas: Four Seasons Foundation, 1974).

Arts at BMC
:   Mary Emma Harris, *The Arts at Black Mountain College* (Cambridge: MIT Press, 1987).

Black Mountain Book
:   Fielding Dawson, *The Black Mountain Book* (New York: Croton Press, 1970).

Boer
:   Charles Boer, *Charles Olson in Connecticut* (Chicago: Swallow Press, 1975).

boundary 2
:   Matthew Corrigan, ed., *Charles Olson: Essays, Reminiscences, Reviews, boundary 2*, vol. 2, nos. 1 and 2 (Fall 1973/Winter 1974).

Call Me Ishmael
:   Charles Olson, *Call Me Ishmael* (1947; reprint San Francisco: City Lights, 1958).

Cech
:   John Cech, *Charles Olson and Edward Dahlberg: A Portrait of a Friendship* (Victoria B. C.: University of Victoria English Literary Studies, 1982).

Clarke's list
:   A list of Olson's books at 28 Fort Square, made by John Clarke in August 1965, supplied to George F. Butterick.

Collected Poems
:   George F. Butterick, ed., *The Collected Poems of Charles Olson Excluding the Maximus poems* (Berkeley: University of California Press, 1987).

Corman Correspondence
:   Charles Olson and Cid Corman, *Complete*

*Correspondence 1950–1964*, ed. George Evans, vols. 1 and 2 (Orono: National Poetry Foundation, University of Maine, 1987 and 1991).

*Creeley Correspondence*     George F. Butterick, ed., *Charles Olson and Robert Creeley: The Complete Correspondence*, vols. 1–8 (Santa Barbara: Black Sparrow Press, 1980–87). Vol. 9 edited by Richard Blevins (1990).

Duberman     Martin Duberman, *Black Mountain, An Exploration in Community* (New York: Dutton, 1972)—pagination used is Doubleday Anchor, 1973.

*Fiery Hunt*     Charles Olson, *The Fiery Hunt and Other Plays* (Bolinas: Four Seasons Foundation, 1977).

*Guide*     George F. Butterick, *A Guide to the Maximus Poems of Charles Olson* (Berkeley: University of California Press, 1978).

*Human Universe*     Charles Olson, *Human Universe and Other Essays*, ed. Donald Allen (New York: Grove Press, 1967).

*In Adullam's Lair*     Charles Olson, *In Adullam's Lair* (Provincetown: To the Lighthouse Press, 1975).

*Maps*     *Maps #4: Charles Olson*, ed. George Butterick (1971).

*Maximus*     Charles Olson, *The Maximus Poems*, ed. George F. Butterick (Berkeley: University of California Press, 1983).

*Muthologos*     Charles Olson, *Muthologos: The Collected Lectures and Interviews*, vols. 1 and 2 (Bolinas: Four Seasons Foundation, 1978).

*OLSON*     *OLSON: The Journal of the Charles Olson Archives*, ed. George F. Butterick (University of Connecticut Library, 1974–1978, ten issues).

*Olson/Melville*     Ann Charters, *Olson/Melville, A Study in Affinity* (Berkeley: Oyez, 1968).

# Introduction

My personal testimony of Charles Olson in the years when he was teaching at Buffalo (1963–65) and when I saw him at the Berkeley Poetry Conference (July 1965) and then later in his own kitchen in Gloucester, Massachusetts, is that he was a man whose eye was on the object. His talk and the reading he always drew on were pressed into identifying the true character of the world. It never struck me that the allusiveness was meant to reflect back on the poet's ego in the slightest. It always seemed a very straight act of taking energy from where he got it—books, to a large extent—and adding to this book knowledge the force of his experience, imagination, and powers of expression. He had achieved his long-stated aim: to be of use. Though the record shows that a time was never reached when Olson rested in his reading, at Berkeley in 1965 he said, "I really have no more than to feed on myself" (*Muthologos* 1, 66), and we felt we were in the presence of the man, for our time, almost complete in knowledge, and therefore a great resource for a general moving forward. The present work is an attempt to tell in outline—and in some detail as regards Olson's reading—the story of how this accomplishment came about.

To my own testimony I add the following, all the more convincing for being oddly casual in tone. Boris Aronson, a theater designer who visited Black Mountain College in the first instance only because he was married to the daughter of a professor there, was recorded by Martin Duberman on his impressions. In his book *Black Mountain: An Exploration in Community* (1973), Duberman transcribed what Aronson said of Charles Olson:

I don't recall ever being influenced by anyone in my life as I was with

3

*Flower* and Jane Harrison's *Themis*), he reserved the right to intuit the essence of a book without. Where we can do so succinctly, some indication will be made in what follows of the kind of attention Olson paid to a book.

Perhaps Olson's schoolboy training as a debater had something to do with it, but all his reading was available to him for argument. It wasn't that he was merely "well-read." He was always on the trail of something, the books scattered behind him. Later, with the *Maximus Poems*, he found a form in which daily reading (the "dailies") could find a place, if it could further the argument. It is not the purpose of this volume to do sources in the way that George Butterick has admirably done in his *Guide to the Maximus Poems* (1978) and before that in *Additional Prose* (1974) and in the *OLSON* journal (1974–78). But it would please me to tell of the personal insight I gained on one occasion of the process in which reading was translated into verse. I once visited 28 Fort Square unannounced, climbing the back stair to the only door, through the glass window of which I saw, more suddenly than I expected, the poet sitting at his kitchen table, refrigerator at his back, walls pinned with photographs, clippings, and maps, the light at 6 P.M. of a summer's day flooding in from the southwest—and he was in the act of writing poetry, almost gymnastically, mouthing the words and beating time with his arm. There was a moment when the real offense of the interruption registered on his face, but the recovery was instantaneous. I told him that the secret of "projective verse" had been revealed! This was six months before Olson's death, and there were premonitions of it (talking of visitors, he said, "I'll reply to letters, but my breath's my own"). But three hours passed quickly with news and talk.[5] He said, learning I had just come down from Gaspé, "You should know that what I was working on when you arrived was Francis Parkman and Canada." Parkman's *Count Frontenac and New France* was open on the kitchen table next to a yellow writing pad. *Webster's Collegiate Dictionary* was in evidence. I noticed Whitehead's *Process and Reality* by the table leg, and other volumes on the floor, but couldn't interrupt things to examine them. I got, anyway, a sense of what it was like when people left Olson alone to write, enough to sustain my present conviction that to follow the evidences of Olson's reading—the books he kept, the books he stored or gave away,[6] the books that the poems, essays, and letters reveal he used, the significant articles in magazines he was sent or read at the drugstore counter or whatever (there is so much evidence, and the abundance is to the point)—to follow Olson's movement within these source works is the best way to get into the poems, which, as I witnessed, are often a direct extension of his reading. The life of the poet was a life within books; hence, "Charles Olson's Reading" and "A Biography."

The approach, therefore, is basically chronological, with an effort to discover how Olson's reading played a part in the major movements of his life. George Butterick (in a personal communication) named Will Durant's autobiography, *Transition* (New York: Simon & Schuster, 1927), as a crucial, formative book for Olson, who told him of reading Durant in the library soon after its publication, at the same time as he found some books on sex; he tied his reading of *Transition* to his sexual awakening. The book is also a "portrait of the artist" in its theme of release from a rigid Roman Catholic upbringing, while dedicated to "a Tender Mother and a Perfect Father." New England workingclass socialism is also a theme that would have fired Olson at seventeen.

Olson was keenly aware of his mother's Irish background, and it was this that led him to W. B. Yeats for one of his first college assignments. His father's Swedish side, though in a vague way translated via Gloucester fishermen into Melville's *Moby-Dick*, had a delayed reaction in Olson's late feeling for the Norse: one of his deathbed books was *Myth and Religion of the North*. Meanwhile, Olson was instinctively ruled in his life actions by sympathy with the underdog, which fueled his resistance to Ezra Pound (the elitist), for example, and contributed to a fight with his best friend of the time over Richard Wright's *Black Boy* (1945).

A similar instinctive disregard for the normally accepted comforts of modern life led him to relish poverty while he explored intellectually the failure of Western Civilization. The great leap may have come through acquaintance with *Gilgamesh* as early as 1941 (edition used unknown), an interest raised to a passion ten years later by Frances Boldereff, who sent him S. N. Kramer's Sumerian work, which led to L. A. Waddell, and the dawning of the notion that the gateway out of the futile Modern is backward to the Archaic.

Olson claimed he was "uneducated" at Harvard. He spent many years in libraries following Professor Merk in the Westward Expansion, only to get his greatest insights during six months out of the country in Yucatan (February–July 1951), and ultimately finding the Way was not only further back to the pre-Homeric, and further out

# 1

## *What Didn't Olson Read?*

Olson is on record as having, in his youth, read one Faulkner novel, *Sanctuary*. He told students at Black Mountain College in 1953 that "W. Faulkner might be as good as several claim he is. But except for his short stories (and those solely DR MARTINO, and other tales), I'm not aware that he is." This implies that Olson tried a few Faulkner novels, but we can't be too sure.[1] For if we ask, "What didn't Olson read?" the answer, in a word, is novels.

In this 1953 presentation to his students, Olson is "starting from where you are,"[2] presuming that they are influenced by the prevailing notion that fiction is the dominant form of the twentieth century; he intends to undermine that received opinion. His skeptical response to the proposition that "stream of consciousness made a difference, Joyce, and all that—P-roost, etc." is to invite the students to read Dostoevsky or Poe (or Hugo, or Dickens, or *Gil Blas*) alongside "Faulk (Juice, hamingway," and compare.[3] Perhaps this was a reaction to the "Proust, Joyce, and Mann" atmosphere that had entered the Harvard English Department with Harry Levin in the years Olson was there (1936–39), and from which Olson had veered away into the new American Civilization program. Olson stopped reading Mann's *Joseph* series after the second volume: "he is a *great fatuity*, Mr. Mann, a master without life."[4] He had been reading Proust and Mann as part of an attempt at "tracing the soundings of the Pacific of the unconscious," as he put it in a letter to Waldo Frank of 12 January 1940. But this is the last we hear of these authors.

James Joyce took longer to wrestle down. Frances Boldereff was a powerful advocate for Joyce. Her books on Joyce came later, but her claim on Olson's attention in 1950 made him "prowl again around the dotus's *History*. And then for good measure, "add today's paper, any edition,[14] including the Black Mt NEWS." Knowing how to read newspapers means we needn't travel as much as Herodotus did.

Olson early developed a preference for nonfiction, witness the fact that he chose to review Hemingway's expository *Death in the Afternoon* (1932) for his college literary magazine. He had read all the preceding fiction, and mentions it: *In Our Time, Torrents of Spring, The Sun Also Rises, Men Without Women,* and *A Farewell to Arms.* He is even willing to say that the bullfight material of *Death in the Afternoon* would have been better used "in a more suitable medium": the "artistically perfect" short stories.[15] But in the end it is not Hemingway's short stories that survive the years. Of the two Hemingway books found in Olson's library, one was the nonfiction *Green Hills of Africa* (New York: Permabooks, 1956). That the other was *For Whom the Bell Tolls* (New York: Scribner, 1940) does not gainsay the proposition that Olson had a leaning toward fiction that was also primarily documentation.

Fielding Dawson reported the following exchange with Olson at their first meeting at Black Mountain in 1949:[16]

> "Mr. Olson, how do you like Wolfe?"
> "No good, bad on public morals."
> "Saroyan?"
> "No good."
> "Scholem Asch?"
> "No good."
> "Why?" He saw the questioned and puzzled look on my face and he said, "Every dog has his own fleas."

An endnote at this point seems the best place to list some of the fleas that we know bit Olson on one fleeting occasion or another. This list is limited to those stray novels actually found on Olson's bookshelves.[17] That there were many other bites is indicated, for instance, by a letter to Creeley on 8 October 1952 where Olson says that during that current baseball World Series he is reading "a novel a night": "And pocketbook crap (not the equal of the dizzy stuff I read Lerma (out of the shrimp boat's library, the Ek-wat-tor): Fitzgerald, Simenon, Mauriac, even. . . . One night, sickened, riz up by reading Mill, on Liberty! And then, an afternoon, Patchen's 'new poems.' How abt that!"[18]

One novelist who was more than a fleabite was Theodore Dreiser, but it is not clear when he came on the scene (perhaps not until Harvard, when F. O. Matthiessen's interest in Dreiser might have infected his graduate student). Olson's copy of *Twelve Men* (New York: Modern Library, 1928) is dated "Cambridge June 1937" and *The "Genius"* (New York: Boni & Liveright, 1923) has a similar signature. *American Tragedy* (which we have no record of Olson owning) was quoted in a manuscript entitled "the mother acquires," dated at Storrs as "ca. 1936–39." But Olson did not otherwise write of Dreiser; he appears to have mentioned *Dawn* ("Newspaper days") in a lecture at Black Mountain College on 27 May 1952;[19] but the only Dreiser he actually kept in his library to the end was *The Financier* (New York: Harper, 1912), having deposited *Twelve Men* and *The "Genius"* with Jean Kaiser in the late fifties with other volumes he did not feel the need to have around.

Let us not suppose that Olson was particularly happy, for instance, to read through *New Directions in Poetry and Prose*, vol. 12 and find that all the fiction was not to his taste. Writing to Cid Corman on 10 June 1951, he sympathized with the problem of finding good prose to print in *Origin*:

> For most of ND XII is made up of narrative which is nothing more than de Maupassant (Elliott Stein's Confessions of a Young Insomniac), necrophilism (bad Poe: Paul Bowles' Dona Faustina—and, a curious combination of same & realism, John Hawkes' Death of an Airman), and WW Jacobs' The Monkey's Claw! (perhaps the most skillful of all, Jack Dunphy's Under the African Trees).
>
> I mean, literally, that the *forms* of narrative have reacted back from the advances of Joyce, say, to these earlier & poorer men, and at the same time, the substance is without any of the rationale which made de Maupassant, Poe, and Jacobs excusable. For these men—all, more or less, creatures of Tennessee Williams' invocation—are ducking their own times, and choosing to make public their own psychic derangements as though they were thus proving the time![20]

Olson was looking for some coolness in prose, and he was finding it only in Robert Creeley's yet unpublished scripts, and previously in certain expository prose. He shared an old enthusiasm with Creeley in a letter of 7 April 1951:

> Or if you ever meet up with a diffident bird named Clarence Graham,

# 2

# *The Boy Historian*
# *and Anecdotes of Late Wars*

"There is a friend here who has a car," Olson writes to a correspondent on 24 July 1950, "and we have been using Sundays (Constanza's only day off) to make quick trips to the extraordinary meadows and rivers on which the Civil War was fought: a week ago Harper's Ferry and Antietam, or, what I prefer the Rebel name of Sharpsburg; before that Manassas. And yesterday, four of the fields of the terror, Fredericksburg, Chancellorsville, Wilderness, Spottsylvania Court House." He is moved to remark of these battlefields "how they sit now, as they did, 100 years ago, a few monuments, but crops, fishing rivers, the same stone bridges, and wilderness roads, even such churches as Salem Church, Wilderness Church, standing where they were."[1] Olson intended to put these excursions to use in a book, anticipating the centenary of the Civil War, "to cut through all propaganda usage of that centenary, and try to say the war as it was—an old dream of mine."[2]

From the autobiographical piece, "The Post Office," we see this antithetical dream as very early indeed:

> It was the Matthew Bradys my father gave me as a child that have influenced my sense of the past to this day. I have the set. It was the *Review of Reviews* issue of the *Photographic History*.[3] They came, by subscription, I suppose, as thin, large, blue paperbound pamphlets which I could lay open page by page on the floor. The photographs cured me that early of romantic history. I preferred Brady to the colored frontispiece each one carried of some fool's oil on Grant at Lookout Mt or Burnside at Nashville. I could take that as narrative in Joseph Altsheler, *The Rock*

*of Chickamauga,* say. Or in the annual play my father made it a ritual to take me to, even though, each year I ducked behind the back of the seat in front of me when the volley came which cut the hero down. It was year after year, one play, "The Drummer Boy of Shiloh." (*The Post Office,* pp. 26–27)

Olson probably never bothered to read the text of *The Drummer Boy,* which styled itself "a new military allegory" but which was a jingoistic melodrama. There were plenty of editions; one was published in Worcester, Massachusetts, where Olson was growing up.[4] He undoubtedly read some of the Civil War Altshelers, which catered to the normal schoolboy.[5] But the boy-historian had already had his eyes opened: "Once Brady had taught my eyes, I broke through the painted surfaces of war. The dead in Devil's Gulch at Gettysburg, this was something I was not shown at school. Or horses puffed up on a field huge beside the corpses of men or humped in a ditch along some Wilderness road" (*The Post Office,* p. 27). We are here in the presence of the old adage: the child is the father of the man, Olson already a realist at age six. Thirty years later, ploughing through the massive Freeman biography of General Lee, he was the same young realist, commenting to a correspondent about this four-volume book: "you never come to the end of the unrelieved facts. The book presents the problem books did when you were a kid: did Lee ever pee?"[6]

When Olson came to write his one poem on the Civil War, "Anecdotes of the Late War"[7] (written by February 1955, the prose book for the centenary become a poem), beneath this scornful, ironic title, he announced the two alternatives for America: "the lethargic vs violence." Being fathered in the way we have seen, he obviously plumped for lethargy, which meant that U. S. Grant could be presented as the tentative hero of the poem. And the romantic civilians ridiculed:

> going out to Bull Run looking for
> Waterloo. the
> diorama. And having to get the fastidious hell home
> that afternoon
> as fast as the carriage horses
> can't make it (Lee Highway
> littered with broken
> elegances.[8]

"The story of the Civil War, if truthfully told, sounds like the group experiences of a nation of madmen": one hears this sentiment under the surface of Olson's poem. There is no evidence that he read W. E. Woodward's *Meet General Grant*, though this 1928 book was reissued in 1946. It is likely he did, for Olson certainly admired Woodward's *Years of Madness* (1951), from the first page of which the above quotation is taken. *Years of Madness* must have been in Olson's mind when he recommended Woodward to Edward Dorn in "A Bibliography for Ed Dorn." He subsequently got Harvey Brown to reprint it in his Frontier Press series.[9] Olson liked Woodward's economic approach, viewing the war in terms of cotton and land; witness the statement in the poem: "you don't get Grant except as you find what he was . . . to real estate," adding the thought that this is what "George Washington also comes alive at," and thereby turning our attention to another of W. E. Woodward's biographies that he read: *George Washington: The Image and the Man* (1926, reissued 1946),[10] and to anecdotes of another war.

The American Revolution was de-romanticized for Olson when he had a homework assignment on George Washington: "The essay was too much for me and I suddenly threw it up in disgust." Again, his father was there to help. "What he had to say about me and George Washington was: do it. And I did it. It took" (*Post Office*, pp. 25–26). Perhaps the young Olson found a way to approach a truth about Washington that Woodward's *George Washington* would later confirm.

The War of Independence was not the nagging thing to Olson that the Civil War was. Being American, and not British, was undoubtedly something to be taken for granted. After a trip during Easter 1949 to Yorktown, the site of the surrender of the British forces, Olson wrote to a friend that he found the place "charming." Next day he wrote "At Yorktown," a poem evocative of a charming afternoon.[11]

The 300th anniversary of the settlement of Gloucester came in 1923, three years after the Plymouth celebrations that Olson attended with his father. The rivalry between the ideologies of these two settlements could have been felt by a thirteen-year-old: the puritan orthodoxy of the south-of-Boston theocracy contrasting with the opportunistic fishing foothold north of Boston. The "military" clash between them, involving Miles Standish vs. Captain Hewes, is given an "epic" place in "Maximus, to Gloucester, Letter 11," where the plaque is quoted in full:

On this site in
1623
A company of fishermen and farmers from Dorchester, Eng.
under the direction of Rev. John White founded
The Massachusetts Bay Colony

from that time the fisheries the oldest industry in the commonwealth
have been uninterruptedly pursued from this port

here in 1625 Gov. Roger Conant by wise diplomacy
averted the bloodshed between contending factors
one led by Myles Standish of Plymouth
the other by Capt. Hewes
a notable exemplification of arbitration
in the beginnings of New England

This "Tablet Rock" is something young Olson knew to play on: "the rock I know by my belly and torn nails." And once, on top of the rock, he came upon a troupe rehearsing for the Historical Pageant, Captain John Smith meeting the Turkish princess Tragabizanda:

Historie
come bang into the midst of
our game!

No members of the Olson family are named in the program as having taken part in the dramatizations, nor would Olson have participated in the "School Children's Essay Contest," being at school in Worcester, but the family was in Gloucester for the actual celebration 25–30 August 1923, and no doubt attended the Historical Pageant on the 28th and witnessed the following as announced by James R. Pringle, the local writer:[12]

Historical Pageant, *auspices Mr. James R. Pringle*   8:00 P.M.
THE GLOUCESTER PAGEANT
The Story of the Most Colorful Fishing Town in America portrayed at the Beautiful Stage Fort Ampitheatre during The Tercentenary Celebration.
It was on this beautiful seashore reservation, fronting Gloucester bay, that many of the historical scenes that will be reproduced occurred. Here it was that the Dorchester fishermen founded the Massachusetts Bay colony in 1623.

The Pageant drama "Gloucester", epitomizes in ten epilogues the history of the most picturesque seaport in America, a community which has carried along in this country for three centuries the perilous business of fishing. Wherever men read of the daring of the men of the seven seas, Gloucester holds a commanding place.

The most prominent of the early navigators of history have visited its shores. Thorwald, the Norseman, was buried on shore. Gosnold and Pring came in 1602 and 1603. Champlain was here in 1605 and 1606 and named the place Beauport, the Harbor Beautiful. He also had a run in with the Indians.

Then in 1614 came Capt. John Smith, he of Pocahontas fame. He named the place Cape Tragabigzanda and the three islands off the southeast coast, Straitsmouth, Thachers, and Milk, the three Turks Heads. As a soldier of fortune in the Austrian army he challenged three Turks to mortal combat, defeating and beheading them, hence the three Turks Heads. Captured by the Turks, he was aided to escape by the Turkish Princess, Tragabigzanda, hence the name of his benefactress for the cape which Prince Charles changed to Cape Ann in honor of his mother, Anne of Denmark. In 1623 Rev. John White, rector of St. Peters church, Dorchester, England, raised L3000 and sent a company of fishermen and farmers to found a colony in New England. The departure of this colony with the whole village turning out on the green, the gentry mounted and the ladies of quality in sedan chairs, the children around the maypole, booths, merry Andrews, etc. will furnish one of the finest examples of pageantry ever seen in this country. Then comes the landing at Stage Fort with the clash between Capt. Hewes and Myles Standish with Roger Conant acting as peacemaker, picturesquely depicted with Hewes' semi-piratical gang singing old Devon sea chanties and mending nets.

This respect for history exhibited by a whole community must have affected the impressionable boy and added to the push given him by the books in the house, which if the direction of the later *Maximus Poems* on migration are any indication, included such items that we find in Olson's library as *An Historical Account of the Circumnavigation of the Globe* and *An Historical and Descriptive Account of Iceland, Greenland, and the Faroe Islands*, published in Harper's Family Library, 1844 and 1854 respectively. What other books were available to young Charles, beyond those already mentioned, are listed in the appendix entitled "Schoolboy Books."

# 3

## A Model Student—
## Phi Beta Kappa, Wesleyan '32

All the evidence indicates that Olson at Wesleyan University was very well-behaved.[1] Isn't it the lot of the immigrant's son not to know better than to do well in everything, both academic and extracurricular activities? So . . . what did one have to do to get one's A at Wesleyan in 1928–32? Read a lot, yes. But not secondary sources, at least not for Wilbert Snow. Olson's Yeats paper for Snow's modern poetry course, probably spring 1930, took care to have no references to Yeats criticism. On the contrary, after a personal introduction (his "kinship with the Irish race" had led him to seek out the Celts in English Literature[2]), the thirty-four page paper is a very direct reaction to the primary texts.

It is quite likely that the young Olson at this time invested in at least three Yeats purchases: *Early Poems and Stories* (1925), *Later Poems* (1928), and *The Tower* (1928).[3] This would bring him up-to-date on the poems—except that, alert beyond any professor's wildest dreams, the watchful scholar had seen in *The New Republic* of 2 October 1929 "a poem of Yeats's later years that I find far superior to anything he has written since the beginning of the last decade, 'Three Things.' " He quotes it in full in his paper, and adds a personal note: "I found it one day during the Christmas season and I haven't got it out of my head since then. I hope I never shall." And then a critical note: "My only regret is that Yeats did not let the poem 'age' a bit more until he had found a different diction in the last two lines the bone speaks." Without reading further, one can well understand why, in his memorial after Olson's death, Wilbert Snow might say: "I still have that essay, and cherish it."[4]

A year later, at the end of his Junior Year, Olson did something that might have been a bit risky; he wrote his term paper for a drama course in the form of a stage script with a flourish of a title page:

An Original New and Audaciously Aboriginal
Erratic Operatic, Historico-plagiaristic,
Pre-patriotic Extravaganza,
being a Per-Version of Ye Trewe
Historie of the American Stage
A CONTEMPORARY NOTE
or
THE DRAMA OF THE 50's
ambling thro'
TWO ACTS
and
SEVERAL SCENES
by Charles J. Olson, Jr.

But the piece was so thoroughly, extravagantly researched that there was really no risk. It is here, for the first time, that we get a sense of the fleetness of foot that later distinguished his Melville research; in compiling a bibliography of John Broughan ("the only one ever made"), Olson picked up items "from Wesleyan, Harvard, Yale, American Antiquarian Society (Worcester), Worcester Public Library, Watkinson Library (Hartford), Hartford Public Library." The main titles in the annotated bibliography are: Laurence Hutton, *Curiosities of the American Stage* (1891): "This is the most interesting and useful book of all"; Meade Minnigerode, *Fabulous Forties* (1924): "A fascinating book based on a great body of reading"; George C. Odell, *Annals of the New York Stage*, vols. 3–7 (1928–31): "These 'tomes' are absolutely necessary to any study of this period. Truly remarkable"; Constance Rourke, *American Humor* (1931): "An excellent book, paying the first modern homage to burlesque and minstrelsy." And so it goes. Olson pulls it off.[5]

"In Professor Alec Cowie's American literature class," Wilbert Snow recalls in his memorial of Olson, "he wrote an essay on George Herbert's influence on the poetry of Ralph Waldo Emerson which was so excellent that Cowie gave it the only A plus Cowie ever gave in his life." Only fragments of this paper exist in the Olson Archives, but one striking footnote predicts future attentions: "Emerson owned three volumes of Herbert (1) Poems (2) Poetical Works (3) The Temple. Through the kindness of Edward W. Forbes of the Fogg Art Museum I am able to record that these are not listed among the volumes found to be annotated by Emerson."[6] It would not be long before Olson would be making widespread inquiries of the same order concerning Melville's reading, and turning up amazing results in his search.

First, however, we must consider two very straight term papers, "Literary Criticism in Emerson" and "Whitman and the Orient," before turning to a very straight M.A. thesis, "The Growth of Herman Melville, Prose Writer and Poetic Thinker." Or perhaps, after acknowledging their demonstration of Olson's proficiency in handling conventional scholarly sources,[7] we can move quickly to concentrate on those occasions in his thesis research when he went beyond the call of duty.[8]

Immediately, we are flabbergasted—what other word can one invoke, being presented with "the first complete bibliography of Herman Melville ever attempted," comprising the first thirty pages of this M.A. thesis? The separate works in chronological order are even presented in proper bibliographical form, with a slash (/) indicating the start of each new line of a title page. "All the major libraries of the east, including the lists of the Library of Congress have been used" (p. i). Besides listing everything by and on Melville in print, Olson obtained knowledge of eight theses either completed or in progress, and contacted Birss of Columbia and Anderson of Duke about forthcoming research. Section 7 of the bibliography, "All The Letters of Herman Melville, Collected and Uncollected, Now Known To Exist," refers to three unpublished collections of letters (N.Y. Public Library, Yale, and in private hands) and seven publications:[9]

1. 4 letters in Hawthorne, Julian. *Hawthorne and His Wife* 2 v. Cambridge, James R. Osgood and Company 1884, I, pp. 385–400 and p. 475.
2. 2 letters in Lathrop, Rose Hawthorne. "The Hawthornes in Lenox." Century Magazine 49: pp. 89–90, November, 1894.
3. 8 letters in The Nation & The Athenaeum (London) 29: 712–713, August 13, 1921.
4. 16 letters, in whole or in part, in Minnigerode, Meade: *Some Personal Letters of Herman Melville and A Bibliography*. N.Y. and New Haven and Princeton. The Brick Row Book Shop, Inc. 1922. This volume is abbreviated in the text as "Minnigerode."
5. 48 letters, in whole or in part, in *Family Correspondence of Herman Melville, 1830–1904. In the Gansevoort-Lansing Collection*, Ed. by Paltsits, Victor Hugo. N.Y. New York Public Library, 1929.
6. 1 letter in New England Quarterly 2: 296–307, April, 1929.

7. 1 letter in American Art Association, Anderson Galleries, Inc., Sale
   Catalogue Number 3911, frontispiece and p. 9, April 29, 1931.

All this preliminary bibliography is exceedingly impressive, but
perhaps not more so than the agile allusiveness of the text. Our job is to
give an account of the enormous amount of reading evidenced by the
thesis without being tedious, that is, without being gulled into assum-
ing that everything mentioned has been read. Let us skim and pinpoint
the allusions with some of the casualness with which Olson inserted
them. In his introduction, Olson states "boldly" (his word) that "the
position of Melville with Whitman, Thoreau, Hawthorne, Emerson,
and Poe is assumed." This takes care of the American classics. In the
body of the thesis there are the following allusions: to Samuel Butler's
John Pontifex[10] (as similar to Melville's father in mediocrity, pp. 3–4);
to Tom Moore's *Lalla Rookh* and to William Beckford's *Vathek*
(Melville's earlier writing akin to, p. 9); to Samuel Johnson's *Rasselas*
(who would not have left the Happy Valley of *Typee*, p. 18); to Emer-
son's essays (similar uplift to *Typee*, p. 18); to Homer's Lotus Eaters (re
*Typee*, p. 19); to Defoe's *Robinson Crusoe* (merely boyhood reading, no
influence, p. 21); to Stevenson, La Farge, London, Maugham, and
O'Brien (as "never equalling their literary father's *Typee*," which is
"Rousseau's dream come true," p. 21); to Eugene O'Neil's *Mourning
Becomes Electra* (its reference to *Typee*, p. 22); to Smollett (influence on
*Omoo*, p. 32, "rambles through" *Redburn*, p. 84); to Fielding (better at
synthesis, p. 38); to Robert Burton and to Thomas Browne ("brought
this to pass," i.e., a passage in *Mardi*, pp. 56–57, Browne predominates
in *Pierre*, p. 166); to Swift's Gulliver (regarding satire in *Mardi*, p. 59); to
Peele's *Old Wives' Tale* (which Melville had not read, p. 64); to Swin-
burne's "Hymn to Proserpine" and "Nephelidia" (a "straining" style
in *Mardi*, p. 65); to Matthew Arnold of "The Better Part" (who found
the same answer, p. 74); to Hemingway ("conveying sensation through
words," p. 85); to the *Iliad* (regarding catalogue of ships in *White-Jacket*,
p. 100); to Yeats ("Melville had a sword upstairs, as Yeats would say,"
p. 102); to *The Mahabarata* (as a measure of *Moby-Dick*'s epic quality, p.
120); to the Russian novels of the nineteenth century (likewise, p.
122)—*War and Peace* specifically mentioned (p. 124); to Oedipus, Sam-
son, and Lear (regarding Ahab, p. 130)—and Satan in *Paradise Lost* (p.
131); to De Quincey, Newman, Pater, and Ruskin ("flowing periods,"
p. 134); to Charles Lamb (similarly chained to daily work, p. 153); to

Hardy and Meredith (affinities with *Pierre*, which "precedes the Goncourt brothers and Zola," p. 157); to Faulkner (the ending of *Pierre* "out-Faulkners Faulkner," p. 158); to Conrad (who wrote nothing as fine as "Benito Cereno," p. 172); to *Apologia Pro Vita Sua, Critik der Reinen Vernunft,* and *Dialogues* (*The Confidence-Man* is Melville's these, p. 173); to Aristotle's definition of tragedy (regarding *Billy Budd*, p. 176); to Tolstoy (a parallel to Melville "in many ways," p. 178); to Wordsworth and Coleridge (who turned to religion whereas Melville had the "strength to go on questioning," p. 178).

As they say of the Ph.D. oral exam, "You'll never know as much again." Olson did not, later, display this kind of knowledge; and indeed, his library as we know it reflects very little of it. Not even *War and Peace* was found on his shelves. The literal fact is that, of all these references, the only author who survived—along with Homer, Shakespeare, Yeats and Hemingway—was Robert Louis Stevenson and his *In the South Seas* (New York: Scribner, 1898).

# 4

## At Once Sane and Sensitive: Olson Before Dahlberg

For Olson, meeting Edward Dahlberg on 9 August 1936 was an event of such momentum that we might look back on all that had gone on before, intellectually, as exploration of the ease and roominess of a cocoon. In *A Guide to the Maximus Poems* (p. 421), Butterick passes on the story, as told to him by Olson, of Willem de Sitter's visit to Wesleyan to lecture on "The Size of the Universe" on 29 October 1931, and Olson "walking late into the lecture from debating practice and comprehending immediately, to his own amazement, all that de Sitter had to say. Indeed, notes taken by Olson during the lecture survive inside the front cover and on the flyleaf of his copy of Foster's *Argumentation and Debating*,[1] which he apparently had with him that evening!" This is a prelapsarian world, in which you can come from varsity soccer to the newspaper editorial board, and where you can meet Vachel Lindsay, Carl Sandburg, W. B. Yeats, and Robert Frost in your professor's living room.[2] For Christmas, you ask for Fowler's *Dictionary of Modern English Usage*.[3] Safe and sound. Wearing *socci* you stride the stage to applause and write your first tragedy in the manner of Synge.[4] Though you have to work summers, you "manage a little reading—'Alice' again, Rabelais, Radiguet, Crane, and a fine bit of criticism—'Discovering Poetry'—by Elizabeth Drew, a woman at once sane and sensitive."[5] You write your professor that you think he would enjoy this latter book. Why not? He has recommended to you George Saintsbury.[6]

From the record of Olson's diaries, the first book of poems he admired was Padraic Colum's *Poems* (New York: Macmillan, 1932), read 11 September 1932 (not owned). Auden's *Poems* (New York: Random House, 1934) was bought and read in the early summer of 1935. In

January 1936 he bought Marianne Moore's *Selected Poems* (New York: Macmillan, 1935). Within this spectrum of current poetry, we can fill in, for this period, only one other name: Conrad Aiken, whom Olson heard in a reading in the Poetry Room, Lamont Library, Harvard: "He's so strikingly different from the idea of him you have from his books—so old and bald and heavy amidships, so little Punch and so much John Bull. But when he opens his sceptical mouth and turns his large saucer eyes upon you he's the Aiken of the Preludes—and 'Landscape West of Eden.' The latter's his new and exciting poem which you probably saw in 'American Poetry Journal' for March."[7] And Olson adds, in this letter to Wilbert Snow, Palm Sunday 1934, that "Delacey at the Dunster Bookstore talks of having Conrad Aiken and myself to lunch this week." Other poetry readings and other lunches have gone unrecorded.

What else, B.D. (Before Dahlberg)? Two: Emily Dickinson and Edgar Allan Poe. Olson's copy of *The Complete Poems of Emily Dickinson* (Boston: Little, Brown, 1924) was, on the evidence of the flyleaf, passed on to him in 1930 by his girl friend Barbara Denny, who had had it since publication. Olson read it in college—little bits of the *Wesleyan Argus* remain in the book as bookmarks. When *Letters of Emily Dickinson*, edited by Mabel Loomis Todd, came out in a "New and Enlarged Edition" from Harper in 1931, Olson obtained a copy and marked it up extensively, obviously very intrigued with the obliqueness of her unusual everyday diction.[8] Of the ten-volume *Complete Works of Edgar Allan Poe* (New York: Fred de Fau, 1902), vols 2, 4, 5, 6, 9, and 10 survived in Olson's library.[9] Annotations in two of the volumes indicate that they were read while Olson was staying with Wesleyanite John Finch in Cambridge in March 1934. In vol 10, "Read: 3/11/34—after J F & I tried some!" appears to refer to treatises on cryptography in Harvard Library referred to by Poe. Olson was having fun, B.D.

If the central core of this world contained Dickinson and Poe, along with Melville, Hawthorne, and Whitman, what were the outside parameters? On the emergent side, we have the books brought up with him from Worcester Classical High School: George Willis Botsford, *A History of Greece for High Schools and Academies* (New York: Macmillan, 1899), Rollin D. Salisbury, *Physiography for High Schools* (New York: Holt, 1908), and Willis Mason West, *The Ancient World* (Boston: Allyn and Bacon, 1904).[10] Then basics, such as the Everyman edition of *Shorter Novels*, vol. 1, *Elizabethan & Jacobean* (London: J. M. Dent; New

York: Dutton, 1929), introduced, by the way, by George Saintsbury. (Nashe's *Unfortunate Traveller* is heavily marked in Olson's copy.) Besides Saintsbury, providing Olson with literary "know-how" was Æ (George William Russell), *Song and Its Fountains* (1932) and John Galsworthy, *The Creation of Character in Literature* (1931), though Olson wasn't dependent on Brits, being acquainted with Norman Foerster's *American Criticism* (1928), Alfred Kreymborg's *Our Singing Strength* (1929), and Ludwig Lewisohn's *Expression in America* (1932). Another pillar of Olson's intellectual world was held up at this time by Frank Thilly's *A History of Philosophy* (New York: Holt, 1929).[11]

There was nothing radical to disturb the innocuousness of all this until Randolph Bourne's *History of a Literary Radical* (1920), one of the first books that Dahlberg talked to Olson about, before giving him a copy of it.[12] In the memorial introduction to this volume, Van Wyck Brooks speaks of Bourne's "intense and beautiful desire . . . for a new fellowship in the youth of America as the principle of a great and revolutionary departure in our life, a league of youth, one might call it, consciously framed with the purpose of creating out of the blind chaos of American society, a fine, free, articulate cultural order" (pp. xi–xii). No exile and cunning here. The authors Olson jots down in his journal after meeting Dahlberg are (after Lenin, Gorky, and Marx) heavily weighted toward the indigenous Left: Randolph Bourne, Charles A. Beard, James Oneal, and A. M. Simons, the list given the heading: "to reduce my socio-politico-economic naivete."[13] Possibly Dahlberg's very first book-gift to Olson was Alexander Berkman's *Prison Memoirs of an Anarchist* (New York: Mother Earth Publishing Association, 1912)[14]—a book not likely to have been pushed at him later, for Dahlberg was increasingly cutting himself off from former Left connections, as indicated by a later entry in Olson's journal that "Dahlberg nudges"

1. Laocoon
2. Frazer
3. Frank, Waldo
      America Hispana
      Rediscovery of Am.
4. Harrison, Jane
      Ancient Art & Ritual
   Migel de Unamuno
      Tragic sense of Life
      The soliloquies & Conversations of Don Quixote.[15]

Waldo Frank is the representative here of the Bourne radicalism, the *New Republic* Left. He was still writing, and Olson had an active correspondence with him during 1938–42, reading many of his books both before and after meeting him in New York.[16] But Dahlberg's list is a widening, and includes one name of future importance: Jane Harrison, whom Olson will later marry (as it were).

So we have a sequence of symbolic gifts. In addition to the two already mentioned: Kenneth Fearing's *Poems* (New York: Dynamo, 1935), praised by Dahlberg in his introduction for its "Marxian lucidity" and "affirmative Communist statement"; R. W. Postgate's *Out of the Past: Some Revolutionary Sketches* (New York: Vanguard, 1926), sent to Olson as late as May 1938; and Stendhal's *On Love* (New York: Brentano's, 1915), inscribed to Olson, 23 August 1940.[17] There was also possibly Theodore Gomperz, *The Greek Thinkers* (London: John Murray, 1901), four volumes, a hefty push.[18] This sequence of signposts suggests the benefit to Olson in being taken up by a Dahlberg already looking back on his socialism. Dahlberg required Olson to grasp instantly this crucial element of recent American past, and then dragged him on immediately to an individualistic, nonsectarian viewpoint. "He has been a liberator," Olson wrote of Dahlberg in a letter to Waldo Frank, 13 March 1939. "I respect the arc of his life and sight even if I too find it limited. You see, I have a gain in my own unshaped and emergent self."

On the endpapers of the Modern Library *Moby-Dick* Olson used in college, he wrote himself a note: "Lovejoy 'The Great Chain of Being' "—referring to Arthur O. Lovejoy's classic work, just delivered as the William James Lectures at Harvard in 1933, and later published as *The Great Chain of Being: A Study in the History of Ideas* (Cambridge: Harvard University Press, 1936). Olson never came to own the book. Dahlberg intervened. Someone who might have been tempted into a career as a historian of ideas suddenly realized that he was meant to be a historian of realities.

# 5

## *Melville's Reading: The Displaced Dissertation*

But for Dahlberg, Olson might have become a Harvard professor of English, famous for work on Melville's sources, just as John Livingston Lowes was for Coleridge's, George Lyman Kittredge was for Chaucer's, and Perry Miller was for the sources of Puritan thought.[1] It was F. O. Matthiessen who brought Olson to Harvard for graduate work in the fall of 1936; he had been impressed when Olson had walked into Harvard Library with some ninety-five of Melville's actual books that one of Melville's granddaughters had entrusted him with after he had persuaded her to donate them. Matthiessen immediately transcribed the annotations in Melville's Hawthorne volumes for his *American Renaissance* (1941), where he acknowledged "Olson's generosity in letting me make use of what he has tracked down in his investigation of Melville's reading."[2] Matthiessen said that he had been "stimulated by Olson's vigorous and imaginative essay,"[3] that is, by "Lear and Moby-Dick," published in the first issue of *Twice A Year* (Fall–Winter 1938), an article that had been an academic term paper for Matthiessen before Dahlberg got at it.

Melville's Shakespeare—that, at least, got done and out. How far did Olson go toward a comprehensive reading of Melville's reading? In his M.A. thesis, Olson called the chapter "Dreams" in *Mardi* an "astounding assembly of writers and thinkers that is overwhelming": "As students of Melville's growth, we con the list and note the qualities he finds significant in each: Homer, Anacreon, Hafiz, Shakespeare, Ossian, Waller, Milton, Petrarch, Prior, St. Paul, Montaigne, Julian, Augustine, Thomas à Kempis, Zeno, Democritus, Pyrrho, Plato, Proclus, Verulam, Zoroaster, Bacchus, Virgil, Sidney."

"Recalling that he had read little or no Shakespeare," Olson adds, "we wonder about the rest" (pp. 64–65). Such doubts must have given him pause. And even when it is the reading behind *Moby-Dick*—how many of the following did Olson check out of the library?

> Browne, Davenant, Lamb,—they are here from his recent reading; and there are his old friends—Shakespeare, Bacon, Milton, Montaigne, Rabelais, Spenser, Waller, Hobbes, Pope, Goldsmith, Falconer, Purchas, Hawthorne. But there are new books, new writers—Holland's *Plutarch's Morals*, Holland's *Pliny*, Tooke's *Lucian*, *Pilgrim's Progress*, Fuller's *Profane and Holy State*, Dryden's *Annus Mirabilis*, Edmund Burke, Cowper, Eckermann's *Conversations with Goethe*. Plato, Bunyan, Cervantes, Byron, "the three Spaniards," Locke, Kant, Spinoza, Dante, Paracelsus, Young, Pascal, Rousseau can be harvested from the text itself. And then there are the scores of histories and voyages on whaling, the "literature" of the cachalot, which made up the bulk of his reading. (Pp. 114–15)

Well, we can score one here: Olson bought Eckermann's *Conversations with Goethe* in the Everyman edition (London: J. M. Dent; New York: Dutton, 1935).[4]

A best guess would be that Olson read Robert Burton and Thomas Browne because of Melville; that, because of Melville, he made himself familiar with Addison, Akenside, Arnold, Balzac, Beckford, Walpole, Burns, Bunyan, Seneca, Carlyle, Defoe, De Quincey, FitzGerald, Hood, Johnson, Lamb, Rousseau, Smollett, Sterne, and Thompson ("B. V."); but none of these writers was in his library and there is little or no evidence of how much or how closely he read.[5] Richard Henry Dana's *Two Years Before the Mast*, which Olson must have read because of Melville if not before, does not turn up in his library; neither does Hawthorne, significantly nothing at all.[6]

Two of Melville's whaleship books caught Olson's attention and were given conspicuous place in *Call Me Ishmael*. The "First Fact" (pp. 3–7) is a summary of Owen Chase, *Narrative of the Most Extraordinary and Distressing Shipwreck of the Whale-Ship Essex, of Nantucket; Which Was Attacked and Finally Destroyed by a Large Spermaceti-Whale, in the Pacific Ocean* (New York: Gilley, 1821). Olson had a chance to examine Melville's own copy,[7] and later purchased the American Experience Series edition (New York: Corinth, 1963). "Fact #2" in *Call Me Ishmael* is based on the circumstance described in William Lay, *A Narrative of the Mutiny, on Board the Ship Globe, of Nantucket, in the Pacific Ocean, Jan.*

*1824* (New London 1828), though it is not clear what access Olson had to this volume.[8] A third Melville source is mentioned by Olson (p. 36): Thomas Beale, *The Natural History of the Sperm Whale* (London 1839), but not really used by him, whereas—so far had *Call Me Ishmael* come from being a dissertation—Olson's actual source for all the whaling economics is concealed.[9]

The direction in which Olson might have been happy to have let a dissertation lead him might have been out from Shakespeare into the other Elizabethan and Jacobean dramatists. Olson notes in his M. A. thesis that Melville brought back from England in 1849 "a 1692 folio of Ben Jonson; a 1673 folio of Davenant; a folio of Beaumont and Fletcher ... and a folio of Marlowe's plays" (p. 96), and adds: "That he had thoroughly digested these ripe old morsels before *Moby-Dick* is certain. They added to the 'fatness' of that great book." In later life Melville "took much pleasure"[10] in reading the Mermaid Series of old plays; Olson began collecting the Mermaids and other like volumes, and when he made a list for himself in April 1949 it was quite a good showing.[11] But by that time all thoughts of an academic dissertation had long gone; he was taking pleasure. In the 1953 talk to Black Mountain students ("Starting from where you are") he was able to say that "for story" he preferred, more than prose fiction, the Elizabethan and Jacobean dramatists: "fletcher, marston, ford, tourneur, dryden (!), lyly, dekker, massinger, peele—as well as such as marlowe (EDWARD II), jonson (THE FOX)."[12]

The kind of scholar Olson would have been—the activeness of his scholarship—is illustrated in a story Olson told Ann Charters in Gloucester in 1968 (*Olson/Melville*, pp. 7–8):

> I got an awful break one day sitting in Eleanor's house.[13] In some dumb way, with my high school French, I began to read Philarète Chasles' review of *Typee* or *Omoo*. Here I suddenly realize that what the French is actually saying is that Melville's brother-in-law was in his house and confirmed all Melville's experiences in the Pacific, 1847. I realize this is Lemuel, or Sam, Shaw. Eleanor's in the kitchen, and I asked her where the Shaw Papers were. "I sent them to the Massachusetts Historical Society—this was long ago, when I was first married." So she calls up to see if I can look at them, and I grab a cab, and within 45 minutes of reading that French review, I was looking at the boxes Eleanor had sent them.

This is thirty-four years after the event, and we still feel the aliveness of it. But there is more, for Olson wrote a letter to Wilbert Snow the evening of the day of the cab ride (letter undated, presumably January 1934):

> I just got in from a day I want to shout about. In Boston today— *today*—in turning over some Shaw (H. M.'s father-in-law) material I uncovered Melville letters and information the like of which has not been seen in twenty years! Diaries and papers and letters, not only of Herman's, but of his wife's, his mother's, his brother's, his brothers'-in-law—the guts of biography. For instance, one of H. M.'s letters establishes the first direct reference to Carlyle—a request to his father-in-law for a letter of introduction to C. from RW Emerson! Another contains a long discussion of what he thinks of "Redburn" and "White-Jacket." And, Bill, I've only stirred the surface of what's there! I'm going back the first thing in the morning. It all came out of a chance remark I spotted in one of those books I brought up from New Jersey—by a Frenchman, and published in 1852.[14] I've just seen Mrs. Metcalf and she's become as wild-eyed as I am after hearing about the discovery.

Behavior like this has been called, by rival graduate students, a "threat." The system can usually eliminate it. As one contemporary of Olson's in graduate school, who later became a professor of English at Harvard, said when asked what Olson was like then: "Mad," he said, "quite mad."

It is our supposition that Dahlberg contributed somewhat to this "madness." Olson was about to enter Harvard in September 1936 as an assistant in English and American Literature. While taking a graduate seminar in Chaucer, he received a postcard from Dahlberg saying: "Remember start work on the Melville book. I believe in you." Let this stand as the continuing, maddening alternative.[15] For, while Professor Kenneth Murdock was laying the foundation for Olson's academic career by commissioning reviews for *New England Quarterly* and Olson was supplying him with good, starched-collar performances, Dahlberg was introducing him to Dorothy Norman and getting her to accept "Lear and Moby-Dick" for the first prestigious issue of *Twice A Year*, no matter how "distraught" Olson might become by rewriting to a deadline. Working on his Melville-Shakespeare paper through the summer of 1937, Olson wrote to Matthiessen: "I've run through with differing pace the old and the new criticism, particularly Johnson, Coleridge, Brandes, Raleigh, Bradley, Barker, Wilson Knight, Spurgeon,

Eliot, and the World's Classics collection."[16] If the term paper referred to any of these (it is not extant), Dahlberg made sure the printed article had no footnotes, and concentrated on *Moby-Dick* rather than "the larger implications of what Shakespeare meant to Melville." Writing to Carl Van Doren on 16 October 1938, Olson still speaks of doing a study "based on the notes in Melville's books and his reading," but to Van Wyck Brooks, 29 November 1938, he reveals a new purpose: to "set Melville off against Dostoevsky" in a "total" judgment. Olson concludes, "M. finally had to lean on Christ like a crutch; D. possessed Christ, in fact to me, in such a passage as Alyosha upon the stone talking to the boys, created Christ." He is "anxious to set Melville's limits."[17] This denotes a major turning-point of which the published "Dostoevsky and The Possessed" gives only a glimmer.

It is not known what caused Olson to turn to Dostoevsky; missing parts of the Dahlberg correspondence would no doubt give a clue. Olson's copy of *The Brothers Karamazov*, which he apparently read first, has not survived, but his copy of *The Possessed* has. The translation by Constance Garnett (New York: Modern Library, 1936) has a flyleaf that reads: "Charles John Olson read March 1939." The copy is heavily annotated as the focus of "Dostoevsky and the Possessed," published in *Twice A Year* 5–6 (Fall–Winter 1940): 230–37. Also heavily marked is Constance Garnett's translation of *The Idiot* (New York: Random House, 1935), mentioned in the essay. Also mentioned are *Crime and Punishment* (Olson's copy not extant) and *A Raw Youth*, which Olson, though he did not own a copy, is known to have read in September 1939, according to a notebook of that time. The notebook indicates he was also reading Nicolas Berdyaev, *Dostoevsky: An Interpretation* (New York: Sheed & Ward, 1934); he did not, however, retain a copy in his library. He owned Avrahm Yarmolinsky, *Dostoevsky: His Life and Art* (New York, 1934), from which he quotes Dostoevsky's *The Diary of a Writer*. On 18 July 1940, while Olson was in the last stages of rewriting the essay for *Twice A Year*, Dahlberg (according to a letter of that date) felt it was important enough to search eight bookstores in order to send Olson a copy of Edward H. Carr's *Dostoevsky 1821–1881* (Boston: Houghton, Mifflin, 1931) to help. The book was subsequently not in Olson's library.

Dostoevsky did not ultimately last the course with Olson. He was given *The Eternal Husband and Other Stories*, translated by Constance Garnett (New York: Macmillan, 1917)—flyleaf: "For Connie & Charles with permanence—from Alice & Harvey April 1946"—and it stayed in his library, but of it he said he "read it on a train and was not interested as I once was interested" (letter to Dahlberg, 20 July 1948). He told Creeley on 26 April 1951 that he "had found it impossible to reread" Dostoevsky (*Creeley Correspondence* 5, p. 184).[18] Nevertheless, in 1939 Dostoevsky provided Olson with a measure for testing Melville's resonance.

Looking back on the previous year, Olson wrote to Waldo Frank on 12 January 1940 about his attempt to get under the surface of things with his "long section on Melville and myth-making":

> I have been reading all the anthropology I can lay my hands on, all the fantastic literature of lost continents with its lovely hidden veracity more true as you have observed than science, tracing the soundings of the Pacific of the unconscious, Freud, and Frazer as well as yourself, Proust and Mann again, and Melville and naturally and necessarily myself. I have felt so often the validity of a heritage beyond my own bones and flesh and now to be exploring and affirming and creating such a past, probing the mysteries of time and space in and with the imagination is a joy and a pain.

Notebooks for 1939–40 reveal with certainty that Olson read the following, though he later had only one of these books:

Robert J. Casey, *Easter Island, Home of the Scornful Gods* (Indianapolis: Bobbs Merrill, 1931).

James Churchward, *The Lost Continent of Mu* (New York: Ives Washburn, 1931)—Olson had this volume and referred to it in the *Mayan Letters* bibliography.

Sigmund Freud, *Delusion and Dream* (New York: Moffat, Yard, 1917).

Sigmund Freud, *Moses and Monotheism* (New York: Knopf, 1939).

Jane Ellen Harrison, *Ancient Art and Ritual* (previously cited).

Thomas Mann, *Joseph and his Brothers* (previously cited).

Lewis Spence, *The Problem of Atlantis*, 2d ed. (New York: Brentano's, n.d.).

There were no doubt other books involved in this effort to get behind the secret that Melville praised Maurice de Guérin for stating so succinctly: "There is more power and beauty in the well-kept secret of one's self and one's thoughts than in the display of a whole heaven that one may have inside one."[19] Having been brought up a Catholic by a strict mother, Olson no less than Melville had a problem with Christianity. It was a personal struggle to find the basis on which to judge the later Melville, whom he finally came to think of as "marred" in Christ's image: "Dostoevsky, Dickinson, Blake, Nietzsche—none resist the Temptation. Shakespeare and Brueghel alone of us all did circumvent the Christ."[20]

It was this wrestling with Melville's beliefs, and his own, that produced a sort of a nervous breakdown in Olson's last term at Harvard, spring 1939. He sought the distractions of New York City and such celebrities as Van Wyck Brooks, Alfred Stieglitz, and Ford Madox Ford.[21] Waldo Frank put him on to Kierkegaard, which did not help.[22] It appears to have been Dahlberg himself, and his prose style, with which Olson was netted and brought down. He had read Dahlberg before he met him in 1936—the novels *Bottom Dogs* (1929), *From Flushing to Calvary* (1932), and *Those Who Perish* (1934). Now he had to face them again, as the author pressed them on him.[23] But Dahlberg had turned from fiction, and right at the time of their meeting was working on the Randolph Bourne essay that, along with others on the general topic of American literature, would be collected into *Do These Bones Live* (1941). Their paths became embarrassingly close. It took Olson many years of persistent effort and residual pain to delineate his separateness.[24] The dedication Olson wrote for Dahlberg at the beginning of part four of *Call Me Ishmael* likens him to Don Quixote and includes quotations from Cervantes.[25] There must have been months when Olson thought he himself had wasted too much time tilting at windmills.

In the end another scholar completed the comprehensive job on Melville's books—not without Olson's help and blessing, nor without occasional fiery criticism. The whole story is laid out fully in Merton Sealts, "A Correspondence with Charles Olson," in *Pursuing Melville 1940–1980* (University of Wisconsin Press, 1982). Sealts first went to see Olson in December 1940 with his essay on "I and My Chimney," and Olson gave him leads to Melville books. The two kept in touch from time to time.[26] When Sealts sent his *Melville's Reading: A Checklist of Books Owned and Borrowed* (Cambridge: Harvard University Press, 1950), Olson's reply was both warm and chilling—or "scorching," as Sealts felt it: "If Olson was excited by the new vistas that my compilation seemed to open, he was dismayed once again to think of things he was sure I knew but hadn't said about the books and what had been done with them since Melville's death. His hot words scorched then, thirty years ago, and they scorch now as I read them over" (*Pursuing Melville*, p. 108). Sealts was reading the response of someone who was feeling guilty for not doing the job himself—but only half-guilty; for Olson was genuinely pleased that a good scholar had finished the work. And, as for himself, he had only one lifetime.

# 6

## *"It Might Take 14 Years"*

In January 1955, Ed Dorn, then a student at Black Mountain College, asked his teacher for some guidance on how to proceed with a study of American history. Within a couple of days he had received two missives on the subject. After years of private circulation they were printed in a pamphlet by Don Allen under the title *A Bibliography on America for Ed Dorn*, Writing 1 (San Francisco: Four Seasons Foundation, 1964). "Best thing to do," Olson told Dorn,

> is to dig one thing or place or man until you yourself know more abt that than is possible to any other man. It doesn't matter whether it's Barbed Wire or Pemmican or Paterson or Iowa. But exhaust it. Saturate it. Beat it.
> And then U KNOW everything else very fast: one saturation job (it might take 14 years). And you're in, forever. (*Additional Prose*, p. 11)

It's what the master did with his Melville. The apprentice can do it, with American history, if he digs for his subject into primary documents:

> Repository #1: THE NATIONAL ARCHIVES, Wash., D.C.
> " #2: Senate Documents (published)
> " #3: Bureau of Am. Ethnology Reports & Bulletins[1]
> (pub. by Smithsonian Inst.)
> & then, depending on subject, all over the place:
> ex., Donner Party, Sutter's Fort Mus., & Cal. State
> Libr., Sacramento
> ex., the Adamses: Mass. Hist. Soc., Boston
> Ex. Whaleship *Essex*: privately owned, Perc Brown, Oilman, Jersey
> —at cruxes, mss will be in private hands. (*Additional Prose*, p. 12)

Although this might appear at first glance to be a mere scattering of references, we can see Olson is here standing by the achievements and procedures of his own fourteen years of assiduity: from the thesis of 1933 to the publication of *Call Me Ishmael* in 1947. Olson had written to Wilbert Snow in a letter of 16 October 1932: "This summer I got acquainted with a person by the name of Herman Melville, introduced to me through a story called 'Moby Dick' and some short 'Piazza Tales.' Now I burn to know, to possess the man completely. With Woodbridge's rather enthusiastic approval I have decided to do my thesis on him."[2] We have already reviewed the fourteen-year saturation job in terms of Melville's reading and Olson's attention to it. We should now recapitulate this exhaustive digging of Melville by looking at the stacks of Melville's works owned by Olson, and the criticism. As he said to Dorn: "the point is *to get all* that's been said on given subject" (*Additional Prose*, p. 12).

We might be prepared to be saturated. Olson read everything, and owned most of it. But in saying that, we have not said too much, for Melville was only just becoming well-known at the time Olson got to him. There was the sixteen-volume Standard Edition (London: Constable, 1922–24) that Olson used for his M.A. thesis and bought soon after.[3] His working copies for the thesis were the Modern Library *Moby-Dick* (1926), *Shorter Novels of Herman Melville* (New York: Liveright, 1928), *Pierre* (New York: Knopf, 1930), and possibly *John Marr and Other Poems* (Princeton University Press; Oxford University Press, 1922), though this last may have been purchased later.[4] Olson went very thoroughly through Raymond Weaver's edition of Melville's *Journal Up the Straits, October 11, 1856–May 5, 1857* (New York: Colophon, 1935). He also picked up Willard Thorp, *Herman Melville: Representative Selections* (New York: American Book Co., 1938). And that's about it before *Call Me Ishmael* (1947).[5]

As for Melville criticism, we have seen how attentive he was to it in his M.A. thesis.[6] As time went on, it was as a reviewer that Olson managed to get Melville books to read and talk about. (In the following list, the review copies were kept by Olson unless otherwise indicated.)

## Reviews for the *New England Quarterly* (1937–1939)

Captain Hartson H. Bodfish and Joseph C. Allen, *Chasing the Bowhead* (Cambridge: Harvard University Press, 1936), in *NEQ* 10 (March 1937): 183–84. Bodfish was a successful whaling captain,

1880–1911, "a Starbuck, not an Ahab." This volume did not stay in Olson's library.

Roger W. Babson and Foster H. Saville, *Cape Ann: A Tourist Guide* (Rockport: Cape Ann Old Book Shop, 1936), in *NEQ* 10 (March 1937): 191–92. "This book is not so good as it should have been. . . . The significant centre of Cape Ann—the fishing industry, its history, its myth, even its economics—is untouched." Interesting in terms of a future "saturation job."[7]

Charles Roberts Anderson, ed., *Journal of a Cruise to the Pacific Ocean, 1842–1844, in the Frigate United States* (Durham: Duke University Press, 1937), in *NEQ* 12 (March 1939): 148–49. The ship's log of the vessel Melville sailed with and subsequently fictionalized in *White-Jacket*.

Clifford W. Ashley, *The Yankee Whaler*, Popular ed. (Boston: Houghton Mifflin, 1938), in *NEQ* 12 (March 1939): 150–51. "Originally published in 1926, . . . unquestionably the great modern book on the subject." Not in Olson's library later.

Dr. K. H. Sundermann, *Herman Melville Gedankengut* (Berlin: Verlag Arthur Collignon, 1937), in *NEQ* 12 (March 1939): 154–56. "This study of Melville's thought is as complete as a concordance—and as undiscriminating. . . . The influence of Plato and Emerson on Melville is exaggerated and that of Hawthorne and Shakespeare is ignored."

Robert Ferguson, *Arctic Harpooner: A Voyage on the Schooner Abbie Bradford, 1878–1879*, ed. Leslie Dalrymple Stair (Philadelphia: University of Pennsylvania Press, 1938), in *NEQ* 12 (June 1939): 389–90. "It is good enough to set beside Lieutenant Gilder's *Schwatka's Search* (Gilder and Ferguson were both at Marble Island the same winter), and to compare with the observations of Freuchen, Rasmussen, and (though farther westward) Stefansson."

Charles Roberts Anderson, *Melville in the South Seas* (New York: Columbia University Press, 1939). Olson was given this volume for review upon its publication in March 1939. He completed a review in typescript (Storrs), but did not submit it. Or perhaps—it is quite a negative review—it was sent back by Kenneth Murdock for revision.[8]

### Review for the *Western Review* (1949)

"I'm busy," Olson wrote to Dahlberg on 8 December 1948, "trying to make 40 dollars, writing a review of three new books on Melville, one of which will interest you, F. Barron Freeman's edition of BILLY BUDD." Besides *Billy Budd*, ed. F. Barron Freeman (Cambridge: Harvard University Press, 1948), the *New Republic* had sent Olson *Piazza Tales*, ed. Egbert S. Oliver (New York: Hendricks House, Farrar Straus, 1948),[9] and *Journal of a Visit to London and the Continent by Herman Melville, 1849–1850*, ed. Eleanor Melville Metcalf (Cambridge: Harvard University Press, 1948).[10] He wrote the review, and told Monroe Engel in a letter of 7 January 1949 to "watch for olson's 1st words on melville since the buch: in the New Republic, issue Jan 17th, I think." The review must have been rejected, for it was next submitted to *Western Review*, rewritten to concentrate only on Freeman's new *Billy Budd*, as we discover from the published "David Young, David Old," *Western Review* 14 (Fall 1949): 63–66.

Besides the reference in this review to W. H. Auden's "Herman Melville," a poem that had been around since its publication in *Southern Review* (Autumn 1939), the casual mention of Richard Chase should also be noted, for Olson at this point had read only Chase's article, "Dissent on *Billy Budd*," *Partisan Review* 15 (November 1948): 1212–18, with which he agreed, and not yet Chase's book, *Herman Melville: A Critical Study* (New York: Macmillan, 1949), with which he ended up disagreeing.[11]

Doing this review roused Olson to think again about Melville, this time in terms of the Bible and Homer—as he tells Sealts on 28 March 1949:

> What the King James piece does, is to argue how clearly and painfully Melville saw his loss in the dying off of *folk* knowledge of the images and narratives of the Bible. . . . The intent of the "Homer" is to suggest in what manner this man . . . is precisely such a "starter" as was Omeros, gave up out of the intelligence and perception of himself a measurement of man and universe so revolutionary that he will stand to the future as fountainhead as has that Greek man. (*Pursuing Melville*, p. 103)[12]

## Review for the *New Republic* (1952)

Presumably through his friend Robert Richman, who became the literary editor of the *New Republic*, Olson was given another chance. He was sent for review the new edition of *Moby-Dick*, ed. Luther S. Mansfield and Howard P. Vincent (New York: Hendricks House, 1952) and Lawrance

Thompson, *Melville's Quarrel with God* (Princeton: Princeton University Press, 1952).[13] To these he added a book which a friend "happened to put in my hands," Ronald Mason, *The Spirit Above the Dust* (London: John Lehmann, 1951), "simply because its intelligence and limpidity measures the soddenness of the scholarship of the new edition of *Moby-Dick* and the perverseness of thinking in *Melville's Quarrel with God*."[14] Olson is able to summarize a whole segment of Melville criticism by saying that Mason's book is "the triumph" of all those who have used "rationalism" as an approach, "that series of critiques which can be said to start with John Freeman's biography, to include Mr. Mumford's more troubled rationalism, and to run the list of the bead-telling books of the last years: Matthiessen's, Sedgwick's, Chase's, Arvin's, and Brooks's—perhaps Yvor Winters's and Auden's *The Enchafèd Flood*—in other words, a rosary of praise which has (with some quietness and a little decency) been the private act of these men."[15]

In the process of setting before his readers "the story of Melville critique and scholarship whole," Olson mentions the following in his review:

Walter Bezanson—"whose work on *Clarel* I only know by snatches."[16]

F. Barron Freeman, ed., *Billy Budd* (Harvard University Press, 1948). Owned by Olson.

Harrison Hayford's unpublished dissertation, *Melville and Hawthorne* (Yale, 1945).

Leon Howard, *Herman Melville: A Biography* (University of California, 1951)—"not yet read."[17]

Jay Leyda, *The Melville Log*, 2 vols. (New York: Harcourt, Brace, 1951).[18]

Henry A. Murray's Introduction to *Pierre* (New York: Hendricks House, 1949)—"continuing application of developed psychological tools to the question of the nature of Melville's personality."[19]

Merton Sealts, *Melville's Reading* (1948–50)—"the scrupulous steady study of Melville's library." Owned by Olson.

Geoffrey Stone, *Melville* (New York: Sheed & Ward, 1949)—"I happen also to like." Owned by Olson.

Nathalia Wright, *Melville's Use of the Bible* (Durham: Duke University Press, 1949.) Owned by Olson.

As for the "soddenness" of the scholarship of the Hendricks House *Moby-Dick*, Olson gives the opinion (not in his review but in a letter to Jay Leyda on 3 March 1952) that it is "mostly Vincent—it does not sound like that certain decency Mansfield has shown from the beginning—from his thesis on M as New Yorker and Pittsfieldian," i.e., L. S. Mansfield, "Glimpses of Herman Melville's Life in Pittsfield, 1850–1851," *American Literature* 9 (March 1937): 26–48, drawing on Mansfield's Ph.D. (Chicago, 1936). Olson objects, for instance, to "such flat words as, Nelson was 'one of Melville's greatest heroes' " (letter to Merton Sealts, 7 March 1952): "How Vincent & Mansfield derogate man's continuing struggle *right now* by speaking so *lightly*, so familiarly, so offhandedly of Melville's involvement with Nelson. For it takes no particular insight to notice that one of the central preoccupations of man today—one of his central necessities—is exactly this problem of *hero*: which is, any time, man's measure of *his own possibilities*—how large is he?" How small Vincent can be is shown, Olson tells Sealts, in the table of American Literature he did for the recent *Compton's Pictured Encyclopedia and Fact-Index* (Chicago, 1950), which Olson had seen in a friend's house:

> He has the gall to expunge the name of Ezra Pound, and his works, from the list. And it obviously must be because Pound is charged as traitor! Imagine: in the face of the Bollingen, and the whole struggle, this little man is in a position to *remove* from the public record in the dark the work of such a man . . . the Melville whom Vincent (and Mansfield, to the degree of his accompliceship) peddle is a scrubbed and school-boy "Classic," is a man so subtracted from his *nature* and his *act* that one has finally to see their re-presentation of him as as *dishonest* an act as the omission of the name of Pound from the encyclopedia.

Olson knows Howard Vincent's *The Trying-Out of Moby-Dick* (Boston: Houghton Mifflin, 1949)—though he "never could afford to buy" it—and Vincent's review of Leyda's *Melville Log* in the *New York Times*. He is heartbroken at "the immorality of the politics and economics of our time walking unseen," he tells Sealts, "right in the midst of something very close to both of us." Behind the review, then, is this plea to "find out *how to clean up our own house*" (letter to Sealts, 7 March 1952).

## Review for the *Chicago Review* (1958)

Olson's copy of Merrell R. Davis, *Melville's Mardi: A Chartless Voyage* (New Haven: Yale University Press, 1952) has on the flyleaf: "Olson

Summer 52 for review (not done)." In fact, Olson did only one more Melville review, when, on the reprinting of *Call Me Ishmael* as a Grove Press Evergreen paperback in February 1958, Paul Carroll of *Chicago Review* sent him Milton R. Stern's *The Fine Hammered Steel of Herman Melville* (Urbana: University of Illinois Press, 1957). "And find it, as always, too much for me," he wrote to Robert Duncan on 6 March 1958, "hate the area of a review (shld know better, than to have taken it. But was all fired up again on Mr Melville—who is my post." From the finished piece itself it is clear that Olson was not concerned about catching up with Melville scholarship, but was eager to have his say on Melville as a precursor of non-Euclidean (the "real") geometry, applying to Melville what he was reading in Hermann Weyl, *Philosophy of Mathematics and Natural Science* (Princeton: Princeton University Press, 1949), a book used both before and after this, but significantly here.[20]

"Equal, That Is, to the Real Itself" is, then, the culmination of twice fourteen years with Melville, the second half being the assured sailing of the authority who has done the "saturation job" referred to in *Bibliography on America for Ed Dorn*.[21] As a footnote to this: Dorn must have asked Olson about "indians"; Olson indicates he does not like the plural. "*Indians* is wicked. I think the thing is to settle on one of em, either literally one, Red Cloud, say; or the Utes."[22] In 1966, Dorn could present Olson a copy of *The Shoshoneans: The People of the Basin-Plateau* (New York: William Morrow, 1966). The Shoshone are Utes. It might take eleven years.

# 7

## *History 62 (Westward Movement) and 'West'*

Red Cloud, recommended as a subject of study to Ed Dorn in *Bibliography on America*, turns up as the frontispiece to Olson's beautifully produced, small volume *'West'* (London: Goliard, 1966). A parenthesis in the first poem of that volume indicates Olson's source was the *Dictionary of American Biography*, but the trail actually goes back all the way to his boyhood reading of Joseph Altsheler. According to the author's preface: "I *have* here a much larger story than would appear."[1] The "Basic Reading List," he tells Dorn, is "Merk (Harvard Press) on *Westward Movement*"—by which he means Frederick Jackson Turner and Frederick Merk, *List of References on the History of the West* (Cambridge: Harvard University Press, 1922; revised 1930)—"you can eat yr way thru this list forever!"[2] Olson's *Bibliography on America* is openly derivative; Olson was willing, in this area, to apprentice himself to at least Frederick Merk and Carl O. Sauer, and Bernard DeVoto up to a point. What did he consume of other people's reading lists on the subject of the West?

As a graduate student at Harvard, Olson took Professor Merk's History 62 (Westward Movement), a year-long course in which he must have worked his way through much of the *List of References*. But we do not have specific assignments, nor do we have Olson's term papers. We only have, from his later use of them, the titles that stuck in his mind:

James Truslow Adams, *The Founding of New England* (Boston: Atlantic Monthly, 1921)—*List of References*, p. 21. Olson kept the BMC library copy.
Thomas H. Benton, *Thirty Years' View*, 2 vols. (New York: Appleton,

1854–56)—*List of References*, p. 73. Olson bought these volumes in November 1956.

Isaiah Bowman, *Forest Physiography* (New York: John Wiley, 1911)—mentioned in the "Washington Summer 1945" notebook.

Consul Willshire Butterfield, *History of the Girtys* (Columbus, Ohio: Long's College Book Co., 1950)—*List of References*, p. 44. Olson finally owned a copy in 1968 as a gift from Harvey Brown.

Katharine Coman, *Economic Beginnings of the Far West*, 2 vols. (New York: Macmillan, 1912)—included in "a useful library for the student to own in connection with the course" (*List of References*, p. 4). Recommended to Ed Dorn, but not later in Olson's library.

Lyman C. Draper, *King's Mountain and Its Heroes* (Cincinnati: Peter G. Thomson, 1881)—*List of References*, p. 46. There is evidence Olson read the reprint (Marietta, Georgia: Continental Book Co., 1954) before writing his poem, "King's Mountain."

J. P. Dunn, *Massacres of the Mountains* (New York: Harper, 1886)—*List of References*, p. 98. Olson known to have used it in the Library of Congress in 1947.

Archer Butler Hulbert, *Historic Highways of America*, 16 vols. (Cleveland: Arthur H. Clark, 1902–5)—the *List of References* includes various volumes on pp. 80–81. Olson acquired a set in 1966.[3]

Ellsworth Huntington, *Civilization and Climate*, 2d ed. (New Haven: Yale University Press, 1922)—in *List of References*, p. 15, found in Olson's library.

Washington Irving, *The Adventures of Captain Bonneville*, vol. 10 of *Works of Washington Irving* (New York: Putnam, 1856)—*List of References*, p. 101. Olson owned the above edition.

A. K. Lobeck, *Physiographic Diagram of the United States* (New York: Geographical Press, Columbia University, 1932)—required for History 62 and recommended to Ed Dorn, but not found in Olson's library.

C. E. Merriam, *American Political Theories* (New York: Macmillan, 1903)—included in list of "a useful library": Olson is known to have borrowed it from Winthrop House library during the spring term of 1939.

Samuel Eliot Morison, *The Maritime History of Massachusetts 1783–1860* (Boston: Houghton Mifflin, 1930)—*List of References*, p. 113. Olson owned and read thoroughly this volume.

E. B. O'Callaghan, *The Documentary History of the State of New York*, 4 vols. (Albany: Weed, Parsons, 1849–51)—*List of References*, p. 53. Olson refers to this work, misremembering it, in "Buffalo Ode."

Francis Parkman, *France and England in North America*, 9 vols. (Boston: Little, Brown, 1865–92)—"especially, for me, his *La Salle*."[4]

Francis Parkman, *The Oregon Trail* (London: Macmillan, 1899)—*List of References*, p. 95. Olson wrote in the flyleaf of his copy: "This book which I have had for years possibly since Cambridge I am now reading with sense and experience January 4th & 5th 1968!"

Nathaniel W. Stephenson, *Texas and the Mexican War* (New Haven: Yale University Press, 1921)—*List of References*, p. 108. Olson owned this volume.

Frederick Jackson Turner, *The Frontier in American History* (New York: Henry Holt, 1920)—required for History 62 and recommended to Ed Dorn, but not found in Olson's library.

In the *List of References*, Merk himself makes an appearance only with the one book he had published up to that time: *Economic History of Wisconsin during the Civil War Decade* (1915). It is not at all certain Olson saw this book. The reference to "how pemmican was born" in *Bibliography on America* has its source in part 2 of appendix B of Frederick Merk, ed., *Fur Trade and Empire: George Simpson's Journal*, vol. 31 of *Harvard Historical Studies* (Cambridge: Harvard University Press, 1931),[5] and Merk's "reprints on the Oregon Triangle" are represented in Olson's library by an inscribed offprint of "The Ghost River Caledonia in the Oregon Negotiation of 1818," *American Historical Review* 55 (April 1950): 530–51.[6] But there were a couple of problems with "my man Merk." One thing was his retentiveness. History 62 was apparently quite inspiring in its breadth and thoroughness; Olson wanted a volume equal to the course: "the unwritten book" that he had been "trying to get out of him for yrs."[7] It took a student of Merk's, Ray Allen Billington, to write a *Westward Expansion* (1949);[8] Merk's own *History of the Westward Movement* (1978) was published posthumously by his widow. And even then it cannot be the book that Olson would have wished for; it is too academic. This is the other problem with Merk: solely a library man—in contrast with, say, Bernard DeVoto, who had walked the western wagon trails and canyons, had been born to it.

The first thing Olson did after finishing the year with Merk was to hitchhike to the West Coast via the Grand Canyon (he did a DeVoto). But there was a problem with DeVoto, too:

> I can only stand DeVoto, say (who knows as much as any literary man
> abt America West), when he ain't cute, and is very damn serious abt the
> facts abt, say, exactly who was there that night that camp a day's drive
> east of Laramie, was it Jim Fitzpatrick who was sitting just inside the
> light, and the Donners, both Jacob and George, didn't know that that man
> was the one man who cld have saved them what they went through . . .
> there you get DeVoto at his best, that, he thought the knowledge of
> a mountain man was the greatest thing in knowledge an American has
> yet had.

So Olson recommends that Ed Dorn read *The Year of Decision, 1846*
(which Olson is remembering here)[9]—with the proviso: "DeVoto's
knowledge is so wide and curious it should be better. He should have
written the unwritten book."

Carl Ortwin Sauer was a fusion of the best qualities of Merk and
DeVoto: high academic attainment plus thorough field work. The one
article of Sauer's that turns up in the *List of References* (p. 57) is "The
Geography of the Ozark Highland of Missouri," Bulletin No. 7 of the
Geographic Society of Chicago (1920), based on his dissertation re-
searched in his native state. Olson may have seen this, for he advises
Ed Dorn in *Bibliography on America* to go back in Sauer's work "all the
way through *Road to Cibola*, back to his first job, for the State of Illinois
handbook (1915?) on the new State Park at Starved Rock."[10] It was *The
Road to Cibola* (University of California Publications, Ibero-Americana
No. 3, 1932) that Olson read in the Library of Congress when he was
thinking he might be traveling west in the spring of 1947. Wouldn't
Olson's eyes have lighted up to see the following passage?

> I had occasion to cover, by car, on horseback, and afoot, virtually all the
> country between the Gila River on the north and the Rio Grande de San-
> tiago at the south. I have seen all but a very few miles of the route herein
> examined, and have been over a good deal of it a number of times and at
> different seasons of the year. In the light of this knowledge of the country
> a reinterpretation of the historical evidence was indicated, which differs
> in numerous particulars from the views previously advanced.[11]

No wonder he sought out Sauer in his office at Berkeley when he fi-
nally made it to the West Coast in the fall of 1947 and was himself cov-
ering afoot the ground of a research project.[12]

In Los Angeles, Olson took the opportunity to follow up some De-

Voto leads on the Donner Party in the Huntington Library. They led him back to Berkeley and the Bancroft Library, as he reported to a correspondent in a letter of 25 November 1947 from Sutter's Fort, Sacramento, California.[13] A trunk of Gold Rush papers had recently been given to the California State Library, and Olson came along just as the librarian, Caroline Wenzel, was examining them. George P. Hammond, Director of the Bancroft Library, University of California, succeeded in interesting the Book Club of California in a series of edited documents from the collection. Olson was commissioned to prepare number two of the "Letters of the Gold Discovery" series, *The Sutter-Marshall Lease*.[14] In this case, the "saturation job" took fourteen weeks, a straight piece of historical scholarship that Merk could have been proud of. But Olson was in no danger of following that master. As he wrote to the Guggenheim Foundation at this time: "The Bancroft Library has asked me to edit a book of uncollected gold diaries, and I am preparing other documents from the McKinstry Papers for the Keepsake series of the Book Club of California. The danger, of course—and it, too, is part of the method—is to allow the scholarship to pull one off course into too much editing, and I shall not accept the offer of the University of California Press to edit the McKinstry Papers as a volume."[15] The way lies elsewhere. And Sauer can be a companion, DeVoto too. Both take their places, twenty years later, in a poem called 'West'.

Nevertheless, Olson's loyalty to his Harvard professor was strong, and when he needed a leg up to get into the third part of the *Maximus*, Olson wrote to Professor Merk. A carbon copy of Olson's letter, 10 September 1953, exists at Storrs:

> As you well know, you are the pivot of my respect for history. And if I turn to you again, it is just because it is a joy to register, once more, my deepest respect. And anything you can give me back—or direct someone else, if there is someone who happens also to have come into this time with a distinct economic, rather than religious attention—shall be exceedingly helpful.
>
> As I say, I have put it thus specifically, not to point any of the pieces at you, but to suggest the sort of saturation that *my own front yard*—literally, that field was where I grew, our house being on "Stage Fort Avenue", Gloucester!—bred in me.

Merk's response of 29 September 1953 provided Olson with the following leads, which he followed up where indicated:

Clifford K. Shipton, *Roger Conant* (Cambridge: Harvard University Press, 1945)—Olson's note: "inter library loan."

Thomas J. Wertenbaker, *Puritan Oligarchy* (New York: Scribner's, 1947).

Samuel Eliot Morison, *Builders of the Bay Colony* (Boston: Houghton Mifflin, 1930)—Olson already owned this volume, and had used it extensively in the *Maximus* poem, "Letter 10."

Charles Edward Banks, *The Planters of the Commonwealth* (Boston: Houghton Mifflin, 1930)—consulted for later *Maximus* poems.

J. P. Donnelly, *Bibliography of the Colonial Fur Trade in the American Colonies* (St. Louis: St. Louis University Press, 1947).

R. O. MacFarlane, "Indian Relations in New England" (Ph.D. diss., Harvard University, 1933).

Francis X. Moloney, *The Fur Trade in New England 1620–1676* (Cambridge: Harvard University Press, 1931)—Olson knew this as an honors thesis "20 years ago" at Harvard; he acquires a copy in 1954 (cited later).

Harold A. Innis, *The Cod Fisheries* (University of Toronto Press, 1954)—Olson acquired a copy in 1957 (cited later).

Ralph Greenlee Lounsbury, *British Fisheries at Newfoundland* (New Haven: Yale University Press, 1934)—there is no evidence Olson consulted this work, but he may already have owned the offprint by the same author: "Yankee Trade at Newfoundland," *New England Quarterly* 3 (October 1930): 607–26.

In writing a review of William Appleman Williams, *The Contours of American History* (Cleveland: World Publishing, 1961) for *Kulchur* 10 (Summer 1963), Olson is still hankering after Merk's book ("sd book now ought to be available soon, after forty years it has been promulgated as lectures") because Merk's postulate about American history (presumably the "frontier thesis") strikes Olson as more valid than a "contour" theory, even if Williams has an edge over Heilbroner, Berle or Galbraith.[16] And in a letter of 21 May 1966, Olson tells Dorn that Harvard University Press "doesn't know that Merk is—any more than I have *ever* been able to persuade him to—working up his lectures"; but adds this testimonial: "my *own* heart was taught by him . . . he—*more* indeed than Sauer . . . —gave me paratacticalness . . . Sauer was etymology and Merk the topology . . . it was *movement* (1st real work in ridding History of 'repose')."

# 8

## "Red, White, and Black"

If *Call Me Ishmael* was an attempt to say, in a kind of a shorthand, that the whole of our world could be found in one man, or in one book of one man, Olson's immediate move after its publication was to propose to his publisher the opposite: *e pluribus unum*, a book on America "to tell another story, this time not as of one man Melville but of several men and women . . . the Indian, white and Negro life here on this continent."[1] The reading, therefore, will not be from a center out, but from the circumference in. This is Olson's first try at a 360° completeness of vision. "The book," Olson thought, "ought to line up something like this":[2]

| | |
|---|---|
| prologue | Hopi myth of the CAVES where human life began |
| Tale 1 | CABEZA DE VACA |
| fact | The Aztec RITE of the cutting out of the heart |
| Tale 2 | CORTEZ and MALINCHE |
| Tale 3 | THE SEVEN CITIES OF CIBOLA |
| Tale 4 | LA SALLE |
| Tale 5 | JIM BECKWITH |
| fact | The Kwakiutls of the Northwest Pacific Coast |
| fact | The Cochiti ICE MOUNTAIN "Inferno" |
| epilogue | THE DONNER PARTY |

The reading behind this book, tentatively entitled "Operation Red, White and Black," is best seen in a cumulative way, from a first formulation in a manuscript at Storrs, "An Outline of the Shape and the Characters of a Projected Poem called WEST," apparently done in the spring of 1941 when Olson read the seminal *History of the Conquest of Mexico* by William Prescott and dated it on the flyleaf:

53

"Spring 1941—towards the 'West'."[3] This is how the shape and characters looked in 1941:

| Prologue | Ulysses | (sea) |
|---|---|---|
| I | Faust[4] | (land) |
| | Columbus | (sea) |
| II | Montezuma | (land—old America) |
| | LaSalle | (land—new America) |
| Prophetic | | (sea) |
| Interlude | Balboa | |
| III | Land America: | |
| |   1 Washington and Boone | |
| |   2 Astor and Crockett | |
| |   3 The Machine and John Henry | |
| IV | Sea America: | |

IV     Sea America:
the figure, yet unnamed, of the leader of the emerging maritime empire, a sea Cortez, an historical Ahab, a man in whom the will of the West shall be bent to the conquest of the world by the machine, a Genghis Khan of production, the last, a sea dictator.

Epilogue   The Figure,
yet unnamed, of the man who, like Ulysses for the West, carries in him the seeds of the way of life which shall replace the West, and in a dying world is restless to open the new; confused, harried, but breathing the air of another Indies while those around him stifle from the dead will.

Olson said later that "it was Parkman, and LaSalle, that stirred up this whole thing."[5] Prescott provided him with Montezuma, Cortes, and Balboa. And if one needs to look for a single source for Boone, Crockett, and John Henry, there is one that Olson is known to have been reading in the spring of 1940—a volume that contains those three and Paul Bunyan for good measure: *Their Weight in Wildcats: Tales of the Frontier* (Boston: Houghton Mifflin, 1936), edited by James Daugherty, who sounds confident in his Introduction: "The immense lore behind these few tales and sketches is, it seems to me, a vast Iliad and Odyssey in the raw."[6]

But Olson is not so sure. "I keep turning over in my mind what use can be made of old American tales," he writes in his notebook on 25 January 1945, when he is setting out to be a professional. "Is there any use they can be put to as did Yeats the stories of an older Ireland?" He lists the stories he hopes to make something of:

1. *Bunyan*
   —either tell them straight or add my own to them—or find they are enough as image, hidden or bold-face
2. *Indian*
   —both Aztec-Maya-Inca— —my princess' people
   —and Southwest U.S.—Cochiti & others: consult Benedict[7]
3. *West*
   —Billy the Kid now, Donner later—Merk
   —B DeVoto's things
4. *South & Civil War*

Two days later, the notebook shows a corrective, when Olson talks of the "fake heroes of our history": "We are small here in this land and to compensate act big." He is only interested in the "fables of the larger elements," where Bunyan huddles small and where "the mystery lies outside, around above below a man." This is the yearning toward the condition that Olson will later call the Human Universe. For the moment, he reminds himself of a little book of Indian myths he had as a boy: "As I remember it HILLS WERE ELEPHANTS."[8] Actually, he had kept the book, and it was still in his library at his death: *The Trot-Moc Book of Indian Fairy Tales* (Hudson, Mass., n.d.), which contains the origin story of "How Wash-Ching-Geka Destroyed the Elephant and Why Elephants are No Longer Native American Animals." Olson would place this "just-so" story on quite a different level from, say, *Tall Tales of the Southwest*, to which he had also given a lot of time.[9]

Olson has in front of him William Carlos Williams, *In the American Grain* (New York: Boni, 1925) as a model of integrity. "What has been wrong with all, except Williams, including Salt, is that it has not been worked hard enough."[10] Nor far enough back: 1500 A.D. is not the beginning, but a halfway point. William Carlos Williams goes back to Eric the Red, 1000 A.D.; but that is not far enough either. As indicated by his "working scheme," dated 20 November 1946 (*OLSON* 5, pp. 20–21), Olson wanted to begin with the prehistoric:

1. Folsom man: a swift summary of what he was, as is known

2. First Indians: 10,000 years—with the incredible story by Cushing of the coming out from under the earth, perhaps set against the African story in Fox's *Genesis*[11]

3. The slow change of the Indian forward into complicated struc-ture—via the Cochiti tales & others I do not know where did those things I saw as kid come from: elephant as hill &c

4. The Mexican and Peruvian:

5. Columbus—no: leave him out purposely to focus attention on the land not the sea adventure, any more the White's than the Indian's

or *Open* here 6. CABEZA DE VACA: and turn back to Indians via de Vaca's medicine, so that you catch all three—White, Indian, Negro at once.[12]

7. The Seven Cities of Cibola[13]

8. CORTEZ, with Malanche, and the first climax of the struggle[14]

9. LASALLE—the northern end of the whip, and the huge Columbian tragedy of his failure to find the mouth of the Mississippi

10. The Plains: Beckwith, & the White Steed of the Prairies[15]

11. The Ohio Land Company—full story[16]
    &

12. The Kwatzikiutl of the Northwest[17]

Thus we are getting closer to the "Red, White and Black" proposed to the publisher in 1947. The book was never done, and one wonders why. Olson was still researching it, early 1948, with added input from Vilhjalmur Stefansson's *Great Adventures and Explorations* (New York: Dial, 1947), especially chapter 4: "China Discovers North America," accounting for the presence of Hoei Sin in the following out-line,[18] pushed further out, and back in time, than even the previous one:

(earliest man in Am: Sandia of New Mexico 15–30,000 yrs ago)

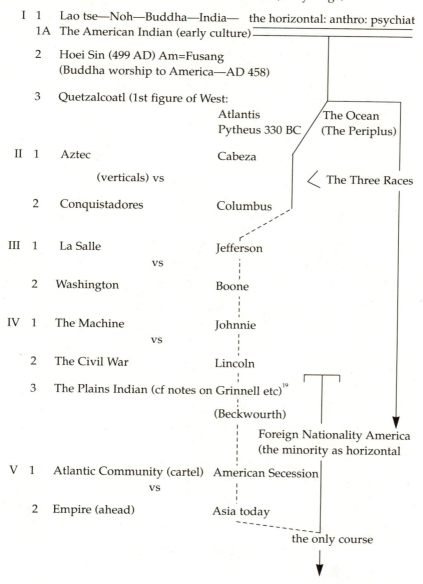

I   1   Lao tse—Noh—Buddha—India—   the horizontal: anthro: psychiat
    1A  The American Indian (early culture)

    2   Hoei Sin (499 AD) Am=Fusang
        (Buddha worship to America—AD 458)

    3   Quetzalcoatl (1st figure of West:

                                    Atlantis              The Ocean
                                    Pytheus 330 BC        (The Periplus)

II  1   Aztec                       Cabeza

            (verticals) vs                            The Three Races

    2   Conquistadores              Columbus

III 1   La Salle                    Jefferson
                    vs

    2   Washington                  Boone

IV  1   The Machine                 Johnnie
                    vs

    2   The Civil War               Lincoln

    3   The Plains Indian (cf notes on Grinnell etc)[19]

                                    (Beckwourth)

                                                Foreign Nationality America
                                                (the minority as horizontal

V   1   Atlantic Community (cartel)  American Secession
                    vs

    2   Empire (ahead)               Asia today

                                            the only course

Olson's own comment on this schemata is: "dispersed beyond imagination." He proposes to himself more work in order to find an aesthetic for a new modern epic of some originality (*OLSON* 5, p. 41):

*Research*

Lao tse
Phyllis Ackerman
Frobenius
Richard Wilhelm's "The Secret of the Golden Flower"
(The aesthetic Salt had?)
Perse's *Anabase*

*Fusang* (1875) Charles G. Leland
*The Dawn of Modern Geography* Charles R. Beazley
*An Inglorious Columbus* Edward P. Vining

The last three titles here were given to Olson by Stefansson's discussion of early Chinese explorations of North America (pp. 109–11); there is no evidence he went further with them. But the approach from the westerly direction has "balked Crane, Macleish, Salt, Aiken," Olson believes. "Reverse the motion of Homer, Dante, Melville: start in Asia with . . . Lao-tse"?[20] Or with Phyllis Ackerman's *Ritual Bronzes of Ancient China* (New York: Dryden Press, 1945), recommended by Henry Murray? Or with *The Secret of the Golden Flower: A Chinese Book of Life*, trans. Richard Wilhelm, commentary by C. G. Jung (London: Kegan Paul, Trench, Trubner, 1945), references to which Olson had noticed in reading Jung's *Psychology and Religion* (1946—cited later), and his copy of which he may have already found? This latter would eventually prove to be Olson's direction, but at this time he still admired St.-John Perse's *Anabase* and wanted "a subject as broad as Perse had."[21] He later came to consider Perse a "phoney Poe," a spreader of "a false spacism" (*Creeley Correspondence* 6, p. 91). These are all explorations,[22] and the most significant leap occurs immediately after in this note to himself, when, under the heading of the Quetzalcoatl Figure, Olson simply writes: "William Stephens, shipwright." He has opened Babson's *History of Gloucester*.

Olson's application to the Guggenheim Foundation for "Red, White & Black" was successful; yet in a letter to Henry Murray of 20 July 1948 Olson declared: "I had to forgo the Guggenheim granted to do the narrative book on the West." He gives no explanation for such a drastic decision. His mind, we know, has turned to poetry; his first book of poems, *Y & X*, had been accepted for publication. A note on "The Long Poem," dated 27 May 1948 (*OLSON* 5, p. 38), begins with a question almost like a rearguard action: "Is it possible to do a long poem called WEST?" He cannot spend time on anything other than what he loves. It is as though, in constructing outlines and reading lists, he has satisfied himself entirely; the subject has found its proper form and has completed itself. Verse is proposing something else to him.

But it isn't only a question of form. America, it seems, has ceased to be a subject he wants to be complete about, and the path dies. Then, just as suddenly, new concerns present themselves: the "prime text" now needed is "a SUMMA based on a putting together, most critically governed, of the work of Frazer, Freud and Frobenius, each bringing the other up, how in the general memory there are old tricks, old events and the oldest dreams and fears, persistent, underneath religion, science and that newest rigidity, collectivism, held there, needing to be registered."[23] This, from an unpublished essay, "About Space," of around June 1948. It proposes another large book that again in the end Olson did not wish to pursue. But it decisively confirms that, for Olson, the urge to completeness is a moveable thing. It can find a proper subject only by continually re-placing itself.

"What does not change is the will to change." The contracted-for history, "Red, White and Black," was dropped in favor of an attempted epic poem, "Proteid" (*Guide*, p. xxiv). Like friezes salvaged from the ruins of that effort, we have the finished poems "The Kingfishers" and "The Praises," which turn epic presumption into tentative personal statement. There is evidence that Olson considered "The Kingfishers" an "Anti-Wasteland";[24] and as the lead poem in Donald Allen's influential *The New American Poetry*, read by the youth of America during a decade of resurgence 1960–70, the poem did gain a status in its own time something like Eliot's poem did in the 1930s. With its quotations from Mao Tse-tung, "The Kingfishers" painted the current political situation in broad strokes. It went to the origins of Western Civilization by means of Plutarch's essay "On the E at Delphi," and to the roots of violence in America by means of William Prescott's *History of the Conquest of Mexico*.[25] It was, at the same time, a personal statement, in which Olson measured himself against not only, by implication, T. S. Eliot, but also more openly Ezra Pound, Dante, and Rimbaud.[26] "The Praises" is cut from the same cloth; but whereas

"The Kingfishers" took its modern definition of "What is Man?" from Norbert Wiener's *Cybernetics*,[27] Olson has since discovered an interesting updating of the Pythagorean tradition: Matila Ghyka's *The Geometry of Art and Life* (New York: Sheed & Ward, 1946), from which he quotes sporadically.[28] Olson had gained a new regard for Pythagoras and his contemporaries from a reading of Diogenes Laertius (previously cited), which he mentioned in a postcard to his old friend Monroe Engel on 28 October 1949: "am thinking very much of you today (of you & Diogenes Laertius) for a clue you gave me some times since ('make a pome of it', sd you), which i suddenly realize is just what i have done (since abt february last.)"[29]

If "The Kingfishers," without belittling the problems, suggests an alternative to the lethargy of T. S. Eliot, "The Praises" might conceivably have Buckminster Fuller in mind with the lines:

> by shipwreck, he perished (Hippasus, that is)
> the first to publish (write down, divulge)
> the secret,
> the construction of, from 12 pentagons,
> the sphere.

That modern wizard of the pentangle had built his first geodesic dome at Black Mountain College in the summer of 1948, and was on campus again the following summer (when Olson was there) with a bigger and better dome. It became understood that it would be either Olson or Fuller who would direct the shape of the future of the College. Olson has described in conversation how Fuller came to his house for a confrontation, and after an hour came out and took his men with him to New York. It does not damage the poem to see behind it a political act of this order, for this is not petty rivalry, but contrasting views of the world's salvation: Fuller's technical improvement versus Olson's essentially conservative attention to the real and its organic processes. When the rather mechanically conceived "Red, White and Black" had transmuted via "The Kingfishers" and "The Praises" into the impulsive and pangenetic *Maximus Poems*, Olson had something which put into the shade such products as Fuller's *Untitled Epic Poem on the History of Industrialization*. After that confrontation, there was nothing for it but to leave and take one's men to the moon.[30]

# Part II
## *Resistances*

Wish some patron or ess wld do for me
what someone did for Ben Jonson—gave
him a swag each yr for books only!
      —Letter to Creeley, 9 October 1951

# 9

## *The Swag of Pound*

To thoughtlessly link Ezra Pound and Charles Olson is a great error. Olson was always annoyed when he saw it happening. Yet he must take a good part of the blame: "next of kin," he called Pound in "The Kingfishers." He placed him conspicuously in the *Maximus Poems*, and at no time refused to name him as one of his masters. The fact is that Olson was very objective about Pound, as every page of the manuscript that was edited posthumously as *Charles Olson & Ezra Pound: An Encounter at St. Elizabeths* testifies. Considering that Olson had not read Pound until he picked up Hemingway's copy of *Personae* in Key West in 1945;[1] considering that he only kept company with Pound for two years (1946–48—and for six months of that he was away, out West); considering that he was a long-time Roosevelt Democrat and publicly declared anti-fascist;[2] and considering that he was very different from Pound, both as a writer and a man—it should be surprising to us that there is any relationship at all to discuss. It happened because of Olson's sense of fair play, his kindness towards a man being brought in chains to what was then Olson's hometown, Washington, D.C. It happened also because Olson had a good idea of the unique value of what Pound, though apparently destitute, was carrying in his swag-bag.

Like a magician, Pound pulled out book after book, and got his young helper to do so, too. The titles are recorded in the minutes of the meetings: "cantos," as Olson dryly headed them.

### "First Canto, January 5, 1946"

"I met Pound for the first time yesterday." How well prepared was Olson? Imperfectly. He misheard Pound, and wrote down a reference to "Cantos 50–61," not aware that the book in question was *Cantos LII–LXXI*, Pound's last U.S. publication before the war cut him off.[3] Olson owned *Eleven New Cantos XXXI–XLI* (New York: Farrar & Rinehart, 1934), which later, on 29 January 1946, Olson brought for Pound to sign (he wrote: "To Chas Olson saviour as it were onlye sustainer Ezra Pound 46"), along with his copy of *Guide to Kulchur* (London: Faber & Faber, 1938), which Pound also signed ("Chas Olson with deep gratitude E. Pound 29 Jan '46"). We know from notebooks that he read in June 1945 *Jefferson and/or Mussolini* (New York: Liveright, 1936) and *Instigations of Ezra Pound, together with An Essay on the Chinese Written Character by Ernest Fenollosa* (New York: Boni & Liveright, 1920);[4] and probably *ABC of Economics* (London: Faber & Faber, 1933—U.S. edition 1940) about the same time.[5]

### "Canto 2, January 15, 1946"

Pound and Olson agreed on the decadence of the surrealist magazine, *View*, published in New York 1940–46, but not on that of newspaper commentators like Westbrook Pegler, Austine Cassini, and John O'Donnell. Pound said he had been reading Ayn Rand's *Fountainhead* (1943) and Ernest Poole's *Harbor* (1915); Olson seems to have been aware of these books, nothing more than that. Pound mentioned Harold Stanley Ede's book on Gaudier-Brzeska, *Savage Messiah* (1931) and Olson noted it in his notebook but did not buy it. Pound also "wildly jotted down two mss for Laughlin's attention": Mary Butts, *Death of Felicity Taverner* (published in England in 1932) and Ronald Duncan, *Journal of a Husbandman* (published by Faber in London, 1944). Olson passed on these recommendations to New Directions the next day. There is no evidence he sought out Mary Butts, but he borrowed a copy of *Journal of a Husbandman* and tried his hand at reviewing it for a magazine he knew called *Tomorrow*. After Pound went through the draft, Olson did not submit it.

### "Canto 3, January 24, 1946, 3:10–3:30"

The only book mentioned this time was Ford Madox Ford's *Some Do Not*, which Pound said had done "more good than anything has, to restore me." Pound told Olson to read it, but there is no evidence that he did.[6]

### "Canto 4, January 29, 2:55–3:15"

Pound is nervous about the sanity trial the next day. He signs the two books Olson brought. Frobenius mentioned for the first time.

### "Canto 5, February 7, 1946, 3:15–3:30"

"Mentioned I had stolen a poem from him." This was a short poem based on the "Make It New" inscription, worked by Olson from his copy of Pound's *Ta Hio: The Great Learning* (New York: New Directions, 1939).[7]

"I had been rereading some passages from the Cantos the night before"—including canto 30, presumably using his copy of *A Draft of XXX Cantos* (London: Faber & Faber, 1933).

Pound said he thought Maritta Wolff's *Whistle Stop* (1941) was good. There is no evidence that Olson agreed.

### "Canto 6, February 14, 2:30–2:45"

Pound gives Olson the typescript of the first two cantos of the *Pisan Cantos* to deliver to James Laughlin. (Before doing so, Olson copied out three pages of the text in admiration.)[8]

Frobenius mentioned again. Olson "did not know of any translation." Pound referred him to Douglas Fox.[9]

### "Canto [7] March 19, 1946"

"Of my raising in Gloucester, he connects Eliot, I register complaint against E's use of Dry Salvages."[10] Arnold Bennett's *Old Wives Tale* is mentioned.[11] Pound proposes that Olson should do a job on Jefferson and Mazzei; Olson will look into it.[12] Olson indicates that he had read, and liked for "the care and the speed," Pound's article, "Ezra Pound on Gold, War, and National Money," *Capitol Daily* (Washington, D.C.), 9 May 1939.[13]

Pound is irritated "at Laughlin's delay on the *Confucius*."[14] Olson is annoyed that Laughlin has sent all of Pound's works to Dr. Kavka:

"I'm damm well going to take them away from K. After all I was the one who gave K your books to start him off."[15]

### "¼POUND: April 30 (after Five Weeks): 20 minutes"

Pound mentions the special Cummings issue of *The Harvard Wake*, No. 5 (Spring 1946); and Goldring's *South Lodge*, "the high period of my life."[16]

### "June 18, 1946: with EP from 1:20–1:45"

Pound brooding about what if he had not left the U.S.—Henry James's story "The Jolly Corner" mentioned in this regard.[17]

### [Stray Notes on Visits, 1946–1947][18]

"MacLeish article—Sat Rev Lit."[19] "Briarcliffe—about Angold (best of the crop—pre–war."[20] "Santayana—at least he's got to the point where he don't lie."[21] "Binyon's trans—fair, mild as he himself."[22] "His job on 'Gabe'."[23] "Pound's insistence: study the Greek for versification, & leave the Greek vision alone—leave off the pagan business—not the Hellenic—H. D. did it."[24] "Pound got on tail of Brooks Adams only in 1937–8."[25] "On HLM."[26] "Eliot's review of *TAR*."[27]

### "February 9, 1948"

Olson, back from the West Coast, mentions Robert Duncan, William Everson, Mary Fabilli, and Kenneth Rexroth.[28]

William Carlos Williams has visited Pound; his article, "With Forced Fingers Rude" (on Eliot and Milton) in the February 1948 issue of *Four Pages*, is discussed.

We have evidence in letters of the time how much Olson regarded Pound as a resource: "Can you direct me to what look like more suppressed stuff—the Hymns and Fragments of Orpheus? (By the way, most remarkable Bellini at National Art Gallery: 'Orphee.') And did you run across any good work on the Priapus cult, how it went underground and where it is beside shit house walls?" Possibly it was Pound's connection with Remy de Gourmont's seminal theories that led Olson to address his questions to him. It was an interest that led Olson to read at least the following books:

Sigmund Freud, *Leonardo Da Vinci: A Study in Psychosexuality* (New York: Random House, 1947)—or perhaps a previous edition; Olson's reading notes are in the "MYTH" notebook of spring 1947.

Remy de Gourmont, *The Natural Philosophy of Love*, trans. Ezra Pound (New York: Liveright, 1942)—half-title page: "Olson."[29]

Richard Payne Knight, *A Discourse on the Worship of Priapus* (originally published 1786)—the "MYTH" notebook indicates Olson read it in the Library of Congress.[30]

Vittorio D. Macchioro, *From Orpheus to Paul: A History of Orphism* (New York: Henry Holt, 1930)—read in Library of Congress, with notes in the "MYTH" notebook.

J. R. Watmough, *Orphism* (Cambridge University Press, 1934)—Olson did not own this volume, but there exist four pages of reading notes at Storrs, made in preparation for the "Imago" essay.

Other letters reveal an ongoing conversation about books, at one point with the practical aim to offer James Laughlin a "low-priced modern classics series," as Olson told him in a letter of 5 May 1946, "the New Eliot 5 ft., the New Loeb." In another connection, in a letter of 29 July 1946, Olson asked Pound for the names of "those two plays you attribute to Woodward": Pound's reply by return mail led Olson, notes indicate, to read in the Library of Congress "William Mahl" (i.e., the historian W. E. Woodward) *Two Plays of the Social Comedy* (New York: privately printed 1935). A letter of Olson's to Dorothy Pound indicates that his attention had been drawn by her to the Oriental Book-shop catalogue listing Ernest Fenollosa, *The Chinese Written Character as a Medium for Poetry* (New York: Arrow Editions, 1936), which he then obtained from them (letter of 26 September 1946). In a letter to Pound on 15 December 1946, Olson comments on the Cavalcanti section of Pound's *Make It New* (New Haven: Yale University Press, 1935), which he owned. Without naming it, he mentions returning to Pound "little Hoffman's big book." At Pound's urging, Olson corresponded with John Berryman at Princeton in February–March 1947. It is not known what Olson had read of this poet (he did not own any of his volumes), but Berryman had a short story in *New Directions 9* (1946) that Pound had handed on to Olson (flyleaf: "Washington Spring '47"). In a letter of 24 August 1947, Olson was offering Pound "2 books on Usury by Geoffrey Mark" that he had in his possesion.[31] Finally (as far as present information goes), in a letter of 14 December 1947, Olson comments on James Laughlin's anthology of the ten years of *New Directions*, *Spearhead* (New York 1947), which, it appears, Pound sent him while on his trip to California. These specific comments were not complimentary, and Olson did not return back East with the volume.

William Carlos Williams always represented the other possibility, the stay-at-home contrast to Ezra's European side. Olson had had his *White Mule* from New Directions when it came out in December 1937, though it was later missing from his library. He called it, in a letter of 5 December 1939, "the best thing to me in American writing in a hell of a while." *The Complete Collected Poems: 1906–1938* (New Directions, 1938) that did survive was probably acquired early, in time for the dinners organized by Ford Madox Ford for "Les Amis de William Carlos Williams" in spring of 1939. *In the American Grain* (New York: Albert & Charles Boni, 1925) goes back even earlier, with its flyleaf signature, "Charles J. Olson Jr." Olson's loyalty to Williams was unwavering and, no matter what remains in his library, he probably read everything as it came out, such things as "Against the Weather" in *Twice A Year* 2 (Spring–Summer 1939), which he claims to have "stolen and stolen from," and "Preface" in *Poetry* (Australia) 10 December 1947. Olson retained his copy of the *New Republic* 133 (31 October 1955) for Williams's "How Verse Forms Create Something New." True affection is evident in all this: Olson sends Williams a get-well message (24 February 1948), saying he has been in California and everybody is reading *Paterson* out there! Williams's play, *A Dream of Love* (New York: New Directions, 1948), seems to him, he tells Creeley on 22 August 1951, "so altogether all right, so exact, so lovely"—something he never got close to saying about anything of Pound's. A high point was receiving *The Beloit Poetry Journal* 5, no. 1 (i.e. Chapbook No. 3, the Walt Whitman issue—Olson had a *Maximus* poem in it), and writing to Williams about "The Ivy Crown," found therein: "You are blessing life all over the place—people (and now this place, for which I am personally moved" (letter, 3 December 1954). He later made a rare (for him) public tribute in reviewing *Paterson (Book Five)* (New Directions, 1958).[32] He was sticking by the choice he had made long before (on 9 February

1948, to be precise), when Pound began to bad-mouth Williams, and Olson walked out on him.

Olson did not visit Pound after February 1948; he was sick of the man, finally. An irresistible antithetical moral force was asserting itself, as we shall see. That the interest in Pound's work did not wane is reflected in Olson's library.[33] One even sees some of the Square Dollar publications there; Olson did not spurn John Kasper out of hand.[34] Olson did not have to become rabidly anti-Pound in order to prove that he had risen from under his predecessor.

One act which takes on symbolic significance happened well before the break with Pound, when Olson bought and gave as a gift to his patron and friend Henry Murray the newly published *Christ Stopped At Eboli* by Carlo Levi (New York: Farrar, Straus, 1947). The preface reads: "Because of his uncompromising opposition to Fascism Carlo Levi—painter, doctor, and writer—was banished at the start of the Abyssinian War (1935) to a small primitive village in Lucania, a remote province of southern Italy. It is his impressions of life in this region, which remains unknown not only to tourists but to the vast majority of Italians, that Levi has given in the following pages." Levi was thus Pound's contrary; he knew what Pound chose not to know, not only about fascism but about a range of life alternative to "the West," to the civilization that Pound had made himself "the ultimate image of the end of."[35]

But no matter how wide the gulf, it seems, the Olson-Pound linkage will not give way. Olson admits he acquired his C. H. Fenn, *The Five Thousand Dictionary*, 6th printing (Cambridge: Harvard University Press, 1948) "fr seeing EP—when yardbird—carry it around the jailyard"; and then adds on the flyleaf: "but 1st appreciated Gloucester 1 Aug. 1959—13 yrs!" And one senses Olson's deep relief at having the chance to do one last "canto" with Pound, Spoleto 1965, after seventeen years.

# 10

## *The Preface to*

It was probably Corrado Cagli who put Olson on to Carlo Levi.
Cagli, too, went into exile from Mussolini's fascism. When his painting
came into disfavor, he left Rome—first for Paris, then to the United
States—where Olson ran into him and was never the same again.
"Talk," he explained to Creeley. "Talk. Reason I like Kaggli. (1st time,
3 days, Gloucester, he not knowing English, I not Italian . . . 3 days, and
all night long mostly. How? Don't know. Just did it, the two of us.
Crazy. May, 1940."[1] And writing in May 1946, Cagli back from his war
service in the U.S. Army, Olson celebrates:

> It is now, precise, repeat. I talk of Bigmans organs
> he, look, the lines! are polytopes.
> And among the DPs—deathhead
> > at the apex
> > > of the pyramid.[2]

But it was not the same, for Cagli had brought back the biggest and
most ghastly news of all time in the form of drawings he had made at
Buchenwald when his artillery unit had opened up the camp: "the first
to look into that compost of civilization."[3] Olson's poem, "La Préf-
ace," commissioned by Cagli for the brochure of the New York and
Chicago showings of the drawings, was the poet's attempt to resist the
utter resistance of this knowledge in such a way that from that stop he
might know a new beginning—while saying to himself in the poem:
"You, do not you speak who know not." Cagli knew. Olson tried to
know, from books such as David Rousset's *L'universe concentrationaire*
(Paris, 1946) and Louis Martin-Chauffier's *L'homme et la Bete* (Paris,
1947).[4]

By a remarkable coincidence, within a few months of writing in the voice of a survivor, "I weigh, I think, 80lbs . . . " Olson met someone to whom that would apply: Jean Riboud, who was among other things (his life would take much space to describe) a French resistance fighter and a survivor of Buchenwald. Olson dedicated his prose piece, "The Resistance," to Riboud, acknowledging that there had been a living model for the defiance of fragmentation he speaks of there.[5] But this is no morbid business: Cagli and Riboud were great friends for Olson; they opened things up, they did not stultify. They taught him "the way a man comes to core . . . the discovery of, his own resistance . . . the way a poet—at least—makes himself of USE to society."[6] It was Riboud who quoted to Olson the words of Mao Tse-tung as his credo, and Olson picked them up for "The Kingfishers": "La lumiere de l'aurore est devant nous. Nous devons nous lever et agir."[7]

If Riboud's contribution was mainly non-literary, Cagli can be seen to have pushed Olson forward on three fronts at a time when such pushes made a great deal of difference to how Olson would develop as a writer. First there was the Tarot. Cagli taught Olson the arcana, and Olson got a number of interesting poems from allowing his fresh sensibility to mingle with the old mystery of the Tarot. The collaborative *Y & X* (1948), five drawings by Cagli and five poems by Olson, was achieved through this "push" into a certain level of archetypal practice. It must have been a great reinforcement to the beginning poet's sense of Muse. But Olson's skill in divination with the cards soon became uncanny to a degree Olson was not at that time prepared for, and at some point in 1950 he swore never to touch the Tarot again. No books on the subject stayed in his library.[8]

Secondly, Cagli was in advance of Olson in utilizing non-Euclidean geometry for an approach to his art, hence the word "polytopes" in the quotation from "La Préface" above. Cagli would have told Olson about Roberto Bonola's *La Geometria non-Euclidea* (1906). Olson quotes Riemann at Pound (in a letter of 15 December 1946) from the English translation of Bonola, in a section on "Projective Geometry."[9] It was Cagli who put Olson on to the four-dimensional models of Paul S. Donchian that Olson then went to the Library of Congress to read about in H. S. M. Coxeter, *Regular Polytopes* (London: Methuen, 1948). This reading was a preparation for his introduction to Cagli's exhibition, brought over from Italy to the Watkins Gallery in Washington, December 1949, entitled "Drawings in the 4th Dimension." Cagli gave

Olson new eyes. "What is involved here," Olson told his audience on that occasion, "is something which both science and art have long been capable of, the act of taking a point of vantage from which reality can be freshly seen."[10]

Cagli's third push was where we might most expect it: Italian painting. When Olson mapped out "Idea for Series of Lectures at Richman's Institute of Contemporary Arts," the "artists and work would be: (1) Bontempelli, (2) Cagli, Mirko, Chirico."[11] Olson had educated himself up to a point; witness *Italian Masters Lent by the Royal Italian Government* (New York: Museum of Modern Art, 1940), which he no doubt picked up at the exhibition, January–March 1940. But it is another matter to be invited up to New York by Cagli for the opening of a show at the Knoedler Gallery: the artist, Mirko Basaldella, again an exact contemporary, born 1910. In other words, Olson had something new and vital to offer the Washington art scene—which, for him, was chiefly Caresse Crosby.[12] So it was to Caresse that he wrote, after the Berlin paintings show in Washington that took place from 17 March to 25 April 1948, of his discovery for himself of Giovanni di Paolo ("one of those half dozen, I suppose, that one finds in a lifetime who seem to have some secret of feeling, statement, method which has your own signature on it"),[13] and of his "Notes on the New Dimension," i.e., the dimension of awkwardness (letter of 23 July 1948): "idea, why we critters take Duccio, Sasetta, Giovanni di Paolo, etc., even up as far as Piero and Uccello, as more interesting than the big and suave boys. The coins I'm handling, the counters, are: awkwardness (as permanent cloth of spirit), the oblique as a via to confront direct—as guerilla, as maquis—the enemy. The enemy being: quantity, materialism, the suave." And then he puts a name to the enemy: "Chiang Kai Check."

Which brings us to the third of those who opened up the world afresh for Olson in the immediate post–war years. For it was not only the maquis Jean Riboud who had news of Mao Tse-tung; Robert Payne had actually visited Mao in the Yenan caves. While still a young man (another exact contemporary of Olson's), Payne had met Hess and Hitler in Munich in 1937 and had been up to the Barcelona front in the Spanish Civil War. He was duty officer of the Singapore Naval Base on the night of Pearl Harbor, spent the war years in China, and when Olson met him in Los Angeles in October 1947 he was fresh from visiting both Jinnah and Nehru in India. What Payne gave Olson at that time was his anthology of Chinese poetry: *The White Pony* (1947),[14] but soon after Olson's return to Washington he received through the mail Payne's book on the freedom movements throughout Asia, entitled *The Revolt of Asia* (New York: John Day, 1947), and wrote Payne a long response to it.[15] Again, a new dimension had become available.

It is important to mention that Cagli, Riboud, and Payne were foreign-born aliens, because it was exactly on the issue of racial and cultural "impurity" into America through immigration that Olson's anger with Pound boiled over: formed by immigrant values, Olson had made his greatest contribution to society through the Foreign Nationals Committee of the Democratic Party. He knew with deep certainty which side he was on.[16] But it is also true that he had had enough of the grievous side of the underdog consciousness and obviously welcomed this new breed of successful supranationals. And through Caresse Crosby he literally received his own "Passeport Citoyen du Monde."[17]

Asia, by all accounts, seemed ready for some new resurgence; the West should look to it. In his "Notes for the Proposition: Man is Prospective" (about May 1948, manuscript at Storrs), Olson has decided that we know enough to make a move:

> The *premise:* that 100 years of analysis into the ways of man and universe
>
>> (Marx Darwin Renan Fourier Sorel
>> Frazer Freud Spengler Kierkegaard
>> Einstein De Sitter Frobenius
>> & some now alive Saint Francis
>
> is enough to go on.

The idea is "to try to see our time at one glance . . . regard its motions and say, swiftly, where it tends"—with the presumption that "those motions actually shape up into a direction as profound as the change of attention which we call the Renaissance."[18] Thus, a preface: a preface to "The Kingfishers," itself a preface to a renaissance called *Maximus*.

The week before Olson's first visit to Black Mountain College, Constantine Poulos, his former associate at the Office of War Information, back from a visit to Greece, put into his hand Lawrence Durrell's novel *Cefalû* (London: Editions Poetry, 1947). Olson wrote to Henry Murray about it on 10 October 1948: "It handles a theme I have interested myself in, blocked out a ballet or dance-play of: the labyrinth."

Olson asked psychologist Murray for anything written on the image of the labyrinth, adding (innocently) "We leave in an hour."

## Appendix

## Art Books

Olson wrote the following letter to Caresse Crosby on 23 January 1950, making evident what an exuberant gallery-goer he was:

c.c.

this is to award you 1st prize in taste    yesterday con & i caught, on its last day, what they call the Austrian show (it shld have been dubbed the Vienna Derby, I never saw such a collection of woman-flesh in my life!)
and wow, does tintoretto win, by all sorts of lengths—and you up isn't it a beauty? i looked over my shoulder & there she was, to dazzle me

otherwise well, the correggio *Io & Jove* next
                    the Durer of the murder of 10,000 xtians
                            another tint.: of the Admiral of Lepanto
                                a wondrous Crespi: of the Sibyl, Aeneas & Charon
                                    & the Cavallino of David playing before Saul

but susanna
        susanna, o!
    And not she alone, the whole canvas, the hedge, the distances,
the peepers, the mirror god keep us, how
can characters not see
the beauty of this world?

                                            i salute you

                                                    o

Despite his cherishing an early book like *Historic Ornament and Art History*, Topic Books of Art Education (New York: Prang, 1913), it seems for all practical purposes Olson's art education began in Washington with Caresse Crosby. Certainly she introduced him into an art world which included luminaries such as Huntington Cairns, whose *The Limits of Art* Olson saw in proof stage, and John Walker, who showed him his forthcoming paper on Bellini's "Feast of the Gods." This led Olson to recommend to Caresse the new Edgar Wind, *Bellini's Feast of the Gods* (Cambridge: Harvard University Press, 1948): "as clean as scholars can be, and alive."[1] Huntington Cairns and John Walker were preparing *Great Paintings from the National Gallery of Art* (New York: Macmillan; Washington: National Gallery of Art, 1952). Olson would have been aware of this volume, as he would (without owning either of them) its predecessor: *Masterpieces of Painting from the National Gallery of Art* (1944).

Olson kept the brochure of the Austrian show mentioned in the above letter, *Art Treasures from the Vienna Collections* (1949). Other brochures and texts not mentioned elsewhere are listed below:

Alfred H. Barr, ed., *Vincent van Gogh*, 2d ed. (New York: Museum of Modern Art, 1935)—light notes and markings.

Nell Blaine, *An Exhibition of Recent Paintings 1964–1965* (New York: Poindexter Gallery, 1966).

Jean Sutherland Boggs, *Picasso and Man: A Catalogue* (Art Gallery of Toronto; Montreal Museum of Fine Arts, 1964).

A. Bredius, ed., *The Paintings of Rembrandt* (Vienna: Phaidon; New York: Oxford University Press, 1937).

W. Norman Brown, *Descriptive and Illustrated Catalogue of Miniature Paintings of the Jaina Kalpasutra* (Washington: Smithsonian Institution, Freer Gallery of Art, 1934).[2]

*Decorative Murals in the Massachusetts House of Representatives* (Boston, 16 December 1942).

Frank Elgar and Robert Maillard, *Picasso* (New York: Praeger, 1956)—flyleaf, in Betty Olson's hand: "July 1960."

Roger Fry, *Cezanne* (New York: Noonday, 1958)—flyleaf: "early October—1959"; markings throughout.

Pierre Gassier, *Goya* (New York: Skira, 1955).

1. Letter to Caresse Crosby (Southern Illinois Special Collections), 23 July 1948. Olson did not acquire this recommended Edgar Wind volume, but the later Edgar Wind volume, *Pagan Mysteries in the Renaissance* (New Haven: Yale University Press, 1958) came into his library via Harry Martin (to whom it was inscribed by Kenward Elmslie).

2. Olson had another volume in the same series by W. Norman Brown, Professor of Sanskrit in the University of Pennsylvania: *The Story of Kālaka: Texts, History, Legends, and Miniature Paintings* (Washington: Smithsonian Institution Freer Gallery of Art, 1933). This was deposited with Jean Kaiser.

Thomas B. Hess, *Willem de Kooning* (New York: Braziller, 1959)—some
   light markings.
Sam Hunter, *Jackson Pollock* (New York: Museum of Modern Art,
   1956)—notes and markings.
Rene Huyghe, *Art Treasures of the Louvre* (New York: Abrams, 1951).
*Iranian Art at the Oriental Institute Museum* (Chicago: University of Chi-
   cago Oriental Institute, 1951).
*Kline* (New York: Sidney Janis Gallery, 1961).
Jean Leymarie, *Monet* (New York: Tudor Publishing Co., 1964).
*Modern Ecclesiastical Art, International Exposition, Chicago, 1933: Ger-
   many* (Berlin: Otto Eisner, 1933).
Frederic Newlin Price, *Ryder (1847–1917): A Study of Appreciation* (New
   York: William Edwin Rudge, 1932)—flyleaf: "Charles John Olson
   February 1940 from Alden Clark" and "For my Constance—be-
   cause she wanted it! All my love, Charles July, 1941."
William Rubin, *Matta* (New York: Museum of Modern Art, 1957).
*Sculpture in Ceramic by Miró and Artlgas* (New York: Pierre Matisse Gal-
   lery, December 1956).
James Thrall Soby, *Ben Shahn* (New York: Museum of Modern Art; West
   Drayton: Penguin Modern Painters Series, 1947).
James Thrall Soby, *Balthus* (New York: Museum of Modern Art, 1956).[3]
James Johnson Sweeney, *Henry Moore* (New York: Museum of Modern
   Art, 1946)—Moore mentioned in "Notes for the Proposition: Man
   is Prospective."


Books owned by Olson which discuss art in a more general way are:


Marcel Brion et al. *Art Since 1945* (New York: Washington Square Press,
   1962)—markings pp. 270–311.
Alex Comfort, *Art and Social Responsibility* (London: Falcon Press,
   1946).
Helen Gardner, *Art Through the Ages* (New York: Harcourt, Brace,
   1947)—flyleaf: "Thomas Field 1948 Fort Wayne Indiana."


3. It seems highly unlikely that Olson did not peruse with interest James
Thrall Soby and Alfred H. Barr, *Twentieth Century Italian Art* (New York: Mu-
seum of Modern Art, 1949).

Susanne K. Langer, ed., *Reflections on Art* (New York: Oxford Galaxy Book, 1961).[4]

Erwin Panofsky, *Studies in Iconology: Humanistic Themes in the Art of the Renaissance* (New York: Harper Torchbook, 1962).

Selden Rodman, *Conversations with Artists* (New York: Capricorn, 1961).

Charles Seymour, *Tradition and Experiment in Modern Sculpture* (Washington: American University Press, 1949).

4. Olson also owned what appears to be a much used second-hand copy of Susanne K. Langer, *Philosophy in a New Key: A Study in the Symbolism of Reason, Rite, and Art* (New York: Pelican Books, 1948).

# 11

## *Throw What Light*

So Olson was ready to go down to Black Mountain College. He packed his "Notes for the Proposition: Man is Prospective"—where he makes good use of Robert Payne and Corrado Cagli:

A treatise on dimensions, springing out of non-Euclidean geometry, would be as contributory to art now as Piero della Francesca's treatise on perspective was in the 15th century.[1]

Add: the persisting failure to count what Asia will do to collectivism, the mere quantity of her people leverage enough to move the earth, leaving aside the moral grace of such of her leaders as Nehru, Mao, Shjarir.[2]

And he gave himself the following schedule.

*Black Mountain College—I: 12–15 October 1948*[3]
Tues:   2:00 strictly 1 hr The Regimen of the Poet—with readings
        8:00 Object and Space or The Dimension of Art
Wed:   2:00 strictly 1 hr—the writing of students
        8:00 The Mystery of Mr William Shakespeare or The Elizabethan
        World[4]
Thurs: 8:00 Mythology—Melville and the Classics
Fri:    2:00 final class in writing.

He visits eight times in the 1948–49 year, a week or so at a time.

*Black Mountain College—II: 17–19 November 1948*[5]
        2:00 writers
        8:30 lecture on non-Homeric myth
        2:00 writers and readers

8:30 readings from contemporary verse
2:00 writers

*Black Mountain College—III: mid–December 1948*[6]

Course descriptions:

> Reading—the work is the examination of writing, both verse and prose, with the end that the individual be led to comprehend the serious intent of the creative writer, whether he be Ezra Pound, William Faulkner, William Shakespeare, Homer, Seami, or the writer who gives the course.

> Writing—the work is the exercise and practice of language by its two means, verse and prose, with the end that the individual learn to see, hear, feel directly, to speak and think likewise (which is to write).

*Black Mountain—IV: 14–19 February 1949*

[Little information:] Olson "lecturing on the ear" [letter to Payne, 24 February 1949].

*Black Mountain—V: 14–19 March 1949*

[Little information:] "Black Mt has helped, for I am able to lecture on those things which concern me at the time, and there is no break in stride" [letter to Monroe Engel, 6 April 1949]. "At Black Mt I took away a book called MELODY & LYRIC by JMGibbon[7] which you might care to look at (do not buy) for the lyrics there printed I do not find elsewhere" [letter to Edward Dahlberg, 8 April 1949].

*Black Mountain—VI: 25 April–1 May 1949*

[Little information:] "These trips tire me very deeply. It is a great effort for me to go, and, back, to return to my work" [letter to Dahlberg, 2 May 1949].

*Black Mountain—VII: 16–20 May 1949*

"I have just bracketed and assigned together DAHLBERG and HOMER: the ODYSSEY & THE FLEA OF SODOM (in mss), BOTTOM DOGS (which they have), and BONES" [letter to Dahlberg, 2 May 1949]—student reading assigned in advance. Olson reports of this session: "You were the one who went home, of all the year. And what will please you, BONES more, much more than DOGS, and, for the illuminated, the FLEA more than BONES! These, the new ones, read yr prose in a romp, the late prose" [letter to Dahlberg, 31 May 1949].

*Black Mountain—VIII: 6–11 June 1949*

[No information.]

Olson's course for the summer session 6 July–29 August 1949 was officially entitled "Verse and the Theatre." At first, Olson's plan was

> to use the eight weeks to mount the first production
> of THE NEW COMPANY now forming here washington
>                                         (i should
> offer a course in the odyssey by omeros which is the clue
> to the re-invention of new theatre)
>         the production to be purposely small, either
>                 TALES AT THE HOUSE OF ALKINOOS omer
>         or WAGADU                               olson.[8]

He could not get his Washington troupe down to Black Mountain, so the final performances, 28–29 August 1949, contained much student improvisation, with Olson reciting "Wagadu" and his own poem, "Not the Fall of a Sparrow."

At the back of all this activity was much reading. For instance, for Homer, Olson had discovered, via Dahlberg, Victor Bérard—not merely the "light quick" *Did Homer Live?*, but the two-volume, untranslated *Les Phéniciens et l'Odyssée*: "It makes me angry and to weep that that work was done 45 years ago, and only now I know of it" (letter to Monroe Engel on 6 April 1949). That Bérard can go behind Homer to more archaic Semitic sources[9] was the breakthrough Olson was groping for through a mass of unyielding material, such as the "biblio on Crete" of October 1948:[10]

> Evans, *The Palace of Minos*
> Edward Bell, *Prehellenic Architecture in the Aegean* (1926)
> E. J. Forsdyke, *Minoan Art* (1929)
> Martin P. Nilsson, *The Minoan-Mycenean Religion* (1927)
> W. Ridgeway, *The Early Age of Greece* (1927).

"I have spent two days in Crete and Mycenae, following the Ariadne thread of my mind," he told Dahlberg (letter, 7 October 1948). "But the words do not go down on paper. . . . So much preparation . . . without production." A nervous bookstore buying spree: "All I was able to do was to divert and prepare myself by buying *Bohns* and *Loebs*: Athenaeus, Hesiod, Catullus, the Anthology, the Morals, Theocritus, Herodotus, Percy's Reliques, John Lyly's Plays, Elizabethan Lyrics. I traded all week" (letter to Dahlberg, 20 September 1948).[11] "Yesterday it was Euripides," he wrote to Dahlberg on 25 March 1949, "his ORESTES, which I was trying to get to by way of Way,[12] angry that I do not have that language." He asks in this letter if Dahlberg knows "any writing by anyone on HOMER, which has illuminations?" He is trying to remember Bérard—"the book you spoke of reading, of the influence of Tyre and Sidon on the Iliad?" By 8 April 1949 he has "fed on" Bérard, and can announce to Monroe Engel (in a letter of that date) that "my heart belongs to VICTOR BERARD!" and that from this "amour" a spate of reading has come: "Theocritus and Ovid (read, one day, in the Heroides,[13] Medea to Jason the day she learns the bastard is taking up with another dame) and the Bacchae of he who wrote it when he was in exile not far from where O was, later. And Maximus of Tyre (now there is a man they don't tell us about either, and on whom I stumbled by chance, reading Sappho)."[14]

What would it take for Olson, after all this dashing in and out of books, to get words to "go down on paper"? It would take, as it turned out, a remarkably intuitive and intellectually energetic woman. Frances Boldereff had read *Call Me Ishmael* when it came out and had written to Olson about it. Olson sent her his poems, *Y & X* (1948). She sent him her tribute to Michelangelo, *A Primer of Morals for Medea* (1949)[15]—no accident that he was reading Medea to Jason in Ovid. It was to Frances that Olson sent the postcard on 29 March 1949 which marks his discovery of Maximus of Tyre; he teased her by giving only the Greek side of the Loeb page (translated it reads: "they were captivated by all beautiful persons"). Then, as a talisman from one scholar to another, Frances forwarded to Olson something she had obtained from its author: an offprint of S. N. Kramer, "The Epic of Gilgameš and Its Sumerian Sources," *Journal of the American Oriental Society* 64 (1944): 7–23. That did it. Olson first dug up an old Gilgamesh poem from 1941 to send; then he wrote a new one, "La Chute," right out of the notes on Kramer that he was making on the flyleaf of his Modern Library Homer. He sent it to Frances on 25 May 1949 with the annotation: "recognize it? my thanks." And for good measure, the next day he wrote a short poem, "Dura," based on frescoes in the temple of Zeus-Baal at Dura-Europos that, again, Frances had directed him to.[16] Olson was launched on the path that, after eighteen months of further work, would result in the essay "The Gate and the Center," his first formulation of the postmodern, with its thesis: "the archaic sought."[17] "We are only just beginning to gauge the backward of literature, breaking through the notion that Greece began it, to the writings farther back: to the Phoenicians, to the Babylonians, behind them the Akkadians, and, most powerful of all, the Sumerian poets, those first makers, better than 2000 years prior to Homer, Hesiod & Herodotus."

The same person ran with him all the laps to the completion of the essay:

*Letter, 28 November 1949.* "it is my big man Sauer who turns my attention back to work by sending me his paper on 'Environment and Culture During the Last Deglaciation,' read before the American Philosophical Society, two years ago . . . it is on the fresh-water fisher folk of Mesolithic time, and sends this child."[18]

*Letter, 10 January 1950.* "have looked into Dunne. But so far he adds nothing to me, in fact irritates me some, he is a salvationist. There is a wrong (and a peculiarly important wrong right now) in such men's overt apocalypsisms. . . . When Dunne comes to talk about the Symphony of All Creation, I reach for a line to slay him with. (Immortality, Bah!). (It was the same when Fjelde kept pressing me to read Sullivan on Beethoven.)"[19]

*Letter, 10 April 1950.* "i have now found in strzygowski your christ horse-mounted, yr havrenah-lands, and i would write and write to you, how beautiful it is, as you so exactly know, to have one's blood reinforced: like cookies, these wonderful stucco things, like archaic myth of the baking of men—my objectism right in front of my nose!"[20]

*Letter, 6 July 1950.* "yr own recent discovery of Pistis Sophia (plus the passage you sent last week, which I want to examine for you)—all this has got me back, today, to this central concern. . . . It is the limit, to mush the archaic into Xty, in order to give it a ride on a new back, when, itself, originally, damn well could walk, and how, BY HERSELF."[21]

*Letter, 13 July 1950.* "Today it is snakes I wish you would tell me all you know abt. Got off on them by way of Apollonius of Tyana (Mead, who writes on PS, writes a book on A of T, which I got to first) . . . ending up, by way of Miss Harrison, on *Zeus, Honey* (it kills me, but that's what it translates, Z Meilichios!), who was worshipped as the most beautiful snake you ever saw, Fig. 1, of Miss Harrison's PROLOGO-MENA. . . . I do not need to tell you that you and I are entwined in a very dark thing, dark not only in its truth (the old dark, which men have strayed away from) but dark, too, for us, no matter how clear we are, because we are also children of that immediate past as well as children and projectors of that more chthonic, archaic thing."

*Letter, 25 July 1950.* "i have so thrown myself down into Sumer i cannot get out! i am 'sealed' 'cylindered' and undelivered! Spent yesterday on my boy Waddell, who continues to be one of the most exciting men i have ever read (yet i am not yet prepared to say whether i buy his package), and have, today, been poking my nose into yr pal Porada, and her boy Frankfort."[22]

It is L. A. Waddell who has captured, for a time, Olson's imagination. In a letter of 26 July 1950 to Frances Boldereff, after quoting Woolley on where the Sumerians came from,[23] Olson uses Waddell to help him formulate his own answer, typing out nine single-spaced sheets of notes on the chronology in Waddell's *The Makers of Civilization in Race and History* (London: Luzac & Co., 1929).[24] He writes to Creeley the next day (*Creeley Correspondence* 2, p. 80):

> Been in one of those periods which come up every so often where I get a teeth-hold on something, and can't give over until I've beat the dog. This time it's a guy I stumbled on accidently in the Sumerian catalogue, Lib. Cong.—and who sends me: I'm bracketing him with the boys who taught me something, with Victor Bérard, Josef Strzygowski, Carl Sauer, & Leo Frobenius (add Lattimore, for one book, his first, I think, The Inner Frontiers of Western Asia). This guy is L. A. Waddell, a crazy Englishman (or maybe he's a Scot). Anyhow, right or wrong, he's got a package wrapped up on who civilization got movin, and who moved it, that jibes with a lot I have found in my own archaisms and previously documented from the above gents.

Waddell is "the GATE," and it is in this letter that the essay "The Gate and the Center" as we know it begins to take shape, a delayed response to Creeley's request for something on education for his proposed magazine. Olson is beginning to see, aided by a lecture by George Sarton he attended the previous spring,[25] that education must get back to a "center" before Plato's Athens, which will be Bagdad, or earlier, Sumer. Thus, while customarily allusive,[26] "The Gate and the Center" comes to rest—solidly or not—on Waddell. A year later, when Creeley is embarking for England, Olson suggests in a letter of 27 July 1951 that he should "prepare himself" with Waddell's *The British Edda*, "in which he dances all over this thing, like some damned witch doctor, trying to squeeze out the old and lost history"—adding that "however nutty he appears, he is a straight application of Frobenius's laws."[27] Olson does not turn his back on Waddell; he lists him in March 1961 among "men worth anyone's study,"[28] a reaffirmation of the effort that went into Olson's first essay written as a pleasure *doceat* sometimes allows.

Concurrent with the months of study that went into "The Gate and the Center" and its revisioning of history to restore the primordial was the writing of that work for which Olson is chiefly known, the new *ars poetica*, "Projective Verse." Olson sent the first version to Frances Boldereff on 11 February 1950. It begins with the comparison of "open" and "closed" verse, with reference to the source, "a French critic" who turns out to be René Nelli.[29] But it differs from the final version in having T. S. Eliot take the main brunt of the argument: "Eliot's line, from 'Prufrock' on down, is a dramatic line, doth stem from Browning(?), certainly hath obvious relation back to the Elizs., especially to the soliloquoth; yet OMeliot is *not* projective, goeth by his personeth instead of by object and by passion."[30] This is later expanded and quietened and put at the end of the essay, but the draft shows where the animus came from: the need to take on the Nobel Prize committee, and state that "it is time we picked the fruits of the experiments of Cummings, Pound, Williams" in composition "by field."[31] Olson was throwing what light he could—in any case, much light on his own poetic methodology.

Influential as "Projective Verse" became, Olson's most immediately effective teaching at this time can be found in those letters to Cid Corman that spell out what a vital magazine the proposed *Origin* could be. Olson had tried earlier with Richard Wirtz Emerson of the Golden Goose Press in Columbus, Ohio, but had been simply too impatient at editorial delays and vacillations,[32] witness Olson's replies to a questionnaire Emerson was sending around. When asked, "Does poetry come from mental and/or spiritual happiness or unhappiness (discontent, frustration, etc)?" Olson wrote (in a letter of around 7 July 1950): "God help us. Just stay sane. But not like Goethe, o, no, no, NOT at such a price. Better be Holderlin (or Christopher Smart), if that's what you have to pay. Anyhow, avoid all such nonsense of da da de da. You will, anyway, if you're putting it out. And for the rest, anybody else? Let it go Hugo: 'l'humanité, c'est l'infirmité.' "[33]

As any literary history of the 1950s now fully records, Olson was more successful with Cid Corman, in such emphatic letters as, for instance, that of 21 October 1950 on "how you, Cid Corman, can, 1951, construct a MAG, which will be pumpkins," i.e., more than a reflection of "this 40 yr end of that essay 'Tradition and the Individual Talent' ":[34] "Well-made poems, stories, pieces—o, say, Harvey Shapiro, or Richard Wilbur, or Miss Hoskins, or Stephen Spender (intimate) or who else do you think of publishing? . . . weary-or-howlyrically lovely (Barbara Gibbs) or o not pretty yet but will be (Rukeyser or the lazy leftists)." Olson is goading Corman into having more than scratch-my-back ambitions as an editor: "But take a look at any little mag, take a look at the PNY issue starring Apollinaire. What happens? The oldest thing here in these States: backtrailing, colonialism, culture scratching! Suddenly Bill Merwin, or whoever is alongside, is, shown up, to be proceeding on culture concepts—humanisms—which are patently NOT HIS. And with no such CORE of ENERGY to offset same fine flowering of PAST: What happens? mag collapses, as FORCE."[35]

Spring cleaning, in Olson's view at this time, calls for the use of "document": "I have in my hand a poem by one RCR, called, "Christmas Comes Early to One Los Angeles Youth"—which is clippings from AP story out of LA, mit comments, including 'phew!' One Paul Valery, when he did edit a magazine, called it—look!—COMMERCE."[36] In this context Olson refers to Charles Reznikoff's *Testimony* (New York: Objectivist Press, 1934): "He is a lawyer. He made his book up of selections from court records, of situations, or words, or 'plots' therein discovered."[37]

> Diana Woelffer (wife of Emerson Woelffer, Chicago Painter)
> sent me Saturday a cat. of SIX STATES PHOTOGRAPHY (Milwaukee
> Museum). Her own photo was of kids under swinging door of
> cantina (very much Cartier-Bresson ::::: if
> > I got you notes by H C-B
> > on trip just now completing
> > self, Peking (Mao's entrance);
> > Shanghai (the Gang's Retreat);
> > India; Indonesia, and auto
> > trip Calcutta to Paris (the
> sort of thing he might well do, yet no one is editing in
> such a fashion as to *call him out*)      short notes—
> WOT WOULD YOU DO WITH IT (alongside Theodore Roethke)?[38]

Photography is document versus creative writing. In surveying the literary scene for Corman, Olson sees document as one possible

way of combatting current fragmentation and angst. A magazine can
be a whole, a totality:

> do you, cid corman, think that you can put out a PUSH,
> now, by not following up on the FIRST PRINCIPLE (the
> non-deductive, but formal totality of a man, say, in each
> issue) to the SECOND PRINCIPLE, the same, from p. 1 to page
> 75 (you say)
>                     AS OF THE WHOLE REALITY NOW?[39]

It was the Woelffers who had put Olson on to the availability of a
cheap waterfront house in Lerma, Yucatan. Olson was already antici-
pating a move, like Apollonius of Tyana's moves, to gain further in-
sight into reality, looking forward to meeting in Mexico Carl Sauer's
protégé, Robert Barlow, who as an anthropologist and a poet has given
signs of knowing the value of document. He offers Corman a model in
Barlow: "His main job, right now, is a life of Montezuma. He has ed-
ited for some years a LITTLE MAG called Tlluocan—in, watch this,
NAHUATL. The last thing of his I saw was two pages in *Circle*—one a
drawing by him of a 'madonna' of rocks and a spring he discovered in
Oaxaca or somewhere. The other page was his impeccable and dis-
criminating description of where he found it and what it is."[40]

Olson was about to embark on a "field trip" as an "archaeologist
of morning." His letters to Robert Creeley will survive as a record of
his experience of the "other," that which might make a totality pos-
sible, a record of where he found it and what it is.

# 12

# Yucatan, Archaeology of the Postmodern

Olson wrote to Frances Boldereff on 16 March 1950:

> A couple of weeks ago I walked into Lowdermilk's bookstore looking for
> Lawrence's *Fantasia*, or anything else I could pick up cheap. Sez the cloik:
> "But look, we've got a Lawrence collection! And some of his paintings."
> My god, I could hardly hold the floor beneath me. And in 3 minutes, there
> I was looking straight into the face of a watercolor I had to own! Of a man
> pissing against a brick wall into a bed of daffodils.

Olson organized the sale of the collection to the Library of Congress,
and got the painting as commission,[1] with, apparently, *Fantasia of the
Unconscious* (London: M. Secker, 1923) thrown in—that "wonderful
questing job," as he termed it in a letter (*Creeley Correspondence* 5, p.
148). This book—as much as anything—got Olson to Mexico in Febru-
ary 1951, not *The Plumed Serpent* or *Mornings in Mexico* or "The Flying
Fish" or any of the moody travel pieces.[2] Just as Olson loved but did
not imitate Lawrence's poetry, so he moved here in a kinship which
was not imitation, except in resisting the high temptation of the mind.
"Lawrence somehow chose the advantage of moral perceptions to
those of the intellect." Olson is speaking of something he noticed Hux-
ley making much of in the introduction to Lawrence's *Letters*, "DHL's
leaving off his intellect's skills."[3] And in *Fantasia of the Unconscious* he
most blatantly and proudly left them off, "trying to stammer out the
first terms of a forgotten knowledge." But then when he goes on to say
that he has "no desire to revive dead kings, or dead sages. It is not for
me to arrange fossils and decipher hieroglyphic phrases"—that's
when Olson feels he can take over. He will do it.

The seed was planted when Olson commandeered a review copy

of *The Maya and Their Neighbors* (New York: Appleton-Century, 1940)—flyleaf: "Olson when he was an editor of COMMON GROUND 1941–2." This volume contains all the greats of Mayan scholarship, including, for instance, Sylvanus Griswold Morley on "Maya Epigraphy," the progress of decipherment up to that point.[4] Olson bought Morley's *The Ancient Maya* (Stanford University Press, 1947) during "summer xlix," and consulted his volumes for the Carnegie Institution, *The Inscriptions at Copan* (Washington, 1920) and *The Inscriptions of Peten* (Washington, 1938), "merely to have the glyphs to look at."[5] He made a lucky buy in *Proceedings of the Twenty-third International Congress of Americanists Held at New York, September 17–22, 1928* (New York: International Congress of Americanists, 1930)—flyleaf: "Olson bmc spring '49 for a buck & ½." He took this large volume with him to Mexico and made good use of it for the poem "To Gerhardt, There, Among Europe's Things," as well as for specific Mayan matters.[6]

There are good guys and bad guys in Mayan scholarship: "the Peabody-Carnegie gang" versus kindred souls, among whom Olson distinguishes John L. Stephens for his two books, *Incidents of Travel in Central America, Chiapas, and Yucatan*, 2 vols. (New York: Harper, 1841), and *Incidents of Travel in Yucatan* (New York: Harper, 1843), with Frank Catherwood's drawings in each, "the only intimate and active experience of the Maya yet in print."[7] The bibliography to *Mayan Letters* gives cautious approval to two "stabs at value, on the language question": "the long work of William E. Gates, from 1910 to 1940, published by the Maya Society, Baltimore, and including his outline dictionary of Maya glyphs, 1931"; and "B. L. Whorf's four papers on Maya, among his many on other languages, and on language itself."[8] And there is an in-between category: "valuable and respectable, of course, but not inspired." Olson places *The Maya and Their Neighbors* in this category, along with J. Eric S. Thompson, *Maya Hieroglyphic Writing: Introduction* (Washington: Carnegie Institution, 1950);[9] A. V. Kidder's Introduction to A. Ledyard Smith, *Uaxactun, Guatemala: Excavations of 1931–1937* (Washington: Carnegie Institution, 1950), pp. 1–12;[10] and "the climax still, of all such work," *Mexican and Central American Antiquities, Calendar Systems, and History*, twenty-four papers by Eduard Seler, E. Forstemann, Paul Schellhas, Carl Sapper, and E. P. Dieseldorff, translated from the German under the supervision of Charles P. Bowditch as Bureau of American Ethnology Bulletin 28 (Washington: Smithsonian Institution, 1904).[11]

Which brings us to the "the Peabody-Carnegie gang." But even here it is not all black and white; Olson makes reference to "whatever they may have done, 50, or 25 years ago"—granting them something, even though they are now "missing the job" (*Creeley Correspondence* 5, p. 25). Very soon Olson is writing to an old Carnegie man, Robert Wauchope of the Middle American Research Institute, Tulane University, about their map of *Archaeological Sites in the Maya Area*.[12] Wauchope sends a map on 5 March 1951, and there is a cordial exchange of letters. Olson did not have the same luck with the Peabody man he tried on the recommendation of Caresse Crosby and on the basis of seeing (presumably in the Archaeological Museum in Campeche) *Tulum: An Archaeological Study of the East Coast of Yucatan* (Washington: Carnegie Institution, 1924). His long letter, raising questions about the importance of the sea to the ancient Maya, was left unanswered by Samuel K. Lothrop of the Peabody Museum, Harvard. It is possible he genuinely did not understand what Olson was getting at; as Olson said in the letter: "It is always a little difficult to say to what ends a poet moves" (letter, 19 March 1951, Storrs). The poet will stand on the ground of aesthetics—Maya hieroglyphs as prosodic entities, for instance. This, anyway, is where Olson certainly saw the divergence, writing to Corman from Lerma on 9 February 1951: "it is wild, the way all the big guns of Carnegie and Peabody etc, actually rest their careers on a people whose whole value, recovered, is aesthetic, and yet, with the possible exception of Tozzer[13] (and among the young Barlow) they themselves are without aesthetic comprehension!"

So that, too, is part of the postmodern, the restoration of beauty! Robert H. Barlow was a poet as well as an expert anthropological linguist; he had proved himself a true follower of Carl Sauer's teaching of culture-morphology, in exactly the way Olson was trying to be:

> a yr ago, unknown to me, he had done precisely what I have now done (and, of course, with supreme equipment, he)—had settled at Telchac (another fishing village like this one, on the north coast of the peninsula, near Progreso) to master this speech, in order, I should imagine from my own temper, to go in by way of it to those passages of man that archaeologists do not get to. . . . In other words, Barlow was taking the steps which the present demands of any worker anywhere: SOUNDS.[14]

But the fragility of the search for beauty is symbolized in Barlow's suicide a month before Olson would have seen him in Mexico.

The difficulty of the task, on another level, is shown in Olson's vain pleas for funding to stay on, the one to the Viking Fund of the Wenner-Gren Foundation taking twenty-five of his working days down there. We do, however, have the document that resulted: "The Art of the Language of Mayan Glyphs," the formal statement to go alongside the *Mayan Letters*. It includes a scholarly survey of the field, with mention of the three codices of Paris, Dresden, Madrid, and also the Book of Chilam Balam, with a glance at the work of Alfred P. Maudslay as well as that of John L. Stephens. There is reference to J. Eric S. Thompson as "the climax of the great decipherers (Forstemann, Goodman, Bowditch, Beyer, Gates, Long and Teeple.)"[15] It is not clear what reading went into this list, beyond the works already mentioned.

The other notable document that reflects the Yucatan experience and Mayan reading is the "Human Universe" essay, where the materials from letters to Creeley and Corman were raised to a semi-formal exposition in the last month of Olson's stay, the first draft written 10–17 June 1951. This draft begins with a postmodern parable resulting from a particular contrast of cultures that Olson was experiencing through having, by accident, brought with him to a Mexican fishing village the latest volume of *New Directions in Poetry and Prose* (no. 12, 1950): "The laws," he writes, "are larger and more durable than these sad modern and personal solutions."[16] The first morning after his arrival back at Black Mountain College, 11 July 1951, Olson started rewriting "Human Universe" by slashing the draft's ephemeral opening. A *Proteus Quarterly* had been waiting there for him, and he noticed in it an article entitled "Law and the Change of Consciousness" by Norman Macbeth. Olson specifically noted the story of Cormac shouting from the back of an early "town-meeting" a judgment that was both commonsense and also, as Olson put it in a letter to Macbeth, "a clear and present noticing of how nature behaves": "This sort of clarity is the issue of particularism (as against, which has been the base of 'law,' deductive and inductive methodologies of universals)."[17] Though the story of Cormac is shrunk in the final "Human Universe" to the one word "shout" in the third paragraph, the theme of particularism versus generalization is strengthened into a frontal attack on Socrates and Plato, and a modern representative like Toynbee.

As a matter of fact, it is in Toynbee's sense of "Post-Modern" (i.e., the latest stage of Western history, after 1875)[18] that Olson uses the word in speaking of "the post-modern world" in a letter to Creeley on 9 August 1951. But in his second use of the word, in a letter of 20 August 1951, he has already attached it to the experience of the archaic to "undo the modern" and its alienation:

> my assumption is
> any POST-MODERN is born with the ancient confidence
> that, he *does* belong.
> So, there is nothing to be
> *found*. There is only (as Schoenberg had it, his
> Harmony) search.[19]

In spite of several uses of "postmodern" in letters around the time of the revision of the essay, the word itself does not appear in "Human Universe." But the definition of it does appear, in terms of belonging— as Olson places himself in the rhythms of life in Yucatan—and through his first use of the statement from Novalis: "he who possesses rhythm possesses the universe."[20] (And this is not just a metaphor: Olson could not travel to the Near East and had to be content with Galpin's book, *The Music of the Sumerians*; but he did work out on old Mayan drums.)[21]

Olson made large claims in the "Human Universe" essay. How many have been prepared, even in the face of the present disarray of Western thought, to name Plato as a culprit? "Nor can I let the third of the great Greeks, Plato, go free—he who had more of a sort of latitude and style my tribe of men are apt to indulge him for. His world of Ideas, of forms as extricable from content, is as much and as dangerous an issue as are logic and classification, and they need to be seen as such if we are to get on to some alternative to the whole Greek system."[22] Lawrence was a clue to the alternative: "For Lawrence knew, as no metaphysician ever does, the discipline and health of form, organic form as distinguished from that false form which the arrangements of the intellect, in its false speed, offer." This was written prior to Olson's trip to Mexico.[23] The people of Yucatan were living confirmation, in the way "they wear their flesh," and the way, for instance, that they "fire clay into pots porous enough to sieve and thus cool water, strong enough to stew iguana and fish, and handsome enough to put ceremony where it also belongs, in the most elementary human acts."[24]

## Appendix

## Mexico Books

Carnegie Institution of Washington publications owned by Olson (not mentioned elsewhere) are:

Samuel Kirkland Lothrop, *Atitlan: An Archaeological Study of Ancient Remains on the Borders of Lake Atitlan, Guatemala* (1933)—from BMC library, later deposited with Jean Kaiser.
Samuel Kirkland Lothrop, *Zacualpa: A Study of Ancient Quiche Artifacts* (1936).
C. L. Lundell et al., *Botany of the Maya Area: Miscellaneous Papers XIV–XXI*, (1940).
A. S. Pearse, Edwin P. Creaser, F. G. Hall et al., *The Cenotes of Yucatan: A Zoological and Hydrographic Survey* (1936).
H. E. D. Pollock, *Round Structures of Aboriginal Middle America* (1936).
Oliver Ricketson et al., *Uaxacutun, Guatemala: Group E—1921–1931* (1937)—cited by Olson in *Mayan Letters* (*Selected Writings*, p. 120).
Alfonso Villa Rojas, *The Maya of East Central Quintana Roo* (1945).
Karl Ruppert and John H. Denison, *Archaeological Reconnaissance in Campeche, Quintana Roo, and Peten* (1943).
J. Eric S. Thompson, *Excavations at San Jose, British Honduras* (1939).
Robert Wauchope, *Modern Maya Houses: A Study of their Archaeological Significance* (1938).

The following items Olson probably picked up while he was in Mexico:

Raul Pavon Abreu, *Metodo Para El Calendo de los Jeroglificos* (1945); *Morales: Una Importante Ciudad Arqueologica en Tabasco* (1945); *Xcalumkin: su serie Inicial* (1949)—all three published by the Campeche Museo Arqueologico Ethnografico, of which Pavon was then director.
Gustavo Martinez Alomia, *Viaje Arqueologico a Los Chenes 1894* (Campeche: Gobierno del Estado, 1941).
Alfonso Caso, *Thirteen Masterpieces of Mexican Archaeology* (Mexico: Editoriales Cultura y Polis, 1938); *Las Estelas Zapotecas* (Mexico: Telleres Graficos de la Nacion, 1928).

Roman Pina Chan, *Breve Estudio Sobre la Funeraria de Jaina, Campeche* (Campeche: Gobierno de Estado, 1948).

Santiago Pacheco Cruz, *Compendio del Idioma Maya* (Mexico: Dep de Divulgacion, 1948).

Juan de D. Perez Galaz, *La Introduccion de la Imprenta en Campeche* (Campeche: Gobiero del Estado, 1942).

Doris Haydn and Arturo Castello, *Archaeology in Mexico Today* (Mexico City: Pemex Travel Club, 1951).

Juan Martinez Hernandez, ed., *Diccionario de Motul: Maya Espanol* (Merida: Tallares de la Compania Tipografica Yucatan, 1929)—"done here in the Yucatan mid–16th century, and not equalled since" (*Selected Writings*, p. 71).

M. Wells Jakeman, *The Origins and History of the Mayas* (Los Angeles: Research Publishing Co., 1945)—mentioned in *Mayan Letters*.

Alberto Ruz Lhuiller, "Universalidad, Singularidad, y Pluralidad de Arte Maya" reprinted from *Mexico en el Arte* 9 (1950).

Manuel Cirerol Sansores, "*Chi Cheen Itsa,*" *Archaeological Paradise of America: A Handy Guide-book for Visitors to Yucatan* (Merida: Talleres Graficos de Sudeste, 1948).

*Tasaciones: de los Pueblos de la Provincia de Yucatan* (Campeche: Gobierno del Estado, 1942).

*Tres Cedulas Reales* (Campeche: Gobierno del Estado, 1942).

The following books were presumably acquired by Olson after his return from Mexico:

*Archaeological Map of Middle America, Land of the Feathered Serpent* (Washington: National Geographic Society, 1968).

*Art Mexicain: Du Precolombien a nos Jours*, Tome 1 (Paris: Les Presses Artistique, 1952).

Bernal Diaz del Castillo, *The Discovery and Conquest of Mexico* (New York: Farrar Straus, 1956).

*Descriptive List of Research Papers and Theses Accepted by the Graduate School of Mexico City College*, vol. 2, 1954–1960 (Mexico City College Press, 1960).

Philip Drucker, *La Venta Tabasco: A Study of Olmec Ceramics and Art*, Bureau of American Ethnology Bulletin 153 (Washington, 1952).

Maud Worcester Makemson, *The Book of the Jaguar Priest: A Translation of the Book of Chilam Balam* (New York: Henry Schuman, 1951)—

flyleaf: "Olson (fr Hazel & Charles Larsen-Archer, Jan 54)", occa-
sional notes.

*Maya Research* (Tulane University), vol. 3, no. 2 (April 1936)—from John
Adams at BMC probably during 1952.

*Mesoamerican Notes* (Mexico City: Department of Anthropology,
Mexico City College)—no. 3 (1953) and no. 5 (1957).

Sylvanus Griswold Morley, "An Introduction to the Study of the Maya
Hieroglyphs," Bureau of American Ethnology Bulletin 57 (Wash-
ington, 1915)—flyleaf: "Olson bot? 53 anyway, 1st used Feb 27, the
day after receiving fr R Creeley the mss of Mayan Letters—to get
on with things."

Robert L. Rands, "Some Manifestations of Water in Mesoamerican
Art," Anthropological Paper no. 48, Bureau of American Ethnol-
ogy Bulletin 157 (Washington, 1955).

J. Avilés Solares, *Descifración de la Piedra del Caledario* (Mexico: Talleres
de Impresión de Estampillas y Valores, 1957).

Gustav Strömsvik, "The Ball Courts at Copan," *Contributions to Ameri-
can Anthropology and History*, no. 55 (Washington: Carnegie Insti-
tution, 1952)—inscribed to Olson by the author, whom he had met
in Yucatan.

Edward Herbert Thompson, *People of the Serpent: Life and Adventure
Among the Mayas* (Boston: Houghton Mifflin, 1932)—flyleaf: "JW"
(a second hand copy, as gift?).

George C. Vaillant, *The Aztecs of Mexico* (Harmondsworth: Penguin,
1951).

Victor Wolfgang von Hagen, *The Aztec and Maya Papermakers* (New
York: J. J. Augustin, 1944)—flyleaf: "To Charles from Charlie &
Hazel 1954," some notes.

Victor Wolfgang von Hagen, *Realm of the Incas* (New York: Mentor
Book, New American Library, 1957).

Gunter Zimmerman, *Kurze Formen—und Begriffssystematik de Hiero-
glyphen der Mayahandschriften* (Hamburg: Im Selbstverlag des
Hamburgischen Museums fur Volkerkunde und Vorgeschichte,
1953).

One classic in the field, Fray Bernardino de Sahagun, *A History of
Ancient Mexico*, available in a two-volume edition (Nashville: Fisk Uni-
versity Press, 1932), was at least known to Olson. When he loses his
patience with Edward Dahlberg over the *Nimbus* article, "Myth of Dis-

covery: The Americas" (previously cited), he explodes with: "my lawd, Sahagun!" (letter to Dahlberg, 12 November 1955).

Olson presumably had with him in Mexico the U.S. War Department's *Spanish: A Guide to the Spoken Language* that he had saved from his days in the Office of War Information when he had produced the bilingual *Spanish Speaking Americans in the War*, also 1943. He later picked up and kept Jose Antonio Echeverria's *Obras Escogidas* (Havana: Ministry of Education, 1960).

# 13

## Olson's University

Well aware of the founding principle of the arts as the center of the curriculum at Black Mountain College[1], Olson threw himself vigorously into dance and theater on his return there in July 1951.[2] By 27 July 1951, he could announce in a letter to Creeley, "have now done three dance-plays, for sundry, here": (1) "Apollonius of Tyana" for Nick Cernovich to dance, "and I to be Tyana, the word or speaking part";[3] (2) "The King of the Wood," an "African shadow-play," based on Frazer's *The Golden Bough*;[4] (3) "The Born Dancer," for "my boy Lafarge," the Nijinsky story, based on his *Diary* and a news item about his last dance.[5] Olson's interest exhibited itself in reviews and pieces of writing done for Black Mountain dancers, e.g., "A Syllabary for a Dancer,"[6] for Nataraj Vashi, who, in the course of teaching dance in the summer of 1952 also gave a lecture, "The Philosophical Foundations of India," which introduced Olson to the Vedas. Olson then cannot write about dance without registering that new knowledge. It is all very well for Olson to quote Artaud in the "Syllabary": "*Arts*, said Artaud, are those things which do not carry their end any further than their reality in themselves"[7]—when clearly dance leads to Vedanta, and the arts as a whole for Olson (one hazards to suggest) are a means to a cosmology.

As for formal theater, Wesley Huss was appointed in 1950 as a full-time drama teacher and stayed with the college till the end in 1956, maintaining a dialogue with Olson, some products of which exist in writing. The one play that Olson is known to have acted in was a reading of *Peer Gynt*, in which he was Button-Molder.

## New Sciences of Man

Black Mountain College held a theater institute, to which Olson contributed a rather off-the-cuff lecture, probably on 11 January 1953.[8] He was already deeply involved in preparations for "Olson's thing," the Institute of the New Sciences of Man. For there was another tradition besides the arts that Olson was eager to pursue: the idea of Black Mountain College as a smaller Princeton Institute for Advanced Studies. As Olson told his fellow faculty, "these two 'Institutes' have the same common intention: the sober, modest concentrated task of penetrating the unknown—Oppenheimer characterizes the IAS as 'a kind of assembly point of ideas.' I wld characterize BMC as ideally a like assembly point of acts."[9] This new attempt at a total vision grew out of Olson's teaching, as Mark Hedden's class notes from about the time of the inception of the Institute indicate. Hedden showed Martin Duberman his diary, and *Black Mountain: An Exploration in Community* presents a summary (pp. 395—96):

> a razzle-dazzle list of important figures and works in the "new sciences," a nonstop recital (the importance of *breath!*) that included Riviere, Bastian, Levy-Bruhl, Ratzel, Frobenius, Berard, Jane Harrison, Freud, Jung, William Carlos Williams' *In the American Grain*, Carl Sauer, Vilhjalmur Stefansson, Owen Lattimore's *The Inner Frontiers of Eastern Asia*, D. H. Lawrence's *Studies in Classic American Literature*, Wilson Knight's *The Wheel of Fire*, the Bohn translations of the classics, Edmund Wilson's *The Shock of Recognition*, Fenollosa's *Essay on the Chinese Written Character*, journals of the Amiel brothers, Stephen Crane's *The Blue Hotel*, and Pound's *ABC of Economics*.[10]

Olson took to the College Board, presumably on 6 May 1952, a "1st Draft of Possibilities for The Institute of the Sciences of Man":[11]

> 1875, the pivot year (Schliemann having opened way by opening Hissarlik-Troy 1868, but without archeological method: that method worked out by Dörpfeld, at Olympia, 1875)
> so,
> I.(base science) ARCHEOLOGY (the re-opening of the backward horizons of man as man NOT as anthropoid:
> ex. of distinction—discovery 1879 of cave of prehistoric paintings, de-

cisive date 1895, Riviere's proof that these were of the Ice Age, 200th century BC

so,

II. emergence of, CULTURE-MORPHOLOGY (the new, & still essentially unadmitted science)

Ancillary to both, and on either side of each, are:

(of ARCHEOLOGY):

III GEOGRAPHICAL SCIENCES (the earth, climate, soils, crops, etc.)

IV BIO-SCIENCES (ontogenetic, phylogenetic, etc)

(of CULTURE-MORPHOLOGY):

V PSYCHOLOGY (Freud, & post)

VI MYTHOLOGY

The first person Olson wrote to, once the Board of Fellows agreed to the institute, was Carl Sauer, on 10 May 1952. When Sauer couldn't come, he thought of Christopher Hawkes, whose book, *The Prehistoric Foundations of Europe to the Mycenean Age* (London: Methuen, 1940) he had just read with great excitement.[12] Olson finally wrote to Hawkes on 3 January 1953, admitting that it was "ridiculously short notice." Meanwhile, he had written to Carl Jung. A carbon copy of a draft of the letter exists at Storrs, dated from Washington, 7 December 1952, and addressed to "My dear and honoured Carl Jung." In inviting Jung to participate in the Institute, Olson is aware (Jung was of an advanced age) that what he was asking might seem extreme: "Yet, great doctor, for you, again, at this time, to make another trip to the United States is as fit as your work has been, as proper a further act of it as all the books I should want to tell you I, for one, would wish that you would still write, as full of total admiration (more than for any living man) as I am for those you have written."

There is no doubt that Olson was sincere in his homage, but it is surprising. Only two and a half years before, he had held a contrary view. Picking up *Psychology and Religion* ("my 1st reading of Jung, by the way") and going through the endnotes, he decided that "Mr Jung is, as I always hunched, a lazy fraud, in this respect, a mere g.d. swiss soft pink hill of learning" (letter to Frances Boldereff, 6 July 1950). Olson would have reason to regret his boast (in the same letter) that he "could smell, by way of a sentence, say, the totality of a man's work." The turn-about would be comical if we did not have some hint of the circumstances: in October 1952 Connie took the baby Kate and left Olson alone in Washington, and it was in his loneliness that he read several volumes of Jung with rewarded intensity.[13] In the end, it was arranged that Marie-Louise Von Franz, Jung's close associate, would come in his place.

Edgar Anderson of the Missouri Botanical Gardens (a Sauer protégé) was invited on 15 January 1953, "for his work on plants and man is crucial to the program as it is conceived."[14] He could not come. Other expected speakers named at one point were Linton Satterthwaite—"on recent Mayan diggings," S. N. Kramer—"to expose Sumerian texts," Frank Frazer Darling—"it was Sauer's insistence that the plan called for some ecology," and Martin Sprengling—"on the alphabet."[15] These were people mentioned to Robert Braidwood in his letter of invitation dated 9 January 1953. None of them came, but Braidwood could come. "Braidwood at least reports accurately what he found," Olson wrote to Creeley on 16 March 1953, after the week's lectures.[16]

As for his own contribution: the surviving pertinent documents were edited by George Butterick under the title "The Chiasma, or Lectures in the New Sciences of Man," comprising the whole of *OLSON* 10. Olson takes it that the "new" sciences will be involved with the oldest of materials, protohistory, and mythology.

Protohistory or Cro-Magnon

William Foxwell Albright, *The Archaeology of Palestine* (Harmondsworth: Penguin, 1949)—Olson had the 1951 printing. Notes and markings.

H. J. D. Astley, "Cup- and Ring-Marking," ed. James Hastings, vol. 4 of *Encyclopaedia of Religion and Ethics* (New York: Scribner, 1924), pp. 363–67—Olson used the BMC set. Butterick dates notes at about November 1951 that indicate Olson was also consulting Lewis Bayles Paton's contributions, "Sanchuniathon," pp. 104–5 and "Phoenicians," pp. 887–97.

William C. Boyd, *Genetics and the Races of Man* (Boston: Little, Brown, 1950)—the second citation in the "BIO" list. Volume not owned by Olson.[17]

Leo Frobenius, *The Childhood of Man* (London: Seeley, 1909)—Olson reminded the students that there was a copy in BMC library; he took this copy when the college closed.

Leo Frobenius and Douglas C. Fox, *Prehistoric Rock Pictures in Europe and Africa* (New York: Museum of Modern Art, 1937)—flyleaf indicates it was acquired in 1952 from John Adams, faculty member at BMC.

R. Ruggles Gates, *Human Ancestry from a Genetic Point of View* (Cambridge: Harvard University Press, 1948)—cited in the "BIO" section of the reading list of the Institute; volume not owned by Olson.

A. L. Kroeber, *Anthropology* (New York: Harcourt, Brace, 1948)—Olson retained the BMC copy in his own library.

Gertrude Rachel Levy, *The Gate of Horn* (London: Faber & Faber, 1948)—flyleaf: "Olson black mt feb '57"; but a copy was borrowed on interlibrary loan in January 1953.[18]

Henry Fairfield Osborn, *Men of the Old Stone Age* (New York: Scribner, 1916)—flyleaf of Olson's copy indicates that it was a birthday gift from a student at BMC, Donald F. Daley, on 27 December 1952.

Max Raphael, *Prehistoric Cave Paintings*, Bollingen Series, vol. 4 (New York: Pantheon, 1945)—cited in *OLSON* 10, p. 55; book not owned by Olson.

Charles Rau, "Observations on Cup-Shaped and Other Lapidarian Sculptures in the Old World and in America," in *Contributions to North American Ethnology* 5 (Washington: Department of the Interior, 1882), 1–112—marked in Olson's copy.

Carl O. Sauer, "American Agricultural Origins: A Consideration of Nature and Culture" in *Essays in Anthropology Presented to A. Kroeber* (Berkeley: University of California Press, 1936), pp. 279–97—cited as Sauer's most noticed piece of work. Volume not owned by Olson.[19]

Carl O. Sauer, *The Morphology of Landscape* (Berkeley: University of California Press, 1938). Reprinted from University of California Publications in Geography 2 (1925)—cited in the reading list of the Institute. Olson acquired his own copy from the University of California Press in June 1960.

The "epigraph to all the Stone Age portion of this Institute" (*OLSON* 10, p. 35) is taken from Frances Densmore, *Teton Sioux Music*, Smithsonian Institution, Bureau of American Ethnology Bulletin 61 (Washington, 1918), p. 205.[20]

Language and Mythology

"I confess I was astonished to find a book three years ago called *Essays on a Science of Mythology*," Olson announced to the first session of the Institute. "I was so struck that another contemporary had been so precise as to see a science in mythology that I was determined to try to bring that man here." Olson twice refers to the quotation from Malinowski (chiefly OLSON 10, pp. 63–64) that he had seen in Jung and Kerenyi's volume.[21] Olson here made first public use of J. A. K. Thomson, *The Art of the Logos* (London: Allen & Unwin, 1935), which he found in the BMC library (and took with him later, when the college closed): the definition of mythology as mutho-logos, "to speak of what is said"—with Herodotus as "the test case."[22] A local legend is referred to, the "Wild Boy of Black Mountain," that Olson could have picked up from a couple of sources.[23] A few items appear casually in these lectures (and nowhere else in Olson's work), items he did not own: Homer W. Smith, "The Kidney," *Scientific American* 188 (January 1953): 40–48, a current article to give a sense of "what you are" (*OLSON* 10, p. 70); and in the same place, a further sense of "the internal environment of ourselves" in "one specific story of Rabbi Nachman, a Slovak Yiddish writer Martin Buber translated into German, about three or seven wise men who went about the world looking for answers";[24] and finally (the name misspelled on p. 49 of the 1 March 1953 lecture), Bernhard Karlgren, *The Chinese Language* (New York: Ronald Press, 1949). For these lectures, Olson is supplementing his Webster's *Collegiate Dictionary* 5th ed. (1945) with *The Shorter Oxford English Dictionary*, 2 vols. 3d ed. (Oxford, 1950), that he had recently acquired.

## "Bibliography on America for Ed Dorn"

In the hiatus between this institute and the next public occasion we have record of at Black Mountain College,[25] there comes "A Bibliography on America for Ed Dorn" (January 1955), from which we have already cannibalized much in considering the West. There is the diagram to consider, "the axes of relevance," millennia:person:process:quantity (*Additional Prose*, p. 10).

Millennia

Under this heading are listed Sauer's "Environment and Culture in the Last Deglaciation"; Lobeck's *Physiographic Diagram of the United States*; and then a new one, Harold Sterling Gladwin, *Men Out of Asia* (New York: McGraw-Hill, 1947), "guessing on migrations."[26] Then Olson mentions "Indian texts on migrations, such as the Toltecs being pushed out of Tula"—referring to Benjamin Lee Whorf, "An Aztec Account of the Period of the Toltec Decline," in *Proceedings of the Twenty-third International Congress of Americanists* (previously cited), pp. 122–29. Olson adds: "also codices in which *feet* (like on floor after bath) are as arrows in Klee," which leaves us guessing.[27] Olson then mentions Herodotus—"At least first chapter"; Frobenius—"anything"; Jung—"when one widens out on any of these four points of the Double-Axe, one begins to hit one of the other 4, in this instance, person"; D. H. Lawrence—"preface to *Fantasia* (don't bother with the rest of the book!)"; Brooks Adams *The New Empire*—"the maps as routes equaled by nothing here except Sauer's";[28] and "like I have said elsewhere, Rider Haggard. And old *American Weekly*."

Person

This is psychology, "the science of the soul," and therefore Olson lists "mister jung," "a vast improvement on almost all the 'creative' men who have gone alongside of same (say, Peek-gas-so, Prrrroost, JJJ-Joys, all but Chaplin. And Eisenstein."[29] Otherwise Olson suggests the Odyssey, and Victor Bérard's work on it.

Process

Alfred North Whitehead, *Process and Reality: An Essay in Cosmology* (Cambridge University Press, 1929). Olson is doing a first reading: "He's just the greatest, if you read only his philosophy. If you read him on anything else ... "[30] Walter Prescott Webb in his first book, *The Great Plains* (Boston: Ginn, 1931)—Olson kept the BMC library copy—"applied process, and some millennia sense," but in *The Great Frontier* (Boston: Houghton, Mifflin, 1952) he did not—and Olson did not own the book. In any case, the great "how to" book is Pausanias, backed up by "Lady Pausanias," i.e., Jane Harrison. Her first book, *Mythology and Monuments of Ancient Athens*, is "nothing but Pausanias on Pausanias."[31]

Quantity

"I can't for the life of me see how books help here ... *50 Families* or Gustavus Myers won't do it.[32] It's why I say one has either to be a banker—or know one, intimately. We need now another set of muckrakers."

## "Tutorial: The Greeks"

We come now to a Bibliography on Greece for whatever students turned up at Black Mountain on 22 June 1955. "Tutorial: the Greeks" is a product of a moment in time; it is how Olson wants, on this occasion, to push his students into action. There are twelve numbered directives.

1. Theocritus' *Idylls* (with a certain fooling around, because the translations available are so bad ((including WCW's)), with one's own transpositions[33]
2. Plutarch's *Morals* (especially the essay *De Isis et Osiris*, and *The E at Delphi*) (Dig all references to P. in Jane Harrison)
3. The murals at *Dura-Europos*[34]
4. E. "The Bacchae"
    "The Cyclops"
    "Hercules Furens"[35]
5. The 6th, or Ionia, Cent. And I know no better quick way to pick up on Heraclitus, Pythagoras, Thales, Anaximander than in the Penguin 2 vol hist of Greek Science (by some English Manchester mathematician)[36]
6. Read Noh plays instead of (or with, for mouthwash) Greek drammer—Japanese Noh theater is the sole poetic theater (both the Greek & the Elizabethan was in the employ of the State)
7. Get a hold of, and read forever, Jaeger's *Paideia* (3 volumes on Greek education of the 5th cent on)[37]
8. Ditto Athenaeus' *The Deipnosophists* (3 vol Bohn translation—abt 6 bucks—on Banqueters)
9. Diogenes Laertius' *Lives of the Philosophers* (also, as 8, for kicks)
10. *L'odysee*
11. Berard: *Les Phoenicien et L'odysee* (or if you read French, read *L'odysee* in B's translation)
12: Evans' *Knossos* (inter-library loan)[38]
    last chapters of Hawkes' *Prehistoric*
    *Fndts of Europe*
    Miss Harrison Miss Harrison Miss Harry's
    son
    Mr. Jung applied
    Bulfinch, I guess, anyhow (unless you
    read German as you read English & can
    get Schmidt) until you know all these
    crazy tales (like one might know fairytales—Grimm)[39]
    plus *American Journal of Archaeology*, the *Illustrated*

*London News*, and the *Encyclopedia of Religion &*
*Ethics* (which, by god, the Black Mt College Library
    does have, even if a couple of vols are missing)
Bibliographical afterthought:
on the Byzantine, the bird to read is a Russian named Vasiliev; Gnosticism
is one of the throws of the 2nd Cent AD (dig Jung correcting this in BMR
#5—very damn fine).[40]


## "The Special View of History"

The synthesis that was the last intellectual act of Black Mountain
College was a series of lectures Olson called "The Special View of His-
tory," delivered during May 1956. It was an attempt, in a fairly small
space, to define postmodern man in terms of ancient man. Two epi-
graphs set the parameters: (1) Heraclitus's "Man is estranged from
that with which he is most familiar," which denotes when "man lost
something just about 500 B.C.,"[41] and (2) Keats's passage about "Nega-
tive Capability," which begins to give an inkling of how to get it back.
Whitehead's "philosophy of organism" is "the metaphysic of the re-
ality we have acquired." Olson here pares down his bibliographical
posts to the essential. On history, Herodotus. On myth, J. A. K.
Thomson and Jane Harrison (long quotations from *Themis*), with Mali-
nowski on the Trobriands again. On physics, two new voices, Schröd-
inger and Weyl, the latter to be heard from again later.[42] To give "an-
other 'natural' than our own," Olson cites Benjamin Lee Whorf, "An
American Indian Model of the Universe," *International Journal of Ameri-
can Linguistics* 16 (April 1950)—Olson kept the offprint, BMC em-
bossed. He did not own the collected papers: *Language, Thought, and
Reality* (Cambridge: M.I.T. Press, 1956). For a further "other" than even
the Hopi, Olson cites a chapter on the "demonic" in Paul Tillich, *The
Interpretation of History* (New York: Scribner, 1936), finally making use
of a book Waldo Frank had given him in 1940.

"The Special View of History," formulated at a time when "Ol-
son's university" was failing, is a contrary: a new cosmology with
which to confront such counsel of despair as "Spengler, the Adam-
ses."[43] Olson posits "actual, willful man," borrowing Jung's dictum,
"The self is at once center and circumference," to help him with his
definition: "The actual, then, is the true word for what has been called
totality."[44]

In order to go further with Keats's notion of staying in the "penetralium," staying in the "process," Olson tries in "The Special View of History" (there and nowhere else) to apply Hegel's philosophy of the "Dialectic." On pages 42–46, he quotes extensively from his one source (which he did not own): *The Logic of Hegel*, trans. William Wallace (Oxford University Press, original edition 1892; reprinted 1950), pp. 150–52. The emphasis Olson culls from Hegel is the view of the "dialectic" as "the dynamic which lies at the root of every natural process" (p. 43). But in the end he has to abandon Hegel, who is interested in *result* rather than staying in the *condition* of things. This is more than a philosophical argument, for "Olson's university" was clearly the latter. Black Mountain College could not survive on the basis of results; like the fourteen "unemployed" scholars of *All Men Are Brothers*,[45] it survived as long as it could without.

# 14

## *The* Black Mountain Review *and Its Editor*

Robert Creeley, though Olson never said it this way, must have been his chief representative of "active, willful man." What he did say, in "Maximus, to himself," was:

> But the known?
> This, I have had to be given,
> a life, love, and from one man
> the world.

It is usually taken that the "one man" is Creeley, to whom Olson dedicated the 1960 *Maximus Poems* as "the Figure of Outward." In his introduction to the first volume of *Charles Olson & Robert Creeley: The Complete Correspondence*, Butterick quotes (p. ix) a note made by Olson toward the end of his life:

> the Figure of Outward means way out way out
> *there*: the
> 'World,' I'm sure, otherwise
> why was the pt. then to like write to Creeley
> daily? to make that whole thing
> double, to
> objectify the extension of an
> 'outward'? a[n] opposite to a
> personality which so completely does (did)
> stay at home?

Or, as Olson put it in a poem "For R. C.," 17 January 1953, "he was so much acknowledgement." We will not, therefore, expect to see Creeley as someone who forced Olson to read more, but as someone so superbly receptive that Olson had to read better. Creeley was there to talk to about current work. So, one expects to find in the letters such flicks of the typing finger as, "suspicion: that FRANCIS THOMPSON is very much of USE"—not, be assured, the dated poet, but a current article: Francis J. Thompson, "Courageous, Not Outrageous," *Hopkins Review* 3 (Summer 1950): 42–44 (*Creeley Correspondence* 1, p. 66). Or, more pertinent to our concerns, Olson reporting his discovery of the Sondley Reference Library in Asheville, "a private library of 35,000 books and pamphlets, the work of a civil lawyer, which he willed to the city . . . for ex, pulled out of it, not only Bérard, and an interesting biz on Elizabethan pneumatology (as of the plays), but such a book as THE MUSIC OF THE SUMERIANS!"[1] And, in this letter of 30 September 1951, Olson not only announced that he is studying Greek for the first time,[2] and, further, has read all of Bérard's introduction to his French translation of the Odyssey "in a couple of hours, without recourse to a dictionary but twice," but is moved to lay out a list for Creeley of "the live ones," most of whom, naturally, we have seen before.

*texts:*

  odyssey
   moby-dick
    herodotus
     ovid (heroides, as much as metamorphs)
      pausanias
       euripides
        sumerian poems (with eye out for discovery,
         coming, of the Phoenician Heraklaid)

*scholarship:*

  bérard
   jane harrison
    waddell
     maspero (conte populaire d'Egypte)
      & anything & anyone on SUMER
       (kramer, porada, frankfort, this galpin
        (the music) even woolley)

*critique:*

  nada nada nada (but there are some shots,
  principally berard, a guy named Thomson, on the
  art of the logos, and a book pub. American 1820 on
  "The Theatre of the Greeks")[3]

& grounds for *logos* and/or the single actor drama or *epos:*

lattimore's (inner frontiers of asia)[4]
strzygowski (on wood, & Gothic
frobenius
& any histories of Ionians, Phrygians,
Cappadocians, Hittites, and
SUMERIANS
　　*beside all of which please place:*
　　THE STATES:　Mayans (language, plus sculpture, plus *tales,*
　　　　　　　　　any Indians') especially, UAXACTUN
　　　　　　　　　the physiography of, these two continents (to
　　　　　　　　　be relevanted to the Caucasus-Himalaya
　　　　　　　　　chain, as of that other past)
　　　　　　　　　Cabeza de Vaca
　　　　　　　　　The Civil War
　　　　　　　　　One, Carl Sauer, on Deglaciation
　　*Add, last,* investigation of *voice* and/or *speech* and/or what was called
*poetics:*
　　　　　　composition, here and now, mister, olson
　　　　　　& as, antistrophe, fenollosa
　　　　　　　　　e.p. ANTHEIL[5]
　　　　　　　　　dante De V E
　　　　　　　　　creeley, notes, on prose

Creeley himself gets in at the last with mention of his "Notes for a New Prose," which Olson read and annotated in manuscript in June 1950. For there is one thing that Creeley forced Olson to do, and that is pay attention to prose, and, out of admiration, to Creeley's own prose. Olson did a two-page introduction for James Laughlin for Creeley's "Mr. Blue and Other Stories" in *New Directions* 13 (1951). He had to have paid attention.

In the fall of 1953 at Black Mountain, Olson tried out Creeley's "The Boat" and "The Gold Diggers" on his American literature class while the stories were still in typescript, using them as a measure for all the prose preceding it. On 11 October 1953 Olson wrote to Creeley: "drives me crazy, how many people, even trained ones, can't take a thing as it is . . . all the damned writing they have been used to, is the nonauthoritative, is that ingratiation of realism, that lie that life is somewhere, and that if it is told realistically, it will show itself. And thus point will come into being. Bah." Creeley has pushed him back into literary criticism by exciting him over the possibility of a reaffirmation of taste.

Example: just to be goddamned pedantic with sd citizens for 11 weeks, i took off this time from Hawthorne! Have this purpose: in 11 weeks to crowd 'em through from 1850 to right now, and do it by a series of doubles at least, that is, Hawthorne & Melville, Poe & Baudelaire, James & Eliot out of Hawthorne, then, say, something like that Norris's Mc-Teague versus a Stendhal—to load it!—and then myself cuffing (while they read same) Lawrence, Pound, Williams, ending, by god, on our-selves. . . . [6] I don't think it is merely the fact that I am enjoying Haw-thorne which persuades me that *the moral* is so much back in business. My own enjoyment of yrself, that is, the damn great pleasure you do give in both these stories, of quite different attack, because a man is present as the hand of the story which *knows* its own making, isn't, for an instant, de-pending on anything, including "life," or any psychology, or any signifi-cances of any mythological reference, to get its point across, *is doing it it-self*. It's just the greatest, who you are. . . . It felt wonderful to see you out loud in my own mouth! And to come in, at the end, with that Note on Canadian Verse socked me, myself.

Olson at the end is referring to the newly arrived *Contact* 8 (September–December 1953), published by Raymond Souster in Tor-onto, which included Creeley's "A Note on Canadian Poetry."[7] The values implicit in Creeley's stories are beginning to be exposed in criti-cal writing and reviews. Creeley's first contact with Olson was as an editor looking for manuscripts and as someone who was willing to comment on submissions. After three years of gaining international contacts (as well as age), he was now to exercise his inherent taste by editing the *Black Mountain Review*.

The *Black Mountain Review* was such a pleasure for Olson that it was as though Creeley, in accepting the editorship, had given Olson the world in the form of a globe to play with. This is where the com-panionship of "the Black Mountain School of poets" comes in, if that label can stick at all. A little magazine gives one the luxury of convers-ing in public with one's like-minded contemporaries, seeing their lat-est work, and sometimes pushing the conversation into a printed re-view of a book. Certainly this applies to Olson and Duncan and the first issue of the *Review*.

### Black Mountain Review 1, No. 1 (Spring 1954)

1. "Against Wisdom As Such" (pp. 35–39; in *Human Universe*, pp.

67–71). This is a disputative tribute to Robert Duncan, responding formally to his "Pages From A Notebook" *Artist's View* 5 (1953), and informally to a December 1953 letter on *Maximus 1–10*, one which Olson welcomed very much, except for Duncan's use of the word "wisdom." We should note that Olson is using as a measure of "wisdom" his recent reading into *The Secret of the Golden Flower*, trans. Richard Wilhelm (London: Kegan, Paul, Trench, Trubner, 1931), the 1945 printing of which he had acquired since his first mention of the book in 1948. Though the tone of the piece could be mistaken for severity, the ensuing years confirm that it was really a welcoming of Duncan fully into his company.[8] (Duncan visited BMC in February 1955 on his way to Europe, and returned there to teach spring and summer 1956).

2. Review of *Captain John Smith, His Life and Legend* by Bradford Smith (Philadelphia: Lippincott, 1953). (*BMR* 1, pp. 54–57; reprinted as "Captain John Smith" in *Human Universe*, pp. 131–34. The copy did not survive in Olson's library.) The emphasis here on John Smith as a writer allows Olson, with a somewhat gleeful gratuitousness, to mention recent critical solecisms: "Williams is damned in London (in the New Statesman & Nation, by G. S. Fraser) for his 'neologisms,' and 'barbarisms.' And thus *Paterson 1 & 2* is thrown down—while Richard Eberhart is raised up! It's all over the place: another smith, Grover by name, in the fall New Mexico Quarterly, also puts down *Paterson*—and the *Cantos* with it, as well, by implication, Crane."[9] Capt. John Smith has already been niched in the *Maximus Poems* with his poem, "The Sea Marke"; now Olson is able to quote some nice bits of Smith's prose from the book under review. Olson later reviewed Philip L. Barbour *The Three Worlds of Captain John Smith* (Boston: Houghton Mifflin, 1964) for the *Boston Globe* newspaper on 27 August 1964 under the title (probably not Olson's title) "Five Foot Four, but Smith Was a Giant." He kept the book in his library, as he did all the following (unless otherwise stated).

### Black Mountain Review 1, No. 2 (Summer 1954)

1. "Mayan Heads" (pp. 26–28, not reprinted). This is an introduction to a photographic collection of Mayan artifacts, and quite possibly goes back to the summer of 1949 when the photographer, Diana Woelffer, and her painter husband were teaching at BMC, and providentially told the Olsons how to rent the house in Lerma. There is no hint in the piece of Olson's 1951 stay in Yucatan.

2. Review of *European Literature and the Latin Middle Ages* by Ernst Robert Curtius (New York: Pantheon, 1953—Bollingen Series 35).[10] (*BMR* 2, pp. 57–60; in *Human Universe* pp. 155–57). Olson is aware that Curtius has mentioned him favorably in a review of Gerhardt's magazine *fragmente* in *Die Tat* (Zurich) 21 July 1951, but, he says, he must show him "Odysseus' paw" as much as he did to Gerhardt, referring to his exhortation in the poem "To Gerhardt, There, Among Europe's Things of which He Has Written Us in His 'Brief an Creeley und Olson'," that he should look out of the "back door" of his inheritance, i.e., the pre–Homeric Europe, Odysseus as bear-son.[11] The references to Stefan George, Bergson, Troeltsch, and Toynbee in the review are from the early pages of Curtius's book, and represent "the literate ignorant men" who will "have the hair off our hands."

3. Review of *The New Empire* by Brooks Adams (New York: Macmillan, 1902). (*BMR* 2, pp. 63–64; in *Human Universe*, pp. 135–36.) Olson offers here a straight book report and footnotes the date 1902 with the question, "Why does this book stay out of print?" At the closing of BMC Olson kept the library copy he was using (flyleaf: "Olson by arrogation") and managed to get the book back in print through Harvey Brown's Frontier Press edition (1967), for which he wrote an introductory note.

## Black Mountain Review 1, No. 3 (Fall 1954)

1. "Notes on Language and Theatre" (pp. 41–44; in *Human Universe*, pp. 73–77). This piece, written in January 1954, is a further try at the archaic, considering drama before Aeschylus.

2. Review of *The Saga of Billy the Kid* by Walter Noble Burns (New York: New American Library Signet Book, 1953). (*BMR* 3, pp. 61–63; in *Human Universe*, pp. 137–40.) This is another slap at the "nuvvel," praising Burns and Stuart Lake (his Bantam edition of *Wyatt Earp, Frontier Marshal*, New York, 1952; another of Olson's pocketbooks) for trying "at least to leave it as it was, to get at it as close as the record will enable them."[12]

## Black Mountain Review 1, No. 4 (Winter 1954)

1. "I, Mencius, Pupil of the Master" (pp. 34–37). This poem records Olson's disappointment at seeing Pound use rhymed verse in translating *The Classic Anthology Defined by Confucius* (Cambridge: Har-

vard University Press, 1954). Olson wrote for a review copy. Olson is not known to have used James Legge's *The Works of Mencius* (1895), but he did own his edition of *The Book of Poetry: Chinese Text with English Translation* (Shanghai: Chinese Book Co., n.d.).

2. Review of *A Thanksgiving Eclogue* by Cid Corman (Flushing, N.Y.: Sparrow Press, 1954). (*BMR* 4, pp. 50–53; in *Human Universe*, pp. 145–48.) Olson received this Vagrom Chapbook from the publishers for review, at the author's direction. He obliged by rewriting the poem, presumably not going beyond the edition he owned, edited by J. Banks (previously cited). Olson wrote to Corman on 5 November 1954: "please always forgive me any harshness, like I think you may find my review of yr Eclogues. It is never the back of my hand. It is that passion, that all things be done right. And take it, please, that I wouldn't talk back if I didn't *love*! And happened to pay attention just because it was you!"[13]

### Black Mountain Review 2, No. 5 (Summer 1955)

"It Was. But It Ain't." (pp. 212–16; in *Human Universe*, pp. 141–43). This review of two Penguin paperbacks published in 1954 compares Thucydides *History of the Peloponnesian War*, translated by Rex Warner, and *Herodotus: The Histories*, translated by Aubrey de Selincourt. The latter historian, "always talking of men and things, not of societies and commodities," wins.

### Black Mountain Review 3, No. 6 (Spring 1956)

1. "A Foot Is To Kick With" (pp. 211–12; in *Human Universe*, p. 79). This short definition of poetry is presumably from a letter not at present known.

### Black Mountain Review 3, No. 7 (Autumn 1957)

1. "Homer and Bible" (pp. 219–25; in *Human Universe*, pp. 149–53). Cyrus H. Gordon, *Homer and Bible: The Origin and Character of East Mediterranean Literature* (Ventnor, N.J.: Ventnor Publishers, 1956), reviewed here, was not in Olson's library at his death, but it was a very important introduction to the work of a man who is bringing to light a

Ugaritic literature before Homer "as S. N. Kramer is, in Sumerian, and Hans Güterbock in Hittite."[14] Olson is alert in this area; he has noticed, even if he could not buy, Michael Ventris and John Chadwick, *Documents in Mycenaean Greek* (Cambridge University Press, 1956), and as research for the review he has ordered on 4 January 1957 Cyrus Gordon's *Ugaritic Literature: A Comprehensive Translation of the Poetic and Prose Texts* (Rome: Pontificium Institutum Biblicum, 1949), which he keeps in his library, perhaps indicating his preference for text over theory.

2. "Quantity in Verse, and Shakespeare's Late Plays"—this essay was meant for *BMR* 7 but did not get in, and there were no further issues. Creeley subsequently rectified the situation by including it in *Selected Writings of Charles Olson* (1966). It is a distillation of a great deal of writing Olson did on Shakespeare in the period 1951–57. Thomas Campion was the early turn to "freedom from the metric *of line*."[15] Olson may have used Campion's *Works* (Oxford University Press, 1909); his reading went beyond the selection of Campion's "Observations in the Art of English Poesie" included in James Harry Smith and Edd Winfield Parks, *The Great Critics* (New York: Norton, 1939), which he owned and used, quoting extensively in this "Quantity in Verse" essay from the book's selections from Dante's "De Vulgari Eloquentia" and "Epistola X."

Do we get any sense of a "Black Mountain School" from a perusal of the seven issues of the *Review*? The first list of "Contributing Editors" drawn up was international and fairly eclectic: Kenneth Rexroth, Paul Goodman, Katue Kitasono, Iriving Layton, Paul Blackburn, Rainer M. Gerhardt, and M. Elath (letter to Creeley, 12 December 1953).[16] This list reduced itself by the first issue to Rexroth, Layton, Blackburn, plus Olson himself. Rexroth did not like some of the reviews, and resigned. Blackburn and Creeley had a personal falling-out.[17] The third issue's "Contributing Editors" were listed as Layton and Olson, with Robert Hellman added[18]—which held firm until issue 6, when Hellman went out of the picture and Allen Ginsberg was added at the last. These moves were, of course, Creeley's, not Olson's; but, in any case, we do not see here a central core of "Black Mountaineers." Layton, who actually contributed more poems than anyone else, was a Canadian who could not even get across the border and was also not projective otherwise, having no form "other than classical English form."[19] Clearly, the enduring, guiding presence was Creeley, at first in dialogue with Olson, later pretty much with his own angel.

Let us re-ask the question about a Black Mountain School by seeing what current poetry Olson adhered to and what books of poetry from the fifties he owned. If there were ever an attempt to make a definition by an anthology of individual poems, Edward Marshall's "Leave the Word Alone" (*BMR* 7) would have high priority. On receiving it, Olson wrote to the young poet: "That's a fine thing you've done here, Marshall—very *true*, and *quick*, very *thick*. It *speaks* very much. It is *very* personal and formal at once. And *form-wise* it is very true—the peopling, the protests, the end."[20] Marshall was really a New England connection, as was his friend Steve Jonas,[21] who with another Boston poet-friend, John Wieners, heard Olson's reading at the Charles Street Meeting House in Boston on 11 September 1954, which, by Wieners's testimony, was an epiphany. Wieners just got in at the end of Black Mountain College, went back to Boston to edit *Measure* (Olson contributed to all three issues), and was a loyal associate of Olson's all through the sixties.[22] Those students who really worked for and found their voices at Black Mountain were Ed Dorn, Tom Field, Fielding Dawson, Michael Rumaker, Jonathan Williams, and Joel Oppenheimer;[23] there one might find a "school." Whatever it was, they stuck with it. But much of their writing was prose—in two cases entirely prose—so the "school of poetry" is shot down here, too. Paul Metcalf, who lived nearby in North Carolina, was writing prose.[24] There is no Black Mountain School of Poets. For section one of the *New American Poetry: 1945–1960*,[25] editor Donald Allen, in order to make up a group beyond Olson, Duncan, Creeley, Blackburn, Dorn, Williams, and Oppenheimer, added Denise Levertov, Larry Eigner, and Paul Carroll, on the grounds that they had poems in both *Origin* and the *Black Mountain Review*.[26] Other writers meet that criterion, William Bronk, Gael Turnbull, Lorine Niedecker, Gary Snyder, and Louis Zukofsky, only serving to further blur the notion of a "school."[27] Well, at least it is usually clear from the books of poems he kept in his library where Olson stood in all this, though he no doubt kept some of the books merely through inertia. He kept Eli Wilentz, *The Beat Scene* (New York: Corinth, 1960), for instance. And, whatever "Black Mountain" may or may not be, it's not that scene.[28]

## *Appendix*

### *Presses*

#### Divers Press

Since Olson was in close touch with Robert Creeley throughout the period in which the Divers Press operated, it would be most unusual if Olson was not sent all of the publications listed below.[1] Those volumes that he retained in his library are indicated by an asterisk(*).

Books Published by the Divers Press

   Paul Blackburn, *Proensa* ([June] 1953)[2]
 * Robert Creeley, *The Kind Of Act Of* ([July] 1953)
 * Larry Eigner, *From the Sustaining Air* (July 1953)
 * Charles Olson, *Mayan Letters* (1953) [January 1954]
   Irving Layton, *In the Midst of My Fever* (February 1954)
 * Robert Creeley, *The Gold Diggers* ([March] 1954)
   Martin Seymour-Smith, *All Devils Fading* [Spring 1954]
   H. P. Macklin, *A Handbook of Fancy Pigeons* (May 1954)[3]
   Katue Kitasono, *Black Rain* ([August] 1954)
 * Robert Creeley, *A Snarling Garland of Xmas Verses* [Xmas 1954]
   Douglas Woolf, *The Hypocritic Days* (January 1955)

1. This list is found in Mary Novik, *Robert Creeley: An Inventory, 1945–1970* (Kent State University Press, 1973). Divers Press books were printed by Mossén Alcover in Palma de Mallorca. Creeley sent from Mallorca another book from the Alcover printing house: Jean Desthieux, *Au Pays des Merveilles* (Nice: Federation des Syndicats D'Initiatives de la Cote D'Azur et de la Corse, 1938). The design for Olson's own Mossén Alcover book, *In Cold Hell, In Thicket*, was adapted by Ann Creeley from plates in that book. Olson deposited it with Jean Kaiser, and it cannot at the moment be traced.

In this period, Creeley also sent Olson his own book of poems, entitled *If You* (San Francisco: Porpoise Bookshop, 1956), acknowledged by Olson on 12 December 1956 but later missing from his library. Creeley's *Four Poems from "A Form of Women"* (New York: Eighth Street Bookshop, December 1959) is found in his library.

2. Olson passed on his copy to Raymond Souster.

3. A letter to Creeley of 30 September 1954 acknowledges receipt of "that damned handsome Pigeon book of Macklin's"; but the volume is not found in Olson's library later.

Paul Blackburn, *The Dissolving Fabric* (March 1955)
* Robert Duncan, *Caesar's Gate* (September 1955)

Books Designed and Printed by the Divers Press

* Charles Olson, *In Cold Hell, in Thicket* (February 1953). Published as *Origin*, no. 8 (Winter 1953)
* Cid Corman, *The Precisions* (New York: Sparrow Press, March 1955)
Iriving Layton, *The Blue Propeller* (Montreal: Contact Press, 1955)

## Jargon

At one time, Jonathan Williams was designated the official "Publisher" of Black Mountain College: his Jargon series thrived beyond the demise of the college and is active to this present time. In the following checklist, the volumes are numbered as in the Jargon series.[4] As likely as not, Olson would be aware of all these books. Those that were found in his library are indicated by an asterisk (*).

(1) *Garbage Litters the Iron Face of the Sun's Child*
poem: Jonathan Williams; engraving: David Ruff
(2) *The Dancer*
poem: Joel Oppenheimer; drawing: Robert Rauschenberg
(3) *Red/Gray*
poems: Jonathan Williams; drawings: Paul Ellsworth
(4) *The Double-Backed Beast*
poems: Victor Kalos; drawings: Dan Rice
(5) *Four Stoppages*
poems: Jonathan Williams; drawings: Charles Oscar
(6) *Fables & Other Little Tales*
Kenneth Patchen
* (7) *The Maximus Poems/1–10*
Charles Olson; caligraphy: Jonathan Williams (1953)
* (8) *The Immoral Proposition*
Robert Creeley; drawings: René Laubiès (1953)
* (9) *The Maximus Poems/11–22*
Charles Olson; calligraphy: Jonathan Williams (1956)
* (10) *All That Is Lovely in Men*

4. Checklist as found in the brochure, *The Jargon Society 1951–75*. See also Millicent Bell "The Jargon Idea," *Books at Brown* 19 (May 1963): 1–12, which Olson possessed an offprint of.

poems: Robert Creeley; drawings: Dan Rice; photograph: Jonathan Williams (1955)

*(11) Poem-Scapes*

Kenneth Patchen

* *(12) A Test of Poetry*

anthology: Louis Zukofsky (1964 ed.)

*(13)*

*a.*

*Amen/Huzza/Selah*

poems: Jonathan Williams; "a preface?": Louis Zukofsky; photographs: Jonathan Williams

*b.*

*Elegies & Celebrations*⁵

poems: Jonathan Williams; preface: Robert Duncan; photographs: Aaron Siskind, Jonathan Williams

*c.* (never released)

*Jammin' the Greek Scene*

poems: Jonathan Williams; note: Charles Olson; drawings: Fielding Dawson

*(14) Letters*

poems & drawings: Robert Duncan

*(15) Some Time*

Louis Zukofsky; song: Celia Zukofsky

*(16) The Dutiful Son*

poems: Joel Oppenheimer; drawing: Joe Fiore

* *(17) The Suicide Room*⁶

poems: Stuart Z. Perkoff; drawing: Fielding Dawson; photograph: Chester Kessler (1956)

*(18) The Improved Binoculars*

poems: Irving Layton; introduction: W. C. Williams

*(19) Overland to the Islands*

poems: Denise Levertov; drawing: Al Kresch; calligraphy: Jonathan Williams

*(20) Passage*

poems: Michael McClure; calligraphy: Jonathan Williams

* *(21) Hurrah For Anything*

5. This volume contained the Olson poem to Williams, "For a Man Gone to Stuttgart," but there was no copy in Olson's library later.

6. Olson associated Perkoff with Alexander Blok (*Creeley Correspondence* 6, p. 189) and with Jaime d'Angulo (letter to Duncan, 9 December 1951); it is not known what he read of these two writers.

poems & drawings: Kenneth Patchen (1957)

*(22) The Red Notebook*

Henry Miller; drawing by Miller; photograph: Wynn Bullock

\* *(23) Lunar Baedeker & Time-Tables*

poems: Mina Loy; introductions: William Carlos Williams, Kenneth Rexroth, (1958) Denise Levertov; drawings: Emerson Woelffer

\* *(24) The Maximus Poems*

Charles Olson; photograph: Frederick Sommer (1960)

\* *(25) Will West*

Paul C. Metcalf (1956)

\* *(26) The Whip*

poems: Robert Creeley; drawing: René Laubiès (1957)

*(27) Sonnet Variations*

Peyton Houston; photograph: Henry Holmes Smith

\* *(28) A Laughter in the Mind*

poems: Irving Layton; photograph: Frederick Sommer

\* *(29) 1450–1950*

visual poems: Bob Brown; photograph: Jonathan Williams (1959)

\* *(30) The Empire Finals at Verona*

poems: Jonathan Williams; drawings & collage: Fielding Dawson

*(31) 14 Poets, 1 Artist*

poems by Paul Blackburn, Bob Brown, Edward Dahlberg, Max Finstein, Allen Ginsberg, Paul Goodman, Denise Levertov, Walter Lowenfels, Edward Marshall, E. A. Navaretta, Joel Oppenheimer, Gilbert Sorrentino, Jonathan Williams, Louis Zukofsky; drawings: Fielding Dawson

\* *(32) Some Deaths*

poems: Walter Lowenfels; introduction: Jonathan Williams; photographs: Robert Schiller (1962)[7]

*(33) A Form of Women*

poems: Robert Creeley; photograph: Robert Schiller

*(34) The Selected Poems of Bob Brown*

introduction: Kay Boyle; drawing: Reuben Nakian

*(35) A Red Carpet for the Sun*

poems: Irving Layton; photograph: Harry Callahan

7. Olson also had Walter Lowenfels, *We Are All Poets Really* (Buffalo: Intrepid Press, 1967). In response to Lowenfels's invitation to contribute to *Where Is Vietnam?* (published as an Anchor Book, 1967—Olson did not have a copy), Olson in a letter of 26 July 1966 suggested that "the only distinguished poem" on the war was Michael McClure's *Poisoned Wheat*, "privately printed as a pamphlet—a year ago" (1965). That volume did not, however, turn up in Olson's library.

(36) *On My Eyes*

poems: Larry Eigner; introduction: Denise Levertov; photographs: Harry Callahan

(37) *What a Man Can See & Other Fables*

Russell Edson; drawings: Ray Johnson

(38) *The Roman Sonnets of G. G. Belli*

translations: Harold Norse; preface: W. C. Williams; introduction: Alberto Moravia; cover: Ray Johnson; collage: Jean-Jacques Lebel

* (39) *Lord! Lord! Lord!*

poem: Jonathan Williams (1959)

* (40) *The Darkness Surrounds Us*

poems: Gilbert Sorrentino: collage & drawing: Fielding Dawson (1960)[8]

(41) *Three Choruses From Opera Libretti*

Lou Harrison

* (42) *A Line of Poetry, A Row of Trees*

poems: Ronald Johnson; drawings: Thomas George (1964)

* (43) *Genoa*

Paul C. Metcalf; iconography: Jonathan Williams (1965)

(44) *Untitled Epic Poem on the History of Industrialization*

R. Buckminster Fuller; collage: Jonathan Williams

(45) *Six Mid-American Chants*

Sherwood Anderson; photographs: Art Sinsabaugh; preface: Edward Dahlberg; postface: Frederick Eckman

(46) *Flowers & Leaves*

Guy Davenport; photograph: Ralph Eugene Meatyard

(47) *Letters to Christopher*

poems: Merle Hoyleman; introduction: George Marion O'Donnell

(48) *Tenderness & Gristle*

poems: Lorine Niedecker; plant prints: A. Doyle Moore

(49) *The Poems of Alfred Starr Hamilton*

introduction: Geoff Hewitt; photograph: Simpson Kalisher; drawings: Philip Van Aver

(50) *The Appalachian Photographs of Doris Ulmann*

introduction: John Jacob Niles; preface: Jonathan Williams

(51) *The Selected Poems of Ian Hamilton Finlay*

(52) *Occasions in a World*

poems: Peyton Houston; drawings: Bob Nash

(53) *The Last Lunar Baedeker*

8. Olson also owned Sorrentino's *Black and White* (New York: Totem, 1964).

poems: Mina Loy; design: Herbert Bayer; introduction: Jonathan Williams

*(54) The Selected Poems of Mason Jordan Mason*
introduction: Judson Crews; photographs: Ron Nameth
*(55) A Long Undressing*
poems: James Broughton; photograph: Imogen Cunningham
*(56) High Kukus*
James Broughton; preface: Alan Watts; drawings: Hak Vogrin
*(57) Friends & Lovers*
poems: Joel Oppenheimer
*(58) Patagoni*
Paul C. Metcalf; iconography: Jonathan Williams
*(59)*
*(60)*
\* *(61) Lullabies Twisters Gibbers Drags*
poems: Jonathan Williams; drawings: R. B. Kitaj (1963)
*(62) Emblems for the Little Dells, & Nooks & Corners of Paradise*
poem: Jonathan Williams
*(63)*
*(64)*

Jonathan Williams designed, and presumably sent to Olson, Raymond E. F. Larsson, *Book Like a Bow Curved* (Detroit: University of Detroit Press, 1961).

## Oyez

Robert Hawley was a student at Black Mountain College who went on to be a publisher of note with his Oyez Press out of Berkeley. He published Olson's *The Special View of History* (1970) and Ann Charters's *Olson/Melville* (1968). The following books from this press were found in Olson's library.

D. Alexander, *Not a Word* (1966)
Gerard Boar, (Ebbe Borregaard) *Sketches for 13 Sonnets* (1969)
Sam Charters, *Days* (1967)
　　　　　*To This Place* (1969)
Robert Creeley, *Way Poems* (1964)—presented to Olson by Mary N. Korte,
　　　　　3 April 1968
Robert Duncan, *Wine* (1964)
　　　　　*Medea at Kolchis* (1965)

> *Up Rising* (1965)—annotated by Olson
> *Of the War* (1966)—annotated by Olson
> *The Years As Catches* (1966)—not later in Olson's library

Gail Dusenbery, *The Mark* (1967)
> *The Sea-Gull* (1968)

Mary Fabilli, *The Old Ones* (1966)

Robert Hogg, *The Connexions* (1966)

Sister Mary Norbert Korte, *Hymn To The Gentle Sun* (1967)

Philip Lamantia, *Touch of the Marvellous* (1966)

Lawrence McGaugh, *A Fifth Sunday* (1965)

David Meltzer, *Oyez!* (1965)—signed by Bob Hawley
> *The Process* (1965)

Josephine Miles, *Civil Poems* (1966)
> *Fields of Learning* (1968)

Lew Welch, *On Out* (1965)

## Other Presses

Audit (Buffalo)

Olson had Robert Creeley's *Contexts of Poetry*, issued as *Audit* 5, no. 1 (Spring 1968), and John Koeth's *Blue Vents* (1968), and several other issues of the magazine.

Angel Hair (New York, later Bolinas)

Olson had no. 5 of the magazine (September 1968), and separate publications:

Bill Berkson, *Shining Leaves* (1969)
Tom Clark, *Bun* (1968)
Larry Fagin, *The Parade of the Caterpillars* (1968)
Lewis Warsh and Tom Clark, *Chicago* (1969)
Lewis Warsh, *Moving through Air* (1968)
John Wieners, *Asylum Poems* (1969)

The Archive (Downington, Pa.)
R. W. Johnson, *Considerations* (1966)

Bear Press (La Grande, Oregon)
Aram Saroyan, *In* (1965)

Birdweed (San Francisco)
Jim Gulyas and Richard Sassoon, *Beaubo* (1967)

**Black Owl Press (Hollywood)**
Barry Seiler, *The Algeria Poems* (1969)

**Black Sparrow (Los Angeles; Santa Barbara)**
Charles Bukowski, *If We Take* (1970)
Robert Creeley, *The Finger* (1968)
Edward Dorn, *Gunslinger Book I* (1968), *Gunslinger Book II* (1969)
Larry Eigner, *The Breath of Once Live Things* (1968)
          *Air the Trees* (1968)
          *Towards Autumn* (1967)
Jonathan Greene, *The Lapidary* (1969)
Robert Kelly, *Finding the Measure* (1968)
          *The Well Wherein a Deer's Head Bleeds* (1968)
          *The Common Shore* (1969)

**Bowery Press (Denver)**
C. H. Hejinian, *Selections from the Winslow Poems* (Broadsheet No. 4, April 1969)

**Burning Deck (Ann Arbor, Michigan; Durham, Conn.)**

Olson had issues 1–4 of the magazine, and the following:
Alan Sondheim, *An Ode* (1968)
Bernard Waldrop, *7 Poems* (1966)
Rosemary Waldrop, *Dark Octave* (1965)

**City Lights (San Francisco)**

Olson kept no. 3, of the *City Lights Journal*, and the following:
Gregory Corso, *Gasoline* (1958)

**Coyote (Eugene, Ore.)**
Douglas Woolf, *Signs of a Migrant Worrier* (1965)

**Desert Review Press (Albuquerque; Santa Fe)**

Olson had *A Poetry Newsletter* (Fall 1967) and *Penny Poetry Sheet* 1–3.
Ronald Caplan, *From Varese* (1967)
Larry Eigner, *The Music, the Rooms* [1965]

**Doones Press**
Raymond DiPalma, *Macaroons* (1969)

**Elizabeth Press (New Rochelle, N.Y.)**

Olson had nos. 2–6, 10, 12, and 13 of *Elizabeth* magazine.
Theodore Enslin, *The Place Where I Am Standing* (1964)

Gena Ford, *This Time, That Space* (1968)
Simon Perchick, *I Counted Only April* (1964)
              *Which Hand Holds the Brother* (1969)
Felix Pollak, *The Castle and the Flaw* (1963)

Friendly Local Press (New York)

Olson had issues 1–5 of the magazine, and the following:
Cleo Nichols, *Farmer's Almanac: a chapter from a novel* (1968)

Golden Quill Press (Francistown, N.H.)
James L. Weil, *The Oboe Player* (1961)

Grove Press (New York)
Keith Wilson, *Graves Registry* (1969)

Hawk's Well (New York)
Robert Kelly, *Armed Descent* (1961)
Jerome Rothenberg, *White Sun, Black Sun* (1960)

Heron Press (Gloucester)

Besides Ferrini volumes cited later:
Hugh Creighton Hill, *Some Propositions from the Universal Theorem* (1954)

Hispanic Publishing Co. (New York)
Allen Katzman, *The Comanche Cantos* (1966)

Interim (New York)
Calvin C. Hernton, *The Coming of Chronos* (1964)

Kayak (San Francisco)

Olson had no. 1 of the magazine, and the following:
Howard McCord, *Fables and Transfigurations* (1967)

Kraft Publications (Philadelphia)
Mimi Goldberg, *The Lover and Other Poems* (1961)—with an introduction
    by William Carlos Williams

Matter (Annandale-on-Hudson, N.Y.)

Olson had *Matter*, nos. 2–4, and the following:
Harvey Bialy, Love's Will (1968)
Theodore Enslin, *The Diabelli Variations* (1967)
Ken Irby, *The Flower Having Passed Through Paradise* (1967)
Gerrit Lansing, *The Heavenly Tree Grows Downward* (1966)

Migrant (Worcester, U.K.; Ventura, California)

> Olson kept no. 2 of *Migrant*, ed. Gael Turnbull, and the following:
> Edward Dorn, *What I See in the Maximus Poems* (Spring 1960)
> Ian Hamilton Finlay, *The Dancers Inherit the Party* (Autumn 1960)
> Roy Fisher, *City* (1961)
> Michael Shayer, *Persephone* (1961)
> Gael Turnbull, *With a Hey Ho* (1961)

New Atheneum Press (Crescent City, Fla.)
Will Inman, *I Am the Snakehandler* (1960)

New Directions (New York)
R. V. Cassill, Herbert Gold and James B. Hall, *Fifteen by Three* (1957)

Ophelia Press (New York)
George Kimball, *Only Skin Deep* (1968)

Paperbook Gallery (New York)
Ray Bremser, *Poems of Madness* (1965)

Paterson Society (Cambridge, Mass.)

> Broadsides (1961):
> Paul Blackburn, *In Recurrent Actions*
> Gregory Corso, *Find It So Hard to Write the How*
> Robert Creeley, *A Poem is a Peculiar Instance*
> Denise Levertov, *I Am Interested in Writing Poems*
> Michael McClure, *From the New Book/A Book of Torture*

Pendle Hill Society of Friends (Wallingford, Pa.)
Elise Boulding, *Children and Solitude* (December 1962)

Perishable Press (Mt. Horeb, Wisc.)

> Olson had *Books* 1968, and the following:
> J. V. Cunningham, *Some Salt* (1967)
> Walter Hall, *Spider Poems* (1967)
> Walter Hamady, *Plum-foot Poems* (1967)
> William Stafford, *Eleven Untitled Poems* (1968)

Poets Press (Kerhonkson, N.Y.)
John Ashbery, *Three Madrigals* (1968)
Diane Di Prima, ed., *War Poems* (1968)
                            *Earthsong* (1968)
                            *The Star, the Child* (1968)
Kirby Doyle, *Sapphobades* (1966)

Jean Genet, *The Man Condemned to Death* (trans. Diane Di Prima)
David Henderson, *Felix of the Silent Forest* (1967)
Herbert Huncke, *Huncke's Journal* (1965)
Timothy Leary, *Psychedelic Prayers* (1966)
Audre Lorde, *The First Cities* (1968)
A. B. Spellman, *The Beautiful Days* (1965)

San Francisco Quarterly
Paul Vangelisti, *Communion* (1969)

Trobar (Brooklyn, N.Y.)

Olson had nos. 1 and 2 of the magazine, and the following:
Robert Kelly, *Round Dances* (1964)
Rochelle Owens, *Not Be Essence that Cannot Be* (1961)
Jerome Rothenberg, *The Seven Hells of the Jigoku Zoshi* (1962)
Louis Zukofsky, *I's (pronounced eyes)* (1963)

Wesleyan University Press (Middletown, Conn.)
David Ignatow, *Figures of the Human* (1964)

White Rabbit (San Francisco)
Helen Adams, *The Queen o' Crow Castle* (1958)
Stephen Jonas, *Love, the Poem, the Sea and Other* (1957)
Jack Spicer, *After Lorca* (1957)

Wild Dog (San Francisco)
Max Finstein, *The Disappearance of Mountains* (1966)

Terence Williams (Lawrence, Kans.)
Kirby Congdon, *When Young, I Quickly Grew* (Dialogue 1964)
Ken Irby, *Kansas-New Mexico* (1965)
Rob Rusk, broadsheet (n.d.)

George Wittenborn Inc. (New York)
Edwin Denby, *Mediterranean Cities Sonnets* (1956)

Noel Young (Santa Barbara)
Jeanne D'Orge, *Voice in the Circle* (1955)

In addition to the books already mentioned, Olson owned the following books by poets:
J. Chester, *An American Sequence* (New York: by the author, 1969);
Jack Collom, *Wet* (1967);
Harold Dull, *The Tree* (n.d.);
Joe Early, *The Pitch* drawings by Fielding Dawson (1968);

Clayton Eshleman, *The Chavin Illuminations* (Lima 1965);

Robert Grenier, *The Minnesota Soldiers' Home* (n.d.);

Don Katzman, *Seventh Street* (New York, 1961);

Taylor Mead, *Excerpts from the Anonymous Diary of a New York Youth* (Venice, California, 1962);

E. G. Molner, *The Voice of Fear* (Vienna: Ars Hungarica, 1959);

Elio Pagliarami, *Lezione di Fisica* (Milan, 1964);

Marcelin Pleynet, *Paysage en Deux* (Paris, 1963); *Comme: Poesie* (Paris, 1965);

Margaret Randall, *Ecstasy is a Number* (New York, 1961);

Louis R. Rowan, *Your Pages Are Not Numbered* (n.d.);

Frank Samperi, *Song Book* (West Babylon, N.Y., 1960), *The Tribune* (Brooklyn, 1969);

Ruth Yorck, *I'll Measure Them for a White White Coat* (New York, 1963), *January Deadlock* (1963), *Poet as Dictator* (1964).

# 15

## *Maximus, Away from Gloucester*

The first two-thirds of the 1960 *Maximus Poems* was written before Olson returned to live in Gloucester in 1957. When one opens the volume and sees the title of the first poem, "I, Maximus of Gloucester, to You," (May 1950), one should be aware that the poem was actually written in Washington, D.C., and that his figure, "Maximus," is "of Gloucester" in the same way that Apollonius was "of Tyana," or the historical Maximus was "of Tyre," travelers who kept an eye on their home city—and in the case of Maximus of Tyre, at least, dispatched "dissertations" to it. Provoked by bits of news that fellow-poet Vincent Ferrini was sending him from Gloucester, these early Maximus poems address him back in kind, drawing as well on Olson's childhood and later memories of Gloucester and its fishermen, the sort of thing that came to mind when he had to do an assignment for Professor Dodd's composition course at Wesleyan, fall 1932,[1] or when, as on 31 January 1945, he made notes to himself on how he could use Gloucester in developing a career as a writer (transcribed by Butterick, *OLSON* 5, pp. 6–7):

> Gloucester—you ought to know all there is to know about her *past* as well as some day to spend a lot of time gathering up all you can out of her *present*: Jim Mason & others, Carl Olsen, Burke
>
> One thing—the unfolding of the races—the Dorchester over first, then when the Irish? the Newfoundlanders, Nova Scotians? the Portuguese? the Italians?
>
> Connolly's stuff is very lively. I should like to make a selection of his stories and then rewrite the best. At first just for my own use, though I might get myself a chance to do it *by proposing a Gloucester volume to a publisher*. Maybe Duell, Sloane & Pierce might be interested in one for that

series of theirs, on American regions (if no book publisher, try
*magazines*—or Adamic's series).[2]
I *Introduction:*
    (1) the *story of Gloucester* 1620 on, with its economics as weighted as its
        dramatics. Our Lady—St. Peter—The coming of the various
        peoples.
    (2) *the craft* (and now the industry) of *fishing*
        Cod—bacalhao—handlining
        the net—mackerel
        the trawl—haddock & halibut
        the beam trawler . . .
II *Stories:*
    (1) *Connolly* rewritten the base
        such as: "Reykjavick to Gloucester"—sail carrier
            "The Wicked Celestine"—a schooner's port
            "The Truth About Oliver Cromwell"—skipper[3]
    (2) *Howard Blackburn:* straight record—no heroics—maybe put him
        first[4] then follow with Connolly's &
end 3) with a story of your own on Cecil Moulton
    *& CARL OLSEN:* a) the heroic moneymaker,
                *the modern highliner*
    but also include:
       *witch stories*—Mitton        MacKaye[5]
       *Captains Courageous*—rewritten? by calling it *selection*[6]
       *Portuguese*—Berger[7]
*Sources:* Gloucester, Rockport, Boston libraries
    —tap S.E. Morison for *Maritime* mss.[8]
    —Rockport bookseller?—for out of way stuff
    —old files of *Gloucester Times*—Connolly himself

A routine visit to his mother's in Gloucester in June 1947 before
traveling west—and suddenly a frantic book-buying spree at the book-
shop on Main Street. Much to his later chagrin, he paid many times
what it was worth for a copy of John J. Babson, *History of the Town of
Gloucester, Cape Ann, Including the Town of Rockport* (Gloucester: Proctor
Brothers, 1860). Why? Because he had had a rather momentous lun-
cheon with Alfred Mansfield Brooks, director of the Cape Ann Histori-
cal Society.[9] Collaboration on a new history of Gloucester was
proposed—something of that order. Some excited veering onto a new
path caused Olson not only to buy heavy volumes of Gloucester his-
tory but to pack them across the country.

Another routine visit to his mother's, June 1949, and Olson had another unexpected meeting of some consequence. In the spring issue of *Imagi* he had noticed a poem by someone called Vincent Ferrini, whose place of residence was given as Gloucester. Olson made a point of seeking him out and discovered someone he could talk to and might even see again. Later, after many poems and many evenings, Olson would call him "the only brother" he'd had.[10] It was this brotherly aggravation that got the *Maximus* poems going.

We deduce from internal evidence what other source materials went into the making of the pre–Gloucester volumes, *The Maximus Poems 1–10* and *The Maximus Poems 11–22*, both published by Jonathan Williams as Jargon Books while he was serving in the U.S. Army in Germany, printed in Stuttgart in 1953 and 1956 respectively. We can cite here two items that appear conspicuously in these early *Maximus* poems and survive in Olson's papers as clippings. The first is "14–Year Hunt Yields 'Missing Link' Fish," *New York Times* 30 December 1952, about James L. B. Smith seeking a coelacanth for over a decade and finally obtaining a specimen. Olson put it into "The Songs of Maximus" the next day:

> and he looked,
> the first human eyes to look again
> at the start of human motion (just last week
> 300,000,000 years ago

—where currency yields with relief to the ache of origin, in a remarkably moving passage. Similarly, on the macabre side, the reference to

> Jericho's
> First Citizens, kept there
> as skulls

in "The Song and Dance of" is explained by an Associated Press dispatch, 12 April 1953, clipped from an unidentified newspaper and kept next to an article from the *Illustrated London News* for 18 April 1953, both describing the archaeological find at Jericho of seven Neolithic portrait heads (skulls covered with plaster) (*Guide*, p. 87). There are many allusions that cannot be pinned down to specific news items; they don't have to be—they come under the category of general knowledge. A good part of these earlier *Maximus* poems is, as Olson used to say, "talking over the fence."

Substantial sources, not previously cited, reveal themselves in the text:

Harold Bowditch, "Nathaniel Bowditch," *American Neptune* 5 (April 1945): 99–110—Olson owned this, and also the January 1944 issue.

John Bartlet Brebner, *The Explorers of North America 1492–1806* (London: A. & C. Black, 1933)—Olson used the BMC library copy and took it with him to Gloucester in 1957.

Henry Harrisse, "The Outcome of the Cabot Quarter-Centenary," *American Historical Review* 4 (October 1898): 38–61—there are notes in an Olson notebook made from a reading of this article.

J. Franklin Jameson, ed., "Letters of Stephen Higginson, 1783–1804," in *Annual Report of the American Historical Association for the Year 1896* (Washington: Government Printing Office, 1879) 1, 704–841—Olson owned the volume.

Charles O. Paullin, *Atlas of the Historical Geography of the United States* (Washington and New York: Carnegie Institution & American Geographical Society, 1932)—Olson used the BMC library copy for the Juan de la Cosa map and brought the book with him to Gloucester.

John Smith, *Travels and Works of Captain John Smith*, ed. Edward Arber, 2 vols. (Edinburgh: John Grant, 1910)—early use of this work is indicated in the poem, though the copy in Olson's library is of later provenance, preempted from the Sawyer Free Library, Gloucester, in 1959.[11]

The poem that begins the last third of the 1960 *Maximus Poems*, "Letter 23," with its authoritative tone: "The facts are: 1st season 1623/4 one ship, the *Fellowship* etc." is not really a new beginning except that Olson had tracked down through interlibrary loan an important new source: Frances Rose-Troup's *John White, the Patriarch of Dorchester (Dorset) and the Founder of Massachusetts, 1575–1648* (New York: Putnam, 1930). This poem was written September 1953 at Black Mountain College, and there was then a four-year break in the *Maximus* series until Olson, fully settled in Gloucester in 1957, could write "a Plantation a beginning" in earnest.[12]

There was a good period of preparation for the move. Soon after the college officially closed, Olson is writing to Mary Shore ("sister" as Ferrini was "brother") on 3 November 1956 that he should now be able "to get back to what I have been split from for the past three years":

> In fact last night had *the* moment in a lifetime: sat down and bought 41 bucks worth of books straight out of catalogues, anticipating return to *Max* work. (By the way, is Choate Alderman still running that antiques and books on lower Main St (West End)? and Saville still in Rockport? and Burnham up in Essex? Do you shop them? I should be interested in any local items they might have and will write them if you confirm they still exist.

We know of only one Gloucester purchase before Olson returned there in August 1957.[13] Meanwhile, catalogue purchases from elsewhere are as follows:

Strand Books, N.Y. (2 November 1956):
> Thomas Perkins Abernethy, *The Burr Conspiracy* (New York: Oxford University Press, 1954).
> Holmes Alexander, *Aaron Burr: The Proud Pretender* (New York: Harper, 1937).
> James B. Connolly, *The Port of Gloucester* (previously cited).
> Edwin Sidney Hartland, *The Science of Fairy Tales* (London: Walter Scott, 1891).
> Frances Rose-Troup, *John White* (previously cited).
> Samuel H. Wandell and Meade Minnigerode, *Aaron Burr*, 2 vols. (New York: Puntam, 1925).

Port Washington, N.Y. (19 November 1956):
> Thomas H. Benton, *Thirty Years' View* (previously cited—Harvard list).

Bookshop unknown (11 November 1956):
> Seton Lloyd, *Early Anatolia: The Archaeology of Asia Minor Before the Greeks* (Harmondsworth: Pelican Book, 1956).
> George Bruner Parks, *Richard Hakluyt and the English Voyages* (New York: American Geographical Society, 1928)—flyleaf: "Olson bmc Nov. 56."

Doubleday, N.Y. (20 November 1956):
> Numa Denis Fustel de Coulanges, *The Ancient City* (Garden City, N.Y.: Doubleday Anchor Book, 1956).

Carolina Book Company, Asheville N.C. (23 December 1956):
> Archer Butler Hulbert, *Forty-Niners* (Boston: Little, Brown, 1931).

University of Chicago (1 January 1957):

> Edward Chiera, *Sumerian Epics and Myths*, Cuneiform Series 3 (Chicago: University of Chicago Press, Oriental Institute Publications, 1934).

> Henri Frankfort, *Kingship and the Gods* (Chicago: University of Chicago Press, 1948).

> I. Gelb, *A Study of Writing* (Chicago: University of Chicago Press, 1952).

> Thorkild Jacobsen, *The Sumerian King List* (University of Chicago Press, 1939).

Orientalia Bookshop (4 January 1957):

> Robert C. Dentan, ed., *The Idea of History in the Ancient Near East* (New Haven: Yale University Press, 1955).

> Theodore Gaster, *The Oldest Stories in the World* (New York: Viking, 1952).[14]

> Bedrich Hrozny, *Ancient History of Western Asia, India and Crete* (Prague: Artia, 1953).

> Swami Sankarananda, *The Rigvedic Culture of the Pre-historic Indus*, 2 vols. (Calcutta: Abhedananda Academy of Culture 1944, 1946).

> Raymond Weill, *Phoenicia and Western Asia to the Macedonian Conquest* (London: Harrap, 1940).

> John A. Wilson, *The Culture of Ancient Egypt* (University of Chicago, Phoenix Books, 1956).

Pantheon Books, N.Y. (1 January 1957):

> Joseph Campbell, ed., *The Mysteries*, Bollingen Series 30.2 (New York: Pantheon Books, 1955).

> C. G. Jung, *Psychology and Alchemy*, Bollingen Series 20 (New York: Pantheon, 1953).

> C. G. Jung, *Symbols of Transformation*, Bollingen Series 20 (New York: Pantheon, 1956).

> C. G. Jung and W. Pauli, *The Interpretation of Nature and the Psyche: Synchronicity: An Acausal Connecting Principle* (Jung); *The Influence of Archetypal Ideas on the Scientific Theories of Kepler* (Pauli), Bollingen Series 51 (New York: Pantheon, 1955).

> Erich Neumann, *The Great Mother*, Bollingen Series 47 (New York: Pantheon Books, 1955).

Yale University Press (8 January 1957):

> Julian Obermann, *Ugaritic Mythology: A Study of Its Leading Motifs* (New Haven: Yale, 1948).

Princeton University Press (8 January 1957):

> James B. Pritchard, ed., *Ancient Near Eastern Texts Relating to the Old Testament* 2d ed. (Princeton: Princeton University Press, 1955).

Blackwell's, U.K. (9–16 January 1957):

> Godfrey Rolles Driver, *Canaanite Myths and Legends* (Edinburgh: T. & T. Clark, 1956).[15]
>
> D. H. Lawrence, *The Complete Short Stories*, 3 vols., Phoenix edition (London: Heinemann, 1955).
>
> D. H. Lawrence, *Mornings in Mexico and Etruscan Places*, Phoenix edition (London: Heinemann, 1956).
>
> William Shakespeare, *Pericles, Prince of Tyre*, ed. J. C. Maxwell (Cambridge University Press, 1956).
>
> Alfred North Whitehead, *Process and Reality* (previously cited).

Unknown bookshop (February 1957):

> John Forsdyke, *Greece Before Homer* (London: Max Parrish, 1956).
>
> G. R. Levy, *The Gate of Horn* (previously cited).

Some of these titles express an exuberance beyond the preparation for returning to New England to write about it. The teacher who lectured on the "New Sciences of Man" is still feeding himself and growing, separate from Maximus. It will be some time before the poet feels a way of allowing Maximus to be as big. Meanwhile, he focuses in.

Goodspeed's Book Shop, Boston (7 January–9 February 1957):

> Charles Knowles Bolton, *The Real Founders of New England* (Boston: Faxon, 1929).
>
> Charles Edward Mann, *In the Heart of Cape Ann, or the Story of Dogtown* 2d ed. (Gloucester: Proctor Bros., 1906).
>
> James R. Pringle, *History of the Town and City of Gloucester* (Gloucester: by the author, 1892).
>
> Frances Rose-Troup, *The Massachusetts Bay Company and Its Predecessors* (New York: Grafton Press, 1930).

And then, sitting in 28 Fort Square, Gloucester, and opening his typewriter case some time during the second week of August 1957, he writes to his friend (*OLSON* 6, pp. 61–62):

> I return to the city and my first thought, Ferrini, is of you who for so long has been my body here and I a shadow coming in like gulls

Now that I am back. . . . I laugh, from my height, and decide to tell you stories, Ferrini, so long as you will listen to me. I'm going to start them today, and I'll send them to you as they get done, just one right after another, to amuse you.

## Appendix

### Black Mountain College Library Books

Olson wrote to Frances Boldereff on 9 June 1957: "Gutted BMC Lib, but only one book looks like anything: 'Celtic Ornament in the Brit. Isles Down to AD 700' by E. T. Leeds, Oxford, 1933, with yum-yum plates. I'll keep to read and bring to you at Woodward!" Apparently the book was given as a gift; it was not among Olson's books later. But many other Black Mountain College library books were. After discarding a number of boxes of books at the North Carolina Wesleyan College Library in Rocky Mount, the following volumes he packed in his car and took to Gloucester in August 1957. (This list is meant to be complete, and includes titles cited elsewhere in this volume.)

Brooks Adams, *The New Empire* (cited elsewhere)—flyleaf: Olson—by arrogation."

James Truslow Adams, *The Founding of New England* (cited—Harvard list); and *Revolutionary New England, 1691–1776* (Boston: Atlantic Monthly Press, 1923)—notes and markings pp. 86–91 regarding Gloucester trade.

Summerfield Baldwin, *Business in the Middle Ages* (New York: Henry Holt, 1937)—flyleaf: "1st dug, *directly* to purpose, March 1960; but read & used since 1955 (?"; heavy notes and markings throughout.

Charles Beard, *An Economic Interpretation of the Constitution of the United States* (cited elsewhere).

Grace Hadley Beardsley, *The Negro in Greek and Roman Civilization* (Johns Hopkins; Oxford, 1929).

Morris Bishop, *The Odyssey of Cabeza de Vaca* (cited elsewhere).

William Blake, *America: A Prophecy*, foreword by Ruthven Todd (New York: United Book Guild, 1947).

Raymond Bernard Blakney, *Meister Eckhart: A Modern Translation* (New York: Harper, 1941).

P. Boissonnade, *Life and Work in Medieval Europe* (New York: Knopf, 1927)

H. N. Brailsford, *Shelley, Godwin, and their Circle* (New York: Holt, n.d.).

Louis D. Brandeis, *Other People's Money, and How the Bankers Use It* (Washington: National Home Library Foundation, 1933).

John Bartlet Brebner, *The Explorers of North America* (cited elsewhere).

M. C. Burkitt, *Our Early Ancestors* (New York: Macmillan; Cambridge University Press, 1926).

*Civil and Mexican Wars 1861, 1846* (Boston: Military Historical Society of Massachusetts, 1913).

Mary Cowden Clarke, *The Complete Concordance to Shakspere* (Boston: Little, Brown, 1871).

Robert M. Coates, *The Outlaw Years* (New York: Macaulay Co., 1930).

W. G. Collingwood, *Scandinavian Britain* (London: Society for Promoting Christian Knowledge; New York: E. S. Gorham, 1908).

Carleton S. Coon, *The Story of Man* (New York: Knopf, 1954)—notes and markings throughout. This book was mentioned to Stan Brakhage during the filmmaker's visit to Gloucester on 17 May 1963, as reported in his article, "Metaphors on Vision," *Film Culture* 30 (Fall 1963), which Olson owned.

W. G. De Burgh, *The Legacy of the Ancient World*, vol. 1 (Harmondsworth: Penguin, 1955).

H. A. L. Fisher, *The History of England from the Accession of Henry VII to the Death of Henry VIII (1485–1547)* (London: Longmans, Green, 1906).

Sigmund Freud, *Totem and Taboo*, trans. A. A. Brill (New York: New Republic, 1931).

Leo Frobenius, *The Childhood of Man* (London: Seeley, 1909).

Leo Frobenius and Douglas C. Fox, *African Genesis* (New York: Stackpole 1937)—Olson had had it on reserve for classes.

James Anthony Froude, *History of England from the Fall of Wolsey to the Death of Elizabeth*, vol. 1 (New York: Scribner, Armstrong, 1872).

Gustav Gluck, *Pieter Brueghel the Elder* (London: Commodore Press, 1937).

Nikolai Gogol, *Dead Souls* (New York: Modern Library, 1936).

C. H. Grandgent, *Italian Grammar* (Boston: D. C. Heath, 1915).

H. J. C. Grierson, ed., *The Poems of John Donne* (London: Oxford University Press, 1939).

Alfred Guillaume, *Islam* (Harmondsworth: Penguin, 1954).

Richard Hakluyt, *Voyages*, vol. 3, Everyman's Library (London: Dent; New York: Dutton, 1926).

Francis W. Halsey, ed., *Great Epochs in American History*, vols. 1 and 2 (New York: Funk & Wagnalls, 1912).

Henry F. Howe, *Prologue to New England* (New York: Farrar & Rinehart, 1943)—notes and markings throughout.

*Human Origins: An Introduction to Anthropology* (University of Chicago Bookstore, 1946)—cover: Charles Olson taken from Black Mountain College by myself as Trustee & Assignee for the Benefit of the Creditors—ex officio President, actually final Rector (of same''; borrowers card indicates Olson used the book around 26 November 1951.

A. Jardé, *The Formation of the Greek People* (New York: Knopf, 1926).

Wassily Kandinsky, *The Art of Spiritual Harmony* (London: Constable, 1914).

Alfred Korzybski, *Science and Sanity: An Introduction to Non-Aristotelian Systems and General Semantics*, 3d ed. (Lakeville: International Non-Aristotelian Library Publishing Co., 1949).

A. L. Kroeber, *Anthropology*, rev. ed. (New York: Harcourt, Brace, 1948).

W. Gabriel Lasker and Charles I. Slade, eds., *Yearbook of Physical Anthropology 1949*; W. Gabriel Lasker and W. L. Straus, eds., *Yearbook of Physical Anthropology 1950* (New York: Wenner-Gren, 1950 and 1951 respectively).

William L. Langer, *An Encyclopaedia of World History* (Boston: Houghton Mifflin, 1940)—notes and markings, pp. 29–67.

Seton Lloyd, *Foundations in the Dust* (Harmondsworth: Penguin, 1955).

S. K. Lothrop, *Atitlan* (previously cited).

L. Macbean, *Elementary Lessons in Gaelic* 5th ed. (Stirling: Eneas Mackay, 1901).

*Maceachen's Gaelic-English Dictionary* 4th ed. (Inverness: Northern Counties Newspaper & Printing & Publishing Co., 1922).

Malcolm MacFarlane, *The School Gaelic Dictionary* (Stirling: Eneas Mackay, 1912).

William Christie Macleod, *The American Indian Frontier* (New York: Knopf, 1928).

Philip Ainsworth Means, *The Spanish Main* (New York: Scribner, 1935).

Marianne Moore, *What Are Years* (New York: Macmillan, 1941).

N. C. Nelson, *South African Rock Pictures* (New York: American Museum of Natural History, 1937).

Curtis P. Nettels, *The Roots of American Civilization* (New York: Crofts, 1945)—occasional notes and markings.

Arthur Percival Newton, *The European Nations in the West Indies*

*1493–1688* (London: A. & C. Black, 1933)—flyleaf: "Olson by ac-
quisition," occasional notes and markings.

C. T. Onions, *A Shakespeare Glossary*, 2d ed. (Oxford at the Clarendon
Press, 1929).

Francis Parkman, *France and England in North America* (cited else-
where).

James Parton, *The Life and Times of Aaron Burr*, 2 vols. (New York: Ma-
son Brothers, 1864).

Walter Pater, *The Renaissance* (London: Macmillan, 1935).

Charles O. Paullin, *Atlas of the Historical Geography of the United States*
(cited elsewhere).

Henri Pirenne, *Medieval Cities* (Princeton University Press, 1946).

Ezra Pound, *Jefferson and/or Mussolini* (New York: Liveright; London:
Stanley Nott, 1936); and *Personae* (New York: New Directions, 1949).

Eileen Power, *Medieval People* (Boston: Houghton Mifflin, 1927).

Arthur Rimbaud, *A Season in Hell*, trans. Delmore Schwartz, 2d ed.
(Norfolk: New Directions, n.d.).

William Hutchinson Rowe, *The Maritime History of Maine* (New York:
Norton, 1948)—light markings.

Gustav Schwabb, *Gods & Heroes: Myths & Epics of Ancient Greece* (New
York: Pantheon, 1946).

*Shakespeare's England*, vol. 2 (Oxford at the Clarendon Press, 1932)—
Olson took this book out on 17 August 1949.

J. Duncan Spaeth, *Old English Poetry: Translations into Alliterative Verse*
(Princeton University Press, 1921)—occasional markings.

Stendahl, *Armance*, trans. Scott-Moncrieff (New York: Boni & Liveright,
1928).

Wallace Stevens, *Ideas of Order* (New York: Knopf, 1936); *Harmonium*
(New York: Knopf, 1947)—Olson had a second copy; *The Auroras
of Autumn* (New York: Knopf, 1950)—and a second copy with fly-
leaf name: "Harvey S. Harmon Black Mountain College April
fifty-one."

*Summary of Archaeological Work in the Americas During 1929 and 1930*
(Washington: Pan American Union, 1931).

Harold G. Thompson, ed., *Smith's First Year Latin* (Boston: Allyn & Ba-
con, 1936).

J. A. K. Thomson, *The Art of the Logos* (London: Allen & Unwin,
1935)—much used (cited elsewhere).

George Macaulay Trevelyan, *England Under the Stuarts* 15th ed. (New York: Putnam; London: Methuen, 1930); and *English Social History* (London: Longmans, Green, 1943).

Walter Prescott Webb, *The Great Plains* (Boston: Ginn, 1931)—much used (cited elsewhere).

Bouck White, *The Book of Daniel Drew* (New York: Doubleday, Page, 1910)

William Carlos Williams, *In the American Grain* (Norfolk: New Directions, 1945)—the second copy Olson owned.

George F. Willison, *Saints and Strangers* (New York: Reynal & Hitchcock, 1945).

John Dover Wilson, *The Manuscript of Shakespeare's Hamlet and the Problem of Its Transmission*, vol. 1 (Cambridge University Press, 1934)—Olson's signature on borrowers card for 15 August 1949 and 8 October 1951.

Leonard Woolley, *A Forgotten Kingdom* (Baltimore: Penguin, 1953)—notes and markings through p. 95.

Irene A. Wright, ed., *Spanish Documents Concerning English Voyages to the Caribbean 1527–1568* (London: Hakluyt Society, 1929); Olson also annotated her article, "Documents: Spanish Policy toward Virginia, 1606–1612," *American Historical Review* 25 (April 1920): 448–79—presumably Olson's copies of this journal were from BMC.

William Butler Yeats, *Last Poems & Plays* (New York: Macmillan, 1940).


Butterick detected Olson's notes and markings in several issues of the *American Journal of Archaeology* which he had retained from the BMC Library:


Elizabeth Pierce Blegen, "News Items from Athens," 46 (October–December 1942): 477–87.

Lionel Cohen, "Evidence for the Ram in the Minoan Period," 42 (October–December 1938): 486–94.

Nelson Glueck, "Archaeological Exploration and Excavation in Palestine, Transjordan, and Syria during 1937," 42 (January–March 1938): 165–76.

George M. A. Hanfmann, "Archaeology in Homeric Asia Minor," 52 (January–March 1948): 135–55.

Stephen B. Luce, "Archaeological News and Discussions," 47 (January–March 1943): 102–24.

Edith Porada, "The Cylinder Seals of the Late Cypriote Bronze Age," 52 (January–March 1948): 178–98.

David M. Robinson, "Archaeological News and Discussions," 42 (January–March 1938): 130–49.

C. A. Schaeffer, "Enkomi," 52 (January–March 1948): 165–77.

Possibly Olson's issues of the *Bulletin of the American Schools of Oriental Research* were from the BMC Library, though they were not stamped as such. Butterick reports notes and markings in the following articles:

William Foxwell Albright, "Stratigraphic Confirmation of the Low Mesopotamia Chronology," 144 (December 1956): 26–30.

Frank M. Cross Jr., "The Evolution of the Proto-Canaanite Alphabet," 134 (April 1954): 15–24.

H. L. Ginsberg, "The North-Canaanite Myth of Anath and Aqhat," 98 (April 1945): 15–23.

George M. Landes, "The Fountain at Jazer," 144 (December 1956): 30–37—mentioned in a letter to Robin Blaser of 3 May 1957.

How many other books and magazines in Olson's library came from this source, but having no library bookplate, cannot be known. The two copies of *The Bibelot* (vol. 9 no. 8, 1903; vol. 20 no. 7, 1914) published by Thomas Mosher in Portland, Maine, found in Olson's library, might be a case in point. *American Mercury* volumes for January–June 1958 and July–December 1958 were "sent to the librarian with compliments," according to an accompanying card. One book that seems clearly to have arrived at BMC after there was no librarian is Nita Scudder Baugh, ed., *A Worcestershire Miscellany, Complied by John Northwood, c. 1400* (Philadelphia, 1956), which has a slip laid in: "Presented by The University of Pennsylvania Library" (added in Olson's hand: "to Editor, BMC"). Olson's second copy of *Webster's Collegiate Dictionary*, 5th ed., with Thomas Field's name in it, was "found in the office March 23/57," according to Olson's note. Olson typed out for Michael Rumaker, 23 December 1956, "The Holly and the Ivy" from Francis J. Sheed, *The Mary Book* (New York: Sheed & Ward, 1950): "Let me show you (fr the Mary Book I found Mary F left behind in her house) what such gentilness (as Chaucer and Sir Philip Sidney had, and died with and about between 1585 and 1603), this beautiful anonymous poem of the sixteenth century." This book may have been returned to Mary Fitton; it is not found in Olson's library later, though a couple of books that have Mary Fitton's signature are: Padraic Colum, *The Voyagers: Being Legends and Romances of Atlantic Discovery* (New York: Macmillan, 1925), and Margaret Mead, *The Changing Culture of an Indian Tribe* (New York: Columbia University Press, 1932). Books in Olson's library from other Black Mountain people (not cited elsewhere) are: W. H. Hadow, *English Music* (London: Longmans, Green, 1931) via John Evarts; Edith Hamilton, *Mythology* (New York: New American Library Mentor, 1955) via Ann Simone; Salomon Reinach, *Orpheus: A History of Religion* (New York: Liveright, 1933) via Donald F. Daley; and from Tony Landreau a copy of Henry Lamar Crosby and John Nevin Schaeffer, *An Introduction to Greek* (Boston: Allyn and Bacon, 1944).

# Part III

## *Instants*

Charles is just like I am. He sits around
and reads all day.
> —Robert Duncan in conversation
with Ann Charters on 25 January 1968

# 16

## *April Today Main Street*

Now, August 1957, settled in, Olson could go out looking for "stories." He picked up Richard Eddy, *Universalism in Gloucester, Mass.* (Gloucester: Procter Brothers, 1892—flyleaf: "Olson bought Gloucester (Ed Kemry's August 15/57"—which became heavily marked and annotated with his reading. Soon he bought the large *Standard History of Essex County* (Boston: C. F. Jewett, 1878)—flyleaf: "bot $2! Pleasant St Gloucester dealer Aug–Sept 1957." He bought a couple of things on a trip to the Essex Institute in nearby Salem: *Records and Files of the Quarterly Courts of Essex County, Massachusetts*, vol. 1 of 8 vols. (Salem: Essex Institute, 1911–21),[1] and Herbert B. Adams, *Salem Commons and Commoners: or the Economic Beginnings of Massachusetts*, reprinted from *Historical Collections of the Essex Institute*, vol. 19 (Salem: Essex Institute, 1882), again notes and markings throughout. And then to another nearby Institute for Alice Gertrude Lapham, *Old Planters of Beverly in Massachusetts and the Thousand Acre Grant of 1635* (Cambridge: Riverside Press for the Beverly Historical Society and the Conant Family Association, 1930)—flyleaf: "Olson bot Beverly Oct 18/1957." And "from Mrs Sanderson, at Sandy Bay Oct 27/57," Marshall H. Saville, *Champlain and his Landings at Cape Ann, 1605, 1606*, reprinted from *Proceedings of the American Antiquarian Society for October 1933* (Worcester, 1934).

All of these supplied something to the *Maximus Poems* eventually. For example, Saville's *Champlain* book provided much, including the title, of "The Savages, or Voyages of Samuel de Champlain of Brouage" (*Maximus Poems*, pp. 453–55); the poem was composed directly into the Saville volume, beginning on page 6 and working backwards (*Guide*, p. 585).

Meanwhile, the poems written after Olson's return to Gloucester that complete the 1960 *Maximus Poems* volume involve the use of the following titles:

"a Plantation a begining" (begun September 1957)
> *John White's Planters Plea*, ed. Marshall H. Saville (Rockport: Sandy Bay Historical Society and Museum, 1930)—Olson utilized this and much more at the Sandy Bay Historical Society in nearby Rockport; he did not need to own it as it was amply quoted in Frances Rose-Troup's *John White* (in his possession, previously cited).

"Maximus, to Gloucester" (probably October–November 1957)
> John Wingate Thornton, *The Landing at Cape Anne* (Boston: Gould & Lincoln, 1854)—a letter to the author from John J. Babson, found only in the Appendix of this volume, is paraphrased by Olson in this poem, though he did not acquire the volume until later (flyleaf: "Olson—bot fr Burstein Feb/59 ($5)").

"So Sassafras" (probably November 1957)
> Francis X. Moloney, *The Fur Trade in New England 1620–1676* (Cambridge: Harvard University Press, 1931)—a background work, acquired by Olson after recommendation by Frederick Merk (letters of 10 and 29 September 1953, Storrs); flyleaf: "Olson Black Mt Feb 1954 $1.06 (List $1.25)"

> Harold A. Innis, *The Cod Fisheries* (Toronto: University of Toronto Press, 1954)—in this and the next poem Olson makes good use of an authority he has known for a while; flyleaf: "Olson black mt july 24 1957."

> George D. Phippen, "The 'Old Planters' of Salem, Who Were Settled Here Before the Arrival of Governor Endicott, in 1628," *Historical Collections of the Essex Institute* 1 (July 1859): 97–110—used for the story of Tilley and the Indians; Olson owned the issue.

"History is the Memory of Time" (probably November 1957)
> *Bradford's History "Of Plimoth Plantation"* (Boston: Wright & Potter, 1898)—flyleaf: "Charles J. Olson Jr Boston, Feb., 1936"; used importantly in one of Olson's earliest poems, "There Was a Youth Whose Name was Thomas Granger," and now in a *Maximus* poem.

> William Hubbard, *General History of New England from the Discov-*

*ery to MDCLXXX*, (Boston: Massachusetts Historical Society, 1815)—presumably consulted at some point, but not necessarily here, for the quotation in the poem could be found in other volumes Olson owned: Frances Rose-Troup's *John White* (previously cited), and her *Roger Conant and the Early Settlement on the North Shore of Massachusetts* (Roger Conant Family Association, 1926).

"The Picture"; "The Record" (probably November 1957)

W. C. Ford, "Dorchester Company at Cape Ann, 1635" in *Proceedings: October, 1909–June, 1910*, Vol. 63 (Boston: Massachusetts Historical Society, 1910)—on John Watts, supplementing Frances Rose-Troup, this volume was ordered from Goodspeed's on 19 February 1958, but was not later in Olson's library.

"Some Good News" (probably February 1958)

Walter H. Rich, *Fishing Grounds of the Gulf of Maine*, Appendix 3 to the Report of the U.S. Commissioner of Fisheries for 1929 (Washington: Bureau of Fisheries, 1929)—used for information on Georges Bank according to a notebook entry, 5 February 1958.[2]

"Stiffening, in the Master Founders' Wills" (probably February 1958)

*Winthrop Papers*, 5 vols. (Boston: Massachusetts Historical Society, 1929–47)—perhaps acquired by 2 January 1958, when in a letter to Corman of that date Olson said he was "running down Puritan emigrations (John Winthrop happens to be the one who is my horse this season at Suffolk Downs)."

Brooks Adams, *The Emancipation of Massachusetts* (Boston: Houghton Mifflin, 1887)—a manuscript note associates this volume with this poem (*Guide*, p. 185).[3]

"Letter-Book of Samuel Sewall," *Collections of the Massachusetts Historical Society*, 6th series, 1 (1886)—possibly used (Olson did not own this volume) for passage on Jeremiah Drummer (*Guide*, p. 187).

"Capt Christopher Levett (of York)" (probably February 1958)

Charles Herbert Levermore, ed., *Forerunners and Competitors of the Pilgrims and Puritans*, 2 vols. (Brooklyn: The New England Society in the City of Brooklyn, 1912)—flyleaf of vol. 2: "Olson Feb 20/58 (fr Goodspeed—2 vols $5)." A notebook indicates that on 12 February 1958 Olson was reading the pertinent document (vol. 2, pp. 608–42): Christopher Levett's *A Voyage into New England* (1628).

"April Today Main Street" (27 April 1959)

> *Note-Book Kept by Thomas Lechford, Esq.* (Cambridge: John Wilson, 1885) Transactions and Collections of the American Antiquarian Society vol. 7—flyleaf: "Olson—bot fr Burstein Feb/59 for 7.50."

> Nathaniel B. Shurtleff, ed., *Records of the Governor and Company of the Massachusetts Bay in New England*, 2 vols. (Boston: William White, 1853)—flyleaf of vol. 1: "bought, happily, fr Jewett 1959 (?—used decently May 1961."[4]

> *Winthrop's Journal "History of New England" 1630–1649*, 2 vols., ed. James Kendall Hosmer (New York: Scribner, 1908)—the most accessible edition, but not owned by Olson.[5]

"Letter, May 2, 1959"

> *Memorial of the Celebration of the Two Hundred and Fiftieth Aniversary of the Incorporation of the Town of Gloucester, Mass. August, 1892* (Boston: Mudge, 1901)—flyleaf: "fr Viola & Homer Barrett years ago"; used here for the John Trask "historical address" pp. 101–35, and the anniversary sermon of Rev. Daniel M. Wilson, pp. 38–54.

> *Johnson's Wonder-Working Providence 1628–1651*, ed. J. Franklin Jameson (New York: Scribner, 1910)—purchased from Goodspeed's on 19 February 1958 and presumably looked at for this poem, although the flyleaf has: "Olson 1st used night of Sun Oct 15 1961."

> Charles Edward Banks, *The Planters of the Commonwealth* (Boston: Houghton Mifflin, 1930), and his *Topographical Dictionary of 2885 English Emigrants to New England 1620–1650* (Philadelphia: Bertram Press, 1937)—consulted in a library for names of Gloucester settlers.

> Eugen Herrigel, *Zen in the Art of Archery* (New York: Pantheon, 1953)—for the novel reference to "Zen archer"; Olson owned the volume.

On 24 February 1958, Olson wrote to Creeley: "Buying books. Marvelous feeling—and maps. Will end up, no matter, loaded with equipment!" The following day he wrote to Robin Blaser, then working in Harvard University Library: "Does Harvard still receive gifts of books from old ladies in Monhegan etc? Here I am looking and buying books on early settlements of Mass Bay Maine and Cape Ann—and suddenly maybe duplicates?????? there??" There were none to be had by the Harvard route, but Olson did acquire by one means or another the following volumes (not previously mentioned) as part of the "*Max* work."

*Massachusetts Historical Society Proceedings, 1910–1911,* vol. 44 (Boston, 1911)—flyleaf: "Olson bot of Goodspeed"; John Franklin Jameson, ed., "Letters of John Bridge, 1623, and Emmanuel Altham, 1624," pp. 178–89—used substantially in "The Gulf of Maine" (*Guide,* p. 397).[6]

J. G. Kohl, *History of the Discovery of Maine,* ed. William Willis (Portland: Bailey & Noyes, 1869)—flyleaf: "bot direct fr Gloucester Library (Miss Heckman) Feb/59 (3.50)."

John T. Hull, *The Seige and Capture of Fort Loyall* (Portland: Owen, Strout, 1885)—cover: "bot Portland—O'Brien's—$5.00 on way with Bet & Chas Peter (to Castine? or Nova Scotia? what year 1961?"

William Willis, *The History of Portland, from its First Settlement* (Portland: Day, Fraser, 1831; Charles Day & Co, 1833)—flyleaf: "given to me by Gerrit Lansing 1961."

Raymond McFarland, *The Masts of Gloucester: Recollections of a Fisherman* (New York: Norton, 1937)—flyleaf: Olson fr Jewett (Ipswich Feb 14/58."

Reider T. Sherwin, *The Viking and The Red Man: The Old Norse Origin of the Algonquin Language* (New York: Funk & Wagnalls, 1942)—Olson used vol. 1 in the *Maximus* poems, but only vol. 2 of 7 volumes was found in his library; flyleaf: "bot fr his widow February(?) 1959—1st looked into (after using Vol I in 1958 & 1959) March, 1960."

John J. Babson, *Notes and Additions to the History of Gloucester: Second Series* (Salem: Salem Press Publishing & Printing Co., 1891)— flyleaf: "Olson—bot of Burke's 1958 (muchos pesos) 7.50? (I therefore lack B's 'Notes & Additions' Part I, or 1st Series)."

John J. Babson, *Notes and Additions to the History of Gloucester, Part First: Early Settlers* (Gloucester: Perley, 1876)—cover: "Olson—fr. Jewett (7.50) April 1959."

George B. Goode, *The Fisheries and Fishery Industries of the United States*

(Washington: U.S. Commission of Fish & Fisheries, 1887)—bought from Harold M. Burstein, Cambridge, 28 April 1959; *"Cashes"* (*Maximus II*) is taken from George B. Goode and Joseph W. Collins "The Fisherman of the United States," section 4 of this volume.

Stephen Willard Phillips, ed., *Ship Registers of the District of Gloucester, Massachusetts, 1789–1875* (Salem: Essex Institute, 1944)—extensive notes and markings.

William Wood, *New Englands Prospect*, introd. Eben Moody Boynton (Boston: 1898)—bought from Harold M. Burstein, Cambridge, 28 April 1959.

N. S. Shaler, "The Geology of Cape Ann, Massachusetts" in *Ninth Annual Report of the United States Geological Survey* (Washington: Government Printing Office, 1889), pp. 529–611—flyleaf: "bot Jewett at some marvelous price some time ago" (possibly May 1959).

Amos Everett Jewett, *The Tidal Marshes of Rowley and Vicinity*, reprinted from *Essex Institute Historical Collections*, vol. 85 (Salem: Newcomb & Gauss, 1949)—cover: "Olson—fr. Everett Jewett May 8/59."

*The Jewett Family of America Yearbook of 1958* (Rowley, 1958).

D. F. Lamson, *History of the Town of Manchester, Essex County, Massachusetts, 1645–1895* (Manchester, 1895)—flyleaf: "Olson June/59 (fr Jewett, May)."

*Town Records of Manchester, From Earliest Grants of Land, 1636* (Salem: Salem Press Publishing & Printing Co., 1889)—cover: "Olson gift of Doris Connors, Librarian Manchester June 4, 1959."[7]

*Essex Institute Historical Collections* 95 (July 1959)—Olson read and marked two articles: Norman Robert Bennett "Americans in Zanzibar: 1825–1845," pp. 239–62, and Ralph W. Dexter, "Common Marine Life at Cape Ann, Massachusetts," pp. 263–68.[8]

*The Probate Records of Essex County, Massachusetts*, 3 vols. (Salem: Essex Institute, 1916–20)—flyleaf of vol. 1: "Olson—bot fr Jewett March 1960"; vol. 2 also came from Jewett, no date; vol. 3 was purchased from the Essex Institute 11 December 1965.

Justin Winsor, ed., *The Memorial History of Boston* (Boston: Ticknor, 1880)—Olson had vol. 1 (of 4 volumes); flyleaf: "Olson bot March 18th 1960 Jewett (2.50)."

Caroline O. Emmerton, *The Chronicle of Three Old Houses* (Boston: Thomas Todd, 1935)—flyleaf: "Olson ($1) at the house September 8, 1960."

Joseph H. Smith, ed., *Colonial Justice in Western Massachusetts* (Cambridge: Harvard University Press, 1961)—flyleaf: "Olson—(fr Hetty, & Leroi??)"

*A Reference Guide to Salem, 1630* (Salem: Board of Park Commissioners, City of Salem, 1959)—cover: "Olson via Vera 1961."

*The One Hundred Years of the Salem Savings Bank: Glances at an interesting and useful past* (Salem: Salem Savings Bank, 1918).

Charles Wendell Townsend, *The Birds of Essex County, Massachusetts* (Cambridge: Nuttall Ornithological Club, 1905)—flyleaf: "Charles Olson bot used 1961 (Jewett? 2 vols? This, 1905—& the Supplement of 1920."[9]

John William McElroy, "Seafaring in Seventeenth-Century New England," *New England Quarterly* 8 (September 1935): 331–64—a note on the cover indicates this was read 12 May 1961; marks and annotations.

*Along the Old Roads of Cape Ann* (Gloucester: McKenzie, 1923)—flyleaf: "Charles Olson fr Cape Ann Historical Sept 15, 1961."

*Journal of Captain Solomon H. Davis, A Gloucester Sea Captain, 1828–1846* (Norwood, Mass.: Privately printed, 1922)—flyleaf: "Charles Olson Cape Ann Historical Sept 15, 1961."

Bernard Bailyn and Lotte Bailyn, *Massachusetts Shipping 1697–1714: A Statistical Study* (Cambridge: Harvard University Press, 1959)—flyleaf: "Olson 1960."

Bernard Bailyn, *The New England Merchants in the Seventeenth Century* (Cambridge: Harvard University Press, 1955)—flyleaf: "Olson oct 1961."

Boston, Mass., *Fourth Report of the Record Commissioners* and *Fifth Report of the Record Commissioners* (Boston: Rockwell & Churchill, 1880).

Charles G. Leland, *The Algonquin Legends of New England* (Boston: Houghton Mifflin, 1884)—*Maximus* poems drawn verbatim from this book.

Fanny Hardy Eckstorm, *Old John Neptune and Other Maine Indian Shamans* (Portland: Southworth-Anthoensen Press, 1945).

Gordon W. Thomas, *Fast and Able: Life Stories of Great Gloucester Fishing Vessels* (Gloucester: William C. Brown Co., 1952)—title page: "Olson."

Frances Manwaring Caulkins, *History of New London, Connecticut* (New London: privately printed, 1852)—many notes and markings.

*United States Coast Pilot, Atlantic Coast Section A: St. Croix River to Cape Cod* 5th ed. (Washington: U.S. Department of Commerce, 1950)—

Olson had the two Supplements to this edition: 1957 and 1958; he also owned the old 1918 edition and its 1926 supplement.

Edmund S. Morgan, *The Birth of the Republic* (Chicago: University of Chicago Press, 1963)—marking indicates one contribution to the *Maximus* poems.[10]

*Annual Report of the City of Gloucester for the year 1895*—Olson also had that for the year 1914.

Horace P. Beck, *The American Indian as a Sea-Fighter in Colonial Times* (Mystic, Conn.: Marine Historical Association, 1959)—notes and markings.

B. Victor Bigelow, *Narrative History of Cohasset, Mass.* (Cohasset Committee on Town History, 1899).

Richard Biddle, *A Memoir of Sebastian Cabot* (Philadelphia, Lippincott, 1915).

*Boston, England, and Boston, New England 1630–1930* (Boston: State Street Trust Co., 1930).

Nathaniel Bowditch, *American Practical Navigator* (Washington: U.S. Navy Hydrographic Office, 1962).

Ralph H. Brown, *Mirror for Americans: Likeness of the Eastern Seaboard 1810* (New York: American Geographical Society, 1943).

Willis T. Lee, *The Face of the Earth As Seen From the Air: A Study in the Application of Airplane Photography to Geography* (New York: American Geographical Society, 1922).

*More Wonders of the Invisible World*, ed. Robert Calef, reprint of 1700 ed. (Salem: Cushing & Appleton, 1823).

*Fifth Annual Cape Ann Festival of the Arts* (Gloucester, 1956).

Edward Vassar Ambler, *The Cape Ann Trail* (Gloucester: Chamber of Commerce, n.d.,[11]—Olson had three copies.

*Cape Ann Scientific, Literary, and Historical Association: The Story of a Venerable Gloucester Society* (Gloucester, n.d.).

Emma Lewis Coleman, *A Historic and Present Day Guide to Old Deerfield* (Boston: privately printed, 1907).

Joshua Coffin, *A Sketch of the History of Newbury, Newburyport, and West Newbury, from 1635 to 1845* (Boston: Samuel G. Drake, 1845).

Frederick Odell Conant, *Life of Roger Conant* (Roger Conant Family Association, 1926)—cover: "Olson"; notes and markings on first two pages.

Melvin T. Copeland and Elliot C. Rogers, *The Saga of Cape Ann* (Freeport, Me.: Bond Wheelwright, 1960)—came to Olson secondhand, formerly owned by Joseph Jeswald of Gloucester.

Ernest S. Dodge, "A Seventeenth-Century Pennacook Quilled Pouch," *Publications of the Colonial Society of Massachusetts: Transactions* 38 (April 1949): 253–59—an offprint with Olson's notes and markings.

Ralph H. Eastman, *Some Famous Privateers of New England* (Boston: State Street Trust Co., 1928).

Frank L. Floyd, *Manchester By The Sea* (Manchester: Floyd's News Store, 1945).

Allan Forbes, ed., *Some Indian Events of New England* (Boston: State Street Trust Co., 1934)—cover: "Olson's copie."

E. G. and Alice W. Foster, *The Story of Kettle Cove* (Magnolia, Mass.: privately printed, 1939).

Emma L. Gartland, *New Bedford's Story for New Bedford's Children* (New Bedford, Mass.: privately printed, n.d.).

Lawrence Henry Gipson, *The British Isles and the American Colonies: The Northern Plantations, 1748–1754*, The British Empire Before the American Revolution, vol. 3 (New York: Knopf, 1960)—notes and markings.

Theodate Geoffrey, *Suckanesset: Wherein May Be Read a History of Falmouth* (Falmouth, Mass.: Falmouth Publishing Co., 1930)—some notes and markings.

*Gloucester Picturesque* (Gardner, Mass.: Charles D. Brown, n.d.)

I. J. Isaacs, compiler, *The City of Gloucester, Massachusetts: Its Interest and Industries* (Gloucester: Publicity Committee of the Board of Trade, 1916).

*Forty-Seventh Annual Report of the Gloucester Fisherman's Institute* (Gloucester: Fisherman's Institute, 1938).

*Inaugural Address of the Mayor with the Annual Report of the City of Gloucester for the Year 1895* (Gloucester, 1896)—Olson also owned that for the year 1914.

*Gloucester Directory 1899–1900* (Gloucester: Sampson, Murdock, 1899).

Richard Hakluyt, *A Discourse on Western Planting*, ed. Charles Deane, Documentary History of the State of Maine, vol. 2 (Cambridge: John Wilson, 1877).

Hildegarde T. Hartt, *Magnolia, once Kettle Cove* (Magnolia, Mass.: privately printed, 1962).

Hannah Josephson, *The Golden Threads: New England's Mill Girls and Magnates* (New York: Duell, Sloan & Pearce, 1949).

Augustus Peabody Loring, *Nathaniel Bowditch (1773–1838) Of Salem and Boston* (New York: The Newcomen Society in North America, 1950).

*Collections of the Maine Historical Society*, vol. 2 (Portland, 1847)— Sawyer Free Library cancellation stamp; notes by Olson.

R. G. Marsden, "A Letter of William Bradford and Isaac Allerton, 1623," *American Historical Review* 8 (January 1903): 294–301—this issue owned by Olson.

Jarvis M. Morse, "Captain John Smith, Marc Lescarbot, and the Division of Land by the Council for New England, in 1623," *New England Quarterly* 8 (September 1935): 399–404—notes and markings.

John Lathrop Motley, *The Rise of the Dutch Republic* (New York: Harper, 1880)—Olson had vol. 1 of 3 volumes.

Wallace Nutting, *Furniture of the Pilgrim Century 1620–1720* (Boston: Marshall Jones Co., 1921).

H. J. Mackinder, *Britain and the British Seas* (London: Heinemann, 1902).

Frederick Clifton Peirce, *Peirce Genealogy* (Worcester: Chas. Hamilton, 1880)—flyleaf: "Olson"; occasional markings.

Wesley George Pierce, *Goin' Fishin': The Story of the Deep-Sea Fishermen of New England* (Salem: Marine Research Society, 1934).

G. W. Prothero, ed., *Select Statutes and Other Constitutional Documents Illustrative of the Reigns of Elizabeth and James I* (Oxford: Clarendon Press, 1913).

John S. E. Rogers, *List of Vessels belonging to the District of Gloucester, August, 1870* (Gloucester: Telegraph Press, 1870)—copy previously owned by Otis Riggs Jr. (name on the cover).

William Otis Sawtelle, *Sir Francis Bernard and His Grant of Mount Desert*, reprinted from Publications of the Colonial Society of Massachusetts, vol. 24, pp. 197–255 (Cambridge: John Wilson, University Press, 1922).

John Scales, ed., *Piscataqua Pioneers, 1612–1775* (Dover, N.H.: Charles F. Whitehouse, 1919).

J. H. Stapleton, ed., *Gloucester Master Mariners' Association* (Gloucester: Association, 1917).

*The Log of the State Street Trust Company* (Boston: State Street Trust Co., 1926).

Leo Francis Stock, *Proceedings and Debates of the British Parliaments Re-*

*specting North America*, vol. 1: 1542–1688 (Washington: Carnegie Institution, 1924)—notes and markings.

Donald K. Tressler, James McW. Lemon, et al., *Marine Products of Commerce* (New York: Reinhold Publishing, 1951).

William P. Upham, ed., *Records of the First Church in Beverly, Massachusetts 1667–1722* (Salem: Essex Institute, 1905).

Reginald Vaughan, "Indians Summered on Cape Ann, Too," *Boston Sunday Globe*, 10 September 1961, p. 86A—clipping kept by Olson.

N. T. Whitaker, *Methodism on Cape Ann* (Gloucester: John D. Woodbury, 1875).

Thurlow Stanley Widger, *The Birth of New England: The True Story of its Discovery and Settlement* (privately published, 1959).

Carlton W. Wonson, "History of a Hall: The Independent Story" *Gloucester Daily Times* 25 September–1 October 1960—clippings.

This is the list of books that Olson seems to have acquired during the major *Maximus* years in Gloucester, 1957–63.[12] By no means do all of them show up in identifiable passages in the poem, as a glance at the bibliography of the Butterick *Guide to the Maximus Poems* would confirm. But no doubt it meant something to Olson to have this kind of overabundance in the house; he was bargaining for poems from a position of strength.

Further, it should be understood that the list implies a false homogeneity; for the poem is more than masts and memories. The trans-Atlantic migration is increasingly seen in its global aspects; usable history gets wider and goes further back. Jeremy Prynne sent over from England *The London Port Books*,[13] but he also knew to send the new fascicles of the revised *Cambridge Ancient History* as they came out and other like materials that culminated in *A Symposium on the Continental Drift*.[14] Prynne was being sensitive to the direction that *Maximus* was going in its "unique process of charting the birth of the real."[15]

## Appendix

### The Fascicles

The revised edition of *The Cambridge Ancient History* was published initially in the form of pamphlets, chapter by chapter. It is safe to say that all of the fascicles that Olson came to own were sent from Cambridge, England, by Jeremy Prynne of Gonville and Caius College. The sequence in which they were sent is not precisely known; they are arranged here in chronological order by date of publication.

## 1962

O. R. Gurney, *Anatolia: c. 1750–1600 b.c.* (fascicle 11)—notes and markings.[1]

C. J. Gadd, *The Cities of Babylonia* (fascicle 9).

William C. Hayes, *Egypt: From the Death of Ammenemes III to Seqenenre II* (fascicle 6).

William C. Hayes, *Egypt: Internal Affairs from Tuthmosis I to the Death of Amenophis III*, parts 1 and 2 (fascicles 10:1 and 10:2).[2]

James Mellaart, *Anatolia c. 4000–2300 b.c.* (fascicle 8).

W. Stevenson Smith, *The Old Kingdom in Egypt* (fascicle 5)—occasional notes and markings.

## 1963

John Chadwick, *The Prehistory of the Greek Language* (fascicle 15)—notes and markings.

C. J. Gadd, *The Dynasty of Agade and the Gutian Invasion* (fascicle 17).

Walther Hinz, *Persia c. 2400–1800 b.c.* (fascicle 19).

J. R. Kupper, *Northern Mesopotamia and Syria* (fascicle 14).

René Labat, *Elam c. 1600–1200 b.c.* (fascicle 16).

Frank H. Stubbings, *The Rise of Mycenaean Civilization* (fascicle 18)—notes and markings throughout.

1. Olson owned Gurney's *The Hittites* (Baltimore: Penguin Books, 1952)—notes and markings throughout. He also had another copy (the 1962 edition) with notes on pp. 46–47.

2. Olson also owned William C. Hayes, *The Scepter of Egypt: A Background for the Study of the Egyptian Antiquities in The Metropolitan Museum of Art*, Part 1 (Cambridge: Harvard University Press for Metropolitan Museum of Art, 1960)—notes and markings pp. 35–40, 58–61.

1964

C. W. Blegen, *Troy* (fascicle 1)—some notes and markings.[3]

John L. Caskey, *Greece, Crete, and the Aegean Islands in the Early Bronze Age* (fascicle 24).

J. M. Cook, *Greek Settlement in the Eastern Aegean and Asia Minor* (fascicle 7).

V. R. d'A. Desborough and N. G. L. Hammond, *The End of Mycenaean Civilization and the Dark Age* (fascicle 13)—notes and markings.

Walther Hinz, *Persia: c. 1800–1550 B.C.* (fascicle 21).

I. E. S. Edwards, The Early Dynastic Period in Egypt (fascicle 25)—notes and markings throughout.[4]

William C. Hayes, M. B. Rowton, and Frank H. Stubbings, *Chronology: Egypt; Western Asia; Aegean Bronze Age* (fascicle 4)—cover: "rec'd (from Prynne) January 2nd (using March 13th (1965?"; notes and markings including marking at a passage used in "ESSAY ON QUEEN TIY."

G. S. Kirk, *The Homeric Poems As History* (fascicle 22)—notes and markings throughout; included in the bibliography of "A comprehension" (*Additional Prose*, p. 46).

René Labat, *Elam and Western Persia c. 1200–1000 B.C.* (fascicle 23).

F. Matz, *Minoan Civilization: Maturity and Zenith* (fascicle 12).

J. Mellaart, *Anatolia Before c. 4000 B.C. and c. 2300–1750 B.C.* (fascicle 20)—two markings.

Frank H. Stubbings, *The Expansion of Mycenaean Civilization* (fascicle 26)—one marking.

1965

J. Černý, *Egypt from the Death of Ramesses III to the End of the Twenty-first Dynasty* (fascicle 27).

C. J. Gadd, *Babylonia c. 2120–1800 B.C.* (fascicle 28).

3. Olson also owned Carl W. Blegen, *The Mycenaean Age: The Trojan War, the Dorian Invasion, and Other Problems* (Cincinnati: University of Cincinnati 1962)—borrowed from Lockwood Library, Buffalo, due on 28 January 1964 but not returned; notes and markings throughout.

4. Olson also owned I. E. S. Edwards, *The Pyramids of Egypt* (Baltimore: Penguin Books, 1964)—notes in the introduction.

Dorothy A. E. Garrod and J. G. D. Clark, *Primitive Man in Egypt, Western Asia and Europe* (fascicle 30).

1966

W. F. Albright, *The Amarna Letters from Palestine: Syria, the Philistines and Phoenicia* (fascicle 51)—cover: "from Jeremy June 1966"; on p. 3: "rec'd fr Prynne Monday June 27th MDCCCCLXVI"; notes and markings.

D. R. Hughes and D. R. Brothwell, *The Earliest Populations of Man in Europe, Western Asia and Northern Africa* (fascicle 50)—notes and markings.

1967

R. A. Crossland, *Immigrants from the North* (fascicle 60)—cover: "Olson fr Prynne February 29th 1968"; notes and markings.

1968

D. L. Linton and F. Moseley, *The Geological Ages* (fascicle 61).

# 17

## Under the Mushroom

It would be convenient if the two peyote sessions that Olson had with Timothy Leary and company in December 1960 and February 1961 "changed everything," as the clichéd phrase has it. But such neatness is denied us. For Olson, the great mind-expansion had clearly come the year before, unconnected with drugs or mushrooms, in the writing of "MAXIMUS, FROM DOGTOWN—I" and "MAXIMUS, FROM DOGTOWN—II," which seem to have sprung fully-armed from Olson's head two weeks apart in November–December 1959 and now stand sentinel at the beginning of *Maximus IV, V, VI*. Preceded by the essay "Proprioception" (October 1959), "MAXIMUS FROM DOGTOWN—I" adds to its depth physiology a depth psychology, taken specifically in this case from Erich Neumann's *The Great Mother*, as amplification of a local legend of Merry and his bull-calf.[1] Olson raises the mythological power of the poem by recourse to Hesiod's *Theogony*, rendering, in a "proem," lines pertaining to the birth of the sea based on Hugh Evelyn-White's Loeb edition.[2] With stress on the glacial rock of Dogtown, a geological depth is added—from N. S. Shaler's "The Geology of Cape Ann"—interplaying with the Whiteheadian concept of "eternal events." In terms of style, the dismemberment becomes even more accentuated in "MAXIMUS, FROM DOGTOWN—II," which is like a charged stream of splintered particles in some reification experiment. In terms of the direction of the *Maximus Poems*, this latter poem is a radical veering to new concerns:

> the Sea—turn yr Back on
> the Sea, go inland

The sea adventure has ended with Jack Hammond's invention of the fathometer and his building "a castle at Norman's Woe."[3] This "leap

onto the land" inaugurates a new epoch, any full explication of which
will draw upon Olson's use of Jung's *Psychology and Alchemy* (cited)
in particular.[4] Much of the poem will remain cryptic. The "Black
Chrysanthemum" we know to be directly from a dream; it remains a
powerful, inexplicable symbol, given a range of meanings in its asso-
ciation with Richard Wilhelm's edition of *The Secret of the Golden
Flower*— though that book is itself mystifying to the general reader. All
in all, "MAXIMUS, FROM DOGTOWN—II" represents a new defini-
tion of the poetic risks Olson is now willing to take. It might seem hal-
lucinatory; hence our stressing that Olson's mushroom experience
came after, not before, this poem, which should be considered gnostic
rather than gastric. Gerrit Lansing knew this when he gave Olson Hans
Jonas, *The Gnostic Religion* for Christmas 1959,[5] and Nick Cernovich,
too, (though perhaps prompted by Olson) when he sent Husaini's
book on *Ibn al 'Arabi: The Great Muslim Mystic and Thinker* in February
1960.[6]

And the drug sessions themselves, as it turned out, proved to be
not the fractious, lurid experience of the proverbial "bad trip" (as it
was for Arthur Koestler, whom Olson was supposed to be guiding),
but "a love feast and a truth pill."[7] These were strictly peyote sessions
(even though Olson liked to talk about "the mushroom"), and this
traditional sacred plant of the Indians induced in Olson, appropriately
enough, the feeling of presiding in a big longhouse as "a peace sachem
holding, as chief, a longhouse ceremony."[8] If he had authority in that
setting, it could be because he had a certain knowledgeability on the
subject, not only from his Yucatan experience but from his reading.
He owned a classic study on longhouse ceremony, William N. Fenton,
*The Iroquois Eagle Dance*, Smithsonian Institution Bureau of American
Ethnology Bulletin 156 (Washington, 1953), and gave evidence in
conversation of knowing Fenton's prolific work in the field very well
indeed. The Bureau of American Ethnology publications pertinent to
the American Indian aspect include, again, Fenton, who with John
Gulick edited *Symposium on Cherokee and Iroquois Culture*, Bulletin
180 (1961)—Mary R. Haas's contribution to the book is marked by
Olson; Julian H. Steward, ed., *Handbook of South American Indians: The
Andean Civilizations*, Bulletin 143 (1946)—flyleaf "Olson black mt
1955"; David I. Bushnell, *Villages of the Algonquian, Siouan, and Caddoan
Tribes West of the Mississippi*, Bulletin 77 (1922)—flyleaf: "Olson"; John
R. Swanton, *Source Material on the History and Ethnology of the Caddo In-*

*dians,* Bulletin 132 (1942) and *Indians of the Southeastern United States,* Bulletin 137 (1946); Frances Densmore, *Seminole Music,* Bulletin 161 (1956) and *Music of Acoma, Islets, Cochiti and Zuni Pueblos,* Bulletin 165 (1957). Olson also had an offprint of Frances Densmore's from the Smithsonian Report for 1952: *The Use of Music in the Treatment of the Sick by American Indians* (Washington, 1953). Olson once stood in a ploughed field in Wyoming, New York, turned some earth with his boot and said, "Indians, they're my people." At that moment he had a book in his house overdue from the library: Allen W. Trelease, *Indian Affairs in Colonial New York* (Ithaca: Cornell Univ. Press, 1960). (He kept the book.)

Whether or not these two "mushroom" sessions in themselves "changed everything," we can sense that several of the major concerns of the final decade of Olson's life—the spiritual side of things— branched out from this point. On the level of current activities, for one thing, Olson could feel himself in tune with the flow of the sixties into these new tribal areas. By the time he was invited by a group at Gratwick Highlands (outside of Buffalo) on 16 November 1963 to give the talk that became the "Under the Mushroom" tape, he had quite obviously made himself an expert, able to refer to Willis W. Harman, "The Issue of the Consciousness-Expanding Drugs," *Main Currents in Modern Thought* 20 (September–October 1963): 5–14 (he had a copy with him then, but not later), and to Richard Evans Schultes, "Hallucinogenic Plants of the New World," *Harvard Review* 1 (Summer 1963): 18–32.[9] Very much up to date. He had obtained offprints of Sanford M. Unger, "Mescaline, LSD, Psilocybin, and Personality Change: A Review," *Psychiatry* 26 (May 1963): 111–25, and R. Gordon Wasson, "The Hallucinogenic Mushrooms of Mexico and Psilocybin: A Bibliography," *Botanical Museum Leaflets* 20 (Harvard University 1962): 25–73. He was able to converse with his audience about such people as Alan Watts, John Lilly, and Andrija Puharich,[10] as well as about recent articles in popular journals.[11] The first issue of *Psychedelic Review* had appeared in June 1963; Gerald Heard's contribution is mentioned.[12]

Olson's tendency would always be to force the discussion into broader areas, and on this occasion he proposed "the triad of politics, theology, and epistemology." If the longhouse session takes care of "politics" for the nonce, "epistemology" is represented by Merleau-Ponty's *Phenomenology of Perception,* or at least passages sent to Olson in a letter that he quotes from.[13] As for "theology," Olson refers to "that actual literal theologian," Huston Smith. Olson had read (but did not own) his Mentor paperback, *The Religions of Man* (1959). But Olson feels that "one needs very much to bring some Mohammedan feeling into this area" (*Muthologos* 1, p. 60). He is thinking of such pieces by Henry Corbin as "Cyclical Time in Mazdaism and Ismailism" in *Man and Time*, pp. 115–72. His remark here was a harbinger of many further attempts to enter the angelology that Corbin offered. Olson purchased Corbin's edition of *Avicenna and the Visionary Recital* (New York: Pantheon, 1960) in Buffalo, on the same day that he also bought the Bollingen volumes, *Spiritual Disciplines*, Alain Daniélou's *Hindu Polytheism* (New York: Pantheon, 1964), and Mircea Eliade's *Shamanism: Archaic Techniques of Ecstasy* (New York: Pantheon, 1964).[14]

It may be that, as a sidelight to the "mushroom" experience, Olson was led occasionally (with Jung as guide) into synchronicity, UFOs, and other aspects of the occult. He welcomed Carlos Castaneda's *The Teachings of Don Juan* in 1968;[15] he did not live to have to face the sequels. He might have given them the benefit of the doubt as he did, say, Robert Graves's *The White Goddess* and, one of the last books to be put in front of him, John Philip Cohane's *The Key*.[16] Olson preferred to believe things, if he could at all fit them into his own cosmology. But (it should go without saying) he was not indiscriminate—witness, for instance, his comment on the *Tibetan Book of the Dead*: "I purposely stay away from it because I have my own book."[17] Presumably he meant the *Maximus*, which increasingly, since the "change," had moved from polis to cosmos, from the satirical to the mythological, subservient to no creed or system—as this survey of Olson's books must cumulatively convince us of, forcing us to agree with Olson that idiosyncrasy is a most powerful creative principle in mythology. So, idiosyncratic in intent ("to put another kind of a plant in there"—*Muthologos* 1, p. 76) and equally in content, Olson gave to the *Psychedelic Review* for its third issue (1964) his long "MAXIMUS, FROM DOGTOWN—IV." To its basic narrative, the war of Zeus against Typhon (lifted from Hesiod's *Theogony*), the poem adds references to Ginnunga Gap and the iotunns Olson found in the much studied essay by Murray Fowler, "Old Norse Religion," in *Ancient Religions*, ed. Vergilius Ferm (New York: Philosophical Library, 1950), pp. 237–50; to Shakti from Heinrich Zimmer, *Myths and Symbols in Indian Art and Civilization*;[18] to "stlocus" from the Table of Roots in Charlton

T. Lewis's *Elementary Latin Dictionary* (New York: American Book Co., 1915); and to Liddell and Scott, and Rose's *Handbook of Greek Mythology*.[19] The essential connection, in Olson's mind, to the "truth pill" and "love feast" of the mushroom experience is made clear in the poet's later characterizing of the poem as "the texture and the condition of love as event" and "an evidence of the process of poetry as approaching truth with no other guise than itself."[20]

The essays of the volume *Proprioception* (Four Seasons, 1965) were written between October 1959 and May 1962, and thus span the mushroom experience. They "can be dug up as signs" (*Muthologos* 1, p. 133).

### "Proprioception"

This essay, with its definition of "proprioception" as "sensibility within the organism by movement of its own tissues,"[21] is itself quite proprioceptive in that there are no outside sources other than the *Webster's Collegiate Dictionary* (previously cited). It is a further proof that Timothy Leary's fiesta was only a confirmation of what Olson already knew a year before.

### "Logography"

Written soon after "Proprioception" and dated 31 October 1959 in manuscript, this piece is entirely a reaction to reading I. Gelb, *A Study of Writing* (previously cited as bought from University of Chicago Press in January 1957), pp. 62–67 (notes and markings in his copy).[22]

### "Postscript to Proprioception & Logography"

Subtitled "Further notes on what would look like fundamentals of any new discourse," this was published in *Kulchur* 2 in the fall of 1960 as a follow-up to the previous two pieces, published together in *Kulchur* 1 (Spring 1960). There is evidence Olson had been rereading Edward Sapir's *Language* (New York: Harvest Book, 1949).[23]

### "Theory of Society"

Olson appears to have been looking at Eric H. Erikson's selected papers in the *Psychological Issues* series, monograph 1, *Identity and the Life Cycle* (New York: International Universities Press, 1959).

## "Bridge-Work"

Subtitled "fr the Old Discourse to the New ," this is a short reading list dated "March, 1961—with acknowledgements to Gerrit Lansing," indicating that it grew out of conversations in Gloucester with Lansing who, according to Butterick's notes in *Additional Prose*, pp. 87–88, would likely be responsible for the inclusion of Edward Carpenter and Aleister Crowley, though Olson would have run into Crowley's *The Book of Thoth* (London, 1944) during his own Tarot period in the 1940s.

<pre>
                    men worth anyone's study:
        Edward Sapir
        Edward Carpenter (Whitman's friend &
                            Eileen Garrett's[24]
                            teacher
        Carl O. Sauer!
        Andrew Lang (on hypnagogic vision,
                        as well as trans. of
                            Homer—& friend of?
        Mead
                        (Pistis Sophia etc
        Aleister Crowley (?: particularly his
                            book on the Tarot
        Ernest Fenollosa!
        B. L. Whorf
        L. A. Waddell
        Edward Hyams
        Victor Berard
        Cyrus Gordon
</pre>

Edward Hyams is another odd one, since apparently all that Olson knew of him was a quotation (sent in November 1953 by Cid Corman) from *Soil and Civilization* (previously cited).[25] Olson had Lang's translation of Homer (London: Thames and Hudson, 1952); in mentioning here "hypnagogic vision," Olson was referring to the piece on "Crystal-Gazing" by Lang that he had noticed in the *Encyclopaedia Britannica*

11th edition (previously cited). The other names are "standard authors" for Olson.

### "The hinges of civilization to be put back on the door"

A synthesis of much reading, this piece cites by name Jane Harrison and Hans Jonas (previously cited). It was presumably part of the March 1961 push, though not sent to *Kulchur* until 8 December 1961 (published in *Kulchur* 5, Spring 1962). Aquinas, Eckhart, Bacon, Locke, Descartes, and Marx are mentioned, but no specific titles given.

### "GRAMMAR—a 'book'"

These are notes drawing upon various reference materials: (1) *Webster's Collegiate Dictionary* 5th ed. (previously cited), (2) Charlton T. Lewis, *An Elementary Latin Dictionary* (previously cited), (3) Liddell and Scott, *A Greek-English Lexicon* (previously cited), and (4) for the discussion of "the middle voice" in Greek, John Williams White, *The First Greek Book* (Boston: Ginn, 1897), which Olson may have owned since his schooldays. In sending the piece to Leroi Jones on 15 March 1961, Olson wrote: "this may be altogether too much but try it on and see in any case it felt damn good to have for FLOATING BEAR"—it was published in number seven of that magazine (1961) soon afterwards, indicating again how open Leroi Jones was to Olson's stubbornly proprioceptive speech.

### "A Plausible 'Entry' for, like, man"

A further historical survey in note form. Hans Jonas, *The Gnostic Religion* (previously cited) is quoted. Published in *Floating Bear* 11 (1961).

### "A Work"

Dated 3 May 1962, this piece was published in *Floating Bear* 21 (1962). The following sources are utilized: (1) Hans Güterbock, "The Hittite Version of the Hurrian Kumarbi Myths" (previously cited); (2) Stephen B. Luce, "Archaeological News and Discussions," marked and annotated in Olson's copy of *American Journal of Archaeology* 47 (January–March 1943): 102–24; (3) regarding Cyrus Gordon on Linear

A, the current news item " 'Cipher' Gives Key to Cretan Tongue: Brandeis Scholar Says His Study of an Ancient Text Shows It Was Phoenician," *New York Times*, 4 April 1962, p. 39—this and other clippings on the subject were saved by Olson;[26] and (4) Robert Graves, *The Greek Myths*, 2 vols. (Baltimore: Penguin, 1961).[27]

Trying in retrospect to understand for himself what special quality this group of essays had, Olson wrote to Peter Anastas on 8 February 1966: "I think in fact the whole PROPRIO: is like a 'stone' in the Sioux sense (which you'll know)—or Hesiod that 'It was not till the stone was vomited up that the thunder(-stone!) could get loose.' (meaning in the instance of course, Zeus)." We have run into the Sioux symbology before:[28] "The outline of the stone is round, having no end and no beginning; like the power of the stone it is endless. The stone is perfect of its kind and is the work of nature, no artificial means being used in shaping it. Outwardly it is not beautiful, but its structure is solid, like a solid house in which one may safely dwell. It is not composed of many substances but is of one substance, which is genuine and not an imitation of anything else." This is longhouse talk—which gets us back to the mushroom experience, "genuine and not an imitation of anything else," a fair description of anything truly one's own, such as the *Proprioception* essays, which Olson himself characterized as "not readable." He produced them like gall stones; "they're incongestible or something" (*Muthologos* 1, p. 133). That he sent them out for publication may be a sign of a burst of confidence in his own idiosyncrasy: this may have been in part the mushroom's doing.

# 18

## From Gloucester Out

After five years of hibernation, the Gloucester bear was coaxed out of his den by Warren Tallman of the University of British Columbia, abetted by Robert Creeley, who climaxed his visiting year in Vancouver by organizing a Summer Session staffed by invited poets: Ginsberg, Duncan, Levertov, Whalen, Avison, and last but not least, Charles Olson. For Olson, this visit inaugurated a period of four years' absence from Gloucester, during which time he found himself buying and reading books on the run.

### Vancouver, July–August 1963

In the first of the two taped sessions in which Olson played a notable part, he leads with his contrast of Herodotus and Thucydides. He demonstrates his currentness by citing several news stories;[1] his poem "Place; & Names" takes the argument to depth. The only new title mentioned is Ibn Khaldun, *The Muqaddimah: An Introduction to History*, 3 vols., Bollingen Series 43 (New York, 1958); Olson was aware of its being published, but did not own it. In the session "On Duende," Olson demonstrates his knowledge of Lorca's essay and refers in passing to "Clark's book on the nude," to "The Enchanted Pony" fairy story, and to "that beautiful story in the Bible of Tobias and the angel."[2] He also speaks at some length on Wordsworth's *Prelude*, almost the only time he is known to have done so (the book was not in his library).

The main point about Vancouver is Olson's interaction with the other participants and the later feedback. Allen Ginsberg is a curious case; we can be sure that Olson read everything he came across but he did not manage to hang on to a single volume of Ginsberg's poetry. There is less reason to think he read Denise Levertov extensively; he retained one of her volumes in his library, *5 Poems* (San Francisco: White Rabbit, 1958). Olson had met Philip Whalen in San Francisco in December 1957, and dedicated the poem "The Company of Men" to him: "for Phil Whalen for Christmas 1957." He retained in his library Whalen's mimeographed issue of *Sourdough Mountain Lookout* (1958); *Self-Portrait From Another Direction* (San Francisco: Auerhahn, 1960); and *Like I Say* (New York: Totem Corinth, 1960). Olson saw some of Margaret Avison's poetry via Cid Corman and praised it in a letter to him of 14 December 1953; she was "featured" in *Origin* 20 (Winter 1957). He told Creeley he was pleased she had been invited to the Vancouver session and hoped to be one of her audience members (letter of January 1963). Avison's *Winter Sun and Other Poems* (Toronto: University of Toronto Press, 1960) is found in Olson's library.

Already, in *Tish* 5 (13 January 1962), the editor Frank Davey had written "One Man's Look at 'Projective Verse' "; in *Tish* 10 (14 June 1962) Samuel Perry had published his essay "Maximus of Gloucester from Dogtown: Charles Olson Personal Locus"; in *Tish* 19 (14 March 1963) George Bowering printed a piece on "Projective Verse" entitled " . . . some notes from 'Universal & Particular'." Olson had received all these issues by mail in Gloucester; Olson and the young poets of Canada's west coast were ready for each other. Besides the three already mentioned, it is safe to say that the following young Canadian writers signed up for the workshop sessions that summer were significantly influenced by Olson: David Bromige, Daphne (Buckle) Marlatt, Judith Copithorne, David Cull, Rona Hadden, William Hawkins, Robert Hogg, Roy MacSkimming, Dan McLeod, Peter Auxier, David Dawson, Jamie Reid, Gladys Hindmarch, Lionel Kearns, and Fred Wah.[3] The following young American writers who came up to Vancouver for the sessions kept in touch with Olson in one way or another: Ronald Bayes, Larry Goodell, Linda Wagner, Clark Coolidge, John Keys, Edward Van Aelstyn, Frederic Franklyn, Drummond Hadley, and David Schaff.[4]

### Buffalo, 1963–1965

It was Albert Cook, the new Chairman of the English Department at the new State University of New York (formerly the University of Buffalo), who talked to Olson in Vancouver by telephone and made him an offer he could not apparently refuse. After about a month among a not unconventional mix of colleagues, Olson wrote to Creeley on 16 October 1963:

> I find it's a pain in the ass to work up against all the dispersed reading and diverse English and Canadian additional persons to the usual American, especially of Buffalo stock—Corso Baldwin Patchen Mailer Miller Joyce—ignorance of Yeats poor knowledge of Pound / & on the other side the ludicrous preparations of the "Harvard" bunch, PhDs in Wallace Stevens or one instance WCW's earliest verse. The joke was I at first thought the problem was neo-classic and worked to find out what *had* happened 1909 on (therefore myself read Hulme, and Peter Quince at the Clavier etc in Miss Monroe's 1917 anthology practically called the New (American) Poetry.[5]

By the time of his letter of 13 November 1963, however, Olson thinks "the place is real live & possible"—mainly because of his students. He names two "scholar-poets," Charles Boer and Charles Doria, who have an enviable classics training and have introduced him to a new book of immediate pertinence, Eric A. Havelock's *Preface to Plato* (Cambridge: Harvard University Press, 1963). The *Niagara Frontier Review* had already been envisaged; Olson sat down and reviewed Havelock, the first piece of such work for some time. Olson concentrates on pages 192–93 of the book, and draws on Notopoulos, Zielinski, Fraenkel, and R. G. Collingwood as quoted by Havelock there.[6]

There was one faculty member, Mac Hammond, who captured Olson's interest when he sent him a linguistics paper. Olson replied with a poem, "FOR MAC HAMMOND" "in appreciation for his Warsaw address on POETIC SYNTAX, 1960," dated Wyoming, New York, December 1963.[7] Other faculty members challenged Olson in a different way, trying to get him to join the fight then going on against the imposition of a Communist loyalty oath. Olson kept clear, but requested and read the pseudonymous pamphlet edited by "Frank Nugent," *The Feinberg Certificate at Buffalo* (Buffalo: Student Bookshop, April 1965).[8]

Olson's main push, almost immediately on settling in at the University, was to arrange that his "own" people were hired for the summer school 1964 vacancies. There was much correspondence, and Olson succeeded in having Ed Dorn, Leroi Jones, and Robert Kelly fill those posts. Dorn's *What I See in the Maximus Poems* (Migrant Pamphlet, 1960) was still the only monograph on Olson. Dorn had published a book of poems, *The Newly Fallen* (New York: Totem, 1961); and many poems in periodicals were ready to be collected. He had been editing *Wild Dog* from Idaho State University in Pocatello.[9] Leroi Jones had edited *Yugen* and *Floating Bear*, publishing much of Olson's poetry and prose under his imprint. Jones's *Preface To A Twenty Volume Suicide Note* (New York: Totem Corinth, 1961) and *Blues People* (New York: Morrow, 1963) were already out and more was on the way.[10] Robert Kelly had been editing *Trobar* and was about to launch *Matter*, from Bard College. *Armed Descent* (New York: Hawk's Well, 1961) was out, with more coming fast.[11] These three were the "high cards" with which Olson led at Buffalo.

Olson's second year at Buffalo (1964–65) seems even more hectic, perhaps because the evidence is fuller—George Butterick's "Notes from Class," for instance, where we hear Olson throw out such remarks as "*Jonathan Wilde* is the most important English novel," "Kierkegaard—a miserable little wretch, the original killer of our non-civilization," "Kafka, Valery, Husserl—those men were the weather of Europe before existentialism seized Grove Press and Europe," "It's better to be a boy scout than a Macleish," "Kerouac's Spontaneous Prose—disease of the single horizontal line, non-interrupted spilling out of the self," and "As post–Europeans, beware of the second conditioning (the Greeks were the first—the abuses we know stem from the second half of the thirteenth century (Aquinas, Grosseteste, Eckhardt, Roger Bacon put Aristotelian generalization back in)." These are splinters of the massive talk that went on after those students who thought seminars ended at five o'clock left.[12]

Someone who knew that things didn't wind down till 5 a.m. was John Clarke, jazz pianist and Blake scholar, who had met Olson when he (Clarke) came to Buffalo in May 1964 for his job interview. Ultimately, Clarke was the one to take over Olson's classes when he left Buffalo and to edit the *Magazine of Further Studies*. Olson could pay tribute by stating, from the platform at the Berkeley Poetry Conference, "Jack Clarke . . . gave me Blake."[13]

Again, visitors: the advantage that a large university offers. Hugh Kenner, Gregory Corso, Marshall McLuhan, Gary Snyder, among others who impinged.[14] And then, for the Spring Arts Festival in April 1965, Olson shared a platform with his handpicked two, John Wieners and Ed Sanders. Wieners had just published *Ace of Pentacles* (New York: James F. Carr & Robert A. Wilson, 1964) and *Chinoiserie* (San

Francisco: David Haselwood, 1965), both of which Olson owned. Olson had been receiving since its start in 1962 Ed Sanders's *Fuck You/A Magazine of the Arts*, and ended up with a complete run. He also had *The Toe Queen Poems* (New York: Fuck You Press, 1964). Harvey Brown's Frontier Press in Buffalo was publishing Sanders's next book, *Peace Eye*; Olson wrote the preface to it.[15]

Perhaps the person who furthered Olson's reading most actively was Jeremy Prynne's student from Cambridge University, Andrew Crozier (who came and signed up for Olson's courses 1964–65), not only in his role as emissary from the U.K.,[16] but also in his own right when he switched his attention (as he put it in his term paper) "from the Greek mythology you proposed us, Charles, to what you call Eddic but which I'd rather call Northern, and which I later found you were working with presently." There was a synchronicity here, for in response to Crozier's request for advanced reading titles, Olson had written on 13 July 1964: "In fact an English-woman (Yorkshire: Miss Jane Harrison, particularly *Themis*—and *Prolegomena* but anything, such as her own earliest *Myths and Monuments of Ancient Athens*," adding a newly acquired title that was exciting him, T. B. L. Webster's *From Mycenae to Homer* (New York: Barnes & Noble, 1960). However, despite this, already in Vancouver in August 1963 Olson was saying in a workshop that "the great back door" is not only Hesiod but also Beowulf,[17] "even purer than Celtic." In spring 1965, while acquiring, as fuel to the mythology course, *A Companion to Homer, Mycenaeans and Minoans, History and the Homeric Iliad*, and *Mycenaean Studies*,[18] Olson was also collecting books on the other "back door": H. R. Ellis Davidson, *Gods and Myths of Northern Europe* (Baltimore: Penguin, 1964)—flyleaf: "a beautiful—'lucky'—book (bought Thursday April 8th 1965"; Henry Adams Bellows's translation of *The Poetic Edda* (New York: American-Scandinavian Foundation, 1957)—flyleaf: "bought in Buffalo spring 1965";[19] E. O. G. Turville-Petre, *Myth and Religion of the North* (London: Weidenfeld and Nicolson, 1964)—flyleaf: "I bought this book at Buffalo in early 1965." On 29 March 1965 he wrote a Norse celebration, a *Maximus* beginning "George Dekker; a fisherman," specifically a response to the explorer Helge Ingstad's sensational article in *National Geographic* 126 (November 1964)—which Olson owned—announcing "Vinland Ruins Prove Vikings Found the New World."[20] So Olson was ready for Crozier's term paper on Northern mythology and could later continue the same dialogue when Crozier, back in England, asked for something for a new magazine, and Olson wrote a series of notes which came to be called "The Vinland Map Review."

### Italy-Yugoslavia, June–July 1965

Olson left Buffalo on 25 June 1965 and flew via Toronto to Rome, to attend Gian Carlo Menotti's Festival of Two Worlds. He then proceeded to Bled, Yugoslavia on 2 July 1965 for the International PEN conference. Olson wrote to Vincent Ferrini from Bled on 10 July 1965: "the poets of Europe are *all* 'umanismo—and you can imagine how I do! (Only *Neruda* sounded like etc—and of course le grande master, EZRA POUND, whom I read in front of, and in homage to, at the Teatro Caio Melissa, Spoleto[21] (here the scene was different—Arthur Miller!"[22]

On a sidetrip, Olson picked up *Assisi: An Illustrated Guide-Book* by Sandro Chierichetti, published in Milan. If, as it seems, he visited Venice, he presumably acquired at this time: Francesco Valcanover, *The Treasures of the "Accademia" Picture-Gallery in Venice* (Milan: Aldo Martello Editore, 1964) and Giovanni Mariacher, ed., *Tesori della Quadreria Correr a Venezi* (Milan: Aldo Martello Editore, 1964). He owned Kathleen Speight, *Teach Yourself Italian* (Philadelphia: David McKay, n.d.).

### Berkeley, July 1965

Because he did not arrive on the scene until 20 July 1965, Olson missed the first week of the Berkeley Poetry Conference: the "Special Reading" by poets David Bromige, Ken Irby, James Koller, David Schaff (Monday 12 July); Gary Snyder (Tuesday 13 July); John Wieners (Wednesday 14 July); Jack Spicer (Thursday 15 July); Robert Duncan (16 July); Robin Blaser, George Stanley, Richard Duerden (Saturday 17 July); "Young Poets" Robin Eichele, Victor Coleman, Robert Hogg, Jim Boyack, Steven Rodefer, David Franks (Sunday 18 July); and "Special Reading" by poets John Sinclair, Lenore Kandel, Ted Berrigan, Ed Sanders (Monday 19 July).[23] He was present at the readings given by Ed Dorn (Tuesday 20 July), Allen Ginsberg (Wednesday 21 July), Robert Creeley (Thursday 22 July), Ron Loewinsohn, Joanne Kyger, Lew Welch (Saturday 24 July),[24] and "Young Poets from the Bay Area": Gene Fowler, Drummond Hadley "and 7 others" (Sunday 25 July). Olson's reading of Friday 23 July was preceded by his more formal lecture, "Causal Mythology," on Tuesday 20 July. Each of these occasions in its way tries for a totality of recapitulation, the lecture by allowing poems ("that which exists through itself") to solely carry the thought ("what is called meaning"), and the reading by making particulars in great quantity fill a world with value. For "Causal Mythology" it is enough here to say that the epigraph comes from *The Secret of the Golden Flower* and the text for the day from Corbin's *Avicenna*. The "Berkeley Reading" is a self-proclaimed political event: "Zander to Sanders. That would be much more important than *Confucius to Cummings* . . . Words are value, instruction, action, and they've got to become political action" (*Muthologos* 1, p. 112). Here Olson is referring to Ed Sanders in his role as peace activist and leader of the protest rock group "The Fugs." Ernst Zander, an independent German radical writer, was editor of *Dinge der Zeit*, which duplicated itself in a London publication, *Contemporary Issues*, of which Olson owned about twenty (1948–1955).[25] In this marathon talk session, Olson is infinitely allusive, but to persons, places, and events, it seems, rather than books. Since poets largely make up his polis, the reading is assumed.

### Drawn to Gloucester, September 1965–September 1966

Returning to Buffalo for the new academic year, Olson managed only about ten days and then returned all of a sudden to Gloucester. Or perhaps it would not appear precipitous to anyone who knew the relief Olson felt in being home after Berkeley and writing "Maximus, in Gloucester Sunday, LXV": "Now date August 1965 returning Gloucester from as far out in the world as my own wages draw me." What tipped the scales? The gift of John Josselyn, *An Account of Two Voyages to New-England, Made During the Years 1638, 1663*, a rare edition (Boston: William Veasie, 1865)—flyleaf: "bot by Stephen Scotti—& given to me by him Monday night Sept 6th LXV"? This gift may have made him want to get started again on the Josselyns of Dogtown—as he did with the poem beginning "Dogtown—Ann Robinson Davis" as soon as he was settled back in Gloucester on 3 October 1965. Or perhaps it was the Fitz Hugh Lane exhibition opening in Gloucester for the centenary of his death? Olson had acquired a copy of John Wilmerding's brochure, *Fitz Hugh Lane: 1804–1865* (Salem: Essex Institute, 1964) the previous year on publication—flyleaf: "arrived Saturday, August 22nd ($4.50) (year? 1964?)"—and had marked it heavily. He bought another on the day he was returning to Buffalo—flyleaf: "bot September 10th (Friday) Cape Ann Scientific, Literary, & Historical Association in Gloucester, 1965." One of the first things he did a month later on his return was to write "An 'enthusiasm'," a verse tribute to Lane for the *Gloucester Times* (printed 16 October 1965), to remind the people of the city of "the marvelous new chance they have to see the things in the museum laid out." Whatever the cause, Olson was irresistably "drawn to Gloucester," as he put it in his new poem of 29 September 1965 that begins "Physically, I am home." He had decided not to be a professor, but only a reader and a writer.

If he is to stay a teacher, it will be through his letters, as we see in following his day-to-day activity in regard to books and reading.

*7 October 1965.* Letter to Buffalo graduate student Albert Glover on Allen Ginsberg's talk at the Berkeley Poetry Conference includes some evidence that Olson actually read Kafka: "even his Metamorphosis surely his best work can be suppressed: who needs the deterioration of the soul?"[26] On the envelope we find an afterwards much repeated comment on pragmatism: "Reason (as Charles Peirce *alone* seems absolutely clear about (even Whitehead I am not sure knew this at least as Peirce did And William James didn't) is only interesting—that is a 'thought' is Or thought is—*when it has already produced belief* (that is, in the person 'thinking') so that the 'thought' in effect is already action, and only valuable if so." Olson gives the source as *The Popular Science Monthly* for January 1878; there is no doubt, however, that Olson read this information in a paperback he had just picked up: Edward Carter Moore, *William James* (New York: Washington Square Press, 1965), where the pertinent passage is marked.

*7 October 1965.* In a letter to Creeley, Olson responds to receiving *New American Story*, edited by Donald M. Allen and Robert Creeley (New York: Grove Press, 1965)—including the comment: "it's Burroughs on bureaus that interested me."[27]

*10 October–28 October 1965.* A series of letters to John Clarke in Buffalo, later issued as *Pleistocene Man* (Buffalo: Institute of Further Studies, 1968), responds to Clarke's questions about Olson's graduate seminar he had been asked to take over. The basic text is still, in Olson's mind, Christopher Hawkes, *The Prehistoric Foundations of Europe* (previously cited), and he mentions other titles from the New Sciences of Man lectures from the Black Mountain College days, to which he adds, for instance, "Mellaart's & others' recent work in Asia Minor" (p. 3); "a *general* & swift pick-up on archeology up to say 1960" (p. 5), i.e., Piggott's *The Dawn of Civilization*; "the Canadian geographer on how the earth got populated anyway" (p. 4), i.e., Griffith Taylor's "Racial Migration-Zones" in *Human Origins* (previously cited); in addition to the classic Sauer piece "Environment and Culture during the Last Deglaciation" (previously cited), "a piece of his originally in *Landscape* ( a magazine published in Santa Fe or Albuquerque it wouldn't be a loss to have the people have) on the date of earliest American Americans" (p. 6); not Coomaraswamy or Campbell, but "Zimmer (that idiot, JC's own teacher)'s *India*" (p. 9); and "Ipswich BC . . . perfect Sandia l'art" (p. 20).[28]

*11 October 1965.* Reading notes, dated, in Alberto Sartoris, *Piero della Francesca The Arezzo Frescoes* (Paris: Fernand Hazan, 1957).

*17–20 October 1965.* Dated annotations in Brooks Adams, *The Law of Civilization and Decay* (previously cited) indicate the beginning of a series of notes for Andrew Crozier's announced magazine, subsequently published in *The Wivenhoe Park Review* 1 (Winter 1965). Olson also turned to Adams's *The New Empire* (previously cited), and a biography of Brooks Adams's contemporary, Douglas Dowd's *Thorstein Veblen* (New York: Washington Square Press, 1964).[29] Olson had in front of him a copy of *Antiquity* 39 (March 1965) containing articles on Norse ship burials.[30] The notes were a response to the announcement of *The Vinland Map*, edited by R. A. Skelton, Thomas E. Marston, and George D. Painter (New Haven: Yale University Press, 1965); Olson acquired a copy later upon publication, by 29 November 1965.

*25 October 1965.* Poem beginning " 'Cut Creek' " indicates Olson was looking again at Marshall Saville's map in his *Champlain and his Landings at Cape Ann* (previously cited), and at Alfred Mansfield Brooks, "A Picture of Gloucester About 1800" *Essex Institute Historical Collections* 87 (October 1951): 333–38, which he owned.

*28 October 1965.* Letter to Andrew Crozier: "One thing would be of *much* help, if you by any chance could pick up for me right away sort of or while there's still time two titles: Gathorne-Hardy, G. M. *The Norse Discoveries of America* (Oxford, 1921); Nörlund, Poul. *Viking Settlers in Greenland* (London, 1936)." These volumes could not be obtained.

*29 October 1965.* James B. Connolly, *The Crested Seas* (New York: Scribner, 1907)—flyleaf: "bought Brown's department store Gloucester October 29th, 1965 & read Thursday night November 4th 1965 now used November 29th—25 days after previous use . . . write Colby College Waterville Maine & ask for information on the James B. Connolly Collection."

*17 November 1965.* Added "Note #5" to the previous pieces for Andrew Crozier, utilizing F. York Powell's introductory chapter to W. G. Collingwood's "not at all to be forgotten" *Scandinavian Britain* (previously cited); John Chadwick's *The Decipherment of Linear B*—Olson owned the paperback (New York: Vintage, 1963); and for Linear A, Cyrus H. Gordon, *Before the Bible* (New York: Harper, 1962) and George Huxley, *Crete and the Luwians* (Oxford: by the author, 1961), both annotated by Olson throughout.[31]

*29 November 1965.* According to two notes to himself in Connolly's *Crested Seas*, Olson intended (1) to order from Ed Budowski's Student Book Shop in Buffalo a copy of "Hal Boner's RR 'classic' "—this appears not to have been done—;[32] and (2) to buy a second copy of Farley Mowat's *Westviking* (Boston: Little, Brown 1965) to send to Louis Douglas—which was done.[33]

*December 1965.* Eric Oxenstierna, *The Norsemen* (Greenwich: New York Graphic Society, 1965)—flyleaf: "bot. December 1965"; extensive notes and markings.

*December 1965.* Eugene P. Wigner, "Violations of Symmetry in Physics" *Scientific American* 150 (December 1965): 28–36—xerox inserted in Olson's copy of Walter Sullivan, *We Are Not Alone: The Search for Intelligent Life on Other Worlds* (New York: McGraw-Hill, 1964).

*7 December 1965.* Charles F. Chapman, *Piloting, Seamanship and Small Boat Handling: 1965–66 Edition* (New York: Motor Boating, 1964)—flyleaf: "bot Building Center . . . Monday December 6th—no Tuesday December 7th!"[34]

*10 December 1965. The Diary of William Bentley, D.D.,* 4 vols. (Gloucester: Peter Smith, 1962), reprint of 1905 edition—flyleaf of vol. 2: "from Peter Smith, gift Friday December 10th 1965"; Olson had ordered it with a check in a letter to Betty Smith, 6 December 1965.

*11 December 1965.* Purchases from the Essex Institute, Salem: (1) John J. Currier, *History of Newburyport, Mass. 1764–1905* (Newburyport: by the author, 1906); (2) vol. 3 of *The Probate Records of Essex County* (previously cited); and (3) vols 4, 7, and 8 of *Records and Files of the Quarterly Courts of Essex County* (previously cited).

*12 December 1965.* Frobenius and Fox, *Prehistoric Rock Pictures* (previously cited)—flyleaf: "Returned to, for new attention, fall LXV

Gloucester"; some notes dated 12 December 1965 including comments on the Edward Lucie-Smith review of several Olson books, "Guru of the Western World," *Times Literary Supplement*, 25 November 1965.

*18 December 1965*. Purchased from the Essex Institute, Salem, the following monographs reprinted from *Historical Collections of the Essex Institute;* (1) Eleanor Bradley Peters, *Hugh Peter: Preacher, Patriot, Philanthropist* (Salem: Salem Press, 1902): (2) Robert S. Rantoul, *The Building of Essex Bridge* (Salem: Salem Press, 1894); and (3) William Lewis Welch, *A Walk Around Salem Neck and Winter Island* (Salem: Salem Press, 1897).

*18 December 1965. Past & Present* 12 (November 1957)—cover: "received this as a present from Jeremy by AIRMAIL Saturday December 18th 1965"; notes and markings in V. Gordon Childe's "The Bronze Age," pp. 2–15,[35] R. A. Crossland's "Indo-European Origins: The Linguistic Evidence," pp. 16–46, and Owen Lattimore's "Feudalism in History," pp. 47–57.

*21 December 1965*. Poem, dated, "The winter the *Gen. Starks* was stuck,"—Olson once more uses Babson's *History of Gloucester* (previously cited) as a source.

*Christmas 1965*. (1) Dorothy Lee, *Freedom and Culture* (New York: Prentice-Hall Spectrum Book, 1965), inscribed from Jonathan Bayliss; and (2) Immanuel Velikovsky, *Earth in Upheaval* (New York: Dell Delta Book, 1955), inscribed from John Clarke.[36]

*26 December 1965*. Benjamin W. Labaree, ed., *Samuel McIntire: A Bicentennial Symposium, 1757–1957* (Salem: Essex Institute, 1957)—flyleaf: "1st used December 26th 1965—Abbott Lowell Cummings' essay p. 37–54."

On the same day Olson wrote to Miss Besson Harris of the Essex Institute: "Would you be so good as to remember my question on Vol II of the Marblehead Records? & A further question of the like sort: the Topfield Historical reports that Vol. I of the Gloucester Vital Records is out of print. Is there any chance the Essex Institute would take the step to photo-reprint the volume?"[37]

[27 December 1965]. Book from John Wieners, presumably birthday gift: *The Pete Johnson Story*, ed. Hans J. Maurer (Bremen: Humburg, 1965)—title page: "To Charles from John 1965."

*30–31 December 1965*. Dated annotations indicate Olson was reading Jung's *The Archetypes and the Collective Unconscious* (New York: Pantheon, 1959), vol. 9, part 1 of the *Collected Works*, and *Aion* (previously cited). He re-embarked on a reading of Matila Ghyka, *The Geometry of Art and Life* (previously cited)—one note: "written New Year's Eve, before Jean found me mopping up the Mazola? And John came in, then (Al 'Ubaid Friday[38] December 31st"; and on flyleaf: "December 31st started used *most* January 2nd & 3rd 1966 (cf. p. 5—& note on rear fly written 11:19 AM (clock-error) Monday morning January 3rd 1966"; on rear flyleaf: "I've hurried along the path, 55 years. When will you stop? and 'rest'? take your 'marks', and have your bearings?"

*15 January 1966.* Annotations dated in Mason A. Walton, *A Hermit's Wild Friends: or, Eighteen Years in the Woods* (Boston: Dana Estes, 1903) prior to the poet's writing "*Sunday, January 16, 1966*" (*Guide*, p. 613) "to honor the memory of Mason A. Walton."[39]

*30 January 1966.* Letter to Henry Rago indicates Olson had read (after it was belatedly forwarded to him) Rago's "T. S. Eliot: A Memoir and A Tribute," *Poetry* 105 (March 1965): 392–95.

*7 February 1966.* In writing the long *Maximus* poem, "a 3rd morning it's beautiful," Olson used, besides Jung's *Psychology and Alchemy* and Zimmer's *Myths and Symbols* (previously cited), such local materials as *The Old Farmer's Almanac* for 1966 and a report on the "Sea Serpent" of Gloucester.[40]

*7 February 1966.* Has received from Ed Dorn the anonymous review of *Geography*, "Down from the Mountain," *Times Literary Supplement* (27 January 1966): 65, and responds to its negativity.[41]

*11 February 1966.* Dated *Maximus* poem beginning "the Mountain of no difference" indicates Olson's further use of Corbin's *Avicenna*, Whitehead's *Process and Reality*, and Jung's *Psychology and Alchemy*, the latter containing reading notes dated 30 January and 10 February 1966.

*12 February 1966.* Letter to Ralph Maud: "Wld you so generously again loan me Ulf's ring or bone or cup or *wat* was Ulf's thing a ma jig," i.e., Cyril G. E. Bunt, *The Horn of Ulf* (York: York Minster, n.d.), which Olson had borrowed previously in April 1965 in Buffalo; it was sent as a gift.

*13 February 1966.* Annotations, dated, in Henry Adams, *The Degradation of the Democratic Dogma* (previously cited) and the Sentry paperback edition of Brooks Adams, *The Emancipation of Massachusetts* (Boston: Houghton Mifflin, 1962). In the latter, p. xxxviii, where Perry Miller footnotes Arthur F. Beringause, *Brooks Adams: A Biography* (New York: Knopf, 1955), Olson writes: "GET immediately." But he made do with the Sawyer Free Library copy.

*15 February 1966*. Thomas Franklin Waters, *Ipswich in the Massachu-setts Bay Colony*, 2 vols. (Ipswich: Ipswich Historical Society, 1905, 1917)—vol 1 flyleaf dated.

*18 February 1966*. Had not received D. H. Lawrence's *Movements in European History* (Oxford University Press, 1921) that Dorn had asked Blackwell's to send. He apparently never did receive it.

*22 February 1966*. "Bot thru Jean R.," bound volume 2 of *Gloucester Daily Times*, part 1 (2 January 1889–29 June 1889).

*23 February 1966*. Acquired from Harold M. Burstein, bookseller, Alexander Brown, ed., *The Genesis of the United States*, 2 vols. (Boston: Houghton Mifflin, 1890), and vol. 2 of John Winthrop's *The History of New England* (previously cited).

*23 February 1966*. Notes, dated, on endpapers of D. A. F. De Sade, *Justine* (Paris: Olympia, 1954), presumably a gift from Creeley long before—flyleaf signed: "Creeley—'54."

*27 February 1966*. Letter to Bruce Loder: "Eliade—and Kerenyi—are useful *informationally* but my own experience is they are *best* (as so many like men to them are) appearing under the auspices of the 'Era-nos' yearly meetings. . . . Campbell I do believe is misleading alto-gether and throughout (his usefulness only exists in his having edited Zimmer's papers . . . on the caves now Hallam Movius's work in the last 10–15 years. . . . My *memory* of Mathews *Wakontah* was the relative cleanness of it as a current report *then* of Indian life: he had, had he not, been the son of an Indian agent at the Pawnee reservation? I *have* the Hymes, but haven't yet read it." Olson also recommends his old stand-by, Victor Bérard's *Did Homer Live*? (previously cited).[42]

*March 1966*. After some correspondence with the author, Olson ac-quired Howard I. Chapelle, *The National Watercraft Collection*, U.S. Na-tional Museum Bulletin 219 (Washington, 1960)—flyleaf: "Olson (present?) from Chapelle March MDCCCCLXVI"; notes and markings throughout.

*4 March 1966*. Bought from Harvard University Press, Gerald Frank Else, *The Origin and Early Form of Greek Tragedy* (Cambridge: for Oberlin College by Harvard University Press, 1965)—flyleaf: "Rec'd Friday March 4th"; many annotations, not always complimentary. Ol-son refers to his Harvard contemporary's "omissions" and "fatu-ities"; but in the notes on p. 107 beside the item Wilhelm Schmid, *Ge-schichte der griechischen Literatur* (Munich: vol. 1, 1929; vol. 2, 1934), Olson writes: "Else put me onto this one—as of one important fact anyway. So I must acknowledge as I have his earliest Ars Poetica as usefulness anyhow."[43]

*9 March 1966*. Letter to Ed Dorn: "Just read, all by myself here at the kitchen table *Idaho Out* and if you don't mind my saying so it feels so much like something I should have written I'm going to rush out and read it the next time I do read for my supper somewhere."[44]

*11 March 1966*. Xerox copy of Maurice Pope, "The Origins of Writing in the Near East," *Antiquity* 40 (March 1966): 17–23—"Sent March 9th, rec'd March 11th"; notes and markings.

*12–13 March 1966*. National Educational Television films Olson reading and talking. Amid much gossip, we note comments on two contemporaries: (1) "even before *Wild Dog* in Pocatello there was a thing called *A Pamphlet* edited by Gino Clays. Gino Clays is a San Francisco poet-man. He's a poet-man: I don't know too much about his writing except the thing that provoked me to write"; (2) "the English novel has been restored in this fucking book by Bayliss! You wouldn't believe it, that guy!"[45]

*14 March 1966*. Letter to Ed Dorn indicates Olson has been reading his copy of Robert L. Heilbroner, *The Future as History* (New York: Harper, 1960).

*18 March 1966* Letter to Jack Sweeney refers to Samuel Eliot Morison, "The Dry Salvages and the Thacher Shipwreck," *American Neptune* 25 (October 1965): 233–47, which Olson had received as an offprint with the author's compliments.

*23, 25 March 1966*. Annotations on vol 2 of *Winthrop Papers* (previously cited): "1st looked into (since reading the Journal of Winthrop's crossing—last fall, 1965? or this winter) May 23rd & 25th MDCCCCLXVI."

*29 March 1966*. Returned to Boston Public Library E. P. Morris, *The Fore-and-Aft Rig in America* (New Haven: Yale University Press, 1927), according to a letter to Stillman Evans. "I got so very angry with the misuse of Gloucester history in this wretched & deliberate—if 'Yale' etc . . . I *annotated* (& excellent corrections, plus *direction* they are)."[46]

*3 April 1966*. In a letter to Albert Glover, Olson made immediate use of Heraclitus, *The Cosmic Fragments*, ed. G. S. Kirk (Cambridge: Cambridge University Press, 1962)—flyleaf: "fr. Prynne, spring 1966 29.3.66—read most 1st Sunday August 14th 1966." Earlier Prynne had xeroxed pp. 306–24 for him.

*12 April 1966*. Thanked Bob Hogg for the gift of the South Atlantic section of Bruce C. Heezen and Marie Tharp, *Physiographic Diagram: Atlantic Ocean* (New York: Geographical Society of America, 1957), the Northern section of which Olson had had on his wall for some time.

*24 April 1966.* In a letter to Wilbert Snow, responding to a poem of his about sea-gulls, Olson quotes Niko Tinbergen, *The Herring Gull's World* (London: Collins, 1953), a gift of Ed Dorn's.[47]

*25 April 1966.* Using Babson's *History of Gloucester* once more for the *Maximus* poem beginning "having developed the differences."

*30 April 1966.* Letter to Albert Cook, responding to the gift of Cook's *The Classic Line: A Study in Epic Poetry* (Bloomington: Indiana University Press, 1966): "My dear Al, I'm reading your book to *learn*, and it is a pleasure."

*May 1966.* Gift of Harvey Brown: Walter Teller, ed., *Five Sea Captains* (New York: Atheneum, 1960).

*2 May 1966.* Reading Jung's essay "On Synchronicity" in *Man and Time* (previously cited), and utilizing it in a *Maximus* poem "JUST AS MORNING TWILIGHT, AND THE GULLS, GLOUCESTER; MAY 1966 THE FULL FLOWER MOON" the following day. Max Knoll's contribution to *Man and Time*, "Transformations of Science in Our Age," is heavily annotated.

*5 May 1966.* In a letter, Olson recommends to Ed Dorn's son the Simon Lash Mystery, Frank Gruber, *The Buffalo Box* (New York: Bantam, 1946), which he owned.

*14 May 1966.* From the author: George Jay Babson, *A Brief and True Report Concerning the Colonial Babsons* (Washington: for the Babson Historical Association, 1958)—flyleaf: "fr Mr Babson May 14th, 1966.)

*18 May 1966.* Letter to Robin Blaser: "I can't get over how powerfully—*anent* Sauer's *Early* Spanish Main, but so many other signs—*The Book of Ammon* (Hennessey), Ives (Wallace Stevens) *Miss Duncan* (Isadora I mean) and all these—like the *Early* Spanish Main—solely now how substance has indeed passed so firmly into the hands of the power of *our* attention, developed so justly from Charles Peirce (Popular Science Monthly, January issue 1878) until today discourse has now re-acquired the means of truth."[48]

*18 May 1966.* Received James W. Mavor, "A Mighty Bronze Age Volcanic Explosion," *Oceanus* 12 (April 1966): 14–23 from the Woods Hole Oceanographic Institution, which, along with Tuzo Wilson, "Continental Drift," *Scientific American* 208 (April 1963): 86–100, was the source for "ESSAY ON QUEEN TIY," sent to Andrew Crozier on 25 May 1966 for publication in *Wivenhoe Park Review* 2 (*Guide*, p. 650).

*22 May 1966.* Purchased *Harvard Guide to American History*, ed. Oscar Handlin, et al. (Cambridge: Harvard University Press, 1963).

*25 May 1966.* Letter to Ed Dorn: "now reading the light-fingered *crookedness* actually crap of the interview Clark has" with Allen Ginsberg in *Paris Review* 37 (Spring 1966)—same issue as "MAXIMUS FROM DOGTOWN—II."

*29 May 1966.* Letter to Ed Dorn: "As you pick up on this Far West stuff let me in, if you wld, on anything which seems to you to show anything *new* there . . . any *tarn* in sense of thought or method—such as *has* happened as of Eastern U.S. History. . . . Ex: is Henry Nash Smith's book any thing more than what Merk taught him, say? . . . How abt Parkman: *Oregon Trail*? And does DeVoto's year *1846* stand up?"[49]

*10 June 1966.* Letter to Allen Ginsberg: "I just can't resist telling you how delicious I found Barry Farrell's superb job on you in *Life*," i.e., "The Guru Comes to Kansas," *Life* (27 May 1966): 79–90.

*15 June 1966.* Used in a *Maximus* poem of that date: Marshall D. Sahlins, "The Origin of Society," *Scientific American* 203 (September 1960): 76–87, an issue Olson owned.

*29 July 1966.* Frank Debenham, "The Ice Islands of the Arctic: A Hypothesis," *Geographical Review* 44 (1954): 495–507—offprint "Sent to me by Jeremy & rec'd July 29."

*10 August 1966.* Gift of Cyrus H. Gordon, *Ugarit and Minoan Crete* (New York: Norton, 1966)—flyleaf: "fr John Spiegel Wednesday August 10th read 1st, Wednesday (August 10th) in Diner (part of Chapter III) again, Friday here at home (August 12th) (Chapters VI, & then V)"; notes and markings. A second copy is inscribed to Olson by Thorpe Feidt.

*11 August 1966.* Letter to Bill Brown: "Just starting to read yr *book* yesterday," i.e., *The Way to the Uncle Sam Hotel* (San Francisco: Coyote Books, 1966).[50]

*14 August 1966.* Prose piece, "A comprehension," sent to Robin Blaser for *Pacific Nation* 1 (June 1967), included a formal "bibliography" (*Additional Prose*, p. 46)—all the items are previously cited:

> *bibliography:* G. S. Kirk, Heraclitus, *The Cosmic Fragments*, p. 3
> Bruno Snell, *The Discovery of the Mind*, p. 17

Sir Kenneth Clark, *The Nude*, p. 57
bottom & over
Add also: G. Else, *Origin & Early Form of Greek Tragedy* (1966) p. 61, top
Add, please:
Stuart Piggott, *Prehistoric India*, p. 255
Also, to date Homer, see: G. S. Kirk Fascicle, for Cambridge Anc. History, #22 on *The Homeric Poems as History*, p. 10

*18 August 1966.* Bound, xeroxed copy of J. Tuzo Wilson, "Did the Atlantic Close and Then Re-Open," *Nature* 211 (13 August 1966): 676–81—cover: "from Jeremy Prynne (rec'd Thursday August 18th 1966."

*30 August 1966.* Letter to Alan Marlowe: "*If* as Diane did mention you *cld* come by both Sir John Woodroffe's *Serpent-Power* and Evans-Wentz *Tibetan Yoga* I do have the money to pay for such!" The latter volume he never got, but Arthur Avalon (pseud.), *The Serpent Power* (Madras: Ganesh & Co., 1964) he did acquire, and from it made notes on Shiva and Shakti on 5 September 1966. Olson also had the edition John Woodroffe did with his wife "Ellen Avalon": *Hymns to the Goddess* (Madras: Ganesh & Co., 1952).

## Europe, October 1966–July 1967

Klaus Reichert, Olson's German translator, invited the poet for a reading at the Berlin Academy of Art that became the excuse for a prolonged sojourn in Europe (mainly London) with ample opportunity for bookstore browsing. For example, "Bought Berlin December 28th? from Schoslers" written by Olson on the flyleaf of his copy of Friedrich Kluge, *Etymologisches Worterbuch der Deutschen Sprache* (Berlin: Walter de Gruyter, 1963) tells the story.[51] And gifts: Karl Wolfskehl and Friedrich von der Leyen, eds. *Alteste deutsche Dichtungen* (Frankfurt: Insel-Verlag, 1964)—flyleaf: "fr Reichert Berlin December 14th 1966—used December 23rd & 24th 1966";[52] and for his birthday, from Renate Gerhardt, Jan de Vries, *Altgermanische Religionsgeschichte*, 2 vols. (Berlin: Walter de Gruyter, 1956–57).[53] In the intensity of his work at the Hotel Steinplatz, Olson dashed off a request to Tom Raworth in London: "Wednesday December 28th could you swiftly by *airmail* send me Penguin #A459 Vikings by Johannes Bronsted"; it was sent.[54]

Back in "England's green"—or rather Panna Grady's 17 Hanover Terrace, London—Olson wrote in his copy of the *Concise Oxford Dictionary*: "If I could be lonely enough and happy enough I'd get out and walk or buy books just like I now stay in bed and read."[55] From flyleaf annotations we know that he did get out to buy the following:

Maurice Ashley, *England in the Seventeenth Century* (Harmondsworth: Penguin, 1965)—flyleaf: "Bot Fleet Street Monday April 10th 1967— afternoon."

T. Burrow, *The Sanskrit Language*, 2d ed. (London: Faber & Faber, 1965)—flyleaf: "Olson bot London 1967—on chance."

R. W. K. Hinton, ed., *The Port Books of Boston: 1601–1640*, Publications of the Lincoln Record Society, vol. 50 (Hereford: The Lincoln Record Society, 1956)—flyleaf: "purchased April/1967—rec'd Thursday April 27th, at London 1st used as such Friday April 28th— evening."

Bruce Mitchell, *A Guide to Old English* (Oxford: Basil Blackwell, 1965)—Olson used dust jacket for trying out some Old English verse, sent the book to Robert Creeley on 27 February 1967.

*The Tower of London* (Ministry of Public Buildings and Works Guidebook, 1966).

E. O. G. Turville-Petre, *Origins of Icelandic Literature* (Oxford University Press, 1967)—flyleaf: "bot at Dillons Bkstore London Friday March 3rd 1967."

We also presume Olson bought the books in the following list. Vincent Ferrini and Peter Anastas remember seeing in 28 Fort Square at the time of Olson's funeral "two huge backpacks filled with books that he had brought home from England several years ago and never unpacked."[56]

*A Brief Guide to Indian Art* (London: Victoria & Albert Museum, 1962).

R. J. Adam, *A Conquest of England: The Coming of the Normans* (London: Hodder & Stoughton, 1965).

J. J. Bagley and P. B. Rowley, *A Documentary History of England I, 1066–1540* (Harmondsworth: Penguin, 1966).

Frank Barlow, *The English Church 1000–1066: A Constitutional History* (London: Longmans, 1963).

Martin S. Briggs, *Puritan Architecture and Its Future* (London: Lutterworth Press, 1946)—markings on pp. 13, 15, and 18.

Richard Burton and F. F. Arbuthnot, trans. *The Kama Sutra of Vatsyayana* (London: Panther Books, 1966).

Agatha Christie, *The Labours of Hercules* (London: Collins Fontana, 1966).

J. G. D. Clark, *The Study of Prehistory: An Inaugural Lecture* (Cambridge University Press, 1954).

R. Rainbird Clarke, *Grime's Graves* (London: HMSO, 1963).

E. Classen and F. E. Harmer, *An Anglo-Saxon Chronicle* (Manchester University Press; Longmans Green, 1926).

Sonia Cole, *The Neolithic Revolution*, 3d ed. (London: British Museum, 1965).

Sonia Cole, *The Prehistory of East Africa* (Harmondsworth: Penguin, 1954).

*Domesday Re-bound* (London: Public Record Office, 1954).

H. J. Fleure, *Guernsey*, British Landscape Through Maps 3 (Sheffield Geographical Association, 1961).

John Bagot Glubb, *The Great Arab Conquests* (London: Hodder & Stoughton, 1963).

E. V. Gordon, ed., *The Battle of Maldon* (London: Methuen, 1966).

Ernst Kitzinger, *Early Medieval Art in the British Museum* (London: British Museum, 1963).

Darius Milhaud, *Notes Without Music* (London: Calder & Boyars, 1967).

Hope Muntz, *The Golden Warrior: The Story of Harold and William* (London: Chatto & Windus, 1949).

Boris Pasternak, *Doctor Zhivago* (London: Collins Fontana, 1967).

R. B. Pugh, *Records of the Colonial and Dominions Offices* (London: Public Record Office, 1964).

C. A. R. Radford, *Early Christian and Norse Settlements at Birsay, Orkney* (Edinburgh: HMSO, 1959).

A. L. F. Rivet, *Town and Country in Roman Britain* (London: Hutchinson Universal Library, 1966).

A. L. Rowse, *Sir Richard Grenville of the Revenge* (London: Jonathan Cape Paperback, 1963)—occasional notes.

Steven Runciman, *A History of the Crusades I: The First Crusade* (Harmondsworth: Penguin, 1965)—occasional notes.

*Shakespeare in the Public Records* (London: Public Record Office Handbook no. 5, 1964)—notes.

A. H. Smith, ed., *The Parker Chronicle, 832–900* (London: Metheun, 1964)—notes.

Muriel Spark, *Ballad of Peckham Rye* (Harmondsworth: Penguin, 1963).

Frank M. Stenton, *Anglo-Saxon England* (Oxford University Press, 1965).

Frank M. Stenton et al., *The Bayeux Tapestry: A Comprehensive Survey* (London: Phaidon Press, 1965).

Geoffrey Tillotson, *Augustan Poetic Diction* (London: University of London Athlone Press, 1964)—markings pp. 18–19.

*The Sutton Hoo Ship-Burial* (London: British Museum, 1966).

D. H. Turner, *Romanesque Illuminated Manuscripts in the British Museum* (London: British Museum, 1966).

Leon Uris, *The Angry Hills* (London: Corgi Books, 1966).

Dorothy Whitelock, *The Beginnings of English Society* (Harmondsworth: Penguin, 1966).

Dorothy Whitelock, ed., *Sermo Lupi ad Anglos* (London: Methuen, 1963).

Colin Wilson, *The Glass Cage* (London: Arthur Barker, 1966).

Except for the obviously recreational books, the main trust of this reading was to get to the roots of English society. Olson had the Great Britain Ordnance Survey, *A Map of Ancient Britain* (1964), both North Sheet and South Sheet, but he does not seem to have traveled widely in Britain.[57] One exception was to visit Dorn and Prynne in Colchester, Essex.[58] The other exception was an extended stay of 8 May–13 June 1967 in Dorchester, to fulfill a long-standing desire to research the Dorchester Company, the founders of Gloucester. His time there was very productive from the first day: on the cover of a monograph reprinted from *Proceedings of the Dorset Natural History and Archaeological Society* 33 (1912), Henry Symonds *Bridport Harbour Through Seven Centuries*, he wrote: "Charles Olson's Bought fr bookseller Church St 1st day in Dorchester (Monday May 8th arr. at 1:32, on 10:30 train out of London—Read that night, and since of use." Olson worked daily in the County Museum. The staff archaeologist gave him his offprint from the *Proceedings* for 1965: R. N. R. Peers, "Dugout Canoe from Poole Harbour, Dorset." The *Proceedings*, vol. 31 (1910) "Acquired Museum Dorset Wednesday May 17 1967" was just the first of several such volumes Olson picked up: 23 (1902), 44 (1922), 52 (1930), 62 (1940), 63 (1941). Also the following:[59]

A. C. Cox, *Index to the County Records in the Record Room of the County Offices* (Dorchester: Dorset Natural History & Archaeological Society, 1938).

Robert Douch, *A Handbook of Local History: Dorset* (Bristol: University of Bristol Department of Adult Education, 1952).

H. J. Moule, *Descriptive Catalogue of the Charters, Minute Books and Other Documents of the Borough of Weymouth and Melcombe Regis, A.D. 1252 to 1800* (Weymouth: Sherren & Son, 1883)—flyleaf: "bot Dorchester May 10th 1967."

H. P. Smith, *The History of the Borough and County of the Town of Poole*, vol. 2: County Corporate Status (Poole: J. Looker, 1951).

Maureen Weinstock, *Studies in Dorset History* (Dorchester: Longmans, 1953)—flyleaf: "bot here—Dorchester May 18th Thursday"; notes and markings.

Maureen Weinstock, *More Dorset Studies* (Dorchester: Longmans, n.d.)

Maureen Weinstock, ed., *Weymouth & Melcombe Regis Minute Book, 1625–1660* (Dorchester: Dorset Record Society Publication No. 1, 1964).

Olson did not entirely ignore Dorchester's other attraction, picking up a copy of C. M. Fisher, *Life in Thomas Hardy's Dorchester 1888–1908* (Beaminster: J. Stevens Cox, 1965), and the Dorset Natural History and Archaeological Society's printing of Hardy's *Some Romano-British Relics Found at Max Gate* (Dorchester, 1966).[60] And to prove that nothing is irrelevant: Wilfred H. Schoff, *The Ship "Tyre"; A Symbol of the Fate of Conquerors As Prophesied by Isaiah, Ezekiel and John . . . A Study in the Commerce of the Bible* (London: Longmans, Green, 1920)—flyleaf: "picked up—crazily enough, Dorchester (England) & from my friend *Hardy's* bookstore! When in there one afternoon this past (June? or May) 1967 with Director of Museum (day we went to the Celtic hill fort of ———? the beauty of them all."

## Home: Celestial Evening

After his European travels, Olson came to home ground with a long automobile trip to Oxford, Ohio: Johnny Appleseed country. On his drive back he apparently stopped for a time at Olean, New York, long enough to check out (on approximately 20 September 1967) a number of volumes from the public library. From the overdue notices he later received in Gloucester, we know that he must have been feeling very American to have chosen the following:

Ralph K. Andrist, *The Long Death: The Last Days of the Plains Indians* (New York: Macmillan, 1964).

Bernard Bailyn, ed., *Pamphlets of the American Revolution, 1750–1776 vol. I: 1750–1765* (Cambridge: Harvard University Press, 1965).

Dee Alexander Brown, *The Galvanized Yankees* (Urbana: University of Illinois Press, 1963).

John Tebbel and Keith Jennison, *The American Indian Wars* (New York: Harper, 1960).

Dale Van Every, *A Company of Heroes: The American Frontier, 1775–1783* (New York: William Morrow, 1965).

Soon after returning, he asked Grolier Bookshop for all of Dale Van Every's *Frontier People of America* series; there exists an invoice of 12 January 1968 for ten volumes, five of which were present in his library.[61]

To be back home in Gloucester meant reading books and writing letters.

*26 September 1967*. Letter to A. J. Mitchell of the Wesleyan *Alumnus* objecting to the definition of "the liberally educated man" in the August issue.

*3 October 1967*. The poem *"Celestial evening, October 1967"*, with the reference to Amoghasiddi, followed a reading of E. Dale Saunders, *Mudra: A Study of Symbolic Gestures in Japanese Buddhist Sculpture*, Bollingen Series 58 (New York: Pantheon, 1960), which he had acquired following his purchase of Christmas Humphreys, *Buddhism*, 3d ed. (Baltimore: Penguin, 1962).

*6 October 1967*. Letter to Chad Walsh of Beloit College, responding to Walsh's article on projective verse[62] and mentioning having read Allen Ginsberg's "Wichita Vortex Sutra," presumably in the *Village Voice*, 28 April 1966, or possibly in the London *Peace News*, 27 May 1966 (which in Olson's view is not "projective").

*8 October 1967*. Request to Grolier Bookshop for a copy of Gertrude Stein, *The Geographical History of America or the Relation of Human Nature to the Human Mind* (New York: Random House, 1936).[63]

*12 October 1967*. Letter to Robert Creeley: "Pleasure to read you on

Zukofsky—hopefully, in fact, that then I might the more be able to read him—You surely make him as attractive as he is, and the Catullus of course anyway wins him hands down the round."[64]

*20 October 1967.* "Talk at Cortland" (*Muthologos* 2, pp. 1–6) includes a cryptic reference to Pierre Teilhard de Chardin, and a glowing reference to two "beautiful poets alive," Giuseppe Ungaretti and Patrick Kavanagh.[65]

*28 October 1967.* Letter to Donald Sutherland regarding his review of *Selected Writings* in *New Leader* 50 (22 May 1967): 28–29: "such a pleasure of recognition and comprehension . . . in fact my first *public* judgment of any relevancy."[66]

*30 October 1967.* Charles H. Lincoln, ed., *Narratives of the Indian Wars, 1675–1699* (New York: Barnes & Noble, 1966)—flyleaf: "acquired October 30th 1967–& read, 1st, October 31st 1967": notes and markings, especially in "Decennium Luctuosum" by Cotton Mather.

*31 October 1967.* William A. Baker, *Colonial Vessels: Some Seventeenth-Century Sailing Craft* (Barre, Mass.: Barre Publishing Company, 1962)—flyleaf: "Bot pharmacy Essex (for 5 dollars) Halloween night October 31 1967—luckily"; notes and markings throughout; quoted in a *Maximus* (*Guide*, p. 323).

*1 November 1967.* Gerald S. Hawkins, *Stonehenge Decoded* (Garden City: Doubleday, 1965)—flyleaf: "Arrived—& used—November 1st (1967) (via Gordon Cairnie, at The Grolier Book Shop"; notes and markings.[67]

*3 November 1967.* Letter to Ed Dorn, acknowledging receipt of *The North Atlantic Turbine* (London: Fulcrum, 1967)—"and delightfully elegant it is."[68]

*6 November 1967.* *Cape Ann Advertiser* 37–38 (1894–95)—flyleaf of bound volume: "Chas. Olson purchased fr Jean & Rene Gross—1964? (1965? 1st used Monday Nov 6th 1967."[69]

*11 November 1967.* Letter to Joyce Benson quotes Oswald Spengler (previously cited).

*12 November 1967.* Letter to Creeley cites Jane Harrison's *Themis*, fig. 138, p. 448, "the metope of Selinus."[70]

*16 November 1967.* Letter to John Taggart on receipt of *Maps* 2. The issue was a "Homage to David Smith": "I had missed Smith, and that picture and the statement by him is very gratifying to know. Also the Oppens—they *are* something. And the Enslin catches, as so much he has done in the last few years has, me, often. I hope you won't mind my acknowledging it this rapidly, reading it tonight but I'm afraid if I don't it might fall back and I not tell you."

*5 December 1967.* Letter to Joyce Benson: "I was quoted to, and checked out my own copy of *Anerca*, particularly the incredible story (a *chola* widow of the Canadian tundra) of a young woman whom Samuel Herne found by snowshoe track there alone in 1772 so composed as to continue etc the whole of her garb so judiciously placed great taste and no little variety of ornament unbelievably lovely." This is the third item (unnumbered pages) in Edmund Carpenter, ed., *Anerca* (Toronto: Dent, 1959)—inscribed from Michael Rumaker on 15 August 1960.

*11 December 1967.* Extensive notes and markings of this date in *The Secret of the Golden Flower* (previously cited).

*14 December 1967.* Extensive notes in Heinrich Zimmer, *Myths and Symbols in Indian Art and Civilization* (previously cited).

*20 December 1967.* Letter to Ed Dorn: "Was fled to Harvey's for a couple of days and had the chance there to read finally *Black Elk*, and though still Neihardt gets in the way, for me, it is a useful book not so much all the shaman evidence—it knocks me out when it all ends up in Buffalo Bill's 1st (?) Wild West Show."[71]

*28 December 1967.* Letter to Fielding Dawson acknowledges receipt from the publisher of his *An Emotional Memoir of Franz Kline* (New York: Random House, 1967) and reacts coldly to it.

*28 December 1967.* Letter to Robert Hogg: "Someone left me *Maine Coast Fisherman* (article 1966) with most interesting suggestion that seagoing canoe of the Beothuks can be shown to be Pleistocene."[72]

*7 January 1967.* Letter to Joyce Benson: "there I was this morning waiting to go to sleep reading Parkman's Oregon Trail with eyes so open to it I felt like all I might have imagined to be—and that book I dare say I bought in Cambridge 30+ years ago! Slow, sd Charles Olson, he is slow!"

*8 January 1968.* Ordered from Grolier Bookshop *Culture in History: Essays in Honor of Paul Radin*, ed. Stanley Diamond, in paperback (there is no evidence that he received it).

*16 January 1968.* Letter to Robert Creeley indicates Olson was reading Thomas Hunt Morgan, *Embryology and Genetics* (New York: Columbia University Press, 1934), "wholly accidentally acquired while I was like they say living in that motel" (i.e., 1964–65 in Buffalo).

*19 January 1968.* Letter to Robert Duncan: "You might even, make

me a *poet* again, it is so beautiful to read the *Passages* you have sent me,
I am reading now (too, in the midst of them." Notes in Olson's copy of
Duncan's *Passages 22–27 Of the War* (Berkeley: Oyez, 1966) indicate he
was reading it on and off up to 3 February 1968, and again on 20 Au-
gust 1968.[73]

  *6 February 1968.* Martin P. Nilsson, *Greek Folk Religion* (New York:
Harper Torchbooks, 1961)—front cover: "1st time Feb 6th 1968 (Tues-
day)"; notes and markings through p. 12.[74]

  *13 March 1968.* Wrote a review of Norman Mailer's "The Steps of
the Pentagon," *Harper's* 236 (March 1968): 47–142, entitled in type-
script "Shortness of Time."[75]

  This period of travel in and out of Gloucester culminates in lec-
tures at Beloit College in Wisconsin 25–29 March 1968. These "beloits,"
as Olson called the lectures later published as *Poetry and Truth*, ranged
widely and allusively but did not add to the bibliography already cited
here.

# 19

## Terrestrial Paradise

Olson was in America for good, but it was impossible not to glance back at what, in the *"Paris Review* Interview," he called his "beloved former nation"—that "I would wish I lived in today, simply because of the grace of life, which is still yours, my dear Europe" (*Muthologos* 2, p. 152). This remark, and much else in that interview of 15 April 1969, was prompted by the inclusion in his morning's mail of Andrew Crozier's *The Park* 4 and 5 (Summer 1969), full of familiar English poets and a stimulating review of *Maximus Poems IV, V, VI* by Jeremy Prynne.[1] Such a recently acquired interest as the poetry of Patrick Kavanagh seems to have moved Olson genealogically to the old country; while trying to get back on track with requests to Grolier for E. P. Morris, *The Fore-and-Aft Rig in America* (cited), *The Mariner's Mirror* 36 (1950), 37 (1951), and *Massachusetts Historical Society Collections*, series 3, vol. 3 (1833), all impossible to find. Olson was at the same time asking for an even more impossible list of old Irish titles.[2] This interest in his maternal ancestry culminated in his borrowing from the Sawyer Free Library in Gloucester L. Russell Muirhead's *Ireland* in the Blue Guides series (London: Benn, 1962) in order to check up on Gort, where both the O'Heynes and the O'Shaughnesseys are buried. The paternal Swedish side received a jolt when Inga Loven from Sweden came to interview Olson in August 1968. He had just been reading Carl Sauer's newly published *Northern Mists*, and could be knowledgeable on Ari Thorgilsson and Snorri Sturlson. Olson also brought up the name of Vilhjalmur Stefansson ("he sounds like a Scandinavian, actually like myself was born in this country," Olson emphasizes—*Muthologos* 2, p. 93), in order to talk about his book *My Life Among the Eskimos*. Olson retained the copy of *Ord och Bild* 5 (1965) that

Inga Loven brought him, containing her translation of William Carlos Williams's poem "The Sparrow." Perhaps no further reading came out of this visit, unless Olson bought his copy of *Burt's Swedish-English Dictionary* (New York: Blue Ribbon Books, 1939) or Carl Hallendorff and Adolf Schück, *History of Sweden* (Stockholm: C. E. Fritze, 1929) at this time, rather than earlier.

Other visitors revived old themes. Ann Charters came to Gloucester 13–14 June 1968 to finalize the book that appeared under the title *Olson/Melville: A Study in Affinity* (Berkeley: Oyez, 1968), with rich photographs from that occasion.[3] They discussed *Call Me Ishmael* almost as if it were incunabula. Olson had not been active with Melville for a number of years. When the full version of *Melville's Reading* had finally been published by University of Wisconsin Press in 1966, Merton Sealts had had the press send a copy, but Olson had not risen to an acknowledgment of it. Likely he was in Europe when it arrived in Gloucester; in any case, it would have seemed to him like a seal upon a storage jar, now briefly reopened by Ann Charters's visit.

Alasdair Clayre of the British Broadcasting Company asked a great deal about Black Mountain College in his interview with Olson on 27 July 1968, as did Andrew S. Leinoff in April 1969 in preparing an honors essay for M.I.T. For the best general statement on BMC, Olson refers Leinoff to Ed Dorn's interview with David Ossman.[4] Olson has seen the obituary of John A. Rice (founder of BMC) in the *New York Times*, 28 November 1968, and is desirous of a xerox. The way in which he talks about the legalities of the ending of the college indicates that it is a matter he has not sealed up.

The greatest intervention—one that Olson likened to the eagle taking Chaucer off to the House of Fame—was Gerard Malanga as nuncio of *The Paris Review* arriving with his tape recorder and camera on 15 April 1969 to induct Olson into the "Writers at Work" series of interviews.[5] Many themes were recapitulated in this long session: the Tarot, for instance, with a reference to Robert Creeley's *Numbers*.[6] Jung is quoted from a passage Olson had been reading on 1 April 1969—"the method of the necessary statement" (*Memories, Dreams, Reflections*, p. 310).[7] Wilhelm Reich, a new concern, is mentioned in conjunction with Otto Rank, whom Olson had read first in the 1940s and had mentioned in the *Maximus* poems.[8] George Oppen had also been included in the *Maximus*, though here he is called "misleading."[9] Robert Duncan's *The Truth and Life of Myth* is referred to in admiration. Olson has read Bob

Dylan's verse in the *Georgia Straight* (14–20 March 1969) and heard the most recent album *Nashville Skyline*. He alludes to Abraham Maslow and D. T. Suzuki—he owned *Zen Buddhism* (Garden City: Doubleday Anchor, 1956). With Harvey Brown and Gerrit Lansing present, Olson felt it was more like "chewing the fat" than an interview. The discussion ranged from Dr. Johnson to Mandrake the Magician, from Memphite Theology to Eadweard Muybridge. This was another cosmology: a "Berkeley Reading," kitchen style.

Olson interrupts one of Malanga's questions with a rather significant comment. Malanga is asking "before the time comes when you will—?"; Olson stops him and says, "I ain't got no time" (*Muthologos* 2, p. 138). This is the only hint in the interview of Olson's awareness of a health problem, unless we take as premonition another comment: "This is all I've been doing, as I said to you, this winter is reading poets whom I have always loved, that's all" (*Muthologos* 2, p. 142). This is in the context of Shakespeare's *Henry IV* Part 1, which he says he had read "for breakfast."[10] If we look closely, as we now must do, at Olson's reading in the last months of his life, we see that it is not literally true that all he did was read his favorite poets. Right up to the end he was capable of pushing into new areas. At the same time, we detect the increasing pleasure he was getting from picking up books he had enjoyed reading before and enjoying them once again. It was 5 August 1968 when, presumably with some awareness, Olson began a long *Maximus* poem with the statement, "I'm going to hate to leave this Earthly Paradise." Our investigation might appropriately begin two months prior to that when Olson spent more than a week in the hospital in Gloucester for reasons not known to us. He was discharged on 10 June 1968. From that milepost a diary of Olson's reading would have the following entries.

*15 June 1968.* Received as a gift from Harvey Brown: Cyrus H. Gordon, *Forgotten Scripts* (New York: Basic Books, 1968)—flyleaf: "fr Harv—at Gerrit's date of gathering of 1st week out of hospital: Sat–Sunday June 15th (AM June 16th: 1968." The date "June 17, 1968" on p. 165 denotes Olson's use of phrasing from that page in a poem, "Take the earth in under a single review"—which, in effect is what Cyrus Gordon was doing in his survey of the ancient languages of the Mediterranean. Further notes indicate that Olson used the book on 21 September 1969 just before going to Connecticut, and that he valued it enough to take it with him.

*29 June 1968.* Looked again at a small poem beginning "the salmon of Wisdom" and sent it to Robert Kelly "for *Matter*, now that it is reborn. Charles Olson, June 29th 1968." Olson deleted the old title on the holograph of the poem ("Cuchulain, born of impregnation by a mayfly"), which he owed to Robert Graves's *The White Goddess*. Nevertheless, it reminded him that he had been hankering for a cloth-bound edition of *The White Goddess* and he requested one the same day from Grolier Bookshop. The store supplied him one within a month.[11] Jumping from Graves's tripartite goddess to the etymological information on the "Fates" in *Webster's 2nd International Dictionary*, and thence to the World-Tree in Turville-Petre's *Myth and Religion of the North*, Olson wrote a prose piece dated "Institute of Further Studies, July 1st, 1968." and published separately with the title *"CLEAR, SHINING WATER," De Vries says, Altgermanische Religionsgeschichte (Berlin, 1957), Vol II, p. 380* (Buffalo: Institute of Further Studies, 1968).

*4 July 1968.* Trying to ensure the publishers got the cover of *Maximus IV, V, VI* right, Olson emphasized to Barry Hall in a letter of 4 July 1968 that *"basic is* the Tuzo Wilson map you have in the Scientific American"; he was also intending to enclose "a bad zerox Heezen of Columbia kindly enough sent" of "Wegener's original 'guess'— circum 1914 or something, as to how those pieces then did fit." However, it was not until 10 July 1968 that he got a copy of the Wegener map to Hall, taken from an article in the *Saturday Review* of 6 April 1968, "The Ancient Relative that Preceded Man to the South Pole," pp. 51–52.[12]

*6 July 1968.* An invoice of that date from Schoenhof's Foreign Books indicates that Olson purchased Julius Pokorny, *Indogermanisches Etymologisches Worterbuch*, vol. 1 (Bern: Francke Verlag, 1959).

*8 July 1968.* Gift from Thorp Feidt: O. C. Marsh, "Description of an Ancient Sepulchral Mound near Newark, Ohio," *American Journal of Science and Arts* 42 (July 1866): 1–11, an offprint.

*9 July 1968.* A note on the cover of Jewett's *Tidal Marshes of Rowley* (previously cited as bought in May 1959) indicates it was "read July 9, 1968."

*10 July 1968.* Telegram and letter to Frances Boldereff on receipt of her privately printed *Hermes to his Son Thoth* (previously cited), inscribed "For Charles—what came out of the Woodward nights."

*21 July 1968.* A poem entitled "That great descending light of day" was sent "to Robt Kelly Sunday July 21st"—though it may have been drafted earlier, perhaps about the time of "AN ART CALLED

GOTHONIC" (June 1966), with which it has affinities and thus can be thought of as drawing upon Otto Jesperson and Eva Matthews Sanford.[13] The inclusion of the Old English "sawol" for "soul" indicates that Olson had about him the xerox Prynne had sent in June 1966 of Morris Swadesh's "Linguistic Overview," pp. 527–56 of Jesse D. Jennings and Edward Norbeck, eds., *Prehistoric Man in the New World* (University of Chicago Press for William Marsh Rice University, 1964).

*22 July 1968.* Visited Gerrit Lansing, who read aloud "the whole first chapter (not very long) of Ko Hung as translated and edited by James Ware" (*Guide*, p. 627). Olson probably borrowed the volume, *Alchemy, Medicine, Religion in the China of* A.D. *320: The Nei P'ien of Ko Hung (Pao-p'u tzu)* (Cambridge: M.I.T. Press, 1967), for the next day he wrote a poem, "*And Melancholy,*" which draws on more than the first chapter. He was also prompted to turn to his copy of Joseph Needham, *Science and Civilization in China*, vol. 1 (Cambridge University Press, 1965)—flyleaf: "from John December 27th 1967—1st used with use July 22nd ('LXVIII) as of Ko Hung (learned of his existence from Gerrit Lansing this day—Monday July 22nd)." It was at this time that Lansing wrote a note (at Storrs) recommending Norman Cohn's *Pursuit of the Millennium* and listing books on loan to Olson:

Scholem, *Major Trends in Jewish Mysticism*
Ferm (ed), *Forgotten Religions*
Guthrie, *The Greeks and their Gods*
Moscati, *Face of the Ancient Near East*
Chang, *Teachings of Tibetan Yoga*
Eliade, *Yoga*[14]

*24 July 1968.* Returned to notes made in 1960–61 from Gloucester town records for a final poem on the founding of Dogtown ("above the head of John Day's pasture land"), utilizing also Babson's *History of Gloucester* and Baxter's *Trelawny Papers*,[15] "a source book for future Maximuses I had despaired of owning" (letter to Jonathan Williams, 21 August 1954).

*28 July 1968.* Wrote notes "on reading, Sunday July 28th 'LXVIII, Sauer on the *Greenlanders Saga*"[16]—presumably with Andrew Crozier in mind; they were published in *The Park* 4 and 5 (Summer 1969) with the title "Continuing Attempt to Pull the Taffy off the Roof of the Mouth."

*31 July 1968.* Seyyed Hossein Nasr, *Science and Civilization in Islam* (Harvard, 1968) from Harvey Brown, 28 July 1968, was "1st read—or started Wednesday night July 31st ('LXVIII," and led Olson to make the long telephone call to Brown in neighboring West Newburyport that is memorialized in the *Maximus* poem entitled "I'm going to hate to leave this Earthly Paradise." Nasr was used for the poem, as well as Zimmer's *Myths and Symbols in Indian Art and Civilization* (previously cited).[17] This poem of nighttime Gloucester celebrates "what Fitz Hugh Lane too saw."[18]

*31 July 1968.* Arrived from England, Larry Eigner, *Another Time in Fragments* (London: Fulcrum Press, 1967)—flyleaf: "Rec'd same day as enclosed letter (Wed Jl 31st 1968)." Olson copied lines from Eigner's first poem in his copy of Nasr's *Science and Civilization in Islam* (p. 250) with the date.

*August 1968.* S. Foster Damon, *A Blake Dictionary* (Providence: Brown University Press, 1965), gift of John Clarke.

*23 August 1968.* Roger Tory Peterson and Margaret McKenny, *A Field Guide to Wildflowers of Northeastern and North-central North America* (Boston: Houghton Mifflin, 1968)—flyleaf: "Olson's—fr. Friday August 23rd ('LX–VIII Gl' (Brown's)"; marking p. 348 at "American pennyroyal."[19]

*18 September 1968.* Making notes in Timothy Leary, *High Priest* (New York: New American Library in association with World Publishing, 1968)—flyleaf: "from Leary's *publishers* the prick Monday in 1968 . . . my own notes made Wednesday September 18th ('LXVIII—8 years afterwards)": after his own trips of 1960–61, that is.

*19 September 1968.* Bernard Lewis, *The Assassins: A Radical Sect in Islam* (New York: Basic Books, 1968)—flyleaf: "bot before Labor Day via Gordon & rec'd Sept 19th!"; notes and markings throughout.

*22 September 1968.* Rereading Walter H. Rich, *Fishing Grounds of the Gulf of Maine* (U.S. Bureau of Fisheries Document of 1929, previously cited)—on cover, beneath signature of R. H. Marchant: "by usurpation from R. H. Marchant so long ago (note acknowledging my arrogation Sunday Sept 22nd 'LXVIII"; p. 98 also dated.

*26 September 1968.* Letter to Joseph Garland, author, also of Gloucester, concerning Olson's possible role in a new edition of Babson's *History* that has been proposed by local publisher Peter Smith.[20] The letter refers to Garland's "*Pattillo* book"[21] and Olson's recent attention to Charles Mann.[22]

*28 September 1968.* Reading John Michell, *The Flying Saucer Vision:*

*The Holy Grail Restored* (London: Sidgwick & Jackson, 1967)—flyleaf: "Acquired—from Panna?—direct from London (Indica?) in Aug? *Sept 1968* & read 1st time really Sat. night September 28th starting fr. the beginning."[23]

*27 October 1968.* Letter to Robert Kelly: "I find I've read a great deal of Caterpillar–5 Or that I keep reading it Which has somewhat to do obviously that you had your hand in editing it (tho it is equally true that that fact also makes it possible like a hand held in front of one's own face to read Eshleman too—as well as Frank Samperi's note on himself etc—And even the lugubrious new-style Ron Hubbard's Dog food style—equally (cf. *Georgia Straight's* latest issue) Buckminster Fuller style biscuits. . . . Also (by the way) the Reynolds interlinear—*&* critique: more? Or *all* of the Sapphos?"

*27 October 1968.* Presumably read *New York Times Book Review*, M. L. Rosenthal on *Selected Writings* and *Human Universe*.[24]

*29 October 1968.* Received invoice for two books purchased from Arthur H. Clark Co.: Frederick Merk, ed. *Fur Trade and Empire: George Simpson's Journal*, rev. ed. (Cambridge: Harvard University Press, 1968)—note on p. 347 on pemmican; Mari Sandoz, *The Battle of Little Big Horn* (Philadelphia: Lippincott, 1966).

*23–24 November 1968.* George R. Stewart, *Ordeal by Hunger: The Story of the Donner Party*, new ed. (Boston: Houghton Mifflin, 1960)—flyleaf: "Olson—bot 1968—used again 1st Monday & Tuesday Nov. 23rd & 24th after having started (ordered—book in October."

*4 December 1968.* Responded to Richard Grossinger's request for an introduction to Charles Doria's translation of Sanchuniathon's *Phoenician History* to be published in the next issue of *Io* (6, Summer 1969). Olson's piece, "What's Back There," speaks of "4 original 'Phoenician' survivals," of which the other three are the *Chronicles of Paros*, the *Chronicles* of John Malalas, and the *Dea Syra* of Lucian.[25]

*7–12 December 1968.* Reading Sylvanus Smith, *Fisheries of Cape Ann* (Gloucester: Gloucester Times, 1915)—flyleaf: "from Homer Barrett I'm pretty sure Read 1st time meaningfully Saturday night December 7th, 1968."[26] On 12 December 1968 Olson began a letter to Joyce Benson by saying, "I'm lost in a bunch of vessels of olden time."

*9–10 December 1968.* Emma Worcester Sargent, *Epes Sargent of Gloucester and his Descendents* (Boston: Houghton Mifflin, 1923)— flyleaf: "bot one day this past summer at the 'House' here Main Street—1968 useful December 9th & 10th 1968."[27]

*18 December 1968.* Poem *"December 18th"* is an elegy for a demolished Gloucester house, the end of a battle fought in the Gloucester *Times* (a measure of Olson's attention to the local newspaper). Against the new fakery, the poet poses a quotation from Melville's *Redburn*.

*27 December 1968.* At a birthday party in Gloucester, Olson was given a book gift by three friends, Peter Anastas, Jonathan Bayliss, and Vincent Ferrini: Sidney Perley's *The Indian Land Titles of Essex County* (Salem: Essex Book & Print Club, 1912"—occasional notes and markings.

*January 1969.* Anselm Hollo, *Tumbleweed* (Toronto: Weed Flower Press, 1968)—"For Charles Olson as it says, on the next page and with love, as ever Iowa City to Gloucester January 1969 from Anselm Hollo."[28]

*[January 1969].* Waited out a blizzard at Vincent Ferrini's and, according to Ferrini's autobiography, "[Olson] reread my last book, *I Have the World*."

*[January 1969].* Wrote poem beginning "As Cabeza de Vaca was" in an undated manuscript (see *Editing Maximus*, p. 72), thus bringing into the *Maximus* poems a long-valued figure from "The Narrative of Alvar Nuñez Cabeça de Vaca" in Frederick W. Hodge (previously cited; especially here p. 108).

*1 January 1969.* In a *Maximus* poem beginning "Between Cruiser & Plato" (i.e., landmarks on the Atlantic Ocean bottom), Olson makes direct use of the *Physiographic Diagram: Atlantic Ocean (Sheet 1)*, done by Bruce C. Heezen and Marie Tharp (New York: Geographical Society of America, 1957).

*3 January 1969.* Sent check to James Laughlin for copy of Ezra Pound's *Drafts and Fragments of Cantos CX–CXVII* soon to be published by New Directions. Laughlin sent Olson a copy as a gift—flyleaf: "Olson from Jas Laughlin April 1969." Olson gave his second copy to Charles Boer, commenting on Pound's "paradiso terrestre": "where Pound and I are related as poets."[29]

*11 January 1969.* Much annotation of Jung's *The Archetypes and the Collective Unconscious* (previously cited as first used 30 December 1965)—flyleaf: "read January 11th 1969 pp. 6–261—& principally part VI."

*20 January 1969.* Reading Gwyn Jones, *A History of the Vikings* (London & New York: Oxford University Press, 1968)—flyleaf: "fr Harv January 1969 read in 1st Sunday January 20th."

*23 January 1969.* Robert Kelly inscribed his *Songs I–XXX* (Cambridge: Pym-Randall, 1968): "for Charles as fast as I can, love to you, all ways Robert 23 January 1969 Gloucester."[30]

*15 February 1969.* Wrote and dated prose piece for *Io* 6 (Summer 1969), "The Animate Versus the Mechanical, and Thought," utilizing what had become standard texts: Merleau-Ponty, Havelock, Whitehead, and Hesiod.

*23–25 February 1969.* Turned once more to vol. 2 of *Records and Files of the Quarterly Courts of Essex County* (previously cited).

*6 March 1969.* Received Robert Duncan, *The Truth and Life of Myth* (New York: House of Books, 1968) inscribed, "This copy for Charles, mythographer and maker maximus." Flyleaf annotations by Olson: "mailed Feb 25th—rec'd March 6th! 9 days across the American continent! Begins to get back to like the Pony Express! Or Butterfield's stage! Read ½ half Thurs night March 6th 1969 in this cold house without eating (except for the clam-chowder Pauli brought up) until I can't go on any more (to top p. 39)."

*[April 1969].* Borrowed from Sawyer Free Library, Gloucester, *Robert Babson Alling's Ancestors, Descendants and Close Relations* (Chicago: privately printed, 1959), and returned before the due date, 15 April 1969.

*1 April 1969.* Reading "On Life After Death" chapter of Jung's *Memories, Dreams, Reflections,* according to a note on the flyleaf.

*19 April 1969.* Wrote what was later published in *Io* as "1st Addition, after some slight studies into present scientific understanding of 'gravity,' to The Animate versus the Mechanical, and Thought." The "present scientific understanding" is contained in Dietrick E. Thomsen, "Searching for Gravity Waves," *Science News* 93 (27 March 1968): 408–9; Barry Paine of Gloucester gave Olson a xerox copy of it.

*20 April 1969.* Eating "Geisha" crab meat from Japan makes Olson bring into his poem (beginning "The first morning was"—*Guide,* p. 731) a comparison between himself and the world of Lady Murasaki's *The Tale of Genji,* a novel he had probably had on his shelves for a long time in Arthur Waley's translation (New York: The Literary Guild, 1935).

A short poem beginning "the left hand is the calyx," written the same day, draws upon E. Dale Saunders, *Mudra: A Study of Symbolic Gestures in Japanese Buddhist Sculpture,* Bollingen Series 58 (New York: Pantheon, 1960).

*26 April 1969.* Wrote, (but never mailed) a statement for Bill Berkson's *Homage to Frank O'Hara.*[31]

*26–27 April 1969.* Dated annotations show intense reading of *The Secret of the Golden Flower* (previously cited). And again on 24–25 June 1969.

*30 April 1969.* From a reading of Henry Corbin's "Cyclical Time in Mazdaism and Ismailism" in *Man and Time* (previously cited), Olson wrote a further short "addition" to "The Animate Versus the Mechanical, and Thought" and sent it off to Richard Grossinger for *Io* magazine.

*6 June 1969.* As recorded in Ralph Maud's "Notes Made After Visiting Charles Olson on Saturday 6 June 1969" in *Iron* 12 (1971), Olson conversed on several topics, including (1) Peter Anastas's "Olson: An Appreciation" in the local weekly *North Shore '68* (28 December 1968): 4–6; (2) Robert Kelly's review of *Pleistocene Man* in *Caterpillar* 7 (April 1969): 234–35; (3) M. L. Rosenthal's *The New Poets* (previously cited), which "made a valuable distinction" in giving Olson a section away from the confessional poets; (4) Lucien Price's *Dialogues of Alfred North Whitehead* (Boston: Little, Brown, 1954), which Olson did not own— Whitehead was not, there, the Master he was in *Process and Reality*; (5) Charles Hartshorne, "Whitehead's Philosophy of Reality as Socially Structured Process," *Chicago Review* 8 (Spring–Summer 1954): 60–77—an important article that had led him in to Whitehead (Olson owned the issue).

*[9 June 1969].* In response to a query from Vincent Ferrini about the history of Gloucester Lyceum, Olson pulled out his copy of Pringle's *History* (previously cited) and jotted down notes from p. 327.

*15 June 1969.* Heavy annotations of this date in Jung's *Psychology and Alchemy* (previously cited), the last of many such readings.

*10 July 1969.* Frank Waters, *The Earp Brothers of Tombstone* (London: Neville Spearman, 1962) inscribed to Olson from Thorpe Feidt, Gloucester.

*19 July 1969.* For a *Maximus* poem, Olson is looking again at Champlain's map of Gloucester as reproduced in *The Fishermen's Own Book* (*Guide*, p. 746).

*22 July 1969.* Births, vol. 1, *Vital Records of Gloucester, Massachusetts to the End of the Year 1849* (Topsfield, Mass.: Topsfield Historical Society, 1917)—flyleaf: "bot, & rec'd from Jewett Tuesday July 22nd, 1969."

*23 July 1969.* Extensive notes in James W. Mavor, *Voyage to Atlantis*

(New York: Putnam, 1969)—flyleaf: "bot. Brown's Book dept & rec'd past week or two—now 1st used July 23rd 1969."[32]

*24 July 1969.* Creeley sends presentation copy of *Pieces* (New York: Scribner, 1969).

*[August 1969].* During a visit of George Butterick to Gloucester, Olson recommended, though he did not own, Theodore Andrea Cook, *The Curves of Life* (New York: Henry Holt, 1914). On this occasion Olson gave to Adam Butterick Charles Peter's old copy of the Classics Illustrated Junior, *The Enchanted Pony* (previously cited).

*20 August 1969.* In a letter to Albert Glover, Olson recommends Valentina Pavlovna Wasson and R. Gordon Wasson, *Mushrooms, Russia, and History*, 2 vols. (New York: Pantheon, 1957).[33]

*[Late August 1969].* In the taped interview with Herbert A. Kenny (printed in *Muthologos* 2 with the title " 'I know men for whom everything matters' "), Olson discusses many Gloucester matters in a sort of recapitulation, including: (1) *The Fisheries of Gloucester* (previously cited), which he attributes to John J. Babson; (2) Charles C. Willoughby, *Antiquities of the New England Indians* (Cambridge: Peabody Museum of American Archaeology and Ethnology, Harvard University, 1935)[34]; (3) the burning of City Hall—he had saved a *Gloucester Times* clipping of 28 August 1964, "Oh, You City Hall How You do Change" by Barbara Erkkila; (4) in connection with Wingaersheek Beach and a 1621 Dutch map, E. B. O'Callaghan, ed., *Documents Relative to the Colonial History of the State of New York* (1856)—not owned by Olson; (5) Capt. Joseph W. Collins and Richard Rathbun, "The Sea Fishing Grounds of the Eastern Coast," edited by Goode (previously cited); (6) Gordon W. Thomas, *Fast and Able* (1952 ed. previously cited)—Olson recommends the new 1968 edition; and (7) study of "the Finder, the Funder, and the Founder," i.e., Capt. John Smith, John White of the Dorchester Company, and John Winthrop.

*1 September 1969.* In a letter to Wilbert Snow, Olson responds to news of Snow's forthcoming autobiography.

*9 September 1969.* Received from Harvey Bialy a xerox copy of Joseph B. Birdsell, "Some Population Problems Involving Pleistocene Man," *Cold Spring Harbor Symposium on Quantitative Biology* 22 (1957): 47–69—notes and markings.

*11 September 1969.* Letter to Peter Anastas acknowledges gift that day of the *New Yorker* for 13 August 1966 with long piece by Joseph Alsop on a Cretan excavation, "A Reporter at Large: Kato Zakro," pp. 32–95—Olson retained the copy with his notes and markings.

*22 September 1969.* Notes in Townsend's *Birds of Essex County* (previously cited):

> p. 60 Great Auk practically the identical dates of the last of the Beothuks—and the Auks
> p. 61 food and fish-bait bred here of the Country
> p. 114 (so large he cld have been the bird upon the Pleistocene stick! today, as my own today on the farthest rock out on the right of the Bridge—and as often cut himself out like an eagle
> p. 115 April 4 to June 18, August 22 to November 24 this year LXIX particularly proven especially the fall presence where I have never noticed or in such numbers before So there are more recently—or is this particular year remarkable?

On 26 September 1969, Olson met Charles Boer in Cambridge and drove down to Connecticut on a visit that would turn into a temporary teaching job, then the hospital, and then his death in New York City on 10 January 1970. He returned to 28 Fort Square, Gloucester, on the weekend of October 5th to settle some practical matters and pick up some books—including the recently arrived Gaston Bachelard, *The Poetics of Space* (Boston: Beacon Paperback, 1969)—flyleaf: "from Ann Charters—& 1st opened essentially Altnaveigh Thurs–Friday Oct 9th–10th 1969 tho 'saw' as there Gloucester—which night, Tuesday(?) of this week October 7th 1969 (rec'd Gl by Cardone week after Friday Sept 26th while I was in Connecticut visiting Charles Boer though returning Sunday October 5th (night Linda walked in." What books did Olson bring back to Connecticut to help with the graduate seminar that had hastily been arranged for him to teach? Two years before, he had jotted down a list of essential titles:

A. N. Whitehead's *Process and Reality*
Noah Webster *Dictionary* before 7th and 3rd.
Charlton Lewis' Roots Table
Weyl's *Philosophy of Mathematics and Natural Science*
Liddell & Scott
Oxenstierna

*Psychology and Alchemy*
Corbin's *Avicenna*
Turville-Petre *Myth and Religion of the North*

Since the seminar at Storrs was announced as "Early English and the Influence of Norse Mythology," the above list would have provided an appropriate core of titles. From dated annotations, we know that he used in Connecticut his copies of Turville-Petre's *Origins of Icelandic Literature* and Brown and Foote, *Early English and Norse Studies*.

According to Charles Boer's account in *Charles Olson in Connecticut*, there was no diminution in the voraciousness of his reading. In the manner of addressing Olson, Boer writes (p. 25):

> You also wanted things to read in bed, and I regularly offered you a book or two that I thought you might not have read. Among other things, you agreed to read *Land to the West* by Geoffrey Ashe, a book on the weather conditions in antiquity by Rhys Carpenter, and an illustrated book called *Secret Societies*. The books had to be informational, no novels and certainly no poetry; and the information had to be of such a kind that the man who wrote it used himself somewhere in the book, drawing out of his own person the theory of the book.
>
> Nonetheless, every time I gave you such a book you were sceptical and reluctant to take it, though the next day (you would get up in the early afternoon of the next day) you would be terribly excited about the previous night's reading, with notes and plans to pursue the book. It would start all over again the next night with the same scepticism and reluctance about the next book. You were a hard man to please.
>
> I remember well that first night, after you had finally gone to bed (the whole ritual could take hours), hearing you in the next room furiously turning the pages of the books, munching vigorously on the lettuce and other food. Every few hours that night I was suddenly awakened by a new burst of frantic munching and page-turning. It went on all night.[35]

One thing that Olson made a point of getting for himself in this period was a Geodesic Survey map of the Mansfield and Windham County area (Boer, p. 91). The other possibility he had offered the University of Connecticut as title for his course was "The Origins of the Thames and Connecticut Rivers"—and that was the River Thames of New London, not the old. He picked up a copy of Helen Earle Sellers, *Connecticut Town Origins: Their Names, Boundaries, Early Histories and*

*First Families* (Stonington: Pequot Press, 1964). He shouted at his semi-
nar students: "I want you to know where you are . . . up the road from
Four Corners in Mansfield is MAN's Field." "We are all cartographic
instances," he added, "topological (rhythm is position)." He read him-
self into his new location.[36]

On a lighter note, Charles Boer describes how a casual remark of
Olson's to Paul Kugler "that every young person should be exposed to
the writings of Thornton Burgess" (p. 100) led to Olson's meeting
Paul's mother, Lee Kugler, who had, as it happens, brought them up
on Burgess and knew well Burgess's "Aunt Sally." Olson borrowed her
copy of Burgess's *Aunt Sally's Friends in Fur* (Boston, 1955); he had
been trying for years to get the original editions of Burgess, who had
lived in Gloucester. Lightheartedness was the general rule in Olson's
Connecticut days as Boer describes them, even after the poet entered
Manchester Hospital on 1 December 1969 for tests. The other side came
in occasionally with the passages from *King Lear* that Boer reports were
in Olson's mind, and sometimes recited. And on 13 November 1969 in
class, student notes indicate that Olson said: "Today I woke up and
looked at my hands like in Tolstoy's Ivan Ilyich . . . *The Death of.*"[37]

Two book gifts became Olson's last reading. The first from Harvey
Brown, an attentive student and genuine patron who had chosen to re-
side near Gloucester at West Newburyport and who, on 18 December
1969, drove down to effect Olson's last move (to a New York City hos-
pital). According to the flyleaf of Stuart Piggott, *The Druids* (New York:
Praeger, 1968) the volume was "opened during the night between
Tuesday November 25th 1969 and Wednesday actually it is 4:30 AM of
November 26th—Altnaveigh (Gift from HB & mailed by Mandrake
November 8th—2 plus weeks ago)." There are several marginal notes
from that first reading, one dated 7:45 A.M. of the 26th: "I've found my
'hole' in the ground (my vatic 'place')"—written on p. 51 after the sec-
tion on the druids' standing in the social order. Then a note "added Sat
Nov 29th after conversation in afternoon with Chas B Jon and Glenis"
at a reference to the *aes dana* ("men of art") performing at "open-air
gatherings" (p. 49): "why T. Hardy probably was greater 'English'
than Shakespeare by going back right through Celtic hill fort and to
Beaker at Stonehenge." Even Shakespeare had become too new for this
New Englander now interested in only the oldest England.

The second gift, and the last book we have record of Olson attending to, was from graduate student John Lobb, who brought it to the hospital on the evening of 4 December 1969: John Philip Cohane's *The Key* (previously cited). Boer once more is the witness (pp. 126–27):

> It was just the sort of book you loved. You said that Cohane bore out what you were yourself thinking about for some time—the migration of various Semitic tribes as far as Polynesia. *The Key* was a book that fit perfectly the Laurentian perspective in your imagination. It made you talk about the Pacific, which you disliked. You said you never wanted to go there, that it was unfriendly—unlike the Atlantic—and the source of earthquakes. The Pacific, you said, was the womb, and primitive, and the moon came out of it. You were a man for Atlantic waters only.
>
> In the margins of *The Key*, you started to keep track of each day's events now, your feelings, your thoughts. Here is one of the first entries:
> Friday Dec. 5 LXIX Hospital Connecticut
> Constant and careful now and forever (There) after
>
> To be to extricate the (soul) from all
> other                                   problems of appetite?
>                        desires          sleep etc.
> To keep the mixtures (sansara?    self conception
> and instead let it have its life by making sure
> (*what solitude very obviously does*
> —as company equally makes one healthy
>      —work for me now
>
> or*Time spent simply for itself wastes one in*
> one's own souls
>                                   *nature* &
>                  special needs    *poetry* - = now
>                                   *Mythology*
>
> Actually place things out in front of me
> They should be placed there in front of one's
> self (as in Pleistocene

There were further similar notes in Cohane's *The Key*—not really reading notes, but diary entries dated 6–7, 8, 9, 13, and 15 December 1969. And then Olson's final piece of writing: "The 'Secret' notes written this day December 16th and to be only opened & by Chas. Boer if & when otherwise still to be retained as mine," published posthumously as "The Secret of the Black Chrysanthemum."[38] We do not look, of course, for new titles here. Most of the items in the London list of 1967 (given above) were mentioned, along with allusions to:

*Secret of the Golden Flower*
Hesiod
Fowler in Vergilius Ferm's anthology
Corbin's "Cyclical Time in Mazdaism and Ismailism" as well as the *Avicenna*
Havelock's *Preface to Plato*

and the latest gift, Cohane's *The Key*. There is nothing sentimental or self-centered in this piece. If totality has been achieved, it is, as always, in the push outward, the process of doing it, not really stopping.

## Appendix

### Schoolboy Books

Helen Bannerman, *The Story of Little Black Sambo* (New York: The Plate & Munk Co., n.d.)—copy in Olson's library.

Arabella B. Buckley, *The Fairy-land of Science* (New York: Appleton, 1894)—bookplate: "Property of the City of Worcester, Abbott St School," inscribed: "Given to Charles Olson for excellent essay on safety."

H. Irving Hancock, *The High School Freshman; or Dick and Co.'s First Year Pranks and Sports* (Philadelphia: Henry Altemus, 1910)—flyleaf: "Charles Olson 4 Norman Ave."

Joel Chandler Harris, *Told by Uncle Remus* (New York: Grosset & Dunlap, 1905)—copy preserved in Olson's library.

Mary Catherine Judd, *Classic Myths* (Chicago: Rand-McNally, 1901)—copy in Olson's library.

Samuel Lover, *Handy Andy* (London: Methuen, 1904)—Olson did not keep a copy, but tells of his father reading it to him "while I recovered from a tonsil and adenoid operation" (*The Post Office*, p. 30).

*Mother Goose Nursery Rhymes* (New York: McLoughlin Bros., n.d.)—"To Charles Olsen from Blanid Reidy Christmas 1914"; this was among the books left with Jean Kaiser.

Beatrix Potter, *Tale of Peter Rabbit*—no specific title mentioned, only the comment at Berkeley: "For the first time, I mean, I hope *I* ran faster than Peter Rabbit" (*Muthologos* 1, p. 100).

The *Maximus* poem, "The Song and dance of," refers to Ralph Henry Barbour, who wrote boys' books such as *The Half-Back* (1899) and *For the Honor of the School* (1900); no specific title is mentioned.

The following books, now at the University of Connecticut, were stored by Olson in the attic of a family friend, Mary Sullivan, in Worcester. They are mainly childhood and high school books, with some from college days.

Victor Appleton, *Tom Swift and his Wizard Camera* (New York: Grosset & Dunlap, 1912)—"From Mrs Collins Gloucester Christmas 1922."

George E. Atwood, *Grammar School Algebra* (New York: Silver Burdett, 1900)—Worcester School Department.

Honoré de Balzac, *Eugénie Grandet*, ed. Eugene Bergeron (New York: Holt, 1906)—Worcester School Department book for French classes.

Mrs. Arthur J. Barnes, *Barnes' Practical Course in Benn Pitman Shorthand* (St. Louis: Arthur J. Barnes, 1916)—flyleaf: "Mildred Blanchard."

J. M. Barrie, *A Window in Thrums* (Philadelphia: Henry Altemus, 1894).

J. M. Barrie, *Courage* (New York: Scribners, 1930)—"C. J. Olson Christmas 1931 with all good wishes W. G. Chanter."

J. M. Barrie, *The Little Minister* (New York: Grosset & Dunlap, 1897).

Nathaniel Horton Batchelder, ed., *Selections from Boswell's Life of Johnson* (New York: Charles E. Merrill, 1912)—Winchester Library stamp, 13 January 1927.

W. J. Baumgartner, *Laboratory Manual of the Foetal Pig* (New York: Macmillan, 1928)—flyleaf: "Harwood Belding '31 Eclectic House"; Olson marginalia.

Peter Bayne, *Essays in Biography and Criticism* (Boston: Gould & Lincoln, 1871)—stamped Leicester Public Library.

John H. Bechtel, *Slips of Speech* (Philadelphia: The Penn Publishing Co., 1915).

Myron T. Bly, *Descriptive Economics: An Introduction to Economic Science* (Rochester: Williams & Rogers, 1898)—"Charles Olson from Alice H. Belding For excellent work"; marginal lines.

Ralph Philip Boas, *The Study and Appreciation of Literature* (New York: Harcourt Brace, 1931)—marginalia.

Halham Bosworth, *Technique in Dramatic Art* (New York: Macmillan, 1927)—markings.

Albert Perry Brigham and Charles T. McFarlane, *Essentials of Geography*, Second Book (New York: American Book Co., 1920).

Stuart R. Brinkley, *Principles of General Chemistry* (New York: Macmillan, 1926)—"Charles J. Olson 8 North College"; many notes.

Gould Brown, *The Institutes of English Grammar*, rev. by Henry Kiddle (New York: William Wood, 1887).

Rollo Walter Brown, *The Writer's Art* (Cambridge: Harvard, 1924)—flyleaf: "Barbara Denny."

William Cullen Bryant, *The Story of the Fountain* (New York: D. Appleton, 1872).

Robert Buchanan, *The Master of the Mine* (New York: International Book Co, n.d.)

Thornton W. Burgess, *Mother West Wind "When" Stories* (Boston: Little, Brown, 1919)—"To Charles Olson, Jr. From Aunt Mary Xmas 1921."

Loomis J. Campbell, *The New Franklin Fourth Reader* with *Lessons in Elocution* by Professor Mark Bailey (New York: Sheldon & Co., 1884)—Worcester School Department Grade 5.

Carmelite Fathers, *The Little Flower Bulletin* (Chicago, 1927).

Frank G. Carpenter, *North America* (New York: American Book Co., 1922).

*Charter of the Massachusetts Bay Colony 1628–29*, facsimile published by Edward J. Cronin, Secretary of the Commonwealth, n.d.

*Christmas Kitties* (Boston: D. Lothrop Co., n.d.)—Olson's flyleaf note: "Dad's—childhood."

*Cicero's Orations* (Philadelphia: David McKay—title page missing).

Sherwin Cody, *Constructive Rhetoric* (New York: Putnam's, 1927).

Albert S. Cook, ed., *Edmund Burke's Speech on Conciliation with America* (New York: Longmans, Green, 1898)—endpaper notes, marginalia.

Council of Baltimore, *A Catechism of Christian Doctrine* (New York: P. J. Kennedy & Sons, n.d.)

Hugh Craig, *Great African Travellers* (London: George Routeledge & Sons, n.d.)

Rachel Crothers, *"As Husbands Go": A Comedy* (New York: Samuel French, n.d.)

Hawthorne Daniel, *Ships of the Seven Seas*, new ed. (New York: Dodd, Mead, 1930).

Alphonse Daudet, *La Belle-Nivernaise*, ed. James Boielle (Boston: Heath, 1902)—Worcester School Department; flyleaf: "C. J. Olson."

Captain Harry Dean, *The Pedro Gorino* (Boston: Houghton Mifflin, 1929).

Walter de la Mare, *Ding Dong Bell* (London: Selwyn & Blount, 1924).

Charles Dickens, *A Child's History of England* (New York: George Routeledge, n.d.)

Charles Dickens, *Barnaby Rudge* and *Edwin Drood* (New York: Hurst & Co., n.d.)—flyleaf: "George E. Reidy Christmas 1892."

*The Boys of Dickens Retold* (New York: McLoughlin Bros., n.d.)— "Charles Olson 4 Norman Ave Worcester Mass. P. R. Please Return."

Sir A. Conan Doyle, *Beyond the City* (New York: Street & Smith, n.d.).

Sir A. Conan Doyle, *Tales of Sherlock Holmes* (Washington: National Home Library Foundation, 1932).

Lieutenant James R. Driscoll, *The Brighton Boys with the Flying Corps* (Philadelphia: The John C. Winston Co., 1918)—"To Charles J. Olson From Mother & Dad Xmas 1921."

J. W. Duffield, *Bert Wilson's Fadeaway Ball* (New York: George Sully, 1913)—"To Charles from Mother Christmas 1922."

A. Dumas, *Les Miserables*—no title page.

Victor Duruy, *A General History of the World*, vol. 3 (New York: The Review of Reviews, 1912).

Michael Earls, S. J., *Ballads of Peace and War* (Worcester: Harrigan Press, 1917).

*Ecclesiastical History Abridged for the Use of Schools* (Baltimore: John Murphy Co., n.d.).

Henry W. Elson, *The Civil War Through the Camera* (New York: McKinlay, Stone & Mackenzie, 1912).

*Europe at War* (Published by Doubleday Page for The Review of Reviews, 1914).

*Everybody's Cyclopedia*, vols. 1-4 (New York: Syndicate Publishing Co., 1912).

Octave Feuiller, *Le Roman d'un Jeune Homme Pauvre*, ed. Edward T. Owen and Felicien V. Paget (New York: Holt, 1897).

*First-Steps*—no title page; inside front cover: "Charls First book From Dad and Mother."

Clyde Fitch, *The Smart Set: Correspondence and Conversations* (Chicago: Herbert S. Stone & Co., 1897).

Percy Keese Fitzhugh, *Roy Blakeley in the Haunted Camp* (New York: Grosset & Dunlap, 1922)—"To Charles Olson From Mother Olson Christmas 1922."

Percy Keese Fitzhugh, *Tom Slade (Boy Scout of the Moving Pictures)* (New York: Grosset & Dunlap, 1915)—"To Charles Olson, Jr From Mother & Dad Xmas 1921."

Percy Keese Fitzhugh, *Tom Slade Motorcycle Dispatch-Bearer* (New York: Grosset & Dunlap, 1918)—"To Charles from Mother Christmas 1923."

Norman Foerster and J. M. Steadman, Jr., *Sentences and Thinking* (Boston: Houghton Mifflin, 1923)—annotations.

William Trufant Foster, *Argumentation and Debating* (Boston: Houghton Mifflin, rev. 1917)—flyleaf: Charles J. Olson Jr. C. J. Olson Jr ΦΝΘ." Notes on Willem de Sitter lecture at Wesleyan 1931 and many other annotations.

Francois, *Introductory French Prose Composition*—title page missing; Classical High School, Worcester.

W. H. Fraser and J. Squire, *A Shorter French Course* (Boston: Heath, 1913)—Classical High School, Worcester.

C. N. French, *A Countryman's Day Book* (London: J. M. Dent, 1929)—flyleaf: "December 22nd 1931 Charles always yours Babs."

Paul M. Fulchet, *Foundations of English Style* (New York: Crofts, 1927).

Hugh S. Fullerton, *Jimmy Kirkland of the Shasta Boys' Team* (Philadelphia: John C. Winston Co., 1915)—"To Charles Olson from Mother Dec. 25 1924."

John Galsworthy, *The Man of Property*, vol. 1, *The Forsyth Saga* (New York: Scribners, 1927).

Gloucester Fishermen's Institute, *Twenty-ninth Annual Report* (Gloucester, 1920).

Johann Wolfgang von Goethe, *Faust* trans. Bayard Taylor (De Luxe Editions, n.d.).

C. H. Graham—two offprints (cited previously).

Edward Everett Hale, *The Man Without a Country* (New York: Barse & Hopkins, n.d.).

Ludvic Halévy, *L'Abbé Constantin*, ed. O. B. Super (New York: Holt, 1894)—Classical High School, Worcester.

H. Irving Hancock, *The Grammar School Boys Snowbound* (Philadelphia: Henry Altemus, 1911).

H. Irving Hancock, *The High School Freshman, or Dick & Co.'s First Year Pranks and Sports*, Dick Prescott Books (Philadelphia: Henry Altemus, 1910).

H. Irving Hancock, *The High School Pitcher* (Philadelphia: Henry Altemus, 1910).

*Harper's New Latin Dictionary* (New York: American Book Co., 1907).

Clair W. Hayes, *The Boy Allies in Great Peril* (New York: A. L. Burt, 1916)—"To Charles from Dad Christmas 1923."

Clair W. Hayes, *The Boy Troopers in the Northwest* (New York: A. L. Burt, 1922)—"To Charles Olson From "Bobby" Chaffin Christmas 1922."

William Hope Hodgson, *Captain Gault* (New York: Robert M. McBride Co., 1918)—"Charles from Meredith Christmas 1923."

*Home Library of Useful Knowledge.*

Rev. Henry N. Hudson, *Classical English Reader* (Boston: Ginn & Heath, 1879)—Worcester High School Library.

*The Iliad of Homer*, trans. Alexander Pope (Boston: Leach, Sherwell & Sanborn, 1986)—City of Worcester label.

*Irving's Oliver Goldsmith*, ed. Lewis B. Semple (New York: Longmans, Green, 1903)—Worcester Classical High School.

Paul Kaufman, *Points of View for College Students* (Garden City: Doubleday, Page, 1927)—"Charles J. Olson ΦΝΘ Eclectic House Wesleyan"; marginalia, especially on Schopenhauer.

Charles Kingsley, *Sir Walter Raleigh and his Time* (Boston: Ticknor & Fields, 1859).

Henry Higgins Lane, *Animal Biology* (Philadelphia: P. Blakiston's Sons, 1929)—many marginalia.

Lockwood, *Lessons in English* (Boston: Ginn, 1888)—title page torn; Garner, Mass., school.

Henry Wadsworth Longfellow, *The Courtship of Miles Standish* (New York: Little Leather Corp., n.d.)—"Charles Olson passed 5 sets of spelling Gr. 4 June 1920."

Mother Mary Loyola, *Jesus of Nazareth: The Story of His Life Simply Told* (New York: Benziger Bros., 1910).

Percy Marks, *Better Themes* (New York: Harcourt Brace, 1933)—some markings.

Luther Whiting Mason, *The New Third Music Reader* (Boston: Ginn 1888)—inside front cover: "Mary Olson."

Howard Lee McBain, *The Living Constitution* (New York: MacMillan, 1928).

James D. McCabe, *Pictorial History of the World* (Philadelphia: National Publishing Company, 1878).

Byron McCandless and Gilbert Grosvenor, *Flags of the World* (Washington: National Geographic, 1917).

*McGuffey's Fifth Eclectic Reader* (New York: American Book Co., 1896).

Molière, *Le Bourgeois Gentilhomme* (New York: American Book Co., 1903).

Thomas Moore, *Lalla Rookh* (Buffalo: George H. Derby, 1850)—flyleaf: "Hyde."

Thomas Henry Newman, *Brilliants* (Boston: Samuel E. Cassino, 1892).

Sam Noble, *'Tween Decks in the Seventies: An Autobiography* (New York: Frederick A. Stokes, 1926).

S. S. Packard and Byron Horton, *The New Packard Commercial Arithmetic* (New York: S. S. Packard, 1890).

Ralph D. Paine, *The Call of the Offshore Wind* (Boston: Houghton Mifflin, 1918).

Francis Turner Palgrave, *The Golden Treasury* (Oxford, 1928).

George W. Peck, *Peck's Bad Boy Abroad* (Chicago: Stanton & Van Vilet, 1905)—"To Charles Olson, Jr. From Mother and Dad Xmas 1921."

Fred S. Piper, *Lexington, the Birthplace of American Liberty* 3d ed. (Lexington Historical Society, 1910).

*The Poems of Winthrop Mackworth Praed*, Frederick Cooper, ed. (London: Walter Scott, 1886)—previous owner M. L. Kellner.

Arthur Quiller-Couch, *The Delectable Duchy* (New York: Scribners, 1899)—stamp of Worcester Hahnemann Hospital.

*The Radio Gunner* (Boston: Houghton Mifflin, 1924)—"Charles, from Aunt Vandla Christmas 1928."

John Crowe Ransom, ed., *Topics for Freshman Writing* (New York: Holt, 1935).

St.-George Rathborne, *Down the Amazon* (Akron: Saalfield Publishing Co., 1905).

John Clark Ridpath, *History of the United States*, vols. 1 and 3 (New York: The Review of Reviews, 1911).

John C. Rolfe and Walter Dennison, *A Latin Reader for the Second Year* (Boston: Allyn & Bacon, 1918)—Worcester Classical High School.

William J. Rolfe, *A Satchel Guide to Europe* (Boston: Houghton Mifflin, 1928)—"To Charles John Olson with the respect and high-hearted wishes of the Faculty of Classical High School Worcester, Mass. June 29, 1928."

*The Rubiyat of Omar Khayyam* (New York: Thomas Y. Crowell, n.d.)—"Charles J. Olson December 27, 1929."

Bertrand Russell, *A Free Man's Worship* (Portland: Thomas Mosher, 1923)—flyleaf: "B. G. Denny."

Francisque Sarcey, *Le Siege de Paris* (Boston: Heath, (1898)—Worcester School Dept.

M. M. Scribe et Legouvé, *La Bataille de Dames* (New York: Holt, 1864).

Vida D. Scudder, *Brother John, A Tale of the First Franciscans* (Boston: Little, Brown, 1927)—Red Star Line Wanted Baggage label, "Charles Olson."

*Selections from Ovid* (Boston: Ginn, 1890)—Classical High School stamp; Olson's note "Page 76 Missing."

*Selections from Voltaire*, ed. George R. Havens (New York: Century, 1925).

Harriette R. Shattuck, *The Woman's Manual of Parliamentary Law* (Boston: Lee & Shepard, 1894).

Mary D. Sheldon, *Studies in Greek and Roman History* (Boston: Heath, 1890)—Worcester School Department.

B. P. Shillaber, *Partingtonian Patchwork* (Boston: Lee & Shepard, 1873).

Frank H. Simonds, *Can Europe Keep the Peace?* (New York: Harper, 1931).

Edmund W. Sinnott, *Botany Principles and Problems* 2d ed. (New York: McGraw-Hill, 1929)—some markings.

Milton Smith, *The Book of Play Production* (New York: D. Appleton, 1928).

Robert Louis Stevenson, *Treasure Island* (New York: Grosset & Dunlap, n.d.)—"From Uncle Charles to Philip Hedges November 1913."

*The Story of Washington: A Reverie* 3d ed. (L. H. Nelson, 1908).

Preston Sturges, *Strictly Dishonorable* (New York: Liveright, 1929).

L. Raymond Talbot, *Le Francais et sa patrie* (Boston: Sanborn, 1912); and *French Composition* (1919)—both Classical High School books.

W. M. Thomson, *Holy Land*, The Land and the Book, vol. 1, (New York: Harper, 1874)—Leicester Public Libary.

Clarence Dewitt Thorpe, et al., *College Composition* (New York: Harper, 1934).

*Trader Horn*, ed. Ethelreda Lewis (Garden City Publishing Co., 1927).

Jim Tully, *Blood on the Moon* (New York: Coward-McCann, 1931).

Louis Untermeyer, *Modern American and British Poetry* (New York: Harcourt Brace, rev. ed., 1928).

J. H. Vanderpoel, *The Human Figure*, 12th ed. (Chicago: Inland, 1922)—"C. J. Olson 4 Norman Ave Worcester."

J. W. Van Der Voort, *The Water World* (Union Publishing House, 1883).

Carl Van Doren, *An Anthology of World Prose* (New York: Reynal & Hitchcock, 1935).

Henry Van Dyke, *A Creelful of Fishing Stories* (New York: Scribners, 1932).

Jules Verne, *From the Earth to the Moon* and *Round the Moon* (New York: A. L. Burt, n.d.)—"To Charles Jr. Xmas 1918."

Jules Verne, *The Mysterious Island* (New York: Scribners, n.d.)—"To all hands."

William Lightfoot Visscher, *Buffalo Bill's Own Story* (John R. Stanton, 1917).

Edith Warburton, *The Crescent and the Cross* (Edgewood Publishing Co., n.d.).

Samuel Warren, *Now and Then*, (New York: Harper, 1861).

*Wesleyan's Next Century* (Wesleyan University, 1931).

Wayne Whipple, *The Story of the American Flag* (Philadelphia: Henry Altemus, 1910)—"Charles J. Olson Jr. Christmas 1917 From Irene & Elizabeth 4 Norman Ave."

Luthera Whitney, *Old-Time Days and Ways* (Boston: Lothrop, 1883).

Jack Wilbur, *Word Pictures of 52 All American Personalities* (New York: Clement-Smith-Rogers, n.d.).

James Albert Winans, *Public Speaking* (New York: Century, 1926).

Homer E. Woodbridge, *Essentials of English Composition* (New York: Harcourt Brace, 1920).

Worcester Bank and Trust Co. *Forty Immortals of Worcester and Its County* (1920).

*Worcester School Dictionary*

Johann Wyss, *Swiss Family Robinson* (Chicago: M. A. Donohue, n.d.)—"Charles Olson Jr. 4 Norman Ave Worcester PR Please Return."

Appended here is a list of childhood books that appear to have been purchased by Olson for his children, more particularly, given the date of some of them, for Charles Peter, born 12 May 1955.

*Andersen's Fairy Tales*—title page missing.

Gustav Eckstein, *Everyday Miracle* (New York: Harper, 1958).
*The Enchanted Pony* (1959—previously cited).
Genevieve Mayberry, *Eskimo of Little Diomede* (Chicago, Follett, 1961).
Eleanor G. Vance, *Adventures of Robin Hood* (New York: Random House, 1953).

# *Epilogue*

On 19 May 1991 I visited Paul Cardone at 28 Fort Square, Gloucester, Massachusetts. It was a Sunday afternoon, and his children and grandchildren came and stayed and went in the customary Sunday extended get-together fashion. In the midst of this happy bustle I was able to see the copy of *Olson/Melville* that Olson had inscribed "for all the Cardones and for my other neighbors of the Fort" at the time of its publication, 23 February 1969. I was also able to read Olson's letter of 3 November 1964 to Mrs. Suzie Cardone. This was when, after Bet's death, he was getting back to work for his second year at Buffalo, and he had forgotten his Gloucester rent: "very dumb." He mentions that it has been reported to him that Charles Peter (his son stayed in Gloucester that year) "seems very much better in school." He continues, referring to the university at Buffalo: "I on the contrary *am not*, in fact *don't like school*, and wish I was home with you all."

I told Paul Cardone of my interest in seeing 28 Fort Square preserved for future generations as "Charles Olson's House," as a memorial, a museum, and an active research center. With this thought he fully concurred. And when I told him that, to this end, I had been collecting a replica of Olson's library so that the flat could some day be restored and be full of books in the way Olson had it, Paul took me to the back porch where there were several boxes of books, and said, "Some of those were Olson's." He explained that when Olson was not well, Mrs Cardone would take him up some soup and chat, and would often come back down with a book. Mrs. Cardone has passed away, so there was no way of knowing for sure which of the books might have come from Olson, but I went through them all, and with great pleasure picked out a few volumes that, because of the date and subject matter, might fall into that category. None of them have inscriptions or any other Olson markings, so the following list is entirely conjectural. However, the circumstantial evidence is positive, and when Paul Cardone looked at the dozen or so books I brought back into the living room he said, "Yes, those would be Olson's."

Ananda K. Coomaraswamy, *Christian and Oriental Philosophy of Art* (New York: Dover Publications, 1956)

T. S. Eliot, *The Complete Poems and Plays 1909–1950* (New York: Harcourt, Brace & Company—1960 printing)

Creighton Gabel, ed., *Man Before History* (Englewood Cliffs, New Jersey: Prentice-Hall, The Global History series paperback—1967 printing)

Carl Gustav Jung, *Psychology and Religion* (New Haven: Yale University Press—1950 printing)—ex-library Grahm Junior College.

George F. Kennan, et al., *Democracy and the Student Left* (Boston: Little, Brown & Company, 1968—second printing)

Jean-Dominique Lajoux, *The Rock Paintings of Tassili* (Cleveland: The World Publishing Company, 1963)

V. I. Lenin, *Imperialism, the Highest Stage of Capitalism* (Peking: Foreign Language Press, 1965)

Karl Marx, *The Civil War in France* (Peking: Foreign Languages Press, 1966)

Robert S. McNamara, *The Essence of Security* (New York: Harper & Row, 1968)

Mary Chalmers Rathbun and Bartlett H. Hayes, Jr., *Layman's Guide to Modern Art* (New York: Oxford University Press, 1949)

Nancy Wilson Ross, ed., *The World of Zen* (New York: Appleton-Century-Crofts, 1955)

Frederick M. Watkins, *The Age of Ideology—Political Thought, 1750 to the Present* (Englewood Cliffs, New Jersey: Prentice-Hall, 1965)—ex-library Grahm Junior College.

To this list can be added two boys' books. The first might have been Olson's, the second possibly Charles Peter's:

James Otis, *The Minute Boys of the Wyoming Valley* (Boston: Dana Estes, 1906)

Edward W. and Marguerite P. Dolch, *Stories from Alaska* (Champaign, Ill.: Garrard, 1961).

# Notes

# Index

# Notes

## Introduction

1. *Massachusetts Review* 12 (Winter 1971): 43–44. This article is a revised version of "Charles Olson: A Tribute," *Wesleyan Alumnus* 54 (Summer 1970):36. Olson also appears in Wilbert Snow's autobiography, *Codline's Child* (Middletown: Wesleyan University Press, 1974), pp. 332–35. We find two of Snow's poetry books in Olson's library: *Sonnets to Steve* (New York: Exposition Press, 1957), and *Spruce Head* (Rockland, Me.: Seth Low Press, 1959).

2. In 1965, when John Clarke made a list of books in Olson's apartment in Gloucester ("Clarke's list"), Olson owned Robert Frost's *West-Running Brook* (New York: Holt, 1928), though it was not in his library later. *A Pocket Book of Robert Frost's Poems* (New York: Washington Square Press, 1946) survived in his library.

3. *Scribner's Magazine* 97 (June 1935): 328–33. A journal entry indicates that Olson had read the piece by 9 July 1935. George Butterick found the periodical stored with other papers and books in Mrs. Sullivan's attic in Worcester, Massachusetts (*OLSON* 7:69).

4. Bob Callahan, ed., "The Correspondences: Charles Olson and Carl Sauer," *New World Journal* 4 (Spring 1979):160. Olson wrote to Sauer, "I figure you alone cld be the Diderot." Sauer replied: "Frankly I think this is one of your weaker ideas" (p. 162). Olson's library contained nothing by Diderot; he does not seem to have been mentioned after this.

5. Ralph Maud, "Notes Made After Visiting Charles Olson on Saturday 6 June 1969," *Iron* 12 (1971).

6. Anyone who presented Olson with a volume which is not mentioned in the present listing should not necessarily be dismayed; it was probably passed on by him with good intent. When I sent him clippings from the *Western Mail* of articles by Richard Deacon that later formed his book, *Madoc and the*

*Discovery of America* (London: Frederick Muller, 1967), Olson told me in a letter that he gave them to a Welsh woman he met and with whom he raised the subject. My own *Entrances to Dylan Thomas' Poetry* (University of Pittsburgh Press, 1963) that I presented to Olson personally in Wyoming, New York, on publication, was not later among his books. I do not assume he disparaged it.

## 1. What Didn't Olson Read?

1. Beyond the 1932 journal reading notes for *Sanctuary*—presumably the then newly published J. Cape and H. Smith edition (New York, 1931)—and the allusion to *Doctor Martino and Other Stories* (New York: Harrison Smith and Robert Haas, 1934), there is no evidence Olson read Faulkner. In a letter to his friend Monroe Engel at Viking Publishers in April 1949, Olson requests a Viking Portable title, and adds "in a whisper, so that no one else sees my blushes—do you think, maybe, the Faulkner?" If he received the Portable Faulkner, it was read covertly and discarded.

2. A carbon copy of the original typescript prepared for students at Black Mountain College was found by George Butterick among a group of Olson's papers from 1953, and published with a title taken from its first sentence, "Starting fr where you are . . . " in *OLSON* 2, pp. 32–36.

3. *OLSON* 2, p. 33. In spite of recommending him here, Olson kept no Dickens in his library, nor a copy of René LeSage's *Gil Blas*. Nothing of Proust survived. Olson's holdings in the other authors will be cited later.

4. Olson's notes from a diary of January 1940 are quoted by Butterick in his "Preliminary Report" under Thomas Mann, *Joseph and his Brothers* (New York: Knopf, 1934), probably a borrowed copy of the four volumes in one. "These notes end the 2nd vol. of Mann's Joseph books. I did not continue with Joseph & Egypt, for by this time Mann is a pall . . . a man to be used by other writers, but himself not a creator—he is a prime ex. of the diff. between a writer & a creator."

5. In a postcard of 30 March 1949 responding to her word "joy-i-city," Olson told Frances Boldereff he wanted to put a nix on a piece he had just read in *Harper's Bazaar* for April 1949, "James Joyce: A Sketch" by Desmond Harmsworth. The following books were designed and published by Frances Boldereff herself under the imprint "Classic Non-fiction Library" from her home in Woodward, Pennsylvania: *Reading Finnegans Wake* (1959)—"For Charles—A gift in return for so many"; *A Blakean Translation of Joyce's Circe* (1965)—"For Charles, because he 'holds hard' "; *Hermes to his Son Thoth: Being Joyce's Use of Giordano Bruno in Finnegans Wake* (1968)—"For Charles—What came out of the Woodward nights." It appears that Olson read them rather fitfully.

6. "Interview in Gloucester, August 1968," *Muthologos* 2, p. 102. Olson's

marked copy of *A Portrait of the Artist as a Young Man* (New York: Modern Library, 1928) looks as though it was used in a college course. His *Dubliners* (New York: Modern Library, n.d.), on the other hand, is unmarked. A journal indicates Olson was reading *Ulysses* in January–February 1934, soon after the publication of his copy (New York: Random House, 1934), which is heavily annotated. His lightly-marked *Finnegans Wake* (New York: Viking, 1939) was presumably a farewell gift in June 1939 when Olson left Harvard; seven undergraduates inscribe it "To Charlie—whose teaching and friendship has meant more to us than anything in college." From M. C. Richards of Black Mountain College he had *Stephen Hero* (London: Jonathan Cape, 1944), though he later deposited it with Jean Kaiser rather than keep it around. During his time at Buffalo, Olson acquired from Oscar Silverman his edition of Joyce's previously unpublished manuscript *Daniel Defoe* (Buffalo: SUNY Buffalo Studies, 1964), which he retained in his library.

7. *Creeley Correspondence* 5, p. 49, included in "Mayan Letters," *Selected Writings*, p. 82. This letter of 8 March 1951 continues with a further thought of Joyce as "Commercial Traveller": "the worship of IARichards—by the same people, accurately enough, who mug Joyce—is more honest: that is, that this internationalizing of language is more relevant to commerce, now, than it is to the aesthetic problem." Olson apparently knows of I. A. Richards and his work with "Basic English," though he owned none of his volumes. Olson had, by the way, one volume by Samuel Beckett: *All That Fall* (New York: Grove Press, 1957).

8. Robert Duncan, taped interview quoted in Ann Charters's Introduction to *Special View of History*, p. 9. Olson tells the story of Pound and *Finnegans Wake* in, for instance, "Reading at Berkeley," *Muthologos* 1, p. 129.

9. Butterick went through these diaries after he had completed his main listing of "Olson's Reading: A Preliminary Report," so these titles all appeared in the "Addenda" in *OLSON* 7.

10. Letter to Wilbert Snow, Olson's thesis advisor, who would have read on p. 156 of the thesis that Tomlinson's preface to the 1929 Dutton edition of *Pierre* was "the best study of Pierre that has been written." According to Olson's inscription on the flyleaf of his copy of the Dutton edition, he tried to give the book to Cornelius Kruse, another of his professors, for Christmas 1933, but it apparently found its way back on to his own shelves.

11. The inscription to the woman who became Connie Olson is dated "Oceanwood Gloucester June 1940." The book stayed with Olson after the separation, as did another such gift, Thornton Wilder's *The Ides of March* (New York: Harper, 1948), which Olson referred to at Berkeley as "that marvellous book of his on the days of Caesar and Catullus" (*Muthologos* 1, p. 146).

12. The few marks (possibly not Olson's) in his copy of Sherwood Ander-

son's *Many Marriages* (New York: B.W. Huebsch, 1923) do not lead us to a "blueberry" passage; indeed, there is none. There is a walk into the country-side (pp. 177–180) for love, not blueberries. (Perhaps Olson equated the two.)

13. *OLSON* 2, p. 32. If Olson had specified a dictionary it would have been the one he always kept at hand: *Webster's Collegiate Dictionary*, 5th ed. (Spring-field: Merriam, 1945). Olson owned the 11th edition of *The Encyclopaedia Britannica* (New York, 1910–11), twenty-nine volumes, much used, as Butterick's listing of notes and markings indicates. Olson also owned and used *Encyclopaedia Biblica* (New York: Macmillan; London: Adam & Charles Black, 1914), and *The Century Dictionary and Cyclopedia*, 10 vols. (New York: Century Co., 1899).

14. "About 1955, he began calling his course 'the Present'; before coming to class, everyone was to have read *The New York Times* and the *Asheville Citizen-Times*—and from there Olson winged it" (Duberman, *Black Mountain*, p. 432). Olson appears to have been an inveterate reader of *Time* and lunch-counter newspapers of all sorts, especially the *Gloucester Daily Times* when in Gloucester.

15. "Death in the Afternoon," *Wesleyan Cardinal* (February 1933): 42–45. Olson was later attracted to Eudora Welty's statement in "The Reading and Writing of Short Stories," *Atlantic Monthly* 183 (February 1949): 54–58 and (March 1949): 46–49 that all the American "novelists" are "in fact no such thing, but short story writers"—as he paraphrases her in *OLSON* 2, p. 33. He kept Welty's *Short Stories* (New York: Harcourt, Brace, 1949) on his shelves, but none of her novels.

16. Fielding Dawson to his sister and her husband, published as "A Letter from Black Mountain," *OLSON* 2, pp. 4–7, quotation on p. 6. A letter of Olson's to Dawson 22 January 1950 includes the comment: "right you are Saroyan is different—he has a little something, no question." This does not mean Olson owned any Saroyan.

17. This list does not include novels found to be pertinent to concerns dealt with elsewhere, and therefore cited later.

Michael Arlen, *The Green Hat* (London: Collins, 1924).
Dom Byrne, *The Wind Bloweth* (New York: Century, 1922)—ex libris Richard P. Doherty.
Raymond Chandler, *The High Window* (New York: Pocket Books, 1969).
Lionel Davidson, *Night of Wenceslas* (New York: Avon, 1960).
André Gide, *Lafcadio's Adventures* (New York: Vintage, 1960).
Robert Graves, *Count Belisarius* (New York: Random House, 1938).
Robert Graves, *Hercules, My Shipmate* (New York: Creative Age Press, 1945).
John Clellon Holmes, *The Horn* (New York: Fawcett, 1959).

George Macdonald, *Visionary Novels: Lilith, Phantastes* (New York: Noonday, 1954).

Walter M. Miller, *A Canticle for Leibowitz* (Philadelphia: Lippincott, 1960)— comment in letter to Creeley, 22 January 1962.

Flann O'Brien, *At Swim-two-birds* (New York: Viking, 1966).

18. Fitzgerald and Mauriac were not represented in Olson's library, but Georges Simenon was: *Inspector Maigret and the Killers* (Garden City: Doubleday, 1954), *The Train* (New York: Pocket Books, 1968), and *The Premier* (New York: Pocket Books, 1968). The edition of John Stuart Mill's *On Liberty* that Olson read is unknown. Kenneth Patchen's "new poems" would have been *"Orchards, Thrones and Caravans"* (San Francisco: The Print Workshop, 1952), but the volume did not remain in Olson's library.

19. Fielding Dawson, *The Black Mountain Book*, p. 97. It is apparently Dreiser the social commentator that Olson was talking about, linking him with Henry Luce of *Time* and "Toynbee—Huge Christian journalist."

20. Olson had in his library a collected Poe (cited later), but no Maupassant or W. W. Jacobs. Writing to Creeley in the same vein around this time (24 June 1951), Olson wondered if "we are a part of the same drive which Tennessee Williams, god help us, or Bowles, are only false agents of" (*Creeley Correspondence* 6, p. 74). Olson had no Tennessee Williams or Paul Bowles. The quotation is from *Corman Correspondence*, pp. 166–67.

21. *Creeley Correspondence* 5, pp. 128–29. Olson had no Hecht in his library, but retained two offprints by C. H. Graham: "Psychophysics and Behavior," *Journal of General Psychology* 10 (April 1934): 299–310, and "Vision: 3. Some Neural Correlations," chapter 15 in *A Handbook of General Experimental Psychology* (Worcester: Clark University Press, 1934), pp. 829–79, a volume to which Hecht had contributed. Olson had stated the same sentiments about Graham and Hecht on 21 October 1950 in *Corman Correspondence*, p. 41. Apparently all three were at Clark University together 1934–36.

22. Jack Clarke noted the titles at 28 Fort Square in 1965 ("Clarke's list"). Those remaining in the collection at Storrs are: *Aaron's Rod* (New York: Grosset & Dunlap, 1930), *The Plumed Serpent (Quetzalcoatl)* (New York: Knopf, 1951), *The Rainbow* (New York: Modern Library, n.d.), *The Trespasser* (London: Duckworth, 1912), and *The White Peacock* (London: Dent's Everyman Library, 1949). The non-fiction *Apocalypse* (New York: Viking, 1932) also disappeared after being on "Clarke's list."

23. Letter of 23 July 1951 (*Creeley Correspondence* 6, p. 189). In a letter the previous April, Olson had stressed how responsive Lawrence was in *Kangaroo* to the landscape, "the Bush and the Pacific" (*Creeley Correspondence* 5, p. 148).

24. *Human Universe*, p. 112. Olson would have had his copy of *Studies in*

*Classic American Literature* (New York: Boni, 1930) at least by 15 March 1939, when in a dated note (at Storrs) he speaks of "vocative prose" and cites Lawrence and William Carlos Williams. Conceivably, Olson's first entry into Lawrence may have been through the review of *In the American Grain* found in *Phoenix: The Posthumous Papers of D. H. Lawrence* (New York: Viking, 1936), pp. 334–36, a volume Olson definitely read even though it was not found later in his library. He refers to the review in discussing *In the American Grain*—(*Creeley Correspondence* 7, p. 83).

The 1930 volume was put aside (it turned up later in the Jean Kaiser collection), and Olson bought *Studies in Classic American Literature* (Garden City: Doubleday Anchor Book, 1953) on publication. "I am more moved than ever," he wrote to Ronald Mason on 25 June 1953, "by his Open Road declaration—and his insights, into us." The only copy of the Anchor edition extant at Storrs bears the signature "Betty Kaiser" on the flyleaf, possibly a copy acquired by Olson's wife before they met.

25. Besides notes on *Etruscan Places* (presumably he was reading the 1932 Viking edition), this same "Key West" notebook shows that Olson was led by Lawrence into perusing Havelock Ellis's *Studies in the Psychology of Sex* (presumably the two-volume Random House edition, 1936–42). He based two poems on dreams described in Ellis, calling them "translations" in manuscripts dated 11 March 1945 (*Collected Poems*, pp. 19–21).

26. Olson's "The Escaped Cock: Notes on Lawrence and the Real" was first published in *Origin* 2 (Summer 1951): 77–80, and included in *Human Universe* pp. 123–25, quotations from p. 123. "Clarke's list" indicates that Olson had a copy of *The Man Who Died* in 1965 (presumably the 1931 Knopf edition), but since he knew of the publication of Lawrence's *Sun* by Black Sun Press in 1928, he might also have come across the Black Sun edition of *The Escaped Cock* (1929).

27. *Selected Poems* with an introduction by Kenneth Rexroth in the New Classics Series (New York: New Directions, 1947). "Clarke's list" also includes the poetry volumes *Amores* (New York: Huebsch, 1916) and *Tortoises* (New York: Thomas Seltzer, 1921).

28. Letters of 9 and 10 March 1950 to Frances Boldereff describe the occasion, discussed in Ralph Maud, "Dylan Thomas and Charles Olson," *Planet* 68 (April-May 1988): 68–72. In a letter to Ronald Mason on 13 July 1953, Olson includes Thomas with "the saddest ones . . . who think reality is desolation. Imagine! that a reality like ours shld be taken so!" He has read three Thomas poems out loud to a student audience at Black Mountain, presumably from the newly published *Collected Poems*, though Thomas was later represented in Olson's library only by *Under Milk Wood* (New York: New Directions Paperbook, 1954).

29. Letter to Monroe Engel, 15 and 17 March 1950. It was thought then

that Mark Schorer would be doing the edition: "i have now wept two nights straight over Schorer and the Collected Poems." Olson kept and annotated Mark Schorer's article, "Magic as an Instrumental Value: Blake and Yeats," *Hemispheres* 2 (Spring 1945):49–54.

30. Olson called Aldington a nasty name in a letter to Frances Boldereff on 29 June 1950, after he had dipped into *D. H. Lawrence: Portrait of a Genius But . . .* (New York: Duell, Sloan & Pearce, 1950), acquired on publication. Nevertheless, Olson kept in his library Aldington's *D. H. Lawrence: An Indiscretion* (Seattle: University of Washington Book Store chapbook 1927), which Olson presumably picked up in Seattle in August 1947. He also owned Frieda Lawrence, *"Not I, But the Wind . . . "* (New York: Viking, 1934), and Harry T. Moore, *The Intelligent Heart: The Story of D. H. Lawrence* (New York: Farrar, Straus and Young, 1954). He read but did not own *D. H. Lawrence: A Personal Record* by "E. T." (Jessie Chambers), presumably the 1936 Knopf edition.

## 2. The Boy Historian and Anecdotes of Late Wars

1. Letter to Edward Dahlberg, 24 July 1950. Olson adds that "there at Spottsylvania, at the Bloody Angle, on the edge of the woods, I stumbled on an abatis, with the sticks still sharpened and raised like snakes to impale a Fed coming in from the forest." We find in Olson's papers the National Geographic Map of the "Southeastern United States" (1947), which he might have used for these excursions.

2. Letter to Caresse Crosby around 30 March 1953. The Civil War book was "planned for fall"; but whatever specific publisher Olson hoped for—back in 1951 it had been Giroux (*Creeley Correspondence* 7, p. 221)—none emerged in the end.

3. Fourteen of the sixteen sections of Benson J. Lossing, *A History of the Civil War 1861–65 and the causes that led up to the great conflict* (New York: The War Memorial Association, 1912) are extant in Olson's library. Captain Hazelton, *Daring Enterprises of Officers and Men* (Washington: National Tribune, 1899) may be another family book that Olson retained. Olson kept the copy of *Hound and Horn* 7 (October-December 1933) in which he had marked Charles Flato's article, "Matthew B. Brady: 1823–1896," pp. 35–41, and later purchased James D. Horan, *Matthew Brady: Historian With a Camera* (New York: Crown, 1955). An unpublished "Memo to a publisher," 17 July 1950, wished to give proper prominence to a colleague of Brady's, Alexander Gardner: "3 quarters of the scenes of the Army of the Potomac were made by him" (quoted in the notes to *Creeley Correspondence* 7, p. 270) This information about Gardner appears to have come from p. 42 of *The Photographic History of the Civil War in Ten Volumes*, published by The Review of Reviews (New York, 1912). This is the work cited in "The Post Office" quotation, though not preserved in Olson's library.

4. Samuel J. Muscroft, *The Drummer Boy; or The Battle-field of Shiloh* (Worcester: C. Hamilton, 1888), "Presented at the Worcester Theatre January 10, 11, 12, 13, and 14, 1899" (Library of Congress catalog).

5. The title Olson remembers in "The Post Office" passage, Joseph A. Altsheler, *The Rock of Chickamauga* (New York: Appleton, 1915), the final volume of six in a Civil War series, was not preserved by Olson. The Altshelers he kept (cited later) were of "The French and Indian War Series."

6. Letter to Ezra Pound, 29 July 1946. A journal entitled "Enniscorthy— June 46" contains Olson's reading notes on Douglas Southall Freeman's *R. E. Lee: A Biography* (New York: Scribner, 1940). He did not own the volumes.

7. First published as Jargon Broadside no. 1 (1955), this anti-romantic poem mocks such works as Frank Moore, *Anecdotes, Poetry, and Incidents of the War: North and South, 1860–1865* (New York: by subscription, 1866). Albert Glover found a copy of this tome for Olson in 1966, but the poet was no doubt aware of it in the early fifties, as he was aware of the other volume Frank Moore edited: *The Rebellion Record: A Diary of American Events, with Documents, Narratives, Illustrative Incidents, Poetry, Etc.*, 11 vols. with supplement (New York 1861–68), referring to it in a letter to Creeley, 1 October 1951, as "the craziest collection of all, like all the Egyptians, Greeks, Babylonians, and Phoenicians, putting down all that happened—wild tales, of guys, behind the lines, home, etc etc" (*Creeley Correspondence* 7, p. 222).

8. This incident is taken from p. 191 of the first of the four-volume *Battles and Leaders of the Civil War*, edited by Robert Underwood Johnson and Clarence Clough Buel (New York: Century Co., 1887). Olson borrowed Theodore Dreier's set at Black Mountain College and it stayed in his possession. He probably used G. F. R. Henderson, *Stonewall Jackson and the American Civil War*, 2 vols. (London: Longmans, Green, 1903) for the poem, though he purchased his copy later, 20 November 1956. He certainly read Kenneth Williams, *Lincoln Finds a General* in 1960 when the last of the four volumes had been published (New York: Macmillan, 1949–59)—"I read Kenneth Williams on Grant," he wrote in the poem " 'abt the dead he sd . . . ' " (*Collected Poems*, p. 500)—but volumes 1 and 2 were out in time for "Anecdotes of the Late War." Olson also owned Lloyd Lewis, *Captain Sam Grant* (Boston: Little Brown, 1950) and paperbacks of books he might have consulted first in their hardcover editions: Fletcher Pratt, *A Short History of the Civil War (Ordeal by Fire)* (New York: Pocket Books, 1956), Burke Davis, *To Appomattox* (New York: Popular Library, 1960), and Bruce Catton, *Mr. Lincoln's Army* (New York: Pocket Books, 1964). Olson marked throughout his copy of Nathaniel W. Stephenson's "A Theory of Jefferson Davis," *American Historical Review* 21 (October 1915): 73–90, but more prominent in the poem is Nathan Bedford Forrest. One wonders if Olson hadn't seen Robert Selph Henry, *"First With the Most" Forrest* (Indianapolis: Bobbs-Merrill, 1944), though there is no specific evidence that he did. Olson retained in his

library two historical novels pertinent to the Civil War: Nathaniel Beverley Tucker's *The Partisan Leader,* edited for the America Desiderata series by Carl Bridenbaugh (New York: Knopf, 1933), concerning the pre-War years, and Hollister Noble's *Woman with a Sword: The Biographical Novel of Anna Ella Carroll of Mayland* (Garden City: Doubleday, 1948), which Olson annotated heavily, especially noting the documentary sources and the map of "The Strategy that Won the Civil War." Olson also owned Matthew Forney Steele, *American Campaigns,* vol. 2, War Dept. Document no. 324 (Washington, D.C.: War Dept., 1909).

9. Olson's copy of W. E. Woodward's *Years of Madness* (New York: Putnam, 1951) was probably given to Harvey Brown from which to set the reprint. Olson's library contained two copies of the reprint (Cleveland: Frontier Press, 1967).

10. Olson did not own this book, but a journal indicates he read it in June 1945. In "Unsticking the Sun," notes for a class dated 10 February 1952 (at Storrs), Olson is telling his students to read *George Washington* "by the man who was first a poor novelist and added the word BUNK to our language as the title of his first novel." Therefore, Olson had seen, even if he didn't own, Woodward's novel *Bunk* (New York: Harper, 1923).

11. On his visit Olson obtained the pamphlet *Yorktown: Climax of the Revolution,* edited by Charles E. Hatch and Thomas M. Pitkin, National Park Service Source Book Series, no. 1 (Washington: U.S. Department of the Interior, 1941). He also owned U.S. Senate Document 318, 71st Congress, 3d Session (Washington, 1931): H. J. Eckenrode, "The Story of the Campaign and Siege of Yorktown," pp. 1–54, along with Senate Document 322, Gaspard de Gallatin, "Journal of the Siege of Yorktown in 1781," pp. 3–15. Olson later acquired the Massachusetts Historical Society Picture Book, Paul Revere's *Three Accounts of his Famous Ride* (Boston, 1961)—for his son? Even if we add that there is record of his borrowing James K. Hosmer, *Samuel Adams* (Boston: Houghton Mifflin, 1893) from Sawyer Free Library, Gloucester, in October 1959, we are still not discovering a great demonstration of interest in the Founding Fathers.

12. Olson did not keep the "Official Program" from which the following passage is taken, but only the program from the Pageant evening itself: "*Gloucester*": *A Pageant-Drama of New England's Oldest Fishing Town,* published by the author, James R. Pringle (Manchester, 1923), who went on to edit *The Book of the Three Hundredth Anniversary Observance of the Foundation of the Massachusetts Bay Colony at Cape Ann in 1623 and the Fiftieth Year of the Incorporation of Gloucester as a City* (Gloucester, 1924), which Olson owned and used.

## 3. A Model Student—Phi Beta Kappa, Wesleyan '32

1. Said of Olson on graduation from high school: "Gifted with a charming

personality, a sterling character and a keen mind, Charles has easily assumed the leadership of our class. A model student, he has guided successfully the student council and the Debating Assembly, where he has made a host of friends"—*Classical Myths* (Worchester: Classical High School Yearbook, Class of 1928), preserved by Olson in his library.

2. Charles Olson, "The Poetry of William Butler Yeats" (Wilbert Snow papers at Wesleyan University Library), p. 3: Irish literature has an "unaccountable, defiant, and titanic quality Arnold speaks of and Renan tries to explain." Olson is relying here on references to Arnold and Renan in Yeats's "The Celtic Element in Literature," *Ideas of Good and Evil* (New York: Macmillan, 1903) pp. 270–95.

3. All published in New York by Macmillan. *The Tower* was missing from Olson's library after 1965 ("Clarke's list"), as was *The Wild Swans at Coole* (New York: Macmillan, 1919), which Olson may also have acquired early. The college paper makes reference to *A Vision*, which at that time was only to be seen in the limited edition (London: T. Werner Laure, 1925), and to the following Yeats books from the library stacks, all Macmillan except the last: *Autobiographies* (1927), *Plays in Prose and Verse* (1924), *Plays and Controversies* (1924), and *A Packet for Ezra Pound* (Dublin: Cuala Press, 1929).

4. "A Teacher's View," *Massachusetts Review* 12 (Winter 1971): 42. There is an endearing quality to the young Olson's preference for Yeats's early poems over those of the newly published *The Tower* (1928) and his innocent conclusion: "Yeats is not as great as Keats or Shelley, but he takes front rank in the minor poets of our literature, I should say. I am inclined to place him ahead of Swinburne and Rossetti. Yeats and Francis Thompson easily step to the front among the poets of the last fifty years" (p. 33). Olson owned (perhaps by this time?) *The Poetical Works of Dante Gabriel Rossetti*, 2 vols. (Boston: Little, Brown, 1909) and Francis Thompson's *Poems* (London: Elkin Mathews & John Lane; Boston: Copeland, 1894), but no Swinburne.

5. Beneath its unusual form, the paper was seriously seeking "to study the influence of burlesque and negro minstrelsy upon the American theatre from around 1830 to the middle of the century." Olson's stated inspiration was Walter Pritchard Eaton's *The Drama in English* (1930). He referred often to the Dunlap Society Publications, 15 vols. (1887–91), particularly William Winter's *Brief Chronicles*. Other works listed as used are: Montrose Moses, *Fabulous Forrest* (1921), Harry Reynolds, *The Story of Burnt Cork Minstrelsy in Great Britain from 1836 to 1927* (1928), and Dailey Parkman and Sigmund Spaeth, *Gentlemen, Be Seated*. None of the works mentioned in connection with this topic are found in Olson's library.

6. This surviving p. 6 of the essay quotes from a work not mentioned elsewhere by Olson: Oliver Wendell Holmes, *Complete Writings* (Boston, 1904).

7. In the case of "Literary Criticism in Emerson," also done for Professor

Cowie (Storrs pages, presumably June 1932), Olson states: "The material for this study was derived fundamentally from" *The Complete Works of Ralph Waldo Emerson*, 12 vols. (Boston, 1903–4) and *The Journals of Ralph Waldo Emerson*, 10 vols. (Boston, 1909–14). Olson lists twenty scholarly works on Emerson consulted for the study plus manuscript letters in Concord Public Library and Harvard. No trace of anything by or on Emerson was later found in Olson's library.

The bibliography compiled for "Whitman and the Orient" included the following standard sources for the time:

Elsa Barker, "Did Whitman Borrow from the Orientals?" *Current Literature* 43 (August 1907): 165–66
Henry Bryan Binns, *A Life of Walt Whitman* (London: Methuen, 1905)
Arthur Christy, *The Orient in American Transcendentalism: A Study of Emerson, Thoreau, and Alcott* (New York: Columbia University Press, 1932)
Emory Holloway, *Whitman: An Interpretation in Narrative* (New York: Alfred A. Knopf, 1926)
Bliss Perry, *Walt Whitman* (Boston: Houghton Mifflin, 1908)
Horace L. Traubel, *With Walt Whitman in Camden*, vol. 1 (Boston: Small, Maynard, 1906)
Horace L. Traubel, et al., eds., *In Re Walt Whitman* (Philadelphia: D. McKay, 1893)
Walt Whitman, *The Complete Writings of Walt Whitman*, 10 vols. (New York and London: G. P. Putnam's Sons, 1902)
Walt Whitman, *The Uncollected Poetry and Prose of Walt Whitman*, ed. Emery Holloway (Garden City, N.Y. and Toronto: Doubleday, Page, 1921)

The only book that turns up in Olson's library is Horace Traubel, *With Walt Whitman in Camden (March 28–July 14, 1888)* (Boston: Small, Maynard, 1906), which he was reading on 27 March 1949 (letter to Merton Sealts the following day). The evidence is that he really got a feeling for Whitman only later. Frances Boldereff sent him a piece she had written on Whitman that, Olson says in his reply of 30 December 1949, "HAS FOR THE FIRST TIME IN MY LIFE GIVEN ME WHITMAN," leading him to read "The Children of Adam" and "Calamus." The Whitman Olson owned and annotated was *Leaves of Grass* (Philadelphia: David McKay, 1900).

8. In the call of duty Olson cites in the bibliography of his M.A. thesis: 3 "full-length biographies"; 13 "shorter biographical studies"; 31 "critical studies"; 37 articles in periodicals and newspapers 1846–1918; and 103 such articles after 1918. However, he cites no more than a dozen of these articles in his footnotes, and chiefly uses the three important Melville studies done up to that time:

John Freeman, *Herman Melville* (New York: Macmillan, 1926)—this copy is entirely without markings (perhaps a replacement for a previous copy).

Lewis Mumford, *Herman Melville* (New York: Harcourt, Brace, 1929)—flyleaf: "Charles J. Olson Jr." Extensive notes and markings.

Raymond Weaver, *Herman Melville, Mariner and Mystic* (New York: George H. Doran, 1921)—Olson's copy heavily marked. (Incidentally, he also owned Weaver's novel, *Black Valley* [New York: Viking, 1926] and was reading it in November 1952, after Weaver's death 5 April 1948.)

The other book from this time that Olson owned and marked— at least, the Melville chapter— was Van Wyck Brooks, *Emerson and Others* (New York: Dutton, 1927). A journal also records that he read Brooks's *Life of Emerson* (New York: Dutton, 1932) upon publication. We can cite here one further title from the M.A. bibliography that Olson came to own: Vega Curl, *Pasteboard Masks: Facts as Spiritual Symbol in the Novels of Hawthorne and Melville* (Cambridge: Harvard University Press, 1931).

9. Of the listed items, Olson owned two: Meade Minnigerode, *Some Personal Letters of Herman Melville and a Bibliography* (New York, New Haven, Princeton: The Brick Row Book Shop 1922)—with occasional markings; and Victor Hugo Paltsits, ed., *Family Correspondence of Herman Melville, 1830–1904, in the Gansevoort-Lansing Collection* (New York: New York Public Library, 1929)—cover: "Ex Libris—Charles J." Notes and markings throughout. A second copy, perhaps a gift from Paltsits himself when Olson visited him, was passed on to Professor Alec Cowie: "with whom I first read Melville," the inscription dated July 1934 (at Wesleyan). Paltsits later sent Olson his "Herman Melville's Background and New Light on the Publication of *Typee*," a reprint from *Bookmen's Holiday* (New York: New York Public Library, 1943), which Olson kept.

10. Olson did not own Samuel Butler's *The Way of All Flesh*, but his library contained *The Authoress of the Odyssey* (London: Longmans, Green, 1897).

## 4. At Once Sane and Sensitive: Olson Before Dahlberg

1. William Trufant Foster, *Argumentation and Debating* (Boston: Houghton Mifflin, 1917).

2. Letter to Wilbert Snow, 2 December 1959: "do you realize it was at *your* house that I met W. B. Yeats, Carl Sandburg and Robert Frost! How much can a man serve up to another—when the other is nothing but an eye and an ear in a corner of the living room." One adds Vachel Lindsay, who was the invited poet at Wesleyan in April 1930, between Frost (February 1929) and Sandburg (March 1931). Yeats's visit was presumably during his American tour of 1932, but there is

nothing to confirm this in the *Wesleyan Argus*. Olson apparently spoke to Yeats about his mother's Irish ancestry, and records that "Yeats told me (on the grounds of my grandfather, who was the immigrant, 'born in Cork and brought up in Galway') that my mother's aunt must have been his 'Mary Hines,' the beloved of the blind poet Raftery and 'the most beautiful woman in all Western Ireland' " (*Additional Prose*, p. 39). Olson later passed this along as a compliment to his mother on Mother's Day, 1946, quoting to her the lines on Mary Hynes in "The Bounty of Sweden," which he found in his copy of Yeats's *Dramatis Personae* (New York: Macmillan, 1936), p. 189. Olson had no Sandburg or Lindsay in his library and only a modicum of Frost (cited in the Introduction).

3. H. W. Fowler, *A Dictionary of Modern English Usage* (Oxford, 1927)—special American edition for Putnam's, New York. Flyleaf inscribed by the poet's father: "To Charles J. Olson Christmas 1928." Olson acquired H. W. and F. G. Fowler, *The King's English*, 3d ed. (Oxford, 1930), presumably on publication. His copy of *Roget's International Thesaurus*, edited by Mawson, is the 1925 edition of Thomas Y. Crowell, New York. Dictionaries presumably acquired early include *Hugo's Pocket Dictionary: German-English and English-German* (Philadelphia: David McKay, 1933)—initially inscribed to his father: "Mr Charles Olsen With kind regards to both of you B Belland".

4. According to the *Wesleyan Argus*, Olson took part in the following productions, basically light fare. Olson did not keep the scripts for further use: Moliere's *Doctor in Spite of Himself* (December 1928); William W. Pratt's *Ten Nights in a Bar-room* (April 1929); *Gammer Girton's Needle* (June 1929)—according to the newspaper, the Stuart Walker adaptation (strangely, the version Olson had stored in a Worcester attic was the Colin Campbell Clements adaptation, Samuel French, New York, 1922); Arthur Hopkins's *Moonshine* (March 1930); A. A. Milne's *Dover Road* (March 1930); Plautus's *Mostellaria*—translated by Professor Nicolson as "The Haunted House" (February 1931): and A. A. Milne's *Ivory Door* (March 1931).

The climax to all this work in drama was Olson's directing his own one-act play, *The Fish Weir*, on 28 May 1931. According to Butterick, who saw it printed in "the Wesleyan literary magazine" (which cannot at the moment be traced), it is "the story of a Gloucester fishing family that loses its only son to the sea" (*Fiery Hunt*, p. vii). In a letter to Gael Turnbull, 12 November 1958, Olson said it was via John Synge that "I wrote my first play, at 18." The one Synge mentioned in the college Yeats essay was *Riders to the Sea*. Olson acquired it later as one of *Three Irish Plays* (Boston: International Pocket Library, 1936)—the other two being Yeats's *Land of the Heart's Desire* and Douglas Hyde's *The Twisting of the Rope*.

*Three Irish Plays* may have been a class text when Olson taught in the English Department at Clark University, Worcester, 1934–36. He is known to have been involved in productions of O'Neill and Clifford Odets (probably *Awake and Sing*). Another playscript stored in Worcester from 1935 was George S. Kaufman and Marc Connelly, *Merton of the Movies* (New York: Samuel French, 1925); this could have been a Clark University production.

5. Letter to Wilbert Snow on 10 June 1933 from Oceanwood Cottage, Gloucester. Lewis Carroll was not an author found later in Olson's library: neither was Rabelais. Olson would be reading Raymond Radiguet's *Devil in the Flesh* (New York: Harrison Smith, 1932); the edition found later in his library was given him by Caresse Crosby, her 1948 Black Sun Press edition. The "Crane" mentioned would be the newly published *Collected Poems of Hart Crane*, ed. Waldo Frank (New York: Liveright, 1933); Olson had already culled an epigraph for his M.A. thesis from Crane's poem "At Melville's Tomb." This poem, it turns out, is discussed on pp. 77–79 of Elizabeth Drew, *Discovering Poetry* (New York: Norton, 1933), which a journal indicates Olson was reading 6 July 1933. He did not keep Drew; he kept Crane.

6. So we deduce from Olson citing Saintsbury, *Loci Critici* (Boston: Ginn, 1903) in his Emerson paper, and *A History of English Prose Rhythm* (London: Macmillan, 1912) in his M.A. thesis.

7. Olson knows much more of Aiken than he ever talks about (a hint of this in *OLSON* 5, p. 38): but, nevertheless, we find no Aiken in his library.

8. The two volumes mentioned were stored after 1957 with Jean Kaiser, along with *Further Poems of Emily Dickinson* (Boston: Little, Brown, 1929) and *Unpublished Poems of Emily Dickinson* (Boston: Little, Brown, 1936), leaving none of her work in his active library. Olson made his judgment on Emily Dickinson in the posthumously published Melville draft entitled "In Adullam's Lair" (probably late summer 1939), for instance: "Dickinson loved Christ but jilted Him and married Death. Her stretch and yawn for the grave strained her nature, poisoned it" (p. 8).

9. Except that, again, Olson put them in storage with Jean Kaiser, keeping only vol. 6 (which includes "The Purloined Letter"). Yet in his 1953 hand-out to his students at Black Mountain College, Olson praised Poe as a short-story writer, and also told them to read Poe's "The Poetic Principle" (*OLSON* 2, pp. 33–34). Olson kept in his library Hervey Allen, *Israfel: The Life and Times of Edgar Allan Poe* (New York: Farrar & Rinehart, 1934), a gift from Barbara Denny for Christmas 1934.

10. Both Botsford and West contain a label: "Property of City of Worcester 'Classical High School.' " Other candidates in this category that we find in Olson's library are: W. E. Lunt, *History of England* (New York: Harper, 1928)—the heavy marking in this volume is probably not by Olson: Henry Smith Williams, *Manuscripts, Inscriptions, and Monuments* (London: Merrill & Baker, 1902)—a portfolio; Holland Thompson and Arthur Mee, *The Book of Knowledge: The Children's*

*Encyclopedia* (New York: Grolier Society; London: The Educational Book Co., 1928)—only vol. 2 survived. Did Olson take biology in high school? He owned J. S. Kingsley, *The Dogfish (Acanthias): an Elasmobranch* (New York: Henry Holt, 1907)—"Guides for Vertebrate Dissection." Olson deposited with Jean Kaiser a high school gift, E. L. Highbarger's *The History and Civilization of Ancient Megara: Part One* (Baltimore: Johns Hopkins Press, 1927)—"For Charles— a brother scholar; may our interests and loves forever remain the same. Jim Beane."

11. Thilly was quoted in the M.A. thesis, mainly for Schopenhauer. Foerster, Kreymborg, and Lewisohn were cited in the college essay "Literary Criticism in Emerson." According to a diary, Æ (George William Russell) was read 11 September 1932 and Galsworthy 25 October 1932. None of these books was owned by Olson.

12. Randolph Bourne, *History of a Literary Radical and Other Essays* (New York: Huebsch, 1920)—flyleaf inscribed: "For Chas. Olson, my Ilium-Faith in His Towers—with deepest love, his devoted friend Edward Dahlberg Christmas '40 N.Y.C. 58 W. 8th St. " An interesting association is that the book's previous owner had been W. E. Woodward, the historian (his signature dated 14 May 1923). Olson later gave this volume to Jean Kaiser. However, he kept in his library Randolph Bourne's *The State* (New York: Resistance Press, 1946–47).

13. Note in "Journal, begun Sept. 1, 1936," quoted in John Cech, *Charles Olson and Edward Dahlberg*, p. 13. James Oneal wrote such books as *The Workers in American History* (1921) and *American Communism* (1927); A. M. Simons wrote *Social Forces in American History* (1911, reprinted 1929). There is no evidence that Olson got around to looking at these recommendations. Beard is represented in Olson's library only by a volume taken from Black Mountain college library (cited later).

Gorky does not appear on Olson' shelves, but he read him: "do you know gorky's days with lenin, AND his reminiscences of tolstoy?" Olson asked Creeley in a letter dated 9 June 1950, "excellent both" (*Creeley Correspondence* 1, p. 91). He owned the following books of a communist stamp:

R. Palme Dutt, *Fascism and Social Revolution: A Study of the Economics and Politics of the Extreme Stages of Capitalism in Decay* (New York: International Publishers, 1935)—no markings.

V. I. Lenin, *"Left-Wing" Communism: An Infantile Disorder* (New York: International Publishers, 1934)—no markings.

Karl Marx and Friedrich Engels, *The Communist Manifesto* (New York: Appleton-Century-Crofts Classics, 1955)—no markings.

Joseph Stalin, *Foundations of Leninism* (New York: International Publishers, 1939)—no markings.

Mao Tse-tung, *On Practice* (New York: International Publishers, n.d.)—no markings.

14. This volume, signed by Emma Goldman and inscribed to Olson by Dahlberg, was given to Harvey Brown for reprinting by Frontier Press. Olson had two books by another famous anarchist, Peter Kropotkin: *The Conquest of Bread* (New York: Putnam, 1907), and *Memoirs of a Revolutionist* (Boston: Houghton Mifflin, 1930)—flyleaf: "Charles Olson."

15. Cech, p. 13. In numerical order: 1. Lessing's *Laocoön* seems to have left no trace in Olson's writing or bookshelves. 2. Olson was reading Frazer's *The Golden Bough* on 12 January 1940 (letter to Waldo Frank); he bought the abridged edition upon publication in 1947 (cited later). 3. Waldo Frank's works are cited in note 16.) 4. Olson was, according to a diary, reading Jane Harrison, *Ancient Art and Ritual* (New York: Henry Holt Home University Library of Modern Knowledge, 1913) early in 1940. The book stayed in his library until at least 1965 ("Clarke's list"). According to a notebook, Olson was reading Miguel de Unamuno, *The Tragic Sense of Life* (London: Macmillan, 1921) in September 1939, but he did not acquire it nor Unamuno's *Life of Don Quixote* (New York: Knopf, 1927).

16. Olson wrote to Waldo Frank from Gloucester on August 1939: "I have read Markand and Bridegroom and reread them, and read again in Hispana, and the Jungle, and am about to read Dark Mother for the first time (I found Mother and Our America in a Boston bookstore on my first trip there last week) . . . I have, for two months and a half, lived with you, been moved and regenerated by your spirit." He is referring to Frank's *Death and Birth of David Markand* (New York: Scribner, 1934) and the then just-out novel *The Bridegroom Cometh* (New York: Doubleday, Doran, 1939); to the books of social criticism *America Hispana* (New York: Scribner, 1931) and *In the American Jungle* (New York: Farrar and Rinehart, 1937)—all these probably sent to him by Frank. He then refers to his new purchases: Frank's second novel, *The Dark Mother* (New York: Boni & Liveright, 1920) and his first nonfiction, *Our America* (New York: Boni & Liveright, 1919). On 4 April 1940, Olson back in Gloucester after meetings in New York with Frank among others, Frank's *Chart for Rough Water: Our Role in a New World* (New York: Doubleday, Doran, 1940) arrived in the mail and Olson immediately read it and wrote his deep appreciation: "such a one as I do thirst to have written and towards which I shall spend my life that one day I may approach you in speech to another generation who may be because by such a book you give us all a future."

There were no letters after 1940. There had been some talk of Olson collaboration on a book on Frank with M. J. Benardete, the editor of *Waldo Frank in America Hispana* (New York: Columbia University Instituto de las Espanas en los Estados Unidos, 1929), but it did not come off. It is not certain Olson read

*Re-Discovery of America* (New York: Scribner, 1929), which Dahlberg had originally recommended. In any case, none of Waldo Frank's books remained in Olson's library later, a sign of some kind of break that has still to be investigated.

17. "For Charles Olson, my dear, good, beautiful Friend, in orison & in belief in his Melville-vision—all love Edward Dahlberg." Olson read and thoroughly annotated *On Love;* on the front paper he writes "the orange groves of Genoa" taken from p. 23, and remembers this and other references when in "The Song and Dance of" in the *Maximus Poems* (1.56) he wants to say

As another such had it,

a writer, love was

Or ought to be,

like an orange tree!

A letter to Frances Boldereff, 21 February 1950, indicates that Olson enjoyed Stendhal's *Memoirs of an Egotist,* or at least the title. He bought and annotated Stendhal's *The Life of Henri Brulard* (New York: Vintage, 1955). Olson knew Stendhal's posthumously published "Les Cenci"; he mentions it in a poem *(Collected Poems,* p. 472), but it is not clear from what source.

18. A push not registered by Olson, however, in any letter or other writing. We only know of this gift from Dahlberg's mentioning of it (in terms of Olson's "ingratitude") in a letter to Isabella Gardner, 8 October 1957, ( Washington University Special Collections).

## 5. Melville's Reading: The Displaced Dissertation

1. Professor Lowes's *The Road to Xanadu* (Boston: Houghton Mifflin, 1927, revised 1930) was so much a "best-seller" around Harvard in the thirties that it is remarkable that anyone in Olson's position should escape having a copy. He certainly knew it, as he knew Lowes's *Geoffrey Chaucer and the Development of his Genius* (1934), which he makes a note of on the endpapers of F. N. Robinson's standard "Student's Cambridge Edition," *The Complete Works of Geoffrey Chaucer* (Boston: Houghton Mifflin, 1933), the text Olson used at Harvard, and kept. Olson also kept through the years the brochure for "An Exhibition of 15th Century Manuscripts and Books in Honor of the 600th Anniversary of Geoffrey Chaucer" (New York: the Rosenbach Co., 1940). When Olson adapted *Troilus* into a masque in 1948 he named Robert Henryson's *The Testament of Cressid* as a source.

Also pencilled into Robinson is a note that Kittredge's lectures on Troilus are "penetrating, even exciting." He did not own Kittredge's *Chaucer and His Poetry* (Cambridge: Harvard University Press, 1915), but he knew it as a "superb book," a model of "how to do *sources*" (letter to Jay Leyda, 7 March 1952).

In notes on a Harvard lecture by Perry Miller on 15 March 1939, Olson jotted down a reference to the Perry Miller book then in print, *Orthodoxy in Massachusetts 1630–1650* (Cambridge: Harvard University Press, 1933). Olson had the Beacon Press reprint (Boston 1959) "bot 1961," which he read 29–30 May 1966 and used in later *Maximus* poems. The lecture notes referred to "the coming Ramus," i.e., *The New England Mind: The Seventeenth Century* (New York: Macmillan, 1939). Olson did not own this volume but he may have consulted it in the Sawyer Free Library, Gloucester; he is known to have used Miller's *The New England Mind: From Colony to Province* (Cambridge: Harvard University Press, 1953) there. He picked up Perry Miller's paperback *The American Puritans, Their Prose and Poetry* (Garden City: Doubleday Anchor, 1956) on publication.

2. F. O. Matthiessen, *American Renaissance: Art and Expression in the Age of Emerson and Whitman* (New York: Oxford University Press, 1941), p. xviii. Olson knew of this book, of course, but no copy was in his library at the time of his death. What was there was Matthiessen's *Russell Cheyney, 1881–1945: A Record of His Work* (Andover, 1946)—flyleaf: "For Charlie with my very best regards from Matty." It is also known from "Clarke's list" that in 1965, Olson owned F. O. Matthiessen, *The Achievement of T. S. Eliot* (Boston: Houghton Mifflin, 1935).

3. *American Renaissance*, p. 458 n. Matthiessen acknowledges further indebtedness to Olson in footnotes on pp. 209, 413, and 415.

4. However, when Olson refers to Johann Eckermann on Goethe in a letter to the Black Mountain College faculty, 21 March 1952, and to Robert Creeley, 30 March 1952, he appears to be relying entirely on quotations found in the periodical *Four Pages* 8 (August 1948)—see *OLSON* 8, p. 33.

5. In a draft of a letter of 7 June 1934 to Professor Weber-Weidig (preserved at Storrs), he makes a revealing reply to a query: "I think perhaps you overestimate Rabelais, Sterne, and Carlyle's effect and neglect Smollett, Browne, and De Quincey's. . . . I should stress, among other English writers you did not mention, Burton, Defoe, and Shakespeare . . . Heine and Schiller were major interests of Melville (I am now working on his copies of their poems." This sort of comment does not settle absolutely the question of how much Olson read of a book in order to satisfy himself about its influence on Melville.

6. Melville read James Fennimore Cooper, but at the end Olson only had a paperback of *The Prairie* (New York: Washington Square Press, 1964). In a few cases, Olson seems to have made a deliberate purchase of a book because Melville had owned or used that title. Olson's copy of Edward T. Perkins, *Na Motu; or, Reef-Rovings in the South Seas* (New York: Pudney & Russell, 1854) is the same edition as Melville's, as is his copy of *Life and Remarkable Adventures of Israel R. Potter* (Providence: Printed by J. Howard for I. R. Potter, 1824) and *The Literary Life and Poetical Works of Victor Hugo* (New York: Hurst, 1883). Melville

owned Diogenes Laertius, *The Lives and Opinions of Eminent Philosophers* in the Bohn Classical Library (London, 1853); Olson obtained the 1891 printing. Melville had George Chapman, *The Odysseys of Homer, Translated According to the Greek,* 2 vols. (London: John Russell Smith, 1857); Olson had the 1874 printing. In the case of *Fables of La Fontaine,* trans. Elizur Wright, Jr., 2 vols. (1879), we find that Olson's edition is earlier (1841). We also imagine that Olson picked up J. A. Lempriere, *A Classical Dictionary,* 5th American ed. (1825) because he saw it was published in New York by Melville's publisher and friend, Evert Duyckinck. If Olson picked up William M. Christy's book-length poem, *Redburn; or the Schoolmaster of a Morning* (New York: by the author, 1845) because he thought it had something to do with Melville's *Redburn,* he would soon have discovered his mistake. He had two copies; would he make the same mistake twice?

7. He probably did not see Chase before his description of it in his 1933 M.A. thesis, but used a quotation from *Books, Autographs, Manuscripts* (New York: American Art Association-Anderson Galleries, 1932), the catalogue of the sale of 9 February 1932. This and the previous year's catalogue would have been shown to Olson by the gallery director himself, John Anderson. "He was a most distinguished man," Olson wrote to Merton Sealts (*Pursuing Melville,* p. 141), "did a *beautiful* book on Turner's drawings, built I think, on his own collection." Olson is here referring to a copy Anderson had inscribed to him on 3 May 1934 of his *The Unknown Turner* (New York: by the author, 1926). Unfortunately, Olson did not retain a copy of the 1932 sale catalogue, or that of the 1938 and 1945 sales catalogues (only an Anderson Galleries catalogue for *A Collector's Sale: Old Chinese Porcelain* was found in his papers). In the final stages of writing *Call Me Ishmael,* Olson made a special trip to New Bedford and Nantucket with some copy of Chase in hand or available to him there, for he wrote the "First Fact" (a section of *Call Me Ishmael*) on the ferry returning from Nantucket on 13 August 1945. He also picked up a few books along the way: Paul Johnston, *Thar She Blows: An Early New Bedford Whaling Yarn* (New York: Random House, 1931), presumably a gift of George H. Tripp of New Bedford; and from Zephaniah W. Pease, in person perhaps, his *Fifty Years on The Morning Mercury, New Bedford, Mass., 1880–1930* (New Bedford: Reynolds Printing, n.d.) and *A Visit to the Museum of the Old Dartmouth Historical Society* (New Bedford: Old Dartmouth Historical Society, 1943). Will Gardner, whom Olson thanks on page 29 of *Call Me Ishmael,* mailed him, soon after, his *Three Bricks and Three Brothers: The Story of the Nantucket Whale-Oil Merchant Joseph Starbuck* (Cambridge: Whaling Museum Publications, Nantucket Island, 1945), inscription dated 19 August 1945. Soon after this trip, Olson was able, via David Randall of Scribners, to get in touch with Perc S. Brown, who had just bought Melville's Chase volume at auction: he went to visit him in New Jersey,

copied out Melville's marginalia afresh, and published them for the first time in *Call Me Ishmael*, pp. 26–32. (The information from David Randall was passed to Olson via Howard Vincent—Robert Bertholf, "On Olson, His Melville," *Io* 22 (1976): 5–36.)

8. Olson told Ann Charters in conversation that he had also examined primary documents, the eye-witness testimonies of the crew of the "Globe" on their arrival in Valparaiso, and consular papers in the National Archives, Washington (*Olson/Melville*, p. 10). He picked up on publication the paperback William Lay and Cyrus M. Hussey, *A Narrative of the Mutiny on Board the Whale-ship Globe* (New York: Corinth, 1963).

9. Robert Bertholf's "On Olson, His Melville," *Io* 22 (1976): 5–36, reveals the source to have been Karl Brandt, *Whale Oil: An Economic Analysis* (Stanford: Stanford University Food Research Institute Fats and Oils Studies no. 7, June 1940). A Library of Congress call slip (preserved at Storrs) indicates that Olson consulted James T. Jenkins, *A History of the Whale Fisheries* (London, 1921). From the M.A. thesis, p. xiii, it is clear that Olson examined a pertinent Melville source: Melville's own copy of Obed Macy, *The History of Nantucket* (Boston: Hilliard, Gray, 1835).

10. Arthur Stedman's testimony, quoted in Sealts, *Melville's Reading*, p. 409. "In general I should agree with you on the Elizabethans as a major influence"—draft letter to Professor Weber-Weidig (cited above).

11. On the back of a Library of Congress user's card, Olson listed "Eliz I own April 1949." They are the following, all found in Olson's library later, except where indicated.

*The Works of Ben. Jonson* (London: Edward Moxon, 1838)—flyleaf: "Charles Olson Washington, Sept 1948."

*The Dramatic Works of Massinger and Ford* (London: Edward Moxon, 1848)—not at Storrs.

*The Works of John Marston*, ed. J. O. Halliwell, 3 vols., Library of Old Authors (London: John Russell Smith, 1856).

*The Plays of Christopher Marlowe*, Everyman's Library (London: Dent; New York: Dutton, 1926).

*Christopher Marlowe*, ed. Havelock Ellis, Mermaid Series (London: Unwin; New York: Scribner, 1893)—not at Storrs.

*John Ford*, ed. Havelock Ellis, Mermaid Series (London: Unwin; New York: Scribners, n.d.).

*Philip Massinger*, ed. Arthur Symons, 2 vols., Mermaid Series (London: Benn; New York: Scribner, n.d.).

*Thomas Heywood*, ed. A. Wilson Verity, Mermaid Series (London: Benn, n.d.)

*Beaumont and Fletcher*, ed. J. St. Loe Strachy, Mermaid Series (London: Unwin; New York: Scribners, 1887).

*Webster and Tourneur,* ed. John Addington Symonds, Mermaid Series (London: Unwin; New York: Scribner, 1903).

*Thomas Middleton,* ed. Havelock Ellis, Mermaid Series (London: Unwin; New York: Scribners, n.d.)—Storrs has vol. 1 of 2 vols., Olson's list is annotated: "but only vol. 1 (need vol. 2)."

*Thomas Dekker,* ed. Ernest Rhys, Mermaid Series (London: Benn, n.d.)—flyleaf: "Olson Wash April xlix."

*John Dryden,* ed. George Saintsbury, 2 vols. Mermaid Series (London: Unwin; New York: Scribners, n.d.)—not at Storrs; Olson's note on list: "but only vol. 2, need vol. 1."

*Robert Greene,* ed. Thomas H. Dickinson, Mermaid Series (London: Unwin, 1909).


In addition to this list, it is likely that some of the related writers found later in Olson's library were acquired around this time.

*Chapman's Dramatic Works,* vol 3 of 3 vols. (London: John Pearson, 1873).

*The Dramatic Works of John Webster,* ed. William Hazlitt, vols. 2 and 3 of 4 vols., Library of Old Authors (London: John Russell Smith, 1857).

John Dryden, *Dramatic Essays,* Everyman's Library (London: Dent; New York: Dutton, 1931)—flyleaf: "Charles John Olson." Notes and markings, especially in "On Translating the Poets."

*The Poems of Robert Greene, Christopher Marlowe, and Ben Jonson,* ed. Robert Bell (New York: Hurst, n.d.).

*Selected Poems from Skelton, Wyatt, and Surrey,* ed. J. Scott Clark (New York: Effingham, Maynard, 1892).


12. Of the two writers not on the previous list, George Peele was not later represented in Olson's library. Olson acquired and kept John Lyly, *Euphues, The Anatomy of Wit and Euphues and His England,* ed. Edward Arber (London: Constable, 1934); also *The Dramatic Works of John Lilly (The Euphuist),* ed. I. W. Fairholt, 2 vols., Library of Old Authors (London: John Russell Smith, 1858).

13. One cannot overemphasize the importance to Olson's research of Eleanor Melville Metcalf, Melville eldest granddaughter, nor their mutual respect. An early gift, inscribed "To Charles from Eleanor M. Metcalf," was Dorothy Wellesley's *Poems of Ten Years: 1924–1934* (London: Macmillan, 1934); to be followed by *Letters on Poetry from W. B. Yeats to Dorothy Wellesley* (London: Oxford University Press, 1940), an inscription dated April 1941; and by Eleanor's own *Poems,* privately printed (Cambridge, 1946), to which Olson responded fully in a letter of 17 May 1947 (carbon copy at Storrs). When she later edited *Journal of a Visit to London and the Continent by Herman Melville 1849–1850* (Cambridge: Harvard University Press, 1948), she inscribed Olson's copy "in

memory of long evenings before the fire at 27 Gray Gardens." She also presented him with her edition of family letters, *Herman Melville: Cycle and Epicycle* (Cambridge: Harvard University Press, 1953).

14. Philarète Chasles, *Anglo-American Literature and Manners* (New York: Scribner, 1852), deposited by Olson in Harvard College Library. This book presumably led him to the review referred to in the previous quotation, as cited in Olson's M.A. thesis on p. xx: " 'Voyages Reels et Fantastiques d' Herman Melville.' Chasles, Philarete. Revue des Deux Mondes 2 (new period): 541–570, May 15, 1849."

15. Postcard from Dahlberg, 14 September 1936, which goes on: "The sooner you start the better. Inaction spawns inferiority." In his next extant letter of 21 January 1937 he reiterates: "I wish you would settle some of the seething things within yourself by writing . . . why are you waiting?"

16. Draft letter to F. O. Matthiessen, end of July 1937. Olson owned and annotated two World Classics collections: D. Nichol Smith, ed., *Shakespeare Criticism: A Selection* (London: Oxford University Press, 1934) and Anne Bradby, ed., *Shakespeare Criticism 1919–35* (London: Oxford University Press, 1936). He acquired Caroline F. E. Spurgeon, *Shakespeare's Imagery and What It Tells Us* (New York: Macmillan, 1936), presumably secondhand ("Ray Willoughby" on flyleaf). The sheet of notes on "1st reading" *Coriolanus* laid in this volume precedes Olson's reading of Spurgeon. G. Wilson Knight, *The Wheel of Fire: Essays in Interpretation of Shakespeare's Sombre Tragedies* came to him as a gift from an unidentified donor—flyleaf: "for Charles from Charles 8 August 1937." The volume was extensively annotated. As for T. S. Eliot, Olson had referred to *The Sacred Wood: Essays on Poetry and Criticism* (1920) in a college essay, but apparently did not have a copy of his own until the University Paperbacks edition (London: Methuen; New York: Barnes & Noble, 1960), which contains occasional notes and markings. Returning as a tutor to John Winthrop House 1937–39, Olson is on record as checking out of the House library in June 1939 Harley Granville-Barker, *Companion to Shakespeare* (edition unknown) as well as, by the way, Franz Oppenheimer, *The State: Its History and Development Viewed Sociologically* (Indianapolis: Bobbs-Merrill, 1914). Olson's use of the Shakespeare criticism of Johnson, Coleridge, Brandes, Raleigh and Bradley has not been determined.

The edition of Shakespeare Olson used at Harvard, with heavy markings, was *The Complete Works of Shakespeare,* ed. George Lyman Kittredge (Boston: Ginn, 1936). Prior to that he may have had Richard Grant White's Riverside edition of *Mr. William Shakespeare's Comedies, Histories & Poems, Tragedies* (Boston, 1901). Olson quotes from that edition in a letter of 29 November 1951 (*Creeley Correspondence* 8, p. 200), but the three volumes did not appear later in his library.

17. Letter to Waldo Frank, 5 December 1938. The Dostoevsky essay found in *Twice A Year* 5–6 (Fall–Winter 1940) was developed into a longer piece and published only posthumously as *In Adullam's Lair* (Provincetown: To the Lighthouse Press, 1975).

18. In spite of the doubts there expressed to Creeley, it should be noted that in the following year Olson named Dostoevsky, with Melville, Rimbaud and Lawrence, as a forerunner of the postmodern (*Additional Prose*, p. 40). And he was still curious enough in November 1963 to check out of Lockwood Library, Buffalo, a new book: Jessie Coulson, *Dostoevsky: A Self-Portrait* (New York: Oxford University Press, 1962).

19. Olson saw this passage from Guérin, and Melville's approving marginal note, in Melville's own copy of Matthew Arnold's *Essays in Criticism* (Boston: Ticknor & Fields, 1865). See *In Adullam's Lair*, p. 16.

20. *In Adullam's Lair*, p. 14. The reference to Nietzsche here should not pass unnoticed since it is possibly the only one in Olson's writings. We have here possibly the only reference to Brueghel also.

As for his mother's Catholicism—

> I do here record
> for eternity no less, lest it be lost, that
> a mother is a hard thing to get away from (*Maximus,* p. 207)

—who knows but that Olson's mother managed to present him, before she died in 1950, with the revised edition of the Baltimore Catechism, *A Catechism of Christian Doctrine* (Confraternity of Christian Doctrine, 1949), or with D. F. Miller, *A Message to Invalidly Married Catholics* (Liguori, Mo.: Liguorian Pamphlets, Redemptorist Fathers, n.d.)? Or Marianus Fiege, *The Princess of Poverty—Saint Clare of Assisi and the Order of Poor Ladies,* 2d ed. (Evansville, Ind.: Poor Clares of the Monastery of S. Clare, 1909)? On his own account, Olson bought and delighted in F. S. Ellis's edition of *The Golden Legend or Lives of the Saints as Englished by William Caxton,* 5 vols. (London: J. M. Dent, 1900), opened on Good Friday in order to quote something to Frances Boldereff (letter of 10 April 1950); and also *The Cloud of Unknowing,* ed. Justin McCann, 6th revised ed. (London: Burns Oates, 1952)—flyleaf: "Cambridge Fri 2 weeks before Dec 6 Nov 22/57 (later chps) read again (notes & markings) Nov 30/58 beginning chapter." He retained in his library an orthodox offprint, Preston Roberts, "A Christian Theory of Dramatic Tragedy," *Journal of Religion* 31 (January 1951): 1–20; also Vincent Sheean, *Rage of the Soul* (New York: New American Library Signet Book, 1953). He acquired Sister Marie, O. P., *Married Saints* (Techny, Ill.: Divine Word Publications, 1960), and, even later, Preston Harold, *The Shining Stranger: An Unorthodox Interpretation of Jesus and His Mission* (New York: Wayfarer Press, 1968).

Olson used the King James Version of *The Holy Bible* (New York: Grosset &

Dunlap, 1931), and it is heavily annotated. Besides the *Encyclopaedia Biblica* (previously cited), he had Stanley Cook, *An Introduction to the Bible* (Harmondsworth: Penguin, 1950). On the other side of the scale, to name the most obvious deconstructive text, Olson had read (though he did not own) R. H. Tawney, *Religion and the Rise of Capitalism*; he mentions it in a satirical poem (*Collected Poems*, p. 478).

21. Van Wyck Brooks was a patron found for Olson by Dahlberg. As we have seen, Olson knew of his writings on Melville at the time of his M.A. thesis, and also probably his *America's Coming of Age* (New York: Huebsch, 1913) and *Letters and Leadership* (New York: Huebsch, 1918), though he did not own these two books and his reading notes on them are in a journal entry of March 1940.

An ardent admirer of Stieglitz, Olson must, we assume, have delved at least into such a notable book as *America and Alfred Stieglitz: A Collective Portrait* (New York: Literary Guild, 1934), edited by Waldo Frank, Lewis Mumford, Dorothy Norman, Paul Rosenfeld, and Harold Rugg.

Olson would have acquainted himself with Ford Madox Ford's work, if only to accept an invitation to the dinner for "The Friends of William Carlos Williams" at Ticino's Restaurant in the Village (Olson attended perhaps only one, on 4 April 1939). The Ford books in his library apparently came via Pound (cited later), except for *The Good Soldier* (New York: Vintage, 1957), which appears to have been borrowed from Gerrit Lansing.

As for "others," perhaps Olson met John Marin, the painter. Marin's privately published poem, *To Paint My Children* (New York: An American Place, 1938) was laid in Olson's copy of E. M. Benson, *John Marin: The Man and His Work* (Washington: American Federation of Arts, 1935). We know Olson met Marsden Hartley at this time (*Guide*, pp. 49–50). He later acquired *Lyonel Feininger/Marsden Hartley* (New York: Museum of Modern Art, 1944).

22. Letter to Waldo Frank, 5 February 1939, Cambridge: "The first week I was back in this region of thick-ribbed ice I followed up some of the urges your conversation stirred in me. I read Wright," (*Uncle Tom's Children*, just published by Harper in 1938, loaned by Frank) "like him, liked him best when he was down in his people, locating his social anger in some tragedy of their own insides: that's why Long Black Song meant more to me. . . . And Kierkegaard. I read a life of him by a man named Allen." (E. L. Allen, *Kierkegaard: His Life and Thought*—but Olson did not own it.) "I'm afraid I shall have to quicken my French before I can get at his thought: the English translations are meagre and poor. Thus far his affair with Regine Olsen has fed me most, twisted as it was with multiple guilt. As sad a thing as poor Murica's in Bread and Wine." (Olson told Anne Bosshard in a letter of March 1939 that he had been reading Ignazio Silone, both *Bread and Wine*, 1937 and *The School for Dictators*, 1938—but

he did not own them.) "I confess it is hard for me to join myself to Kierke-gaard: I still stiffen at the Xtian vocabulary, for I too was marked by it when I was young."

23. Edward Dahlberg, *From Flushing to Calvary* (New York: Harcourt, Brace, 1932)—flyleaf: "For Charles Olsen as a momento of our Melville con-versations & with friendship—Edward Dahlberg Sep. 22, '36 N.Y.C."; *Bottom Dogs* (London: Putnam, 1929)—inscribed: "TO CHARLES OLSON—whose genius I believe in & again *affirm* from his devoted & loving friend, Edward Dahlberg Nov. 21 '38 N.Y.C."; *Those Who Perish* (New York: John Day, 1934)—no inscription, perhaps not a gift.

24. His purchased copy of *Do These Bones Live* (New York: Harcourt, Brace, 1941) Olson loaned to Robert Payne "when he left for Tibet" (letter from Olson to Dahlberg on 2 February 1949); so it must be a further copy Olson is referring to when he writes to Pound (letter possibly of 12 May 1947): "Of an-other Turk, Dahlberg by name: the letter duel continues, so I am mailing to you his BONES." On 2 February 1949, in a period of friendship, Olson asks for an inscribed copy of *Do These Bones Live,* but the copy found in his library is not inscribed. Neither is his copy of the U.K. edition, *Sing, O Barren* (London: Rout-ledge, 1947). *The Flea of Sodom* (London: Peter Nevill, 1950) was sent to Olson by Dahlberg at the end of July 1950 with a note rather than an inscription (there was already a dedication within the text). Dahlberg inscribed the U.S. edition (Norfolk, Conn.: New Directions, 1950) to Olson, 24 August 1950. Olson started a review of *Flea* while he was in Yucatan, but Edouard Roditi's review in *Poetry* 77 (January 1951): 236–38 and Dahlberg's onslaught "How Do You Spell Fool," *Poetry* 78 (April 1951): 54–59 might have made him duly cautious. There was an "up" moment in their relationship when Dahlberg wrote "Laurels for Borrowers," *Freeman* 26 (17 December 1951): 187–90, defending Olson's *Call Me Ishmael* from some supposed plagiarism on the part of a Melville scholar. Olson thanked him (letter of 19 December 1951), but later in a letter to Creeley on 18 February 1952 he called it an embarrassment, "something I cannot stand the public display of—the coup of it: so done, ultimately, as a love token." It was Olson's failure to come through with the promised review that rankled up to the final break.

There was no correspondence after a last spat over Dahlberg's article "Myth of Discovery: The Americas," *Nimbus* 2 (Winter 1954): 38–48. Dahlberg was invading Olson's territory, the West. Olson heavily annotated Dahlberg's "Moby Dick—An Hamitic Dream," *The Literary Review* 4 (Autumn 1960): 87–118; there exists at Storrs a reply to it in manuscript but it was not sent for publication. Olson acquired a copy of Dahlberg's *Cipango's Hinder Door* (Aus-tin: Humanities Research Center, University of Texas, 1965), but nothing after that.

25. Miguel de Cervantes, *Don Quixote* (New York: Modern Library, 1930), signed on the flyleaf "Charles John Olson," an early signature and marginalia. The copy came to light recently in boxes of books owned by Jean Kaiser, having failed to be included in the inventory made by George Butterick.

26. Sealts inscribed an offprint to Olson in July 1941 of his "Herman Melville's 'I and My Chimney,' " *American Literature* 13 (May 1941): 142–54. Other offprints Olson received and kept were: "Did Melville Write 'October Mountain' ?," *American Literature* 22 (May 1950): 178–82; "Melville's 'Neoplatonic Originals,' " *Modern Language Notes* 67 (February 1952): 80–86; and "Melville's Reading: A Supplementary List of Books Owned and Borrowed," *Harvard Library Bulletin* 6 (Spring 1952): 239–47. Sealts sent Olson the Melville Issue of *Modern Fiction Studies* (Autumn 1962), but it did not apparently survive in his library.

## 6. "It Might Take 14 Years"

1. These publications of the Bureau of American Ethnology from the Government Printing Office in Washington D.C. were very inexpensive on first publication. Of the Bulletins, Olson owned nos. 28, 57, 77, 98, 132, 143 (vol. 2), 151, 152, 153, 156, 157, 161, 162, 165, and 180. Of the Annual Reports of the Bureau of American Ethnology, Olson owned the 1st, 8th, 16th, 19th, 22nd, 24th, 26th, 27th, 34th, and vol. 5 of the *Contributions to North American Ethnology.* Insofar as these volumes are utilized by Olson, they are cited in the appropriate place in subsequent discussion. Butterick's "Preliminary Report" indicates notes and markings in Cosmos Mindeleff's contribution to the *Sixteenth Annual Report* (1897), pp. 73–198 and in Frances S. Nichols, *Index to Schoolcraft's "Indian Tribes of the United States,"* Bulletin 152 (1954).

2. "The vivid entry was either *Benito Cereno* or *Bartleby* Middletown Conn spring 1933 getting out of the infirmary after weeks of illness, and (as it might be) starved, and throwing myself down on my cot in my own room of a spring afternoon with the lovely Constable small edition of the Piazza Tales. That did it"—*Olson/Melville*, p. 5. In 1929 there was a Constable reprint of the Standard edition, *Piazza Tales* (1923). Olson speaks of it again, in a letter to Albert Erskine on 22 April 1949, as "my 1st Melville, Benito, in a slim volume never seen since, by Constable."

Of course, Olson was acquainted with Melville long before. Whether or not on his prompting, his parents had bought for his nineteenth birthday the Raymond Weaver edition of *Moby Dick* (New York: Modern Library, 1926); it still exists for all its wear and markings, so we can read the notable inscription:

When o'er this book, you cast your eyes,

Forget your studies and Mobylize.

Each minute spent, some thought should bring
Of Gloucester scenes, and your old Viking,
Dad & Mother Dec. 27, 1929.

One sees the father's engaging charm in what Olson later called "a bad pun" (*Olson/Melville*, p. 5), and how parents always get it the wrong way round—it being at that time unimaginable that the book would become Olson's chief study and not his recreation.

3. As Olson remembered it later, he "bought via John Grant the Bookseller Edinburgh George the IVth Bridge the Constable edition complete. For I think $25. In 1939 (or 1938 probably)"—*Olson/Melville*, p. 5. Butterick notes that the invoice from John Grant is dated 12 July 1934. Almost every one of the fifteen volumes of this Standard Edition contains extensive notes and markings.

4. Olson's notes on the contents page of *John Marr and Other Poems* indicate a disatisfaction with this "poor selection," which left out "Timoleon," "After the Pleasure Party," and a number of other poems Olson names.

5. Two old first editions survived in Olson's library (at least until 1965): *Omoo* (London: John Murray, 1847) and *Pierre* (New York: Harper, 1852). In a letter written from Black Mountain on 28 September 1957, on his final return to wind up the place, Olson noted that a building had been "busted into and some of my Melville 1sts stolen." For instance, Henry Murray had given Olson a *Redburn* in 1934, which was not in his library later.

6. Evidence for Olson's continued attention to Melville criticism exists in a page of titles of articles from current journals such as *American Literature, New England Quarterly,* and *Notes and Queries* for the year 1935, done while Olson was at Clark University. The sheet was later inserted in his copy of Anderson's *Melville in the South Seas,* as if for future use.

7. It was the 4th edition, *Cape Ann Tourist's Guide* (Gloucester: Cape Ann Community League, 1952–54) that we see Olson annotating and using in the *Maximus Poems.* This edition included "comments on Business Cycles"— Babson had become a successful business consultant, the founder of the Babson Institute business school. Olson was interested enough in this side of him to borrow from Mary Shore, presumably on his return to Gloucester in 1957, Roger W. Babson, *Actions and Reactions: An Autobiography* (New York: Harper, 1950). Olson also owned two of his pamphlets on local history: *Story of Bear Skin Neck, Rockport, Mass.,* extract of an address given at Rockport 8 August 1939; and *Sargent-Murray-Gilman-Hough House Association,* privately printed— the 1941 original and the 1964 reprint.

8. Murdock had passed on to Olson a couple of offprints pertinent to the subject: Robert S. Forsythe, "Herman Melville in Tahiti" and "More Upon Herman Melville in Tahiti" in *Philological Quarterly* 16 (October 1937): 344–57 and 17 (January 1938): 1–17, respectively. Olson kept them laid in his copy of

*Melville in the South Seas.* A letter to Merton Sealts on 7 March 1952 reveals that Olson had actually been a reader of the Anderson book for Harvard University Press and had refused it after "reading for a long time in Ellis, say, and in such modern anthropologists as Linton, and other publications of the Bishop Museum," i.e., William Ellis, *Polynesian Researches,* 4 vols. (London, 1833) and Ralph Linton, *Archaeology in the Marquesas Islands* (Honolulu: Bishop Museum, 1925)—neither of these became part of Olson's library. He kept Thomas Trood, *Island Reminiscences: A Graphic, Detailed Romance of a Life Spent in the South Sea Islands* (Sydney: McCarron, Stewart, 1912). Olson also had *New England Quarterly* 8 (September 1935) in which he marked the article by Daniel Aaron, "Melville and the Missionaries," pp. 404–8.

9. It is to this Oliver edition that Olson referred when, on receiving Jay Leyda's *The Complete Stories of Herman Melville* (New York: Random House, 1949) from its publisher, he wrote back: "It is such a pleasure to have someone undo the damage of the HendricksHouseFarrarShts . . . to have a text of the stories I can trust" (letter to Albert Erskine, 22 April 1949).

10. Olson kept in his library both this review copy and the presentation copy from the author (previously cited).

11. On 9 March 1950 Olson is telling Frances Boldereff that Chase "has moved me most of anyone who ever wrote on melville"; but on finishing Chase's book he was "horrified" (letter of 10 April 1950), and did not retain it in his bookshelves. He disliked Chase's review of Leyda's *Melville Log* in *The Nation* (1 December 1951).

12. Olson's Bible was the King James Version previously cited. His first Homer was probably *The Iliad of Homer,* trans. Andrew Lang, Walter Leaf, and Ernest Myers (New York: Modern Library, 1929), with notes and markings throughout, as Butterick saw when he examined it in the Jean Kaiser collection. (It has since been lost sight of.) Olson then acquired *The Complete Works of Homer* (New York: Modern Library, n.d.), where the above *Iliad* text is joined by *The Odyssey,* trans. S. H. Butcher and Andrew Lang. Olson's name is on the flyleaf and it is heavily marked throughout, especially the front and endpapers, where Olson has made extensive reading notes of Bérard's *Did Homer Live?,* Rhys Carpenter's *Folk Tale, Fiction and Saga,* Kramer's *Epic of Gilgamesh* (all cited elsewhere), and of Velikovsky from an unidentified source. His library also contained *Homeri Odyssea,* (Lipsiae: Teubneri, 1893) and *The Iliad of Homer with an Interlinear Translation* by Thomas Clark (Philadelphia: McKay, 1888). Olson later picked up two paperbacks of the *Iliad*: The Penguin Classics (trans. E. V. Rieu), 1950, and the Bantam Classic (trans. Alston Hurd Chase and William G. Perry), 1960.

13. Letter to Robert Richman of 15 March 1952 reports that *Melville's Quarrel with God* "came in last night." The volume was later passed on to Jean

Kaiser, and cannot at the moment be found. Olson also asked for *Collected Poems of Herman Melville,* ed. Howard Vincent (Chicago: Packard, Hendricks House, 1947)—flyleaf: "Olson bmc April 52 (fr Farrar Straus as of N R review of Vincent's ed. of MD)." But the review was apparently finished before it arrived.

14. *Human Universe,* p. 109. The review originally ran in two issues of *New Republic* as "The Materials and Weights of Herman Melville," numbers 128 (8 September 1952): 20–21 and 128 (15 September 1952) 17–18, 21. Although copies inscribed to Jonathan Williams bear Olson's written complaint, "This was so unstraightened by Michael Straight that it bears little resemblance to the original," Olson did not effect any changes for its collection into *Human Universe,* pp. 109–116.

15. *Human Universe,* p. 109. Olson's library contained two copies of William Ellery Sedgwick, *Herman Melville: The Tragedy of Mind* (Cambridge: Harvard University Press, 1944), neither of them marked. One copy came with the following note from William Sedgwick's widow: "Dear Charlie, Here is Ellery's book which would have reached you long ago had I known your address. He would have particularly wanted you to have it, for you shared a common slant of mind. It dwells in my memory always, the very tall figure and the very short, poised indefinitely on the corner of Brattle St and Appian Way, talking, talking—"

Newton Arvin, *Herman Melville,* American Men of Letters Series (New York: William Sloane Associates, 1950) was not owned by Olson. Listing it here gives it more dignity than one would expect, given Olson's statement in a letter to Dahlberg of 19 December 1951 that Arvin was one of the three he was "most after" in *Letter for Melville.*

"Herman Melville, and the Problems of Moral Navigation" in Yvor Winters's *Maule's Curse: Seven Studies in the History of American Obscurantism* (Norfolk: New Directions, 1938) had just been reprinted in his *In Defense of Reason* (New York: Swallow Press-William Morrow, 1947), but Olson owned neither volume. W. H. Auden, *The Enchafèd Flood or The Romantic Iconography of the Sea* (New York: Random House, 1950), which has a part three, "Ishmael-Don Quixote," was in Olson's library. The other Melville critics mentioned are cited elsewhere. The discovery of Ronald Mason's *The Spirit Above the Dust* led to a substantial correspondence, both sides of which are now at Storrs.

16. The printer's error in the review means we do not know if Olson was going to specify a particular work of Bezanson's. He was probably aware both of the dissertation *Herman Melville's Clarel* (Yale, 1943), and of Bezanson's fence-sitting review of *Call Me Ishmael* in *New England Quarterly* 20 (September 1947): 410–13.

17. *Human Universe,* p. 110. Olson apparently never acquired a copy of

Howard's book, though he later picked up (from a library) his *Herman Melville* in the Pamphlets on American Writers series (Minneapolis: University of Minnesota, 1961). He had read Howard's early article "Melville and Spenser—A Note on Criticism," *Modern Language Notes* 46 (May 1931): 291–92, and mentioned it to Sealts in the 7 March 1952 letter along with like studies "that do not claim to be other than they are": Wilson L. Heflin, "Melville's Third Whaler," *Modern Language Notes* 64 (April 1949): 241–45; Harrison Hayford, "Two New Letters of Herman Melville," *English Literary History* 11 (March 1944): 76–83; and William H. Gilman, "Melville's Liverpool Trip," *Modern Language Notes* 61 (December 1946): 543–47—see *Pursuing Melville,* p. 120 and notes p. 366. Olson also knew William Gilman's book, *Melville's Early Life and Redburn* (New York: New York University Press, 1951), asking Leyda on 15 March 1952 if he had a copy to swap; he is not known to have owned the book.

18. When Leyda sent the typescript of the *Melville Log* in draft form, Olson thought it would make "a vivid book" (letter of 4 February 1946). However, he added; "It was precisely such documentation I spent 13 years to assemble in order to discard! For my aim was to master such an intense interpretation that I could make the man come alive without biography." The two-volume work was sent to Olson by the publisher (acknowledged to Robert Giroux, 6 December 1951). He was "much delighted" with it (*Creeley Correspondence* 8, p. 128). Olson was not so delighted with *The Portable Melville*, ed. Jay Leyda (New York: Viking, 1952); he annotated the introduction with derogatory expletives and later stored the volume with Jean Kaiser.

19. *Human Universe,* p. 110. Responding very positively to Murray's *Pierre* in a letter of 31 March 1949, Olson was grateful for some of the footnote references: Claude Bragdon, *More Lives Than One* (New York, 1938) and M. C. D'Arcy, *The Mind and Heart of Love* ((London 1947)—though there is no evidence he followed up on them. The third he mentions, Denis de Rougemont's *Love in the Western World* (New York: Harcourt, Brace, 1940), he had actually quoted in a letter to Waldo Frank on 4 May 1940, though the book was not owned.

Olson quarreled with him whenever Murray stepped outside his expertise as psychologist, as the marginal notes to *Pierre* indicate. When he received an offprint of "In Nomine Diaboli," *New England Quarterly* 24 (December 1951): 435–52, Murray's address at the Williams College centennial celebration, Labor Day 1951, Olson composed the most powerful rebuttal imaginable (letter to Murray, 16 February 1952). Murray magnanimously termed it "full of corrective truth" in a postcard of 21 May 1952, but their long friendship had just about run its course.

20. "Equal, That Is, to the Real Itself," *Chicago Review* 12 (Summer 1958): 98–104, collected in *Human Universe*, pp. 117–22 and *Selected Writings*, pp. 46–52. Weyl's *Philosophy of Mathematics and Natural Science* is quoted several

times in the review without being named. Olson's copy is extensively and thoroughly marked, and was used in *Special View of History* and the *Maximus*. It came to Olson as a gift from one of the long-surviving faculty of BMC, the musician Stefan Wolpe, in the year of closure—flyleaf: "to my friend charles, with four years of Black Mt'n behind us, mutually shared, and with years in front of us Stefan II 3.1956."

While writing the review, Olson's attention was drawn to an unsigned article, "Assumptions of Symmetry," *Time* 71 (5 May 1958): 53–54. The torn-out pages with marginal notations were inserted in his copy of Weyl. Olson later bought Irving Adler, *The New Mathematics* (New York: New American Library, 1962), P. W. Bridgman, *The Logic of Modern Physics* (New York: Macmillan paperbacks, 1960), and E. A. Burtt, *The Metaphysical Foundations of Modern Physical Science* (Garden City: Doubleday Anchor, 1954); but none of these served him as Weyl did.

21. The winding down. C. L. R. James, *Mariners, Renegades and Castaways: the Story of Herman Melville and the World We Live In* (New York: by the author, 1953)—"a crazy book fr a crazy man came in here, surprise, yesterday . . . sounds like a sort of Waddell & Ignatius Donnelly diminished a seventh by some sort of critic like G. Wilson Knight" (letter to Creeley, 13 February 1953). Letter to Ed Marshall on 20 August 1956: "last week picked up (thru John Wieners) this "Ishmael Complex" in article in *Commonweal* on the book on Melville called *Ishmael*: I am asking the publishers to send me it for review." The volume, James Baird, *Ishmael* (Baltimore: Johns Hopkins, 1956), was apparently not sent.

He picked up two paperbacks: *Billy Budd, Foretopman* (New York: Popular Living Classics Library, 1962), which comprises the novel as edited by Frederic Barron Freeman and a play adaptation by Louis O. Coxe and Robert Chapman; and *Selected Poems of Herman Melville*, ed. Hennig Cohen (Doubleday Anchor, 1964). He received from the publisher in March 1963 *Billy Budd, Sailor*, ed. Harrison Hayford and Merton Sealts (Chicago: University of Chicago Press, 1962), and made occasional notes in it. The *Directory of Melville Dissertations* compiled by Tyrus Hillway and Herschel Parker (The Melville Society, 1962) was sent to Olson by Sealts for unknown reasons; and finally *Melville's Reading* (cited in full later) for obvious reasons.

22. "Bibliography on America for Ed Dorn," (*Additional Prose*, p. 13) dated January 1955.

## 7. History 62 (Westward Movement) and *'West'*

1. Untitled preface to *'West'*, unnumbered pages. Olson kept on his shelves two Joseph A. Altsheler books: *The Sun of Quebec*, The French and Indian War Series (New York: Appleton, 1919) and *The Shadow of the North* (New

York: Appleton, 1924). In a *Maximus* poem he remembers a further Altsheler by name, *The Eyes of the Woods* (New York: Appleton, 1917). Olson does not have in mind any Altsheler specifically on Red Cloud. According to a journal, by 15 May 1947 he had read in the Library of Congress George E. Hyde, *Red Cloud's Folk: A History of the Oglala Sioux Indians* (Norman, Okla.: University of Oklahoma Press, 1937); he may also have known from those days Grace Raymond Hebard and E. A. Brininstool, *The Bozeman Trail: Historical Accounts of the Blazing of the Overland Routes into the Northwest and the Fights with Red Cloud's Warriors*, 2 vols. (Cleveland: Arthur H. Clark, 1922)—the copy in his library was apparently borrowed from Harvey Brown about the time of the opening poem of *'West'*, "as of Bozeman." He also owned Mari Sandoz, *Crazy Horse: The Strange Man of the Oglalas*, A Bison Book (Lincoln: University of Nebraska Press, 1961). Olson's stated source, the *DAB*, 22 vols. (New York 1928–1944), was presumably in the BMC library or the Sondley Library in nearby Asheville; or perhaps Olson's notes for this poem, finished in 1959, go back to 1947 and the *Dictionary of American Biography* in the Library of Congress.

2. *Additional Prose*, p. 11. It seems that Olson still had his copy of the *List of References* at this time (January 1955), but it was not in his library later. He should have been aware of the *Harvard Reading List in American History* that came out in June 1937, while he was at Harvard. Perhaps he was not impressed by it; there is no evidence that he was. (See *Merk and Olson*, ed. Ralph Maud, Simon Fraser University, 1970, where the list is reproduced.)

3. Of the 16 volumes, there remained in Olson's library numbers 1, 2, 4, 10, 13, 14, 15, and 16. Olson also owned Hulbert's *Red-men's Roads* (Cleveland: Arthur H. Clark, 1900) and the well-known *Forty-Niners* (cited later). He was interested in Hulbert enough to read and mark his article "Western Ship-Building," *American Historical Review* 21 (July 1916): 720–33, and to recommend for Harvey Brown's Frontier Pamphlet series his *A New Basis for the Study of Local History* (Cleveland: Frontier Press, 1966), which he owned.

4. *Additional Prose*, p. 11. In Olson's library at the time of his death were various parts of Parkman's *France and England in North America*: part 3, *La Salle and the Discovery of the Great West* (Boston: Little, Brown, 1903); part 6, *A Half-Century of Conflict*, 2 vols. (Boston: Little, Brown, 1918); and part 5, *Count Frontenac and New France Under Louis XIV* (Boston: Little, Brown, 1886). The latter was the one volume Olson kept when, in moving to Gloucester in 1957, he stored the rest of the BMC library's set of 9 volumes with Jean Kaiser.

5. *Additional Prose*, pp. 7 and 11. Olson did not own the first edition, but bought the revised edition in 1968 (cited later).

6. *Additional Prose*, p. 8. Merk inscribed to Olson another of his offprints, "Eastern Antecedents of the Grangers," *Agricultural History* 23 (January 1949): 1–8.

7. *Additional Prose*, p. 13. In this remark of 1955 Olson suggests the title of Merk's future book should be *Land*, which seems to have been the kind of grounding Merk would not be interested in. Nevertheless, Olson finds "poor" when compared to Merk a work like Stanley Vestal, *Queen of Cowtowns: Dodge City*, which he had just picked up in Pennant paperback (New York, 1954) along with J. Frank Dobie, *A Vaquero of the Brush Country* (New York: Pennant. Books, 1954), which he doesn't mention in this context but could have.

8. Olson did not own this title, but bought Billington's *The Far Western Frontier 1830–1860* (New York: Harper Torchbook, 1956). The contrast here would be W. J. Ghent, *The Early Far West: A Narrative Outline, 1540–1850* (New York: Longmans, Green, 1931), written without benefit of Turner's frontier thesis. But Olson does not comment on this work. The copy he owned was a late gift—flyleaf: "Olson—fr Harvey spring 1968."

9. *Additional Prose*, pp. 8 and 11. In the Sentry paperback, which Olson owned (Boston: Houghton Mifflin 1960), the incident being recalled is on pp. 184–85, where Jim Clyman (not Fitzpatrick) is seen to be DeVoto's protagonist. The other book of DeVoto's that Olson owned was his nonfiction story of the fur trade, *Across the Wide Missouri* (Boston: Houghton Mifflin, 1947).

10. Carl O. Sauer, Gilbert H. Cady, and Henry C. Cowles, *Starved Rock State Park and Its Environs*, Bulletin 6 of the Geographical Society of Chicago (University of Chicago Press, 1918) was available at Black Mountain College according to a letter to Sauer of 20 October 1949, but was not in Olson's library later.

11. As reprinted in Sauer's collected papers, *Land and Life* (cited later as owned by Olson), p. 54. A notebook indicates Olson read the original *Road to Cibola* by 15 May 1947, and another Sauer volume which he never owned, *Man in Nature: America before the Days of the White Man* (New York: Scribner, 1939). Olson was also likely to have made a point of looking at Sauer's "The Morphology of Landscape," *University of California Publications in Geography* 2 (1925): 19–54, though he did not own this influential piece until much later when he noticed that it was available as a monograph reprint (Berkeley: University of California Press, 1938) and sent for it—cover: "Olson (bot fr U of C Press June 1960"—and read it thoroughly with annotations.

12. Olson and Connie, traveling by automobile with a friend, stopped at Yellowstone Park where they perused the handbook, *Haynes Guide* (it seems that some facts about Jim Bridger stuck in Olson's mind for later use). Is it possible that they had also gone through Deadwood, Colorado, and picked up the Souvenir Program "The Trial of Jack McGill for the Killing of Wild Bill Hickok in Deadwood, 1876" (which survives in Olson's library)? In any case, with Sauer as a goal, they are likely to have used the *Atlas of American Agriculture* (Washington: U.S. Department of Agriculture, 1924)—which also survives—as a road map.

13. Letter to Ezra Pound. He was then in his third week at Sacramento—he had had a copy of *Sutter's Fort Historical Museum* (Sacramento: State of California Documents Division, 1947) inscribed by the curator on 7 November 1947.

14. This facsimile of the lease, with "Introductory notes by Charles Olson," published for its members by the Book Club of California, is dated February 1948 though it appeared later in the year. Olson refers to only one source, Governor Mason's letter in U.S. House Executive document No. 17. It would be idle to speculate on what scholarly works Olson consulted in order to feel he could present himself as an authority in this area. The one book in his library that he might have acquired at this time for California history is John Bigelow, *Memoirs of the Life and Public Services of John Charles Fremont* (New York: Derby & Jackson, 1856). Or the tribute to the founder of the U.S. Geological Survey, *Clarence King Memoirs: The Helmet of Mambrino* (New York: Putnam's 1904). Olson wrote to Robert F. Heizer, Assistant Professor of Anthropology at Berkeley, and received an offprint of his, "The Direct-Historical Approach in California Archaeology," *American Antiquity* 7 (October 1941), and another from the same issue: Franklin Fenenya and Robert F. Heizer, "The Origin and Authenticity of an Atlatl and an Atlatl Dart from Lassen County, California." Heizer's book, *Francis Drake and the California Indians, 1579* (University of California Press, 1947), had just been published; Olson picked up or was given a copy. Years later he put a cap on this subject by purchasing Herbert M. Hart, *Old Forts of the Far West* (Seattle: Superior Publishing Co., 1965).

15. "Guggenheim Fellowship Proposal, 1948," *OLSON* 5, p. 35, where Olson indicates that he also has ready "the material for two other articles, one a statement of the true chronology of the Donner Party, another the '46 crossing as a whole."

16. "The Contours of American History," reprinted from *Kulchur* in *Human Universe*, pp. 159–60. There is no knowledge of what Olson read of A. A. Berle, but he owned Heilbroner's *Future as History* (cited later) and John Kenneth Galbraith *American Capitalism* Sentry Ed. (Boston: Houghton Mifflin, 1962). He also mentions that William Appleman Williams has a feeling for history similar to R. G. Collingwood; Olson owned Collingwood's *The Idea of History* (New York: Oxford Galaxy Book, 1956).

## 8. "Red, White, and Black"

1. "Operation Red, White & Black," *OLSON* 5, p. 27. This proposal is presumably the one sent to Monroe Engel at Reynal & Hitchcock with the returned page-proofs of *Call Me Ishmael*. Engel is talking about a contract (letter to Olson of 31 January 1947), and when he moves to Viking in March 1947 he takes the project with him. Hence, Olson's reference in his "Guggenheim Fel-

lowship Proposal, 1948" to Viking's having commissioned "Red, White & Black" (*OLSON* 5, p. 36).

2. *OLSON* 5, p. 30. Under the heading of "Background to the Maximus Poems (Notes and Essays, 1945–1957)," George Butterick gathered practically all the unpublished material pertinent to this segment of Olson's reading as issue no. 5 of *OLSON: The Journal of the Charles Olson Archives* (Spring 1976).

3. William H. Prescott, *History of the Conquest of Mexico and History of the Conquest of Peru* (New York: Modern Library, n.d.). This heavily annotated volume in the Jean Kaiser collection was, unaccountably, not seen by Butterick, and therefore does not appear in his "Preliminary Report." It seems clear now that this "Outline" is not "ca. 1946" as the contents page of *OLSON* 5 suggests, but 1941, what the Key West Notebook of 1945 mentions as "notes on the poem to be called 'West' you wrote 4 yrs ago" (*OLSON* 5, p. 11). Olson's use in the "Outline" of W. B. Yeats, *A Vision* (New York: Macmillan, 1938)—the reference to Giraldus and "the last turn of the wheel before the new gyre begins" (*OLSON* 5, p. 16)—suggests a date close to the time of his first acquiring the book, presumably not long after publication.

4. Faust, like Ulysses, was dropped later when Olson envisaged a Maximus without such a traditional burden of guilt. He had no copy of *Faust* in his library.

5. "Guggenheim Fellowship Proposal, 1948," *OLSON* 5, p. 36: "so little has been done since Parkman."

6. Daugherty, p. xvii. Olson later owned B. A. Botkin's *A Treasury of American Folklore* (New York: Crown, 1944), which covers the same ground and more but he seems to have paid less attention to it.

7. *OLSON* 5, pp. 3–4. A later reference on p. 30 to "The Cochiti ICE MOUNTAIN 'Inferno' " makes it clear that Olson was especially struck with the last tale, "A Visit to the Underworld," in Ruth Benedict's *Tales of the Cochiti Indians*, Bulletin 98 (Washington: Bureau of American Ethnology, 1931), which he owned. Olson also owned and annotated tales in George A. Dorsey, *Traditions of the Caddo* (Washington, D.C.: Carnegie Institution, 1905).

8. *OLSON* 5, p. 6. Butterick presents a long section from the "Trot-Moc" story (pp. 8–9), and reproduces an illustration in *Guide* (unnumbered plates); Olson remembers the story again in *Maximus*, p. 139.

9. The profuse marginalia in Olson's copy of *Tall Tales of the Southwest*, ed. Franklin J. Meine (New York: Knopf, 1930) suggest that Olson gave lectures on the subject from the book (at Clark University?).

10. *OLSON* 5, p. 19. Sydney Salt's *Christopher Columbus and Other Poems* (Boston: Bruce Humphries, 1937) had an introduction by William Carlos Williams, who, though speaking of the title poem's "placid beauty," does not really seem to disagree with Olson's judgment. Salt was a personal acquaintance

through Connie's sister, and inscribed *Christopher Columbus* to them, and also his previous book, *Thirty Pieces* (Majorca: Caravel Press, 1934). The copy of Salt's *New Journey* (Prairie City, Ill. and Rochester N.Y.: Black Faun Press, 1940) in Olson's library is inscribed to "Barbara Wilcock April 6, 1942." Salt wrote a play on the life of Poe that Olson apparently read in manuscript (see Butterick note, *Additional Prose*, p. 81).

11. Olson read Frank Cushing's telling of the Hopi creation myth as a quotation on pp. 188–91 of Paul Radin, *The Story of the American Indian* (Garden City Publishing Co., 1937—edition used by Olson unknown), making reading notes in a journal on 24 November 1945. The African story is the Kabyl creation story, "The First Human Beings, their Sons and Amazon Daughters," which leads off *African Genesis,* compiled by Leo Frobenius and Douglas C. Fox (New York: Stackpole, 1937). Olson must have read this first in a borrowed copy since his own copy came later, requisitioned from the BMC library.

12. The inception of "Red, White & Black," then, is associated with Cabeza de Vaca. This "healer" of "The Kingfishers" would be known to Olson at this time mainly through John Gilmary Shea, *Discovery and Exploration of the Mississippi Valley* (Albany: Joseph McDonough, 1903), probably read in the Library of Congress in 1946 (not owned). He had just acquired *Spanish Explorers in the Southern United States 1528–1543,* ed. Frederick W. Hodge and Theodore H. Lewis (New York: Scribner, 1907), and marked up the "Narrative of Alvar Nuñez Cabeça de Vaca" section edited by Hodge, writing on the inside of the front cover "Olson fall, 1946." A notebook indicates that within a short time he was determined to know more about Cabeza de Vaca, and read in the Library of Congress Cleve Hallenbeck, *Alvar Nunez Cabeza de Vaca: The Journey and Route of the First European to Cross the Continent of North America, 1534–1536* (Glendale, Calif.: Arthur H. Clark, 1940); Walter Goodloe Stuck, "Alvar Nunez Cabeza de Vaca (1490–1564), First European 'Physician and Surgeon' in the United States," reprinted from *Texas State Journal of Medicine* 32 (May 1936): 15–21; and Morris Bishop, *The Odyssey of Cabeza de Vaca* (New York: Century Co., 1933). "Is Cabeza an equivalent Aeneas," Olson asks (*OLSON* 5, p. 38), and suggests to himself: "Read *Aeneid.*" There is no further investigation of this parallel.

13. A title taken, most immediately, from Coman, *Economic Beginnings of the Far West* (cited previously), chapter 1, section 2. Olson associates her with Cibola (*OLSON* 5, p. 12).

14. Olson came to own at some point Haniel Long, *Malinche (Dona Marina)* (Santa Fe: Writers' Editions, 1939), but Prescott, as we have seen, is Olson's source at this time for the Cortez story. Among these documents (*OLSON* 5, p. 41) Olson makes a note to himself to "try Stechert" for a title: F. Gomez de Orozco, *Dona Marina, La Dama de la Conquista* (Mexico: Ediciones Xochitl, 1942); presumably he got his copy from that bookseller.

15. Olson owned and used *The Life and Adventures of James P. Beckwourth,* ed. T. D. Bonner (New York: Knopf Americana Deserta series, 1931)— flyleaf, early signature: "Charles J. Olson, Jr." The "White Steed of the Prairies" is one of the catalog of whitenesses with which Melville compares "the Whiteness of the Whale" (chapter 42 of *Moby-Dick*). There is no evidence that Olson went to Melville's source, James Hall, *The Wilderness and the War Path* (1846), but he may have done.

16. Olson could have read a page of information of the land dealings of the Ohio Company (1788) in Edward C. Kirkland, *A History of American Economic Life* (New York: Crofts, 1939), which a notebook indicates he looked at in the summer of 1945.

17. Olson is misremembering the name of the Kwakiutl Indians, having read of them on pp. 318–36 of Paul Radin's *Story of the American Indian* (cited previously).

18. "WEST" (*OLSON* 5, pp. 40–42) is undated, but a notebook indicates Olson was reading his copy of Stefansson in late 1947, and the *Kinsey Report,* mentioned on p. 42, was released in January 1948; hence, the conjectured date of early 1948.

19. Olson was reading George Bird Grinnell, *The Fighting Cheyennes* (New York: Scribner, 1915) in the Library of Congress in May 1947 when, a notebook also shows, he was reading J. P. Dunn, *Massacres of the Mountains: A History of the Indian Wars of the Far West* (New York: Harper, 1886) and Col. Henry B. Carrington's account of the Fetterman Massacre of 1866, in U.S. Senate Document 33, *History of Indian Operations on the Plains,* 50th Congress, 1st Session, 1888.

20. *OLSON* 5, pp. 38–39. Olson acquired *The Wisdom of Laotse,* trans. Lin Yutang (New York: Modern Library, 1948) about this time, and perhaps earlier his *Laotzu's Tao and Wu-Wei,* trans. Bhikshu and Dwight Goddard, 2d ed. (Thetford, Vt.: Dwight Goddard, 1939).

21. *OLSON* 5, p. 22. Olson read the first edition, *Anabase* (1938), but did not own it. Robert Giroux sent him the second edition, *Anabasis,* trans. T. S. Eliot (New York: Harcourt, Brace, 1949) on publication; Olson kept it.

22. There are three additional references under the heading "WEST— THE NEGRO" (*OLSON* 5, p. 42): Frank Tannenbaum, *Slave and Citizen* (New York: Knopf, 1946), Gilberto Freyre, *The Masters and the Slaves* (New York: Knopf, 1946)—there is no evidence Olson read these—and a note, "Sherburn Cook's census studies—watch for." In his library, with light notes and markings, we find 3 of the 4 volumes of S. F. Cook, *The Conflict Between the California Indian and White Civilization* (Berkeley: University of California Press, 1943). As for the item under "Witches (Salem)," (*OLSON* 5, p. 42), Butterick footnotes the standard source: Charles W. Upham, *Salem Witchcraft,* 2 vols. (Boston, 1867), any specific source not having been identified.

23. Frazer and Frobenius are dealt with elsewhere; Freud here, since there is no more obvious place. According to a notebook, Olson read Freud in the fall of 1939 when trying to understand Melville's psychology; he acknowledges *Moses and Monotheism* (New York: Knopf, 1939) came into *Call Me Ishmael* from that reading (presumably with the "brother horde" of p. 82), but it would be wrong to "make too much of it" (*Olson/Melville*, p. 8). Again, it is a notebook that tells us Olson was reading Freud's *Leonardo Da Vinci: A Study in Psychosexuality* early in 1947; he did not own the book. He owned at this time *An Autobiographical Study* (London: Hogarth Press & Institute of Psychoanalysis, 1946) and *The Interpretation of Dreams* (London: Allen & Unwin; New York: Macmillan, 1945), though the second of these at least was not really read until later—flyleaf: "Charles Olson *read* or *reread* for the 1st time? Oct 25, 1960." It was in 1960 that he picked up a couple of paperbacks: *Civilization and Its Discontents* (Garden City: Doubleday Anchor, 1958) and *A General Introduction to Psychoanalysis* (New York: Washington Square Press, 1960). Freud's influence was not conspicuous, even if we add the Freudians:

Otto Fenichel, *The Psychoanalytic Theory of Neurosis* (New York: Norton, 1945)—mentioned irreverently in the poem "The Morning News" (1950). (Now in the possession of Olson's daughter.)

Erich Fromm, *Psychoanalysis and Religion* (New Haven: Yale University Press, 1950). Olson offers Corman a couple of quotations from this volume on the envelope of a letter of 24 November 1951 (*Corman Correspondence*, p. 220); but it was not later in his library.

Patrick Mullahy, *Oedipus, Myth and Complex: A Review of Psychoanalytic Theory* (New York: Hermitage Press, 1948)—flyleaf: "Olson."

Geza Roheim et al., eds., *Psychoanalysis and the Social Sciences* (New York: International Universities Press, 1950)—Olson owned vol. 2 and annotated thoroughly Roheim's "The Oedipus Complex, Magic and Culture," pp. 173–228.

Frederick Wertham, *Dark Legend, A Study in Murder* (New York: Duell, Sloan & Pearce, 1941)—i.e., Orestes story, not owned, but reading notes January 1942.

24. *Guide*, p. xxiv. See also George Butterick, "Charles Olson's 'The Kingfishers' and the Poetics of Change," *American Poetry* (Winter 1989): 28–69 and Ralph Maud, " 'The Light is in the East': Notes on 'The Kingfishers,' " *intent.* no. 2 (Summer 1989): 1, 2, 7, and no. 3 (Fall 1989): 25.

25. Prescott (cited previously). "*Olson* many years many times many poems" is the inscription on the flyleaf of Olson's copy of *Plutarch's Morals: Theosophical Essays*, trans. C. W. King, Bohn's Classical Library (London: George

Bell, 1908), probably bought in Washington during September 1948. It was quoted at length in the writing of "The Kingfishers" around April 1949. Olson also owned vols. 2 and 4 of Plutarch's *Lives* and 3, 4, and 5 of the *Essays and Miscellanies* in A. H. Clough and William W. Goodwin, eds., *Plutarch's Lives and Writings* (Boston: Little, Brown, 1909).

26. Olson quotes Rimbaud's "A Season in Hell" in the last part of "The Kingfishers," but we do not know what edition he was using at this time. He may have had *Prose Poems from The Illuminations*, trans. Louise Varese (New York: New Directions, 1946), but *A Season in Hell*, trans. Delmore Schwartz (Norfolk: New Directions, n.d.) was a BMC library book, appropriated later. His copy of Rimbaud's *Oeuvres Completes* (Paris: Gallimard, 1951) has a flyleaf inscription: "Olson fr Gallimard Nov 54," and therefore was available for "Variations Done for Gerald Van DeWiele," but not earlier. In using Rimbaud as the ultimate modern (and therefore with Melville, Dostoevsky and Lawrence as precurser of the postmodern), Olson is thinking of a specific sentence in Wallace Fowlie, *Rimbaud* (New York: New Directions, 1946): "Rimbaud moved on to the despair which lies beyond sin and then sought what lies beyond despair" (p. 42). Olson quotes this in paraphrase a number of times in letters later, but even in "The Kingfishers" Rimbaud is a pivot, the rock bottom from which some action must ensue. (Fowlie is on "Clarke's list.") Olson's notebooks at the time indicate he was reading Edith Starkie's *Arthur Rimbaud* (New York: W. W. Norton, 1938) as early as February 1945.

27. Olson saw the galley proofs of *Cybernetics: or, Control and Communication in the Animal and the Machine* (New York: John Wiley, 1948) at Black Mountain College through Natasha Goldowski, who knew Wiener. Olson never owned the book, but he picked up Wiener's *The Human Use of Human Beings: Cybernetics and Society* (Garden City: Doubleday Anchor Books, 1954).

28. Caresse Crosby must have passed on to Olson the copy she received from the author—flyleaf: "To Mrs Crosby with author's compliments Matila Ghyka 1947." Olson annotations in this copy date from 1966, for example, "Dec 31st started used *most* Jan 2nd & 3rd 1966"; so perhaps Olson used a different copy earlier. The poem moves from the geometric circle to the ritual wheel—a draft of "The Praises" indicates that Olson was thinking of the Orphic mysteries described in Jane Harrison, *Prolegomena to the Study of Greek Religion* (Cambridge University Press, 1903)—flyleaf: "Charles Olson Washington 1948." But he had also acquired William Simpson *The Buddhist Praying-Wheel* (London and New York: Macmillan, 1896)—flyleaf: "*Olson* via Lekakis *Wash 1948?*" (he actually asks for the book on a post card to Michael Lekakis, 24 May 1949).

29. Monroe Engel was important to Olson, both as a friend and as a contact in the publishing world. His library at the end contained none of Engel's

own books, but Engel was the means by which several items came to be there, perhaps, from the R & H days: Gontran De Poncins, *Kabloona* (New York: Reynal & Hitchcock, 1941), certainly Malcolm Lowry, *Under the Volcano* (New York: Reynal & Hitchcock, 1947), though the latter did not remain long. The big gift—in terms of the rise—was Graham Greene, *The Heart of the Matter* (New York: Viking, 1948), which "stirred up so many things, and I am, as I think you know, a precise specialist in his matter" (letter, 9 June 1948). Olson writes two close pages: "Greene goes over his depth and is washed ashore a Somerset Maugham. Up to then I was willing to hail him as a moralist to go in Mr Dostoevsky's younger shoes. Or a Bernanos." Olson had read Georges Bernanos, *The Diary of a Country Priest* (New York: Macmillan, 1937) in March 1940, according to a notebook. He didn't own it, but was willing to say to Engel that "Bernanos has no equal on man's problems in the Catholic frame . . . Greene goes wishy on us." Greene was not later in his library.

30. Olson did not own R. Buckminster Fuller's *Nine Chains to the Moon* (1938) any more than the *Untitled Epic Poem*, which Olson berated Jonathan Williams for publishing in the Jargon series (letter, 26 April 1961). Olson had kept from BMC days a couple of pamphlets from the Fuller Research Foundation, *Designing a New Industry* (1945–46) and *Fluid Geography* (1946).

## 9. The Swag of Pound

1. As Olson told Paul Blackburn, "1st caught him, in Hemingway's copy, of *Personae*, living in Hem's swimming-house, K W, 1945" (letter, 4 May 1953)—adding, "I did as I do long before I ever read the master." "Clarke's list" shows a copy of *Personae, the Collected Poems of Ezra Pound* (New York: Boni & Liveright, 1926), now missing (was it Hemingway's?). Olson's other copy of *Personae* (New York: New Directions, 1949) was the BMC library copy.

2. We have to assume that Olson was conversant with all current political writing in the period 1939–45, and by instinctive habit beyond that. Only a few traces remain in his library of the war years. His own anonymous 1943 *Spanish Speaking Americans in the War*, done with Ben Shahn, typifies the kind of work produced in the Office of War Information. He hung onto Gunnar Myrdal's two-volume *An American Dilemma: The Negro Problem and Modern Democracy* (New York: Harper, 1944). Olson's pent-up feelings had their say in an article "People v. The Fascist, U.S. (1944)," *Survey Graphic* 33 (August 1944: 356–57, 368, in which he urges tougher laws against hate propaganda. Here Olson uses large chunks of several offprints he had obtained from his old acquaintance David Riesman, then at the University of Buffalo Law School: "Democracy and Defamation," *Columbia Law Review* 42 (1942): 727–80, 1085–1123, 1282–1318; "Equality and Social Structure," *Journal of Legal and Political Sociology* 1 (October 1942: 72–95; and "Civil Lib-

erties in a Period of Transition," in *Public Policy,* Yearbook of the Graduate School of Public Administration, vol. 3 (Cambridge: Harvard University, 1942): 33–96. Also a mimeographed article, "The Politics of Persecution" (New York: Council for Democracy, 1941), with an attached typescript, very much on Olson's subject: "Proposal Model Group Libel Bills,"—"to appear in *Public Opinion* Quarterly Spring 194–?"

It is rumored that Olson almost went off to the Spanish Civil War. He would, in any case, know such anti-fascist books as José Ortega y Gasset, *Invertebrate Spain* (New York: Norton, 1937), for instance. He actually retained a pamphlet of a speech André Malraux gave on 8 March 1937 at Harvard, *The Fascist Threat to Culture,* under the auspices of the Cambridge Union of Teachers and the Harvard Student Union. He read Malraux, *Man's Fate* (New York: Modern Library, 1936) in October 1939; there are many notes and markings in his copy.

3. Seelye, p. 41. Olson later owned the volume, *Cantos LII-LXXI* (Norfolk: New Directions, 1940).

4. Olson's interest in Pound had obviously quickened after Pound's arrest in May 1945, and he was preparing himself to make the statement that became "This is Yeats Speaking," where he urges poets to make their own judgment on Pound regardless of other notions of treason. Olson is thought to have used Charles Norman, "The Case For and Against Ezra Pound," *PM* (25 November 1945); he certainly turned to an article in a volume of *American Historical Review* that he owned: Samuel Rezn_eck, "Constructive Treason by Words in the Fifteenth Century," 33 (April 1928): 544–52, making occasional markings. He also marked Richard P. Blackmur, "Masks of Ezra Pound," *Hound and Horn* 7 (January–March 1934): 177–212, perhaps at this time.

5. The copy in Olson's library is the 2d edition, *ABC of Economics* (London: Peter Russell, the Pound Press, 1953)—flyleaf: "Olson bmc nov/53," with extensive notes and markings. Olson wrote to Creeley on 14 November 1953 that he had "reread ABC of ECO last night": "crazy, how thin it seems, when, 8 years ago, I took it as, The Very Damned Best:" Now he objected to the chapter on "Volition," and wrote in the margin: "One cannot fight bulls at will"—a quotation from Manuel Chaves Nogales and Leslie Charteris, *Juan Belmonte, Killer of Bulls* (New York: Bantam, 1953), which he had from Joel Oppenheimer and was reading at the same time. Olson preferred Pound's *Money Pamphlets,* all six of which appeared in his library, presumably from the publisher Peter Russell (London, 1950–52).

6. Seelye, p. 58. Pound seems to have passed on to Olson copies of three of Ford Madox Ford's books: *Portraits from Life* (New York: Houghton Mifflin, 1937)—flyleaf in Pound's hand: "from 35 W 53 N.Y. 19 L. Littlefield E Pound"; *The March of Literature* (New York: Dial Press, 1938)—flyleaf: "E Pound for L.L.

Jan '47 35W 53''; and *Great Trade Route* (New York: Oxford University Press, 1937)—"swapped" (letter to Pound 13 March 1947).

7. Seelye, p. 69. The poem was written the previous November (*Collected Poems*, p. 646). "Clarke's list" shows that Olson had not only the 1939 edition but also *Ta Hio: The Great Learning* (Seattle: University of Washington Bookstore, 1928), both missing later.

8. Seelye, pp. 72–75. Olson purchased *The Pisan Cantos* (New York: New Directions, 1948) on publication—flyleaf: "Olson Black Mt Dec 13, 1948."

9. Seelye, p. 76. Olson wrote to Douglas Fox in September 1946, and they met when Fox visited Washington: "between us we are trying to get a Katharine Cowan to translate the Paideuma volume," Olson reports to Pound 24 March 1947. "From my own study I take *Erythraea* to be no. 2." This translating did not get done. Olson had to be content to read (about February 1947, according to a notebook) Douglas Fox's exposition, "Frobenius' Paideuma as a Philosophy of Culture," *New English Weekly* (3 September–8 October 1936)—Olson came to acquire the five issues (from Fox?)—a sixth part was missing—in June 1948, and had them bound together at Black Mountain for circulation. In a letter to Fielding Dawson on 11 April 1951, where Fox is praised for his "excellent jobs," Olson refers to his "small creepings through PAIDEUMA" in the German; a phrase he uses several times, "Der Weg stirbt," comes from p. 84 of the 1928 edition. Olson had *Langenscheidt's Pocket-Dictionary*, 2d part, German-English (Berlin, 1929).

10. Olson copied out parts of "The Dry Salvages" into a notebook, 22 November 1945. He was objecting to what he thought was Eliot's misappropriation of Gloucester's Lady of Good Voyage. At some point Olson acquired T. S. Eliot's *Four Quartets* (New York: Harcourt Brace, 1943).

11. "I allowed I couldn't read prose of such long wind" (Seelye, p. 81). However he did keep the copy of Arnold Bennett's *Lord Raingo* (New York: George H. Doran, 1926) that Pound gave him, signed.

12. Seelye, p. 80. Later in the month Olson writes from New York: "no leads on Mazzei"; so perhaps he never tracked down *Memoirs of the Life and Peregrinations of the Florentine Philip Mazzei 1730–1816*, ed. Howard R. Marraro (New York: Columbia University Press, 1942).

13. It is not clear when Olson read the article, but no doubt Pound's talk of Major Douglas and Social Credit led Olson to the Dumbarton Oaks Research Library where he picked up the *Handbook of the Collection* (Washington, 1946) and *Acquisitions December 1, 1946–November 1, 1947* (1947). A February 1947 notebook indicates he read Willis Overholser, *A Short Review and Analysis of the History of Money in the United States* (Libertyville, Ill.: Progress Publishing Concern, 1936).

14. Seelye, p. 83. *Confucius: The Unwobbling Pivot and The Great Digest*

(Norfolk: New Directions, 1947) was published as *Pharos* no. 4 soon after this complaint, for Olson's copy, with markings and inscription by Pound, was given to him on 20 March 1947. Next day he wrote to Pound: "it is beautiful, and an historic act. You fix yourself as pivot." Olson saw, but did not buy the 1951 New Directions edition: "his misuse of 'stone,' of Fenollosa, of ideogram does rankle" (letter to Creeley, May 1952).

15. Seelye, p. 81. Olson may have retrieved *The Fifth Decad of Cantos* (Norfolk: New Directions, 1937), which he seems to have taken with him out West, July 1947.

16. Olson saw the special issue and wrote to Cummings on 12 May 1946 that it was "heartening" to see "WAKE honor you."

Pound gave his copy of Douglas Goldring, *South Lodge: Reminiscences of Violet Hunt, Ford Madox Ford and the English Review Circle* (London: Constable, 1943) to Olson—flyleaf: in Pound's hand "Ezra Pound," in Olson's hand "to Olson."

17. Olson owned no James, but once mentioned "The Figure in the Carpet" in a letter to Creeley of 1 October 1950 (*Creeley Correspondence* 3, p. 65).

18. There is no "canto" for 15 July 1946, but we know that on a visit that day Pound passed on the author's presentation copy of Patrick F. Kirby, *Poet on Mule* (Whittier, Calif.: Western Printing Co., 1940), which Olson kept in his library. In a letter to Harvey Breit on 1 March 1947 Olson mentions visiting Pound and discussing Basil Bunting. Olson later owned Bunting's *Poems: 1950* (Galveston, Texas: Cleaners' Press, 1950), and much later received from Tom Picard *The Spoils* (Newcastle: Morden Tower Book Room, 1965). Butterick thinks the notes and markings in the introduction by Porter Sargent to *A Handbook of Private Schools for American Boys and Girls*, 13th ed. (Boston: Porter Sargent, 1947) are by Pound; if so it was another gift.

19. Seelye, p. 111. Archibald MacLeish, "Victory Without Peace," *Saturday Review of Literature* 29 (9 February 1946): 5–7.

20. J. P. Angold was an English poet killed in World War II. On Pound's prompting, Olson wrote to *Circle*, the California magazine, about publishing Angold, if not also to *Briarcliffe Quarterly*. The project did not come to fruition.

21. Seelye, p. 110. Olson owned no Santayana.

22. *The Portable Dante*, ed. Paolo Milano (New York: Viking, 1947) had just been published, reprinting in full Lawrence Binyon's translation of *The Divine Comedy.* Olson later had it as a gift from Monroe Engel, 11 May 1948.

23. There is no evidence that Olson read any Gabriele D'Annunzio.

24. Seelye, p. 113. Olson owned *Collected Poems of H. D.* (New York: Liveright, 1940), and kept on his shelves the gift from Robert Duncan of the specially bound *Three Books of the War: The Walls Do Not Fall, Tribute to the Angels,* and *The Flowering of the Rod* (London: Oxford University Press, 1944, 1945, 1946); but maintained practically a total silence on H. D.'s work.

25. Seelye, p. 113. First mention of Brooks Adams, a writer of great importance to Olson later.

26. Olson owned the 1945 printing of H. L. Mencken, *The American Language,* 4th ed. (New York: Knopf, 1936).

27. Seelye, p. 113. Olson did not own *Tarr* nor any other Wyndham Lewis novels.

28. Before going to the West Coast, Olson had seen Robert Duncan's poem "The Years as Catches" in *Circle* 7/8 (Fall 1946), which he had from George Leite and kept (as also later Duncan's "Towards an African Elegy" in *Circle,* 10 Summer 1948). He also had *The Ark* 1 (Spring 1947) with Duncan's "Homage and Lament for Ezra Pound: May 12, 1944." While Olson was in California in November 1947, Duncan published his first volume, *Heavenly City Earthly City.* If Olson brought a copy back with him, it has since been misplaced.

On Olson's return, Duncan sent him his magazine, *Berkeley Miscellany* 2 (1949), containing a story "The Garden" by Mary Fabilli that Olson considered "so fine it will last" (letter to Monroe Engel, 8 April 1949).

William Everson, writing as Brother Antoninus, is represented in Olson's library by two early publications from his own Untide Press, Waldport, Oregon: *War Elegies* (1944) and *Poems: MCMXLII* (1945), possibly gifts from the poet in 1947.

Kenneth Rexroth did not apparently appeal to Pound—nor to Olson. There are only two small items in Olson's library, both gifts; one sent by the author for Christmas 1948, a poem from *The Signature of All Things,* and the other brought in person by Jonathan Williams, *Thou Shalt Not Kill* (Sunnyvale, California, 1955), which Olson called that "gruesome Thomas thing" (letter to Duncan 31 May 1955).

29. "I wld guess, it is here that this bad science of EP's was picked up: a biological mechanistic romanticism abt how nature behaves"—letter of 29 November 1951 (*Creeley Correspondence* 8, p. 205; and on p. 225 "you must read" Pound's "Postscript"). Olson had mentioned Remy de Gourmont's "decadence" in a college paper, 14 October 1932, and may have acquired early the two-volume *Remy de Gourmont: Selections from All His Works,* chosen and translated by Richard Aldington (New York: Covici-Friede, 1929). He eventually deposited the latter with Jean Kaiser.

30. It was on the basis of this one reading that Olson had the temerity to assign Knight as the sole text in the Myth Seminar at Buffalo 1964, and ended up working from a xerox copy, which remained in his papers.

31. Olson did not later own Jeffrey Mark, *Modern Idolatry* (London: Chatto & Windus, 1934) or *Analysis of Usury* (London: Dent, 1935), so perhaps they were sent to Pound.

32. The review appeared in *Evergreen Review* 9 (Summer 1958), an

issue Olson kept. Volumes by WCW in Olson's library, not mentioned above, are:

*A Beginning on the Short Story,* The Outcast Chapbooks 17 (Yonkers: Alicat Bookshop Press 1950)—this copy inscribed from Denise Levertov to Mitchell Goodman, August 1952; probably therefore coming to Olson via Creeley.

*The Build-Up* (New York: Random House, 1952)—flyleaf: "Olson." Letter to Creeley, 16 January 1953: "what a mystery to me, as always, his 'novels'! . . . white mule, and now this one."

*I Wanted to Write a Poem,* ed. Edith Heal (Boston: Beacon Press, 1958)—on "Clarke's list."

*Paterson,* The New Classics (New York: New Directions, 1950). Another copy (1951) came to Olson as a gift from Mary Shore.

*Paterson (Book Five)* (New York: New Directions, 1958)—review slip laid in; much response to the text in the margin.

*Selected Poems,* The New Classics (New York: New Directions, 1949)—flyleaf: "Mary Fitton July 1949" crossed out, and "Michael Rumaker 1952 Black Mountain" added.

It is strange that this list does not include *Desert Music and Other Poems* (New York: Random House, 1954), and even more so *The Autobiography of William Carlos Williams* (New York: Random House, 1954), where Williams did an act of high confirmation in including a large segment of Olson's "Projective Verse" essay because of its importance in his life.

In letters, Williams is a constant topic of discussion, for example, his piece "The Present Relationship of Prose to Verse" contributed to *7 Arts* (Doubleday Permabooks, 1953) (not owned) in a letter to Creeley, 25 May 1953. It is through the *Creeley Correspondence* 7, pp. 63–74 that we read Olson's most sustained engagement with Williams's work in a letter to Louis Martz that was sent to Creeley instead. It is here (p. 70) that Olson indicates he knows Vivienne Koch, *William Carlos Williams,* The Makers of Modern Literature (Norfolk: New Directions, 1950). In a marginal note to Creeley, he says that Martz's "William Carlos Williams: On the Road to Paterson," *Poetry New York* 4 (1951): 18–32 is "an improvement on Koch." Linda Wagner sent her critical study *The Poems of William Carlos Williams* (Middletown: Wesleyan University Press, 1964) to Olson "with admiration" in December 1964—Olson annotates: "read in and acknowledged Dec 9th." Olson had a xerox copy of Walter Sutton's "A Visit with William Carlos Williams" from *The Minnesota Review* 1 (1961).

33. Olson's library included the following Pound books not listed above:

*The Classic Anthology Defined by Confucius* (Cambridge: Harvard University

Press, 1954)—Olson's response to this publication was the "I, Mencius" poem.

*Drafts and Fragments of Cantos CX–CXVII* (New York: New Directions, 1968)—flyleaf: "Olson from Jas Laughlin April 1969."

*How to Read, Followed by The Spirit of Romance Part I* (Le Beausset, Var, France: TO Publishers, 1932).

*The Letters of Ezra Pound, 1907–1941,* ed. D. D. Paige (New York: Harcourt, Brace, 1950).

*Literary Essays of Ezra Pound,* ed. T. S. Eliot (Norfolk: New Directions, 1954)— flyleaf: "Olson," with "Creeley—54."

*Make It New* (New Haven: Yale University Press, 1935)—on "Clarke's list."

*Provença: Poems, Selected from Personae, Exultations, and Canzoniere of Ezra Pound* (Boston: Small, Maynard, 1930)—flyleaf: "Edward Dorn Dec 19th, 1953 Seattle."

*Section: Rock-Drill 85–95 de los cantares* (New York: New Directions, 1956)— ordered from publisher; flyleaf: "Olson black mountain 1/7/57."

*Thrones 96–109 de los cantares* (New York: New Directions, 1959)—gift of James Laughlin.

Pound's translation of *Sonnets and Ballate of Guido Cavalcanti* (London: Stephen Swift, 1912) was borrowed by Olson from the Public Library of the District of Columbia in June 1946 and never returned. Olson did at one time (though later it was missing) own *ABC of Reading,* presumably the 1934 edition (London: Routledge; New Haven: Yale University Press). In a letter to Creeley on 2 April 1953, Olson wrote: "Have just (for 1st time) gone slow, and then swiftly through EP's ABC of Reading . . . and find him of course, on Chaucer very damned thick and fine ((It *is* his time."

Olson kept *An Examination of Ezra Pound* (Norfolk: New Directions, 1950), which may have been a gift from editor Peter Russell; and Eustace Mullins's *This Difficult Individual, Ezra Pound* (New York: Fleet, 1961), which came to him via Ted Berrigan. He had words of praise for Lawrence Richardson, "Ezra Pound's Homage to Propertius," *Yale Poetry Review* 6 (1947): 21–29, but did not own the issue (*Creeley Correspondence* 6, p. 24).

34. Kasper actually visited Olson at Black Mountain 17–23 November 1951 to discuss publishing plans, but it doesn't seem that Olson talked him into anything. He opposed the "planned issuance of Agassiz": "rather than such, or de Gourmont, I'd say, republish Pliny's Natural History!" (*Creeley Correspondence* 8, p. 215). Pliny was not in Olson's library, but he accepted and kept *Gists from Agassiz,* ed. John Kasper (New York: Kasper & Horton Square Dollar Series, 1953). He also had Eustace Mullins, *A Study of the Federal Reserve* (New York: Kasper & Horton, 1952), Kasper's own *Segregation or Death* (Washington: Seaboard White Citizens Council, n.d.), and Del Mar, *A History of Mon-*

*etary Crimes* (Washington: Cleaners' Press, for the Del Mar Society, n. d.)—"fr gasper" (Creeley letter, 23 January 1952). There is also found in Olson's library a Government Document: U.S. Senate, Committee on the Judiciary, *Hearing Before the Subcommittee to Investigate the Administration of the Internal Security Act and Other Internal Security Laws . . . on Communist Propaganda* (83d Congress, 2d Session, 1954)—stamped on the cover: "Compliments of Make It New Bookshop, New York" (the bookshop John Kasper ran on Bleecker Street).

35. Olson's comment in the essay entitled "GrandPa, GoodBye"—Seelye, p. 99.

## 10. The Preface to

1. Letter, 25 October 1950 (*Creeley Correspondence* 3, p. 132). Olson's Italian dictionary was *Nuovo Dizionario Italiano ed Inglese*, ed. John Millhouse, 7th ed. (New York: Appleton, 1893)—he had vol. 2.

2. "La Préface," written May 1946 (*Collected Poems*, pp. 46–47; *Selected Writings*, pp. 160–61). "Bigmans," Olson told Butterick (*Guide*, p. xxxi), came from a poem he had seen in "The Greenberg Manuscripts: A Selection of the Poems of Samuel Bernard Greenberg, the Unknown Poet who Influenced Hart Crane," ed. James Laughlin, *New Directions* 4 (1939): 353–81 (not owned). Olson kept a copy of *Southern Review* with an article on the subject: Philip Horton, "The Greenberg Manuscripts and Hart Crane's Poetry," 2 (Summer 1936); 148–59.

3. A searing phrase, from lecture notes (at Storrs) written by Olson in preparation for the Northwest Writers Conference, Seattle, August 1947. Some of the Buchenwald drawings are reproduced in *Cagli*, ed. Roberto Barzanti (Siena, 1972). Olson had read, but did not own, Hitler's *Mein Kampf* (New York: Reynal & Hitchcock, 1939). He owned Konrad Heiden, *Der Fuehrer: Hitler's Rise to Power* (Boston: Houghton Mifflin, 1944), and there are reading notes in a notebook of summer 1945 on a three-part series, "I Was Hitler's Buddy" by Reinhold Hanisch, *New Republic* 98 (5 April 1939): 239–42, (12 April 1939): 270–72, (19 April 1939): 297–300. Nothing here would have prepared him for Cagli's drawings.

4. Martin-Chauffier's book was in Olson's library and supplied a phrase in "The Resistance": "the way of the beast—of man and the Beast" (*Human Universe*, p. 47; *Selected Writings*, p. 13). David Rousset was not owned, but it seems definite from a letter to Creeley on 30 May 1950 (*Creeley Correspondence* 1, p. 60) that Olson knew the book in French before its translation as *The Other Kingdom* (New York: Reynal & Hitchcock, 1947). He preferred this document of the camps to Rousset's fictionalized account, *Les Jours de Notre Mort* (Paris, 1947).

5. Olson wrote to Ben Shahn on 10 May 1949: "There is a fine friend by

name Jean Riboud, yes, French, Lyon, now NY, though soon back to France. Have known him some two years since he has been here. Has great eyes in his heart. Is one of the rare ones." In opening a New York office for Schlumberger, Riboud was on his way to being the chief executive officer of one of the most profitable private companies in the world—so that *The New Yorker* gave him a "profile" (6 June 1983). From this in-depth study by Ken Auletta we learn much about Riboud's experience in the French underground, his capture in 1943, and his two years in Buchenwald ("when he emerged, he had tuberculosis and weighed ninety-six pounds"—*New Yorker*, p. 46). That experience, his brother is quoted as saying, made him "very strong, very capable of resisting anything" (p. 59). The author of the article noticed about him an impression of delicacy, and his eyes, "which are deep brown and cryptic" (p. 44).

"The Resistance" was an essay written on the occasion of Jean Riboud's wedding on 1 October 1949 (Olson was best man), or soon thereafter. The bride was Krishna Roy, Rabindranath Tagore's niece. Tagore's *The Gardener* (New York: Macmillan, 1915) was in Olson's library.

6. Quotation from a letter to Vincent Ferrini as published in *Origin* 1 (Spring 1951). Olson had sent "The Resistance" to Ferrini in November 1949, saying "it is for you, as well as Riboud"; it was published in Ferrini's *Four Winds* 4 (Winter 1953). The direct allusion in the essay to "Bogomolets' researches into the nature of connective tissue" means that Olson had been looking into Alexander A. Bogomolets, *The Prolongation of Life* (New York: Duell, Sloan & Pearce, 1946), though he did not own it.

7. Mark Riboud, the brother, was one of the first photographers into Communist China, and eventually published the photographic study, *Three Banners of China* (1966), which Olson saw but did not own. This was the connection to Henri Cartier-Bresson, whose *The Decisive Moment* (New York: Simon & Schuster in collaboration with Editions Verve of Paris, 1952) was a gift to Olson from Jean Riboud; and whose *China: Photographed by Henri Cartier-Bresson* Olson picked up in the Bantam Gallery Edition (New York, 1964).

Olson attended a number of Jean Riboud parties in New York. There is no knowing whom he met there and what developed. Perhaps he met Paul Richard there; his library contains Richard's two publications from Paradox Publications (New York, 1966); *Land of the Rising Sun* (on Japan) and *The Twin Space of "Quasars"* (on Einstein). Some of the following books from France may have been passed on to Olson by Riboud:

Jean Noir, *33 Sonnets Composés au Secret* (Paris: Aux Éditions de Minuit, 1944).
Géraud Lavergne, *Des Monts d'Auvergne à l'Antique: La Dordogne et ses Pays*, 2 vols. (Paris: Editions U.S.H.A. Aurillac, 1930).
Raymond Queneau, *Zazie dans le metro (Paris: Olypia, 1959).*
Jules Martha, *Manuel d'Archeologie Etrusque et Romaine* (Paris: A. Quantin, n.d.).

Claude Augé, *Nouveau Petit Larousse Illustre* (Paris: Libraire Larousse, 1932).

8. Olson's notebook for the summer of 1946 indicates that he read in the Library of Congress at least the following: Gervais Bouchet, *Le Tarot Egyptien* (Vichy: Bouchet-Dreyfus, 1922), J.-B. Bourgeat, *Le Tarot*, 4th ed. (Paris: Chacornac Freres, 1923), and Etudes Picard, *Manuel Synthetique and Practique du Tarot* (Paris: H. Daragon, 1909). Olson told Robert Kelly (letter, 3 October 1960) that it was "via the tarot cards" that he came to know André Breton.

9. Bonola translated by H. S. Carslaw as *Non-Euclidean Geometry* (New York: Open Court, 1912), p. 142. Or, since we know Olson also consulted around this time H. S. M. Coxeter, *Non-Euclidean Geometry* (Toronto: University of Toronto Press, 1942), he could have found the identical quotation from Riemann there on p. 11. Reading notes for Coxeter are found in the "Verse and Geometry" notebook dated 1946 (at Storrs) along with reading notes for Stephen A. and Margaret L. Ionides, *Stars and Men* (Indianapolis: Bobbs-Merrill, 1939).

10. Typescript "4th dimension" (Storrs). On Olson inquiring, Donchian wrote that the models were "badly banged and bent on their return trip from the Chicago Fair in 1934," and could not be sent to Washington (*Muthologos* 2, pp. 72–73, and note p. 186). Olson was constantly seeking to take advantage of investigations into "the infinitely small"; for instance, two examples among the many we do not know about: Jerome Rothstein, "Information, Measurement, and Quantum Mechanics," *Science* 114 (17 August 1951): 171–75—notes made from this article in Olson's papers of 1951–53; and Tobias Dantzig, *Aspects of Science* (New York: Macmillan, 1937)—typed notes exist from the late 1940s.

11. Olson owned Massimo Bontempelli's brochure, *Corrado Cagli* (Rome: Studio D'arte Palma, 1947), done for Cagli's show there; and Cagli's own *Dieci disegni e uno scritto su La rotta del Po* (Rome: Edizioni de Cultura Sociale, 1951), inscribed to Olson. What Mirko publications might have been available to Olson is not known, but he referred in a manuscript "De Priapo" (1947, Storrs) to Giorgio de Chirico's "book with the ambiguous title"—likely *Commedia dell'Arte Moderna* (Rome, 1945). He linked himself with de Chirico when proposing to Caresse Crosby a series of "tuppenny pamflets of painter-poet now: each issue a poem and drawing or repro: Eluard-Picasso, Lorca-Frances, Pound-Cagli, De Chirico-Olson, St Perse-who?, Montale-Morandi, etc. etc." (letter, 23 July 1948). Here, it seems, is the idea that within six months gave birth to *Y & X*, five Olson poems with five Cagli drawings (Black Sun Press, 1948), though the model for its production technique and high quality may have come from Pierre Emmanuel, *Le Poète Fou* (Monaco: Editions du Rocher, 1944), which Caresse Crosby may have given Olson for that purpose.

12. Olson kept Caresse Crosby's memoir, *The Passionate Years* (New York: Dial Press, 1953), but unsigned, because he couldn't get to the publication party. She must be responsible for the presence in Olson's library of rare Harry Crosby books, all from the Black Sun Press in 1931: *Chariot of the Sun*, *Sleeping Together*, *Torchbearers*, and *Transit of Venus*. Another gift was Paul Eluard, *Misfortunes of the Immortals* (New York: Black Sun Press, 1943), inscribed to Olson by Caresse in 1948 at the time she was trying to get Eluard into the U.S. Olson helped by writing to Monroe Engel; but to no avail. On Eluard's death, Olson wrote to Caresse, 30 March 1953: "My consolations to you, over this loss. Tho I still have no clear sense of his work, the feeling of the man is rare." Olson bought Robert D. Valette, *Eluard: Livre d'identité* (Paris: Claude Tchou, 1967) on publication.

There were undoubtedly many other gifts. The only gift going the other way that we have record of is *The Winston Dictionary* (1942), inscribed "for Caresse the writer the writer 1948 Olson."

13. "Notes on the New Dimension," typescript for a talk at the American University Art Center, Washington, 29 July 1948 (Storrs). The catalog, which Olson kept, *Paintings from the Berlin Museums* (New York: Metropolitan Museum of Art, 1948) includes plate 27, "Saint Clare Saving a Ship in Distress," by Giovanni di Paolo.

14. The inscription on Olson's copy of *The White Pony: An Anthology of Chinese Poetry from the Earliest Times to the Present Day* (New York: John Day, 1947) is from Payne to Ezra Pound "in homage and deepest love for his poetry and his delight in China, Los Angeles October 22, 1947." Presumably Olson was to deliver the book, but didn't.

15. Olson's letter is unfortunately not extant (Payne's reply is), and the poet seems to have passed the book along to somebody else, as he did several of the books that we know from letters he received from Payne: *Alexander the God* (New York: A. A. Wyn, 1954); *The Wanton Nymph: A Study of Pride* (London: Heinemann, 1951); *Report on America* (New York: John Day, 1949); even the volume dedicated with the printed dedication "for Charles and Constance Olson," *Zero, The Story of Terrorism* (London and New York: Wingate, 1951). He donated to BMC library in March 1952 Payne's *The Marshall Story: A Biography of General George C. Marshall* (New York: Prentice-Hall, 1951), which had been inscribed "for Kate Constanza & Charles with love from Robert montevallo january 1952 (the copy now with the residue of BMC library books at North Carolina Wesleyan, Rocky Mount, N.C.). Olson picked up the Pocket Books edition of *The Chieftain: A Story of the Nez Perce People* (New York, 1954), and mentioned it in a letter to Payne on 17 January 1955, but did not keep the book. Olson did retain in his library: *Mao Tse-Tung: Ruler of Red China* (New York: Henry Schuman, 1950), inscribed "for Charles & Connie with the abounding love of Robert, November 1949"; *The Fathers of the Western Church* (New York:

Viking, 1951), inscribed "For Charles & Connie with love from Robert montevallo ala oct 1951"; *The Canal Builders* (New York: Macmillan, 1959), inscribed "for Charles with my love Robt"; and the Leonardo da Vinci "novel" discovered by Payne and published as *The Deluge* (New York: Twayne, 1954). No doubt Olson glanced at from curiosity other Payne books through the years. Payne did over a hundred. Olson called him "that extraordinary slayer of books" (letter to Payne, 24 February 1949).

16. He was his father's son in this, witness the stories of *The Post Office* written in tribute to his father's immigrant workingclass values, in February 1948, immediately upon his break with father Pound. Olson makes the point to Creeley in a letter of 5 February 1952: "if you ever want to catch the bottom of EP's plot, get a hold of Stoddard's book on RACE—I happened to pick it up once in a bookstore, and give it a go: the incredible low brain of it, the hate, the fixed premise about homogeneity." Lothrop Stoddard wrote several books that could be so described; perhaps most vivid in its title is *The Rising Tide of Color against White World-Supremacy* (London: Chapman & Hall, 1920).

17. Included with the passport is a statement about World Community membership signed by J. C. and R. G. King. Olson also owned their joint *Manifesto for Individual Secession Into World Community* (Paris: Crosby Continental Editions, 1948). During his trip to Italy in 1965, Olson stayed at Roccasinibalda, "Caresse Crosby's Castle—365 rooms, literally, and flying the flag of the Citizens of the World above it like the *only* Renaissance I have seen" (letter to Vincent Ferrini, 10 July 1965).

18. "Notes for the Proposition: Man is Prospective," *boundary 2* (Olson issue) p. 1. Of the writers mentioned, Olson owned Georges Sorel, *Reflections on Violence*, trans. T. E. Hulme, 3d ed. (New York: Huebsch, 1912), and Albert Einstein, *Essays In Science* (New York: Philosophical Library, 1934). Olson made notes on W. de Sitter, *Kosmos* (Cambridge: Harvard University Press, 1932) in a notebook labeled "Verse & Geometry" Washington November 1946. There is no evidence for direct contact with the works of Darwin, Renan, and Fourier. The other names are dealt with elsewhere, except for the "now alive Saint Francis," a reference that remains cryptic.

## 11. Throw What Light

1. *Boundary 2* (Olson issue), p. 3. In March 1948 Cagli had sent Olson a copy of Mario Salmi, *Piero della Francesca*, 2d ed. (Bergamo: Instituto Italiano D'Arti Grafiche, 1944) from New York.

2. *Boundary 2* (Olson issue), p. 3. "It is significant that Soetan Shjarir, Jawaharlal Nehru, and Mao Tse-tung are scholars in their own right, with the historian's understanding of the political forces at work and the poet's sensitivity"—Robert Payne, *The Revolt of Asia* (cited above), p. 4.

3. This schedule is found in a Storrs file: "Notes for lecture on the Search in Art and the New Dimension." Olson wrote to Henry Murray on 10 October 1948: "I will do one lecture on space and I'm thinking it might be best to read the text of About Space as a point of departure." "About Space" (typescript at Storrs) is a rewriting of "Notes for the Proposition: Man is Prospective."

4. Pound had given Olson copies of *Tomorrow* magazine containing a two-part article by Charles Wisner Barrell, "Verifying the Secret History of Shakespeare's Sonnets," 5 (February 1946): 49–55 and (March 1946): 54–60—Pound had added a note, "1st intelligent article on the Sonnets I have ever seen" (*Creeley Correspondence* 8, p. 263). Following one of Barrell's leads, Olson suggested to Monroe Engel in August 1948 that Viking might republish Thomas Looney's *Shakespeare Identified*, though Olson may have seen no more of it than Barrell's citations. About the same time he borrrowed Eva Turner Clark, *The Man Who Was Shakespeare* (New York: Richard R. Smith, 1937) from the District of Columbia Library, and never returned it. He borrowed, or was given, a friend's copy of Tucker Brooke's edition of *Shakespeare's Sonnets* (London & New York: Oxford University Press, 1936)—flyleaf "Sam Rosenberg 1943 wash." He made notes about this time from Frank Harris, *The Man Shakespeare and his Tragic Life-Story* (New York: Mitchell Kennerley, 1909), though he did not own the book. He purchased a copy of Denys Bray, *The Original Order of Shakespeare's Sonnets* (London: Methuen, 1925)—endpapers: "1st reading—1948: 1, 6, 25."

5. Information from a letter to Joseph Albers, Rector of Black Mountain College, 6 November 1948. A page of notes entitled "mythography & geometry" exists from around this time (Storrs), where the first section is headed: "non-Homeric myth || non-Euclidean geometry." Olson considers non-Homeric myth "multiple narration and finite," but does not specify further.

6. BMC course description from the files of the College deposited by Olson in the North Carolina State Archives, Raleigh, in 1957.

Seami, whose *Hagoromo* is named in "Projective Verse" (1950), is mentioned here for the first time. Olson had been reading Seami's plays in Arthur Waley *The Nō Plays of Japan* (New York: Knopf, 1922)—borrowed from a library, due date 11 May 1948, but never returned. Olson presumably had had for some time Ernest Fenollosa and Ezra Pound, '*Noh' or Accomplishment: A Study of the Classical Stage of Japan* (New York: Knopf, 1917), but this volume does not feature Seami by name. Olson also had, by the way, Arthur Waley's translations, *The Temple and Other Poems* (New York: Knopf, 1923), and later acquired his *One Hundred and Seventy Chinese Poems* (London: Constable, 1947—flyleaf: "Olson bmc feb 53."

7. John Murray Gibbon, *Melody and the Lyric from Chaucer to the Cavaliers* (London: Dent; New York: Dutton, 1930). Olson must have returned the book to the BMC library; he did not later own it.

8. Letter to Natasha Goldowski, Secretary of Black Mountain College, 1 June 1949 (Raleigh Archives). The "Kyklops" episode performed was not really Homer, but an adaptation of Euripides's satyr play. "Wagadu" was from "Gassire's Lute" in Frobenius and Fox, *African Genesis* (cited previously), which Olson had on reserve in the BMC library at this time. Somebody remembered Olson as associated with a production of Garcia Lorca's *Lament for Ignacio Sanchez Mejias* (Duberman, p. 308), but there is doubt about that.

9. The best statement of this reiterated point is in Olson's letter to Creeley of 1 April 1951 (*Creeley Correspondence* 5, p. 118):

> what Berard seems to me to prove is, that Homer was writing his poem on the base of another poem, a Phoenician predecessor, and that the accuracies are sailor's accuracies (or his predecessor's) not, his. Only, again, it ain't that simple, for, what is the most wonderful thing of all abt Berard's work, is, the way it argues that Homer's inventions of his incidents & personages rest entirely on an animation of geographical features which sailors after sailors had noticed until the names of "remarkable" rocks, headlands, etc. had got fixed as nouns characterizing sd shapes. And that what Homer did (or maybe, the Phoenician before him, or, maybe, some guy of Lagash) anyway, what he did was to spin a tale riding out fr these nouns! That is, Circe-Kirke means nothing in Greek but, in Phoenician periploi, the name for the island precisely in her spot on the coast of Italy just north(?) of Cumae (which seems to have been a Phoenician point of call before it was the 1st Greek settlement in Italy) translates as SHE-HAWK (as I remember it). Which leads on, in Homer's hands, to the presentation of, her nature.

It is not clear whether or not Olson owned *Did Homer Live?* (New York: Dutton, 1931) at this time; the copy that was in his library later was a gift, inscribed "Wieners From Morgan Memorial to Charles Olson for his *Homer and Bible* 2.12.58." He did not own *Les Phéniciens et l'Odyssée*, 2 vols. (Paris: A. Colin, 1902–3; rev. 1927), nor the three-volume translation, *L'Odyssée*, that he announced to Dahlberg on 20 April 1949 that he was using.

10. Manuscript at Storrs. Evans was recommended later, "Tutorial: the Greeks" (1955), and is cited there. The Nilsson volume Olson attempted to get through interlibrary loan on 24 January 1953; there is no record that he was successful. The other titles in this list are not mentioned elsewhere. Olson did not pick up J. D. S. Pendlebury's *The Archaeology of Crete* until he found the paperback (New York: W. W. Norton, 1965), but he must have seen it earlier. In another Storrs manuscript, "Creatively we are Neolithic" (1948), Olson refers to a further work he would like to see: H. Th. Bossert, *The Art of Ancient Crete* (London: Zwemmer, 1937).

11. The named volumes can be found in Olson's library:

*A Book of Elizabethan Lyrics,* ed. Felix E. Schelling (Boston: Ginn, 1895).

Athenaeus, *The Diepnosophists, or Banquet of the Learned,* trans. C. D. Yonge, 3 vols. (London: Bohn's Classical Library, 1854)—markings in vols. 1 and 3.

*Catullus, Tibullus, and Pervigilium,* Loeb Classical Library (London: Heinemann; New York: Macmillan, 1914)—"Clarke's list."

*The Dramatic Works of John Lyly* (cited previously).

*Herodotus: A New and Literal Version,* trans. Henry Cary (New York: Harper's New Classical Library, 1878)—notes and markings through p. 139.

*The Idylls of Theocritus, Bion, and Moschus,* ed. J. Banks, Bohn's Classical Library (London: George Bell, 1891).

*Lyra Graeca,* ed. J. M. Edmonds, Loeb Classical Library (London: Heinemann; New York: Putnam, 1922)—Olson had vol. 1 of 3 vols.

Thomas Percy, *Reliques of Ancient English Poetry,* ed. J. V. Prichard, 2 vols., Bohn's Standard Library (London: George Bell, 1878).

*Plutarch's Morals,* Bohn's Classical Library (previously cited).

*The Works of Hesiod, Callimachus, and Theognis,* trans. J. Banks, Bohn's Classical Library (London: Bohn, 1856)—heavy notes and markings through p. 83.

12. Arthur S. Way translated the four volumes of Euripides in the Loeb Classical Library (London: Heinemann; New York: Macmillan 1912)—flyleaf of vol. 2: "Olson April 1947." Notes and markings in "The Phoenician Maidens" of vol. 3. Olson was also using his Everyman Library, *The Plays of Euripides in English,* 2 vols. (London: Dent; New York: Dutton, 1920, 1917)—on contents page against the title "The Bacchanals": "lovely—'47." Olson later had, via Wesley Huss, the Penguin Classics edition: *Three Plays: Hippolytus; Iphigenia in Tauris; Alcestis,* trans. Philip Vellacott (Baltimore: Penguin Books, 1953).

There is no evidence that he gave the same kind of attention to Sophocles, though he may have had his Jebb translation of *The Tragedies of Sophocles* (Cambridge University Press, 1905) at this time. Later he had the Penguin Classics, Sophocles, *Electra and Other Plays* (Baltimore: Penguin Books, 1953)—flyleaf "Joseph Dunn Beacon Hill Boston" with "Charles Olson's (ok)" below. He also picked up C. M. Bowra, *Sophoclean Tragedy* (Oxford Paperbacks, 1965), but there is no indication that he read it.

As for Aeschylus, if it were not for the reference to his *Agamemnon* in the first draft of "Projective Verse" (later Euripides' *Trojan Women* was substituted as a more satisfactory example), we would hardly know that Olson read him. There is no Aeschylus edition in his library. Richard Lattimore's translation of *Agamemnon* was included in Dudley Fitts's edition of *Greek Plays in Modern Translation* (New York: Dial, 1947), as was Edith Hamilton's *Prometheus Bound,* mentioned in "Notes for the Proposition" (*boundary 2,* p. 4). Olson certainly used the Fitts anthology though it was not in his library later. (Olson kept his copy of Dudley Fitts, *More Poems from the Palatine Anthology* New Directions, Poet of the Month, 1941.)

13. *The Heroides or Epistles of the Heroines, The Amours, Art of Love, Remedy of Love, and Minor Works of Ovid*, trans. Henry T. Riley, Bohn's Classical Library (London: George Bell, 1879)—flyleaf: "Olson Wash 1949." Olson also had the companion Bohns, *The Fasti, Tristia, Pontic Epistles, Ibis, and Halieuticon of Ovid* (London: George Bell, 1892)—flyleaf: "Olson Wash—Dave Ornstein—Mr 1949" and *The Metamorphoses of Ovid* (London: George Bell, 1898)—flyleaf: "Olson—from Con Wash (Orenstein's) April XLIX." Olson's library contained two other Ovids: *Selected Works*, Everyman's Library (London: Dent; New York: Dutton, 1939) and *The Metamorphoses of Ovid, Books VIII–XV*, trans. Henry T. Riley, The Students' Literal Translations (New York: Translation Publishing Co., 1925).

14. Maximus of Tyre's *Dissertations* is quoted in "Life of Sappho," vol. 1 of *Lyra Graeca* (cited above), p. 155. So we see that one aspect of the Maximus figure came out of a major push into older texts, not merely confined to the above mentioned titles. To these we can add the following "stragglers," owned by Olson:

*Aristophanes*, 3 vols., Loeb Classical Library, trans. Benjamin Bickley Rogers (London: Heinemann; New York: Putnam, 1924)—"Acquired Aristophanes today. But of whom I am suspicious" (letter to Dahlberg 31 May 1949).

*Ausonius*, trans. Hugh G. Evelyn White, 2 vols., Loeb Classical Library (London: Heinemann; New York: Putnam, 1919–21).

*Clement of Alexandria*, trans. G. W. Butterworth, Loeb Classical Library (Cambridge: Harvard University Press, 1953).

*Corpus Poetarum Latinorum*, ed. Gulilmus Sidney Walker, 2 vols. (London: Henry G. Bohn, 1849).

*The Ecclesiastical History of Eusebius Pamphilus*, trans. C. F. Cruse, Bohn's Ecclesiastical Library (London: George Bell, 1903)— "picked up for 2 bucks" (letter to Frances Boldereff, 27 February 1950).

*The Moral Discourses of Epictetus*, trans. Elizabeth Carter, Everyman's Library (London: Dent; New York: Dutton, 1910).

*Pausanias' Description of Greece*, trans. Arthur Richard Shilleto, 2 vols., Bohn's Classical Library (London: George Bell, 1886)—flyleaf: "Olson Washington xlix"; notes and markings throughout both volumes.

Strabo, *Geography*, trans. Horace Leonard Jones, Loeb Classical Library (London: Heinemann; New York: Putnam, 1923–24)— Olson had vols. 2 and 3 of 8 vols.

Xenophon, *The Anabasis or Expedition of Cyrus, and the Memorabilia of Socrates*, trans. J. S. Watson, Bohn's Classical Library (London: Henry G. Bohn, 1864)—mentioned *boundary 2*, p. 10.

We glimpse Olson's activity around these texts in his postcard to Michael Lekakis, 10 July 1949, asking if he could find a copy of Andrew Robert Burn, *The World of Hesiod* (London: Routledge & Kegan Paul, 1936)—which didn't materialize, one assumes, partly because Olson got the name wrong on the card.

There are a few additional texts that one suspects Olson picked up in the midst of the 1949–50 push of reading:

*Aucassin and Nicolette and Other Medieval Romances and Legends,* trans. Eugene Mason, Everyman's Library (London: Dent; New York: Dutton, 1937)—bought 24 April 1947 to adapt "Our Lady's Tumbler" for a ballet (letter to Herman Engel, 17 May 1947).

*Gesta Romanorum: Entertaining Moral Stories,* trans. Charles Swan (London: George Routledge; New York: Dutton, 1905).

Giovanni Pico della Mirandola, *The Very Elegant Speech on the Dignity of Man,* with an appendix by Robert Grosseteste, *Man Is A Smaller World,* Classics of the St. John's Program (Annapolis: St. John's College Press, 1949).

*Ideal Commonwealths: Plutarch's Lycurgus; More's Utopia; Bacon's New Atlantis; Campanella's City of the Sun; and a fragment of Hall's Mundus Alter et Idem,* ed. Henry Morley, 10th ed. (London: George Routledge; New York: Dutton, n.d.)—flyleaf: "Olson" and some notes in the introduction.

Niccolo Machiavelli, *The Prince,* trans. Luigi Ricci, World's Classics (London: Oxford University Press)—Olson also acquired the same translation, revised by E. R. P. Vincent as a Mentor Classic (New York: New American Library, 1960).

*John Skelton: A Selection of his Poems,* ed. Roland Grant, Crown Classics (London: Grey Walls Press, 1949).

Tom Taylor, *Ballads and Songs of Brittany,* The New Universal Library (London: Routledge; New York: Dutton, 1865).

Lynn Thorndike, *University Records and Life in the Middle Ages* (New York: Columbia University Press, 1944).

Olson asked Dahlberg (letter of 20 April 1949) what was the "best Chrysostom." Dahlberg recommended that he read "Trojan Discourse," but there is no evidence Olson did.

15. Text by Frances Ward [Boldereff] to photographs of Michelangelo sculpture, published from the author's home in Woodward, Pennsylvania, under the imprint of the Russian Classic Non-Fiction Library. Frances was not herself Russian, but was brought into the émigré world by her first husband.

One book-gift she inscribed to Olson was David Talbot Rice, *Russian Icons* (London: King Penguin Book, 1947).

16. In a letter of 10 May 1949, Frances recommended Franz Cumont's "volume of plates in color on the frescoes found at Dura-Europa,", i.e., the second part of *Fouilles de Doura-Europe 1922–1923* (Paris, 1926), presumably seen by Olson in the Library of Congress, where he also consulted at this time James Henry Breasted, *Oriental Forerunners of Byzantine Painting: First Century Wall Paintings from the Fortress of Dura on the Middle Euphrates* (Chicago: University of Chicago Press, 1924). It is hard to believe that Olson would not know and use Breasted's well-known *The Dawn of Conscience* (New York: Scribner, 1947), but there is no specific evidence that he did.

17. A phrase from the poem, "Dura" (*Collected Poems,* p. 85). The quoted passage is from the essay entitled "The Gate and the Center," first published in *Origin* 1 (Spring 1951): 35–41, reprinted in *Human Universe*, pp. 17–23, quotation on p. 20.

18. Carl O. Sauer sent Olson this offprint, "Environment and Culture in the Last Deglaciation," *Proceedings of the American Philosophical Society* 92 (1948): 65–77—cover: "Chas Olson with regards Carl Sauer." Writing to Sauer on 25 October 1950, Olson says: "One day, maybe, you'll have a chance to see how I have drawn up from it"—referring to his essay, "The Gate and the Center," *Human Universe*, p. 17, and adding: "It is this concept of CENTER as the thing knowledge goes for, or it's not worth its keep, that I was pushing."

19. Frances had recommended J. W. Dunne, *An Experiment with Time* (London: A. & C. Black, 1927); Olson obviously read it, but refused to own it. (She also recommended Trignant Burrow, whom Olson stayed away from.) Rolf Fjelde was the editor of *Poetry New York* and actively supervised the publication of "Projective Verse"; there is no evidence Olson took up his suggestion to read John W. N. Sullivan, *Beethoven: His Spiritual Development* (New York: Knopf, 1927).

20. Fig. 70, "Stucco ornaments from the Deir es-Sûryani," in Joseph Strzygowski, *Origin of Christian Church Art* (Oxford: Clarendon Press, 1923). Olson bought his copy of this book, continually used by him as a signpost, two years later—flyleaf: "Olson bmc aug 52"; notes and markings throughout.

21. In response to Frances's mention of *Pistis Sophia,* Olson in this letter adds some leads he has picked up from the footnotes in Jung's *Psychology and Religion* (read 1947—cited elsewhere). It is not at all certain that he followed up these particular references himself.

Charlotte A. Baynes, *A Coptic Gnostic Treatise Contained in the Codex Brucianus* (Cambridge University Press, 1933).

G. R. S Mead, trans., *Pistis Sophia* (London: John M. Watkins, 1921; reissued 1947).

G. R. S. Mead, *Fragments of a Faith Forgotten*, 2d ed. (1906)—"which sounds, fr
    Jung, as worth a look at."
R. Reitzenstein, *Poimandres* (1904).
Carl Schmidt, *Pistis Sophia* (1925).

22. Olson would have been in the Library of Congress looking at two
classic scholarly works in the field: Henri Frankfort, *Cylinder Seals: A Documen-
tary Essay on the Art and Religion of the Ancient Near East* (London, 1939) and
Edith Porada and B. Buchanan, *Corpus of Ancient Near Eastern Seals in North
American Collections I: The Collection of the Pierpont Morgan Library*, Bollingen Se-
ries (Washington, 1948). Olson mentions this title in "The Gate and the Cen-
ter" (*Human Universe*, p. 18) and also Porada's previous *Mesopotamian Art in
Cylinder Seals of the Pierpont Morgan Library* (New York: Pierpont Morgan Li-
brary, 1947), from which he quotes. He later appropriated the BMC library
copy of the *American Journal of Archaeology* 52 (January–March 1948) that con-
tained Edith Porada, "The Cylinder Seals of the Late Cypriote Bronze Age,"
pp. 178–98.

23. Leonard Woolley, *The Sumerians* (Oxford University Press, 1928), p. 7.
Olson did not own this volume but he had probably acquired by this time
Woolley's *Ur: The First Phases* (London: King Penguin Book, 1946) and *Digging
Up the Past* (Harmondsworth: Pelican Book, 1950).

24. According to a note at Storrs, George Butterick examined the Library
of Congress copy of *The Makers of Civilization* and noticed partly-erased mark-
ings on pp. 131–32, 135, 151, 186, 189, 209, 221, 226, 238, 241, 253–54, 306–7.
Olson never came to own a copy.

25. Lecture at the Library of Congress on 29 March 1950, published as a
pamphlet, "The Incubation of Western Culture in the Middle East" (Washing-
ton: Library of Congress, 1951). Olson did not have a copy of it, but later picked
up George Sarton, *Ancient Science and Modern Civilization* (New York: Harper
Torchbook, 1959).

26. Olson alludes to "Steffanson on diets" (*Human Universe*, p. 17). He is
presumably thinking of *Not By Bread Alone* (New York, 1946)—not owned by
Olson—on Eskimo eating. He alludes—since the essay does not change very
much the text of the letters to Creeley—to such a topical thing as the use of
"euhemerism" as applied to *Call Me Ishmael* in a review of it by Stanley Edgar
Hyman, "The Critic as Narcissus," *Accent* 8 (Spring 1948): 190. The allusion to
Maspero's Egyptian folk tales (*Human Universe*, p. 20) is actually something
taken over from Victor Bérard; he does not give evidence of having seen Gas-
ton Maspero's *Popular Stories of Ancient Egypt* (1915) for himself. He alludes to
current news stories involving Leo Szilard's researches, an allusion that has
not been pinned down.

The most notable allusion is Olson's turning from the ancient to the living prime, to see the "FIRST WILL back in business" (*Human Universe*, p. 21), referring to the vision quest of the Omaha boy or girl, as recounted in one of the large ethnology volumes he owned, *27th Annual Report of the Bureau of American Ethnology*, Alice C. Fletcher and Francis La Flesche on "The Omaha Tribe" (Washington, 1911), pp. 17–654.

27. *Creeley Correspondence* 6, p. 213. L. A. Waddell, *The British Edda* (London; Chapman & Hall, 1930) was not owned by Olson; nor was the other volume Olson specified that Creeley should try to find him in England, *The Phoenician Origin of Britons* (London, 1924). Within the next year Creeley, or someone, did find him Waddell's *The Aryan Origin of the Alphabet* (London: Luzac, 1927)—flyleaf: "Olson bmc oct 51"; *The Indo-Sumerian Seals Deciphered* (London: Luzac, 1925)— flyleaf: "Olson bmc oct 51"; *Egyptian Civilization: Its Sumerian Origin and Real Chronology* (London: Luzac, 1930)—flyleaf: "Olson bmc august 52" (notes and markings throughout).

28. "Bridge-Work" (*Additional Prose*, p. 24). On 21 August 1950 Olson ordered from the publisher James P. Montgomery and Zellig P. Harris, *The Ras Shamra Mythological Texts*, Memoirs of the American Philosophical Society, vol. 4 (1935), but was told it was out of print. On the cover of his *Annual Report of the Smithsonian Institution for 1937* (Washington, 1938) he wrote, "Olson's copy Important: Ras Shamra," referring to Zellig S. Harris, "Ras Shamra," pp. 479–502. As more gates into the center Olson picked up *The Great King—King of Assyria: Assyrian Reliefs* (New York: Metropolitan Museum of Art, 1945), Francois Lenormant, *Chaldean Magic: Its Origin and Development* (London: Samuel Bagster, 1880), and Isaac Taylor, *The Origin of the Aryans* (New York: Scribner & Welford, 1890).

29. "Mais y a-t-il une poesie *ouverte* sur le reel et une poesie fermee sur les mots?"—Rene Nelli, *Poésie Ouverte Poésie Fermée* (Paris: Cahiers du Sud, 1947), p. 12 (not owned by Olson). Olson once said Mallarmé's Preface to *Un Coup de Dés* was close to his own view (Boer, p. 63).

30. Olson kept the following T. S. Eliot books in his library, and presumably had them by this time: *Collected Poems: 1909–1935* (New York: Harcourt, Brace, 1936), *Murder in the Cathedral* (New York: Harcourt, Brace, 1935), *Old Possum's Book of Practical Cats* (New York: Harcourt, Brace, 1946), *Selected Essays 1917–1932* (New York: Harcourt, Brace, 1932), plus *The Sacred Wood* and *Four Quartets*, previously cited.

31. After hearing E. E. Cummings read in Washington on 21 November 1950, Olson wrote to Creeley about his disappointment at the "uninventive" verse of "this man who was so long a poet to me." He had looked at Cummings's play, *Him* (New York: Boni, 1927) the next morning, but it didn't help (*Creeley Correspondence* 4, pp. 41–43). He alludes to *The Enormous Room* as "in-

fantilism," and kept nothing of Cummings in his library later. However, he did let the name remain in "Projective Verse."

32. Emerson came to Washington in August 1950 and contracted for a chapbook of Olson's poems. In this period of friendly relations, Olson, on 27 September 1950, gave Emerson a full and favorable critique on a 56-page typescript, "The Origins" (now at Storrs), and received his volume of poems *The Greengrocer's Son* (Denver: Alan Swallow, 1950). The following volumes from Emerson's Golden Goose Press, Columbus, Ohio, were owned by Olson:

Robert Creeley, *Le Fou* (1952).
Frederick Eckman, *XXV Poems*, Golden Goose Chap Book 2 (1949).
*Five Poets: Robert Lawrence Beum, Leslie Woolf Hedley, Harold G. Miller, Scott Greer, Nathan R. Teitel* (1949).
Patricia Northway Harris, *Perception of Duer* (1949).
Christopher Maclaine, *The Automatic Wound* (1949).
Henry Rago, *The Travelers*, Golden Goose Chap Book 4 (1949).
Robert Thom, *Viaticum*, Golden Goose Chap Book 3 (1949).
William Carlos Williams, *The Pink Church*, Golden Goose Chap Books 1 (1949)—"Clarke's list."

33. Olson's answers were published out of context, as though part of a round table discussion, in "Symposium on Writing," *Golden Goose*, series 3, 2 (Autumn 1951): 89–96. The May 1951 issue had contained a selection of Olson's poems, but the promised chapbook did not materialize and there were recriminations.

The quotation indicates Olson was familiar with Holderlin and Christopher Smart—it appears from a letter that he gave Dahlberg a volume of Smart as a gift in September 1948. He presumably had by this time his Oxford Library of German Texts edition of *Goethe's Poems and Aphorisms* (New York: Oxford University Press, 1932). Victor Hugo is cited earlier.

34. *Corman Correspondence* 1, p. 39. "Tradition and the Individual Talent" is included in T. S. Eliot's *The Sacred Wood* (previously cited). The poets mentioned in the quotation, several of them associated with current issues of *Poetry New York*, are not represented in Olson's library. Olson at one time read Muriel Rukeyser "with pleasure" (letter to Waldo Frank, March 1940).

35. *Corman Correspondence* 1, p. 43. *Poetry New York* no. 1 contained a long translation of Apollinaire, "which," Olson adds, "any alert man would have gone to, at source, as part of process of learning his trade in this hear time and day (or to some equivalent of same—as Rimbaud, say, or Edgar Allen Poe (as WCW mined him, *not* Baudelaire)." In a note dated 20 November 1946, "Homage to Baudelaire" is listed as a project, but Olson appears not to have owned him. William Merwin, contemporary poet and translator, was recommended to

Jonathan Williams in July 1951 ("AM-O," *Parnassus* 4 [Spring–Summer 1976]: 245), but none of his books survived in Olson's library.

36. *Corman Correspondence* 1, p. 41. Olson called Paul Valery a "stuffed bird" in a letter to Corman, 26 January 1953, and owned none of his work. Creeley's "found" poem is mentioned by him in a letter to Olson of 25 October 1950 (*Creeley Correspondence* 3, p. 130).

37. *Corman Correspondence* 1, p. 40. Olson did not own the 1934 edition of *Testimony,* but he was apparently sent in page proofs the 1965 edition, published jointly by New Directions and the San Francisco Review.

38. *Corman Correspondence* 1, p. 40. There was no Roethke in Olson's library. Cartier-Bresson is cited previously. Diana Woelffer's "The Children of Yucatan" is illustrated in the exhibition catalog *Six States Photography* (Milwaukee Art Institute, 8–30 September 1950); Olson must have passed the catalog on to someone else.

39. *Corman Correspondence* 1, p. 40. Olson is afraid Corman might settle for "an eclectic selection of aesthetic work."

40. *Corman Correspondence* 1, p. 40. Robert H. Barlow, "The Malinche of Acacingo," *Circle* 10 (Summer 1948): 52–53 is, in effect, a documentary prolegomenon to a study of the methodology of the *Mayan Letters*.

## 12. Yucatan, Archaeology of the Postmodern

1. Olson had to forgo the gem of the book collection, *The Paintings of D. H. Lawrence* (1929) "with inscription to Orioli (who published Lady Chat)" (letter to Monroe Engel, 17 March 1950). He later purchased *Paintings of D. H. Lawrence,* ed. Mervyn Levy (New York: Viking Studio Book, 1964), and ultimately gave it as a gift to Harry Martin of Gloucester.

2. "The Flying Fish," a story of Lawrence leaving Mexico, "that impeccable thing" (letter to Frances Boldereff, 10 March 1950), is found in *Phoenix: the Posthumous Papers* (cited previously). In one of the "Mayan Letters" Olson told Creeley: "don't let even Lawrence fool you (there is nothing in this Mexican deal, so far as 'time in the sun' goes . . . the arrestment, is deceptive: it is not what fancy outsiders have seen it as, seeking, as they were, I guess, some alternative for themselves (like DHL & his Ladybird)" (*Selected Writings,* pp. 78–79).

3. Quotations from a typescript dated 21–22 January 1950 (Storrs), published posthumously as *D. H. Lawrence, & the High Temptation of the Mind* (Santa Barbara: Black Sparrow Press, 1980), first unnumbered page. Olson owned *The Letters of D. H. Lawrence* (London: Heinemann, 1932), where Aldous Huxley writes:

> Lawrence had, over and above his peculiar gift, an extremely acute intelligence. He was a clever man as well as a man of genius. (In his boy-

hood and adolescence he had been a great passer of examinations.) He could have understood the aim and methods of science perfectly well if he had wanted to. Indeed, he did understand them perfectly well; and it was for that very reason that he rejected them. For the methods of science and critical philosophy were incompatible with the exercise of his gift—the immediate perception. (p. xv)

In Olson's essay, the contrasting figures (those who do not resist the "high temptation of the mind") are Schopenhauer—no particular work specified, but his Philosophy professor at Wesleyan, Cornelius Kruse, "ruined" him with Schopenhauer—and, among contemporaries, Ortega Y Gasset, whose "brilliant essay on Goethe" is cited, i.e., "In Search of Goethe from within," *Partisan Review* 16 (December 1949): 1163–88, which Olson kept a copy of. It was reprinted in *The Dehumanization of Art* (Garden City: Doubleday Anchor, 1956), which Olson also owned, as well as the popular *The Revolt of the Masses* (New York: Mentor, 1950).

4. *The Maya and Their Neighbors*, pp. 139–49. Oliver G. Ricketson's contribution, "An Outline of Basic Physical Factors Affecting Middle America" (pp. 10–31), Olson described as "a beaut of a job I first read 10 years ago" (*Creeley Correspondence* 6, p. 60), and specifically recommended in the bibliography added to the *Mayan Letters* (*Selected Writings*, p. 125). The general impression is that the piece Olson made most use of while in Yucatan was "Diffusion of Maya Astronomy" by Herbert J. Spinden, pp. 162–78.

5. *Selected Writings*, p. 126. Olson did not own these large Morley volumes, but he did purchase, in the summer of 1949, Arthur Posnansky, *Tihuanacu: The Cradle of American Man* (New York: J. J. Augustine, 1945), 2 vols. in one; and, at date unknown, J. T. Goodman, *The Archaic Maya Inscriptions* (London: Biologia Centralia-Americana, 1897).

6. At Berkeley in 1965 Olson was willing to say that the poem "To Gerhardt" was the one he believed in the most, "because it really has such a weak backbone that there's a nerve in it, only" (*Muthologos* 1, p. 141). The "nerve" is a string of direct quotations from bear ritual which had its source in prehistoric times, taken from N. P. Dyrenkova, "Bear Worship Among Turkish Tribes of Siberia" in the *Proceedings*, pp. 411–40. The poem was written in June 1951, just before the Olsons left Yucatan.

The *Mayan Letters* specifically mentions Ruth Benedict's contribution to the *Proceedings*, "Psychological Types in the Cultures of the Southwest," pp. 572–81 (*Selected Writings*, p. 94). Butterick noticed evidence of Olson's having read other contributions to the *Proceedings of the Twenty-third International Congress of Americanists*: Herman Beyer, "The Infix in Maya Hieroglyphs Infixes Touching the Frame," pp. 193–99; Stansbury Hagar, "The Symbolic Plan of

Palenque," pp. 220–210; Warren King Moorehead, "Prehistoric Cultural Areas East of the Rocky Mountains," pp. 47–51; Gladys A. Reichard, "Form and Interpretation in American Art," pp. 459–62; Franz Termer, "Uber die Maya-asprache von Chicomucelo," pp. 926–36; Alfonso Toro, "Las Plantas Sagradas de los Aztecas y su Influencia sobre el Arte Precortesiano," pp. 100–121 (used by Olson in "Experience and Measurement." *OLSON* 3, p. 60); James Williams, "Christopher Columbus and Aboriginal Indian Words," pp. 816–50; and Thomas Gann, "Recently Discovered Maya City in the Southwest of British Honduras," pp. 188–92. Olson also marked up Gann's "Mounds in Northern Honduras" in *19th Annual Report of the Bureau of American Ethnology* (Washington, 1900), pp. 655–92, and inserted there some reading notes he had made on John B. Adams, "Contributions to the Study of Maya Art and Religion" University of Chicago, (Ph.D. diss., 1946).

    7. *Selected Writings,* p. 127: "Prescott and Parkman are a triad: Stephens is the unacknowledged third." Olson had both titles with him in Mexico but the latter book was not found in his library later. Olson quotes approvingly (*Selected Writings,* p. 113) from Tatiana Proskouriakoff, *A Study of Classic Maya Sculpture,* Carnegie Institution Publication 593 (Washington, D.C.: Carnegie Institution, 1950).

    8. *Selected Writings,* pp. 126–27. As part of his preparations for the Yucatan, Olson made notes on William E. Gates's "Glyph Studies" and "The Birth of the Vinal" in *Maya Society Quarterly* 1 (1931–32): 32–33, 37–44, likewise consulting at the same time presumably Gates's *An Outline Dictionary of Maya Glyphs,* Maya Society Publication no. 1 (Baltimore: Johns Hopkins Press, 1931).

    Olson would have studied, though he did not own, Benjamin Lee Whorf's "A central Mexican inscription combining Mexican and Maya day signs," *American Anthropologist* 34 (1932): 296–302; *The Phonetic Value of Certain Characters in Maya Writing,* Papers of the Peabody Museum (Cambridge: Harvard University Press, 1933); "Maya writing and its decipherment," *Maya Research* 2 (1935): 367–82; and "Decipherment of the Linguistic Portion of the Maya Hieroglyphs," *Smithsonian Institution Report for 1941* (Washington, 1942): pp. 479–502. The *Mayan Letters* "Bibliography" adds a note (*Selected Writings,* p. 127): "how questionable Whorf's work is may be judged by the free ride it is just now getting from those sinister rightists, the semantic people, who come out of that 'human engineering' one, Non-A Korzybski." He does not go further to clarify the battle lines here; he owned two Korzybski books, but only later.

    9. "He's a respectable worker, this T, but, I very much surmise he's playing with things he ain't bought the rights to" (*Creeley Correspondence* 5, p. 103). Olson is apparently drawing on the copy of Thompson's book in the Anthropological Museum in Campeche for the myth of the sun and the moon

which he tells to Creeley and retells in the "Human Universe" essay (*Selected Writings,* pp. 103–4, 64–66), for he acquired his copy later—flyleaf: "Olson ordered Lerma June bought BMC July 51."

10. Olson did not own this volume but had the use of it in Campeche to quote passages in letters (*Creeley Correspondence* 5, pp. 187–88; 6, pp. 25–26).

11. Olson did not have a copy of this collection when he inquired about it to Frank Moore 28 March 1951. His copy came to him later, via Fielding Dawson (his mother's name, "Mrs. Clarence H. Dawson," is embossed on the flyleaf).

12. In his letter of 24 February 1951, addressed to the Middle America Research Institute at Tulane, Olson said that he had seen their map mentioned in Earl P. Hanson and Raye R. Platt, eds., *The New World Guide to the Latin American Republics,* 2d ed. (New York: Duell, Sloan & Pearce, 1945). Olson did not own this reference work later; nor, apparently, did the map he received from Tulane survive.

13. If Olson had in mind Alfred M. Tozzer's "Maya and Toltec Figures at Chichen Itza" in the *Proceedings of the 23rd International Congress of Americanists* (previously cited as being with Olson in Yucatan), pp. 155–164, it seems only barely possible as an exception to the unaesthetic. Cid Corman, at Olson's request, sent Tozzer's *A Maya Grammar* (Cambridge: Peabody Museum, Harvard University, 1921) by mail—flyleaf: "Olson lerma, campeche March 1951."

14. This and the previous quotation are to be found in *Corman Correspondence* 1, pp. 93–94. Olson had seen *Meso-American Notes,* which Barlow founded at Mexico City College, and *Tlalocan,* which Barlow was currently editing. He had no doubt looked at, though never owned, Barlow's scholarly publication: *The Extent of the Empire of the Culhua Mexica* (Berkeley: University of California Press, 1949). Among Olson's books is a copy of Barlow's poems, *View From a Hill* (Azcapotzalco D.F., 1947), with the author's autograph on the cover.

15. Published as "Project (1951): 'The Art of the Language of Mayan Glyphs,' " *Alcheringa* 5 (Spring–Summer 1973): 94–100, quotation from p. 94.

16. Typescript of "The Human Universe" (Corman Collection, Texas), transcribed in Albert Glover, *Charles Olson: Letters for Origin* (Ph.D. dissertation, State University of New York at Buffalo, 1968), pp. 258–90, quotation from p. 259. See chapter 1, above, for Olson's discussion of this issue of *New Directions.* It was, by the way, where Olson read possibly all he ever read of Richard Eberhart: "his 'variety' is mere eclecticism" (*Corman Correspondence* 1, p. 168).

17. Draft letter to Norman Macbeth on 14 July 1951 (Storrs), quoted by Butterick in notes to a Creeley letter (*Creeley Correspondence* 7, p. 252). The Macbeth article was in *Proteus Quarterly* 2, no. 2 (Spring 1951): 2–11; it espoused the ideas of Rudolph Steiner, whom Olson otherwise seems to have paid little attention to. A similar discovery in the concept of law was Simone Weil's "Beyond Personalism," *Cross Currents* 2 (Spring 1952): 59–76, which Olson used right away in some unpublished essays; he kept the issue of the magazine. An

allied work Olson owned later was Friedrich A. Hayek, *The Road to Serfdom* (Chicago: University of Chicago Press, Phoenix Books, 1961).

18. Olson did not own any Toynbee, but he is likely to have seen the use of "Post-Modern" in D. C. Somervell's abridgment, *A Study of History* (Oxford University Press, 1946), p. 39. A thorough investigation of the matter is George F. Butterick, "Charles Olson and the Postmodern Advance," *Iowa Review* 11 (Fall 1980): 4–27.

19. *Creeley Correspondence* 7, p. 115: "tho, I should wish to kill that word, too—there is only examination." Olson did not own Arnold Schoenberg, *Theory of Harmony* (New York, 1948), but he did keep in his papers *Black Mountain College Bulletin* 3, no. 1 (November 1944) containing Ernst Krenek, "Arnold Schoenberg at Seventy" and "The Composer and the Interpreter."

20. *Selected Writings*, p. 61. Butterick traces the Novalis quotation to *Fragmente*, ed. Ernst Kamnitzer (Dresden, 1929), p. 584, but does not cite any translation Olson is known to have used (*Creeley Correspondence* 7, p. 273). There are notes and markings in Heinrich Eduard Jacob, "Novalis: Magician and Seeker," *Hemispheres* 2 (Spring 1945): 60–68, but the quoted words are not found there.

21. *Selected Writings*, p. 79: "five, so far, cut out of trees." Francis W. Galpin, *The Music of the Sumerians and Their Immediate Successors the Babylonians and Assyrians* (Cambridge University Press, 1937)—flyleaf: "Olson bmc November 1951," contains occasional notes and markings. Olson had just applied for a Fulbright to Istanbul or Teheran (as close as he could get to Mesopotamia). The application is printed, in part, as an endnote to "Transpositions," *Alcheringa* 5 (Spring–Summer 1973): 11–12, where he compares his approach to that of Henri Frankfort in the recently published *The Birth of Civilization in the Near East* (Bloomington: Indiana University Press, 1951), which he owned—flyleaf: "Olson," with notes and markings throughout.

22. *Selected Writings*, p. 55. Olson's library contained no Plato at the end, and we have no clue to what editions he may have used. Refining his sense of what "the whole Greek system" might be, Olson acquired along the way F. M. Cornford, *From Religion to Philosophy: A Study in the Origins of Western Speculation* (New York: Harper Torchbook, 1957) and Bruno Snell, *the Discovery of the Mind: The Greek Origins of European Thought* (New York; Harper Torchbook, 1960)—much marked.

23. *D. H. Lawrence, & The High Temptation of the Mind* (previously cited). The Olsons were in Mexico 23 January–4 July 1951.

24. "Human Universe," *Selected Writings*, pp. 57–58.

## 13. Olson's University

This chapter title is taken, with respect, from a chapter heading in Mary Emma Harris's definitive study and immaculate book, *The Arts at Black Moun-*

*tain College* (Cambridge: MIT Press, 1987). As Mary Emma Harris has written, "After 1949 Black Mountain College was essentially a community of artists working together" (p. 182). Inviting Bernard Leach, the potter, in a letter of 19 March 1952, Olson described it as very much like "some Chinese out of Shui Hu Chuan's time on the western roads or some hillside," referring to the Chinese classic novel that he owned in Pearl Buck's translation, *All Men Are Brothers* (New York: John Day, 1933).

1. The founder John A. Rice was a "maquis" in the American educational system and Olson had followed his career from the first shot, "Academic Freedom and Tenure: Rollins College Report," *Bulletin of the American Association of University Professors* 19 (November 1933): 416–38, which Olson remembered thirty-five years later had been penned by the distinguished Arthur O. Lovejoy (*Muthologos* 2, p. 58). He also remembered John Rice's "Fundamentalism and the Higher Learning," *Harper's* 174 (May 1937): 587–96. Since Olson was associated with the magazine, he would have read Rice's "Inside the South" in *Common Ground* 1 (Spring 1941): 26–34. He knew, although he did not own, Rice's autobiography, *I Came Out of the Eighteenth Century* (New York: Harper, 1942). So Olson knew why Rice took to the hills. But he had also taken to heart the positive side of it, and kept a reprint of "Black Mountain College: A Foreword" as it was in the original catalogue, "written by Mr. Rice, anonymously, and it says, in so many words, that this place shall be that place in the world in which the arts shall share the center of the curriculum with the more usual studies" (*Muthologos* 2, p. 60).

2. As for painting, resident for a short time after Olson's arrival was his old friend Ben Shahn, who did a poster, "Tonight at 8 Chas. Olson Will Read His Poetry," and, in response to an Olson poem, "Glyphs," for the Shahns, painted "A Glyph for Charles." Soon after, Olson received, and kept, *Paragraphs on Art by Ben Shahn* (New York: The Spiral Press, 1952). He also preserved in his papers the Shahns's New Year's Gift for 1957, *Love and Joy*.

3. *Creeley Correspondence* 6, p. 210. G.R.S. Mead's *Apollonius of Tyana* (London and Benares: Theosophical Publishing Society, 1901) was the sole source for Olson's dance-play; he must have had a copy available to him at BMC. It was not in his library later. He knew of Philostratus, *In Honour of Apollonius of Tyana* (Oxford, 1912), but only through a reference in Jane Harrison's *Prolegomena*; there is no trace of it in the script. In October 1954 Olson apparently wrote for a review copy of Alice Winston, *Apollonius of Tyana* (see Creeley letter of that date), but there is no evidence he received it.

4. Olson owned the abridged edition of James G. Frazer, *The Golden Bough* (New York: Macmillan, 1947)—flyleaf: "Olson Washington, May, 1947": occasional notes and markings throughout. Also he had part 2 of the complete edition, i.e., *Taboo and the Perils of the Soul*, 3d ed. (London: Macmillan, 1911).

5. *Creeley Correspondence* 6, p. 211. Butterick's introduction to *The Fiery Hunt* (pp. xv–xvi) indicates that Olson made notes of his reading of *The Diary of Vaslav Nijinsky* (New York: Simon & Schuster, 1936) in a journal of 1941; and that William Walton's report in *Life* (10 September 1945) on Nijinsky's last dance is a likely source also.

6. "A Syllabary for a Dancer," dated 4 August 1952, was published with "The Syllabary (II)" and "Syllabary III" in the Olson issue of *Maps* 4 (1971): 9–15. The word "syllabary" was suggested by Samuel Noah Kramer, *Sumerian Mythology* (Philadelphia: American Philosophical Society, 1944)—flyleaf: "Olson Wash. aug 50"—which Olson turned to with renewed interest at the same time as he purchased Kramer's *Lamentation Over the Destruction of Ur* (Chicago: University of Chicago Press, 1940) in July 1952, and *Sumerian Literary Texts from Nippur in the Museum of the Ancient Orient at Istanbul,* published as the *Annual of the American Schools of Oriental Research* 23 (1943–44)—flyleaf of Olson's copy: "Olson bmc Aug 52—& worked bmc Jan 57." He had recently acquired Alexander Heidel, *The Babylonian Genesis,* 2d ed. (Chicago: University of Chicago Press, 1951)—flyleaf: "Olson bmc october 51"; occasional notes and markings. Olson sustained an interest in the earliest literature of mankind, acquiring, in the last year of his life, William W. Hallo and J. J. A. Van Dijk, *The Exaltation of Inanna* (New Haven: Yale University Press, 1968).

7. *Maps,* p. 10. David Tudor brought an Antonin Artaud typescript over from France, and M. C. Richards (at BMC) decided to translate it. Olson arranged for its first publication as "From *The Theater and Its Double*" in *Origin* 11 Autumn 1953): 145–92.

David Tudor also brought news of Pierre Boulez, and specifically Boulez's contribution to "4 musicians at work," *trans/formations* 1 (1952): 168–70), which Olson described to Creeley on 15 May 1952 as "a new terrific slick, a magazine called *transformations,* a fine package of Bauhaus turned Backhouse." Soon, however, through Tudor's playing of it, Olson became a complete convert to Boulez's music.

8. "Theatre Institute Lecture on Language," *OLSON* 8, pp. 50–55, where Olson mentions Christopher Fry's "vulgar" reputation, without specifying plays, and ends: "I have yet to see a verse drama (or to read one) which approaches Milhaud's *Orestes.*" Also in *OLSON* 8, in a piece called "The Theatre" (p. 48), Olson refers to Gordon Craig, "The Actor and the Uber-Marionette," in *The Mask* (March 1908) or some more recent not identified discussion. Olson also knew of Heinrich von Kleist, "Essay on the Puppet Theatre," *Partisan Review* 14 (January–February 1947): 67–72, but did not own that issue.

9. "A Letter to the Faculty of Black Mountain College," *OLSON* 8, p. 28. Olson quotes from Lincoln Barnett, "J. Robert Oppenheimer," *Life* (10 October 1949): 120–38, which article he apparently kept up to that point. He later

bought Haakon Chevalier, *Oppenheimer: The Story of a Friendship* (New York: Pocket Books, 1966)—occasional notes and markings.

10. Of this list, Riviere, Bastian, Levy-Bruhl, and Ratzel are not represented in Olson's library; neither is Amiel's *Journal Intime,* though Olson refers to it a number of times prior to this. Edmund Wilson and Stephen Crane are not mentioned very often; none of their works are in Olson's library. The remaining names on the list are dealt with elsewhere.

In regard to the bio-sciences, especially pertinent are Gavin de Beer, *Embryos and Ancestors* (Oxford University Press, 1930), which Olson read (presumably the revised edition of 1951) around 18 March 1952 (letter to Creeley that date) but did not own; and one that he may have had in his possession for years, Harris Hawthorne Wilder, *The History of the Human Body,* 2d ed. (New York: Henry Holt, 1923)—flyleaf: "Olson"; notes and markings throughout.

11. *OLSON* 10, p. 3. Olson took the information on Dörpfeld and Schliemann from Emil Ludwig, *Schliemann: The Story of a Gold-Seeker* (Boston: Little, Brown, 1932).

12. Hawkes is first mentioned in a letter to Creeley of 9 May 1952. He agreed to come to the Institute, but apparently could not get a visa in time. This did not prevent Olson making much use of *The Prehistoric Foundations of Europe,* his copy having first been borrowed from John Boman Adams of the BMC faculty and then bought from him—flyleaf: "Olson (bought fr Adams for $5 check, Aug, 52 bmc"; notes and markings throughout. In August 1968 Olson could still say "it is to my mind one of the most precise and specific books that I have ever read" (*Muthologos* 2, p. 91).

13. Olson's first testing of Jung was apparently in conjunction with Connie; the flyleaf of his much-marked copy of *Psychology and Religion* (New Haven: Yale University Press, 1946) is inscribed: "the Olsons." It is through Olson's letters to Connie during October–December 1952 that Butterick was able to note (at Storrs) that the following were read at that time:

*The Integration of the Personality,* trans. Stanley Dell (New York: Farrar & Rinehart, 1939)—flyleaf: "Olson"; markings throughout.
*Psychology of the Unconscious,* trans. Beatrice M. Hinkle (New York: Dodd, Mead, 1947)—notes and markings throughout.
*Psychological Types,* trans. H. Godwin Baynes (London: Kegan Paul, Trench, Trubner; New York: Harcourt, Brace, 1946)—heavy markings.
(with Kerenyi), *Essays on a Science of Mythology,* trans. R. F. C. Hull, Bollingen Series (New York: Pantheon Books, 1949)—flyleaf: "Olson personal private"; notes and markings throughout.

It is conjectured that Olson would have acquired around this time Jolan Jacobi, *The Psychology of Jung* (New Haven: Yale University Press, 1943)—flyleaf: "Olson (private)"; notes and markings throughout. He later acquired as a gift Frieda Fordham, *An Introduction to Jung's Psychology* (Baltimore: Penguin, 1953)—flyleaf: "Michael Rumaker 1954"; occasional notes and markings. Olson's later attentions to Jung, which have been the subject of a study by Charles Stein, *The Secret of the Black Chrysanthemum* (Barrytown: Station Hill Press, 1987), are in a subsequent chapter.

14. Letter to Joseph Willits of the Rockefeller Foundation on 13 January 1953 as part of a request for funds for the Institute. On Sauer's suggestion, Olson had written to Edgar Anderson for an offprint of C. R. Stonor and Edgar Anderson, "Maize Among the Hill Peoples of Assam," *Annals of the Missouri Botanical Gardens* 36 (September 1949): 355–404, which was acknowledged by Olson in a letter of 10 June 1952 (carbon copy at Storrs). Olson put Anderson's book, *Plants, Man and Life* (Boston: Little, Brown, 1952), on the reading list for the New Sciences (*OLSON* 10, p. 108), but it was not in his library later.

15. A letter of 9 October 1951 (*Creeley Correspondence* 8, p. 32) indicates that Olson was reading Martin Sprengling's *The Alphabet, Its Rise and Development from the Sinai Inscriptions,* Oriental Institute Communications no. 12 (Chicago: University of Chicago Press, 1931), though it was not in his library later. What Olson read of Darling and Satterthwaite is not known. Darling was originally recommended to Olson by Sauer in a letter of 19 May 1952 that also mentioned Roderick Seidenberg. Olson bought Seidenberg's *Posthistoric Man: An Inquiry* (Chapel Hill: University of North Carolina Press, 1950). There is no indication what he thought of it, except that Seidenberg was not contacted and the book was put into the BMC library (now at North Carolina Wesleyan).

In a letter of 12 October 1951 (*Creeley Correspondence* 8, p. 47) Olson recommended to Creeley, who was then resident in the south of France, Abbé Breuil on the Altamira caves, but did not specify which of Breuil's many titles he had in mind.

16. Olson owned and made use of the recent *Scientific American* 187 (October 1952) that included Robert J. Braidwood's article "From Cave to Village," pp. 62–66. Braidwood may have brought the following with him to the Institute in March 1953 or sent them soon afterwards:

"Ksar'akil, Its Archeological Sequence and Geological Setting: Prefatory Remarks," *Journal of Near Eastern Studies* 10 (April 1951): 113–14.
(with Linda Braidwood) "The Earliest Village Communities of Southwestern Asia" *Journal of World History* 1 (1953) 278–310—an offprint.
(with Linda Braidwood), "Jarmo: A Village of Early Farmers in Iraq," *Antiquity* 24 (December 1950): 189–95—an offprint.
*The Near East and the Foundations for Civilization* (Eugene: Oregon State System of Higher Education, 1952)—cover: "Olson (re-read April 1/59—due to Dan sending me clipping within." The clipping (pinned to p. 30) was

"Civilization's Cradle," *Time* 73 (23 March 1959); 76. Olson looked at that page again in June 1962 when he wrote a *Maximus* poem from it (*Guide*, p. 406).

17. *OLSON* 10, p. 108: "back files of *Scientific American* have articles of his"—presumably, though Olson did not own the issue, William C. Boyd, "Rh and the Races of Man,"*Scientific American* 185 (November 1951): 22–25. Other reading on heredity about the time of the Institute was Earnest Hooton, *Up from the Ape* (originally 1931; revised ed. 1947), but the book did not stay in Olson's library. He did own Amram Scheinfeld, *You and Heredity* (Garden City: Garden City Publishing Co., 1945), and H. Kalmus and Lettice M. Crump, *Genetics* (Harmondsworth: Penguin, 1952). He borrowed a copy of Edmund W. Sinnott, *Cell and Psyche* (New York: Harper, 1951) in March 1952 (*Corman Correspondence*, p. 247).

18. Footnotes in Levy led Olson to ask for further books from the Pack Library: W. F. Jackson Knight, *Cumaean Gates* (1936) and T. Zammit, *Prehistoric Malta* (1930) (letter to Ida Padelford, 24 January 1953). There is no record of his receiving them.

19. Of allied interest is Mark Graubard, "Food Habits of Primitive Man," *The Scientific Monthly* 55 (October 1942): 342–49, which Olson marked in his copy. We might note here that Olson saw Sauer in Berkeley on a trip soon after Black Mountain closed and received as offprints: "The Education of a Geographer," *Annals of the Association of American Geographers* 46 (September 1956): 287–99, and "The End of the Ice Age and Its Witnesses," *The Geographical Review* 47 (1957): 29–43.

20. Olson did not own *Teton Sioux Music*, but he had three other similar Densmore studies, cited later.

Other works in archaeology that Olson could have been using at this time are:

Uvo Hölscher, *Excavations at Ancient Thebes 1930/31,* Oriental Institute Communications (Chicago: University of Chicago, 1932)—cover: "Olson bmc july 52."

Frederick Johnson, ed., *Radiocarbon Dating,* Memoirs of the Society for American Archaeology no. 8 (Salt Lake City, 1951).

Walter W. Taylor, *A Study of Archeology,* Memoir no. 48 (American Anthropological Association, 1948)—markings. Inserted in Olson's copy is an offprint: J. Richard Carpenter, "The Biome," *The American Midland Naturalist* 21 (January 1939): 75–91.

A. S. Schultz, *Beitrag Zur Analyse Sudafrikanischer Felsbilder* (Frankfort am Main: Institut fur Kulturmorphologie, 1933).

About this time Olson picked up the current book of "stone age" travel, Thor Heyerdahl, *Kon-Tiki* (Garden City: Permabooks, 1953)–two copies were found in his library.

21. *Essays on a Science of Mythology* (previously cited), p. 7. Letter of 7 April 1951 (*Creeley Correspondence* 5, p. 129): "as of malinowski, can't say how readable he is—have picked up what i know of him from others' quotes, not, fr him, direct." Butterick indicates that Bronislaw Malinowski's *Magic, Science and Religion, and Other Essays* (Garden City: Doubleday Anchor, 1954) was used in class 1964–65 at Buffalo, though it was not in Olson's library at his death.

22. *OLSON* 10, p. 63. This is the source of Pindar's remark about Homer that Olson used in the *Maximus* poem, "Letter 23" (see quotations from J. A. K. Thomson in *Guide*, pp. 145–47).

23. Marion L. Starkey, *The Cherokee Nation* (New York: Knopf, 1946), p. 8, and James Mooney "Myths of the Cherokee," *19th Annual Report of the Bureau of American Ethnology 1897–98*, Part 1 (Washington, 1900). pp. 3–548, both of these sources in Olson's library. He might, however, have heard the story verbally from David H. Corkran, a Cherokee expert who was on the faculty of BMC 1945–50.

24. Butterick's note (*OLSON* 10, p. 112) supplies us with a citation, Buber, trans., *Die Geschicten des Rabbi Nachman* (Frankfurt am Mein, 1906), which Olson did not own. There would appear to have been no English translation available to him in print. The story is not in the Buber that Olson owned: *Tales of the Hasidim: The Early Masters* (New York: Schocken, with Farrar, Straus & Young, 1947). Olson is reported to have quoted from Buber's *Moses: The Revelation and the Covenant* (New York: Harper Torchbooks, 1958) in a tutorial at Vancouver 1963 (*OLSON* 4, p. 62). On the subject of the Old Testament in a Berkeley seminar 1965, Olson said he "preferred Louis Ginzberg," i.e., *Legends of the Jews* (rev. ed. 1961)—though he did not own it. His long-time possession in this area was *Hebraic Literature: Translations from The Talmud, Midrashim and Kabbala*, Universal Classics Library (New York: M. Walter Dunne, 1901).

25. The year 1954 was a somewhat fallow period. Olson lost his Washington residence and was increasingly estranged from his wife. On 26 December 1954 he wrote on the flyleaf of Joseph Hone, *W. B. Yeats: 1865–1939* (New York: Macmillan, 1943): "Sour cross and rue, sour herb of grace Dec 26 '54 another day on this earth stolen from me." During all this period, Shakespeare (here specifically *Richard II*) was his consolation.

26. *Additional Prose*, p. 5. Olson did not own Gladwin and actually could not remember his name, but he considered it important enough to mention again on p. 11, again by title only.

27. Olson quotes from Paul Klee's *On Modern Art* (London: Faber & Faber, 1948) in a letter of 7 November 1950 (*Creeley Correspondence* 3, p. 157),

but there are no arrows in that volume. Olson did not own that work, nor any other Klee.

28. Olson would not have forgotten the maps in C. G. Seligman, "The Roman Orient and the Far East," *Annual Report of the Board of Regents of the Smithsonian Institution. . .1938* (Washington, 1939), pp. 547–68—notes and markings in Olson's copy.

29. *Additional Prose*, p. 6. Besides the films, Olson would have known Sergei Eisenstein's books: *The Film Sense* (New York: Harcourt, Brace, 1942) and *Film Form* (New York: Harcourt, Brace, 1949), because they were edited by Olson's friend Jay Leyda; he did not own them. He received as a gift from Frances Boldereff in the summer of 1953 Marie Seton's *Sergei M. Eisenstein* (New York: A. A. Wyn, n.d.).

30. *Additional Prose*, p. 7 and p. 8: "we should start from the notion of actuality as in its essence a process"—Olson quoting Whitehead's *Adventures of Ideas* (New York: Macmillan, 1933), though he did not own a copy. He owned *The Aims of Education and Other Essays* (New York: Mentor, 1952). And, of course, *Process and Reality: An Essay in Cosmology* (Cambridge University Press, 1929)—flyleaf: "1st read spring 55 again spring 56 now spring 57." That is, he bought his own copy in January 1957. Many later readings are dated in the copy. The importance of this work for Olson could not be overexaggerated. See chapter 3 of Robert von Hallberg, *Charles Olson: The Scholar's Art* (Cambridge: Harvard University Press, 1978), and Robin Blaser, "The Violets: A Cosmological Reading of a Cosmology," *Process Studies* (1983): 8–37. Ann Charters transcribed the following from Olson lecture notes of 1956 (*Olson/Melville*, p. 84): "I am the more persuaded of the importance and use of Whitehead's thought that I did not know his work—except in snatches and by rumor, including the disappointment of a dinner and evening with him when I was 25 and he was, what, 75!—until last year. So it comes out like those violets of Bolyai Senior on all sides when men are needed, that we possess a body of thinking of the order of Whitehead's to catch us up."

31. Olson is still using his Bohn edition of Pausanias (previously cited), but soon afterwards he received the J. G. Frazer 6 volume edition, *Pausanias's Description of Greece*, 2d ed. (London: Macmillan, 1913)—flyleaf: "given to me by Robt Creeley circum 1956." Creeley had remembered Olson's cry in a letter of 9 October 1951: "the books I need are all 5 and 10 buck goes! Frazer's PAUSANIAS, goes $75!" (*Creeley Correspondence* 8, p. 36).

*Mythology and Monuments of Ancient Athens* (London: Macmillan, 1890) is a translation by Margaret de G. Verrall of part of the "Attica" of Pausanias, with an introductory essay and archaeological commentary by Jane E. Harrison. The copy in the Olson archive contains no markings.

32. *Additional Prose*, p. 14. Olson is referring to two books he did not ap-

parently own: Ferdinand Lundberg, *America's 60 Families* (New York: Vanguard Press, 1937), and Gustavus Myers, *History of the Great American Fortunes* (New York: Modern Library, 1936). Olson at one time owned E. James Ferguson, *The Power of the Purse: A History of American Public Finance* (Chapel Hill: Univ. of North Carolina Press, 1961); it was on "Clarke's list" but is now missing. With reference to the category name "Quantity" itself: René Guénon, *The Reign of Quantity and the Sign of the Times* (London: Luzac, 1953)—flyleaf: "Where did I get this book? Nick's? & at same time as Buber's Tales from the Hassidic? 1951 oh no 1954, on way back to Black Mountain." Olson liked only the title; the notes in the book are mainly derogatory. Olson was interested in econometrics, and encouraged Harvey Brown to bring out, as Frontier Pamphlet no. 1, *The Decline and the Fall of the "Spectacular" Commodity-Economy* (1967).

33. *OLSON* 2, p. 43. Olson had tried his hand at translation in responding to Cid Corman's attempts—see next chapter. William Carlos Williams had done a "Theocritus: Idyll I," included in *Desert Music and Other Poems* previously cited as not present in Olson's library. He may have passed on his copy to Creeley for him to do the review which appeared in *Black Mountain Review* 2 (Summer 1954).

34. Olson is thinking of Breasted's *Oriental Forerunners* (previously cited). He then makes an excursus (not quoted) into the second and third centuries A.D., mentioning Maximus of Tyre and Marinus of Tyre, and "a lovely homosexual poet," whom Butterick (*OLSON* 2, p. 48) suggests is Phanocles, author of *Erotes* (not owned by Olson). This digression includes a mention of William Dunbar, who is not represented in Olson's library later but who caught Olson's attention at one time—letter 8 June 1950: "I took a crack at translating same into american some two months ago" (*Creeley Correspondence* 1, p. 90). He also mentions "that Scot now," i.e., Hugh MacDiarmid, whose *In Memoriam James Joyce* (Glasgow: W. McClellan, 1956) Olson picked up later.

35. These are not the form of the titles in any edition of Euripides that Olson is known to have owned (cited previously). "Euripides ought to be read first without reference to Aeschylus and Sophocles," Olson advises. (*OLSON* 2, p. 45). "He ought to be read in connection with the fact that he made Racine Racine, for example." Neither the *Phèdra* nor anything else of Racine is present in Olson's library.

36. Olson owned the 2 volume edition of Benjamin Farrington, *Greek Science* (Harmondsworth: Penguin, 1949)—flyleaf: "Olson's copie"; occasional notes. Creeley quoted John Burnet, *Early Greek Philosophy* (1892, reprint 1958) in his "Some Notes on Olson's *Maximus*," to which Olson responded in a letter on 18 February 1961 that he had never seen the book. He did, however, own B. A. G. Fuller, *History of Greek Philosophy: Thales to Democritus* (New York: Henry Holt,

1925). In conversation Olson mentioned Milton C. Nahm, *Selections from Early Greek Philosophy* (New York: Appleton, 1947), but it was not found in his library.

37. Olson did not own the 3 volume Werner Jaeger, *Paidea: The Ideals of Greek Culture* (New York: Oxford University Press, 1943–45), but picked up the volume 1 that came out in Oxford's Galaxy paperback in 1965. According to "Clarke's list," Olson also had in his library in 1965 Jaeger's *Die Antike* (Berlin, 1927).

38. Presumably Arthur Evans, *The Palace of Minos: A Comparative Account of the Successive Stages of the Early Cretan Civilization as Illustrated by the Discoveries at Knossos,* 4 vols. in 6 (London: Macmillan, 1921–35), not owned by Olson.

39. Olson had *Grimm's Fairy Tales,* ed. Rose Dobbs (New York: Random House, 1955). It is not recorded that he had Bulfinch's *Age of Fable,* but he owned the adaptation of it, Charles Mills Gayley, *The Classic Myths in English Literature* (Boston: Ginn, 1893), presumably a very early gift—"Charles Olsen" written by the giver inside the front cover. Marie-Louise von Franz, visiting Black Mountain in March 1953, passed on information about Father Wilhelm Schmidt's *Der Ursprung der Gottesidee* (Munich, 1912) being expanded from 1926 to 1955 into twelve volumes, apparently not knowing H. J. Rose's translation, *The Origin and Growth of Religion* (1931). Olson owned Maxime Collignon, *Mythologie figurée de la Grèce* (Paris: A. Quantin, 1885).

40. C. G. Jung, "The Mass and the Individuation Process," *Black Mountain Review* 5 (Summer 1955: 90–147, translated by Elizabeth Welsh. (Actually, Olson kept only issues 1, 2, and 4 of the *Review.*)

Notes among Olson's papers of the late 1940s indicate that he read in the Library of Congress A. A. Vasiliev, *History of the Byzantine Empire,* 2 vols. (Madison: University of Wisconsin, 1928–29).

41. *The Special View of History,* ed. Ann Charters (Berkeley: Oyez, 1970), p. 15. The epigraph is Olson's paraphrase of Heraclitus's fragment 93 as he found it translated by John Burnet in *The Portable Greek Reader,* ed. W. H. Auden (New York: Viking, 1948), p. 751—the volume a gift from the publisher via Monroe Engel.

42. Weyl is quoted without being named on p. 49 of *Special View;* Olson had just received the book as a gift (cited previously). Erwin Schrödinger's *What is Life?* had just come out as an Anchor Book (1956). Olson comments on it on p. 42; he did not own it later.

43. *Special View,* p. 48. Olson had the two volumes of Oswald Spengler *The Decline of the West* (New York: Knopf, 1926–28)—flyleaf: "Charles John Olson N.Y. March 1940"; notes and markings. As for the "Adamses" in their doom and gloom aspect:

Brooks Adams, *The Law of Civilization and Decay* (New York: Knopf, 1943)—notes.

Brooks Adams, *The Theory of Social Revolutions* (New York: Macmillan, 1913)—occasional markings.

Henry Adams, *The Degradation of the Democratic Dogma,* Introduction by Brooks Adams (New York: Macmillan, 1919)—flyleaf: "Olson working text"; occasional notes.

Worthington Chauncy, ed., *Letters of Henry Adams (1858–1891)* (Boston: Houghton Mifflin, 1930)—notes inside back cover.

Henry Adams, *The Education of Henry Adams,* (Boston: Houghton Mifflin, 1918)—Olson used the BMC library copies, now at North Carolina Wesleyan.

44. *Special View,* p. 36. About this time Olson bought the old classic, W. Robertson Smith's *The Religion of the Semites* in a paperback edition (New York: Meridian Books, 1956), but there is no evidence for his use of it.

45. Previously cited. Olson makes the comparison in both "On Black Mountain" tape recordings: *Muthologos* 2, p. 78, and *OLSON* 8, pp. 77–78.

## 14. The *Black Mountain Review* and Its Editor

1. *Creeley Correspondence* 7, p. 210. Galpin was previously cited as purchased by Olson the following month. The borrowed book referred to is Robert H. West, *The Invisible World: A Study of Pneumatology in Elizabethan Drama* (Athens: University of Georgia Press, 1939).

2. Olson owned Helen Pope, *Why Not Learn Greek?* (New York: Cosmos Greek-American Printing Co., 1941). He also had White, *The First Greek Book* (cited later); but markings went only up to page 6. It is doubtful that Olson got very far into Augustus Nauck, ed., *Tragicorum Graecorum Fragmenta* (Lipsiae: B. G. Teubneri, 1856), which he owned.

3. *Theatre of the Greeks, Containing, in a Compendious Form, a Great Body of Information Relative to the Rise, Progress, and Exhibition of the Drama* (Cambridge, England: Printed for W. P. Grant, 1825)—occasional markings. A comment on Aeschylus from p. 111 was quoted on July 1951 (*Creeley Correspondence* 7, p. 27).

4. Olson apparently never owned Owen Lattimore, *Inner Asian Frontiers of China* (New York: American Geographical Society, 1940), though we note him referring to it numerous times.

5. Olson had previously called attention to Pound's *Antheil and the Treatise on Harmony* (Chicago: Covici, 1927) in a letter of 22 June 1950 (*Creeley Correspondence* 1, p. 139). He did not own a copy.

6. Later in the same letter Hawthorne's *The Marble Faun* and *The Blithedale Romance* are named; no Hawthorne appeared in Olson's library later, nor Frank Norris's novel, *McTeague.*

7. Raymond Souster published Olson in *Contact* and invited him to read

in Toronto in April 1960 and February 1962, where he met, for instance, Kenneth McRobbie, who presented Olson with his verse *Eyes without a Face* (Toronto: Gallery Editions, 1960) in June 1960 on a visit to Gloucester. Olson kept the following gift volumes of Souster's poetry in his library: *Shake Hands with the Hangman* (Contact, 1953), *What Time Slays* (Contact, 1955), *The Selected Poems* (Contact, 1956), *Crepe-hanger's Carnival* (Contact, 1958), and *Place of Meeting* (Gallery Editions, 1962).

8. Olson had been instrumental in having Corman "feature" Robert Duncan in *Origin* 6 (Summer 1952), writing to him, for instance, on 6 February 1952: "as of DUNK, will try to enclose to you with this, or shortly thereafter, the huge mt of stuff from him which i have—both those things you sent me and a flock of other stuff he has kept putting to me" (*Corman Correspondence* 1, pp. 238–39).

Regarding *Faust Foutu,* Duncan remembers: "In 1953 when this play was completed, I rented a mimeograph machine and ran off, 100 copies I think it was. . . . Copies were mailed to Black Mountain College where Act I was performed in 1954, with music composed by Stefan Wolpe"—*Robert Duncan: A Descriptive Bibliography,* compiled by Robert J. Bertholf (Santa Rosa: Black Sparrow Press, 1986), pp. 34–35. Olson retained one of the embossed BMC copies.

9. Olson's marked up copy of Grover Smith, "On Poets and Poetry," *New Mexico Quarterly* 23 (Autumn 1953): 317–29 exists at Storrs. Olson's letter to the editor was published in the *New Mexico Quarterly* 24 (Spring 1954): 112–14, and reprinted as "On Poets and Poetry" in *Human Universe.*

10. This was apparently a review copy received from *New Mexico Quarterly;* Olson retained it in his library. Occasional notes and markings.

11. The notion of Odysseus as Bear-son is developed in Rhys Carpenter, *Folk Tale, Fiction and Saga in the Homeric Epics* (Berkeley: University of California Press, 1946). Olson made notes on it inside the front cover of his Modern Library *Homer,* perhaps in 1949. We know he was reading Carpenter's *The Greeks in Spain* (London: Longmans Green, 1925) then. These two books were not in his library later.

Neither Gerhardt's magazine *fragmente* nor his book of poems, *Umkreisung* (1952) turns up in Olson's library, but he kept a copy of *Ferrini and Others* that Gerhardt edited and printed in Germany 1955; also Wolfgang Weyrauch *Feuersbrunst* (1952) from the *fragmente* press.

12. *Human Universe,* p. 140. Olson also owned Walter Noble Burns, *Tombstone, an Iliad of the Southwest* (New York: Doubleday, Page, 1927). Olson refers in his review to Stewart H. Holbrook, the prolific writer on American frontier history; no specific title is mentioned.

13. As a contrast: Judson Crews, *The Anatomy of Proserpine* (n.d.) came in for review; Olson did a page, but then dropped it: "Damd if 'll speak in public for him" (letter to Creeley, 19 February 1955), though he kept the book. Cor-

man's *Thanksgiving Eclogue* was not in Olson's library later but the following gift volumes from Corman were:

*The Precisions* (New York: Sparrow Press, 1955).

*The Responses* (Ashland, Mass.: Origin Press, 1956).

*Stances and Distances* (Ashland: Origin Press, 1957).

*Sun Rock Man* (Kyoto: Origin, 1959).

*The Descent from Daimonji* (Ashland: Origin Press, 1959).

*Cool Melon* (Kyoto: Origin, 1959).

*For Instance* (Kyoto: Origin, 1962).

Presumably also sent by Corman was Shimpei Kusano, *Selected Frogs* (Kyoto: Origin, 1963). Corman had sent Olson a birthday gift, 27 December 1957, of John Esquemeling's *The Buccaneers of America,* but it was not later in his library. He kept another gift, Ferdinand Lallemand, ed., *Journal de Bord de Maarkos Sestios* (Paris: Editions de Paris, 1953)—flyleaf: "Cid Corman 30 November 1957."

14. There is at Storrs a letter from Hans Güterbock to Olson on 14 February 1957 talking of the possibility of coming to BMC with Kramer, and adding: "I see from my mailing list that you got my Ullikumi at the time it came out." He is referring to "The Song of Ullikumi: Revised Text of the Hittite Version of a Hurrian Myth," an offprint from the *Journal of Cuneiform Studies* 5 (1951): 135–61, and 6 (1952): 8–42 (New Haven: American Schools of Oriental Research, 1952). For Olson's own "Song of Ullikumi" see *Muthologos* 1, pp. 72–75, 91–93. He also had Güterbock's "The Hittite Version of the Hurrian Kumarbi Myths: Oriental Forerunners of Hesiod," in *American Journal of Archaeology* 52 (January–March 1948): 123–34, presumably the copy from the BMC library.

15. Letter to Creeley, 10 December 1954. In a letter to William Carlos Williams, Olson wrote on 21 December 1954: "it was suddenly circum 1602 when, so far as I can see, Campion soundly up and sounded a blast against rime and meter (meeter he spelled it). I was led into this by pleasure in Shakesp. own late verse" (carbon typescript at Storrs). We can list the following books owned by Olson as reflecting his long love affair with the Bard (besides items mentioned elsewhere):

*Elizabethan and Jacobean Pamphlets,* ed. George Saintsbury (London: Percival & Co., 1892)—flyleaf: "Olson 56."

*Hamlet,* ed. John Dover Wilson (Cambridge University Press, 1954)—Olson also specifically recommended, but did not own, *Measure for Measure* in the same series (*Creeley Correspondence* 8, p. 223).

John Middleton Murry, *Keats and Shakespeare* (London: Oxford University Press, 1926)—mentioned in a letter to Ronald Mason, 15 July 1953.

Wyndham Lewis, *The Lion and the Fox: The Role of Hero in the Plays of Shakespeare*

(New York and London: Harper, n.d.)—notes and markings heavy throughout; mentioned in letter to Creeley in January 1954.

John Dover Wilson, *Life in Shakespeare's England* (Harmondsworth: Penguin, 1951).

16. Olson was aware of Paul Goodman's books, but he did not own any of them and apparently didn't like what he had seen of Goodman when he was at BMC—see "Black Mt. College Has a Few Words For A Visitor" (*OLSON* 8, p. 40).

Olson introduced one of Kitasono's poems in *Right Angle* (May 1949), with information presumably from Kitasono himself in Tokyo, when his magazine *Vou* 33 (1949) published Olson's "La Préface." Any of Kitasono's books that may have been in Olson's library were not there later.

Olson and Creeley both saw, and liked, a piece by an unknown M. Elath, "In Another Direction: Commentary and Review of Three Anthologies," *Intro* 1 (1952): 3–4. Olson wrote of him in a letter 3 June 1952 as "a guy to catch" (*Corman Correspondence* 1, p. 260), but apparently nothing came of it.

The other persons named are dealt with elsewhere.

17. See Robert Buckeye, "The Principle, The Demarkation is Use: Selected Letters of Paul Blackburn in the Abernethy Library," *Credences* 3 (Spring 1985): 53–90, especially p. 15. Perhaps the break was the reason Olson apparently never got a copy of *The Dissolving Fabric* (Majorca: Divers Press, 1955). He later owned *Brooklyn-Manhattan Transit* (New York: Totem, 1960), *The Nets* (Trobar, 1961), and *The Cities* (New York: Grove Press, 1967). It was Blackburn, as an editor at *The Nation,* who commissioned Olson to review Creeley's *For Love: Poems 1950–1960* (New York: Scribner, 1962), and when his editor-in-chief vetoed the review, took it over to *The Village Voice* where it was published 13 September 1962.

18. Creeley met Robert Hellman in Europe, and published him in *BMR* 1. Olson hired him for BMC summer sessions 1954 and 1955 and kept in touch, but nothing of his work remains in Olson's library.

19. Letter to Creeley, 11 October 1953. In September 1953 Layton sent Olson the anthology *Cerberus,* poems by Louis Dudek, Irving Layton and Raymond Souster (Toronto: Contact Press, 1952), along with his own *Now is the Place* (Montreal: First Statement Press, 1948), *Here and Now* (Montreal: First Statement Press, 1945), and *The Black Huntsman* (Montreal: by the author, 1951), the last of which remained in Olson's library along with presentational copies of *The Long Pea-Shooter* (Montreal: Laocoon Press, 1954),*The Bull Calf* (Toronto: Contact Press, 1956), and *A Laughter in the Mind* (Jonathan Williams, 1958). Layton also apparently sent *Music on a Kazoo* (Toronto: Contact Press, 1956), but it was not found later in Olson's posssession. At first, Olson was very interested in Layton as a phenomenon, a present-day Martial; but he was later

annoyed with him on a couple of scores—see Tim Hunter, " 'The North American States': Charles Olson's Letters to Irving Layton," *Line* 13 (Spring 1989): 123–52.

20. Letter to Edward Marshall of October 1955. This poem was actually not included in Marshall's volume of poems, *Hellan, Hellan* (San Francisco: Auerhahn, 1960), sent to Olson by the publisher, Andrew Hoyem. Olson also had Marshall's *Transit Gloria* (New York: Carp & Whitefish, 1967).

21. Olson owned Stephen Jonas, *Love, the Poem, the Sea and Other* (San Francisco: White Rabbit, 1957), and *Transmutations* (London: Ferry Press, 1966).

22. Living for a time in San Francisco, Wieners published his first book there, *The Hotel Wentley Poems* (San Francisco: Auerhahn, 1958). Olson also had the 1965 2d edition as a presentation copy, and the translation published in Milan in 1967. He also had the following:

*Ace of Pentacles* (New York: James F. Carr & Robert A. Wilson, 1964).
*Asylum Poems* (New York: Angel Hair, 1969); and 2d ed. (Press of the Black Flag Raised, 1969).
*Chinoiserie* (San Francisco: David Haselwood, 1965).
*Pressed Wafer* (Buffalo: The Gallery Upstairs, 1967)—inscribed to "Charles Olson on the occasion of his birthday 1967 John Wieners (with love)."

23. Edward Dorn published his first significant story in *BMR* 7. Tom Field published poems in *BMR* 3—but developed into more of a painter than a poet. Fielding Dawson had a story in *BMR* 6 and went on to publish many volumes of stories, of which Olson had *Elizabeth Constantine* (Asheville: Biltmore Press, 1955), *Thread* (London: Ferry Press, 1964), *Man Steps into Space* (New York: Shortstop Press, 1965), and *Krazy Kat/The Unveiling* (Black Sparrow, 1969). Michael Rumaker had stories in *BMR* 5 and 6; Olson owned his *The Butterfly* (New York: Scribners, 1962) and *Gringos and Other Stories* (New York: Grove Press, 1966). Jonathan Williams had poems and essays in *BMR* 5, 6, and 7. The appendix to this chapter lists the titles of Williams's Jargon Press, with Olson's holdings indicated. In October 1951 Williams gave Olson a book gift: E. W. Tedlock, Jr., *The Frieda Lawrence Collection of D. H. Lawrence Manuscripts: A Descriptive Bibliography* (Albuquerque: Univ. of New Mexico Press, 1948) with a warm inscription. From Aspen in 1962 Williams inscribed to Olson his *In England's Green &* (San Francisco: Auerhahn, 1962). Joel Oppenheimer had several poems in *BMR* 4, 5, 6, and 7, but any volumes of his poetry that Olson may have had were not later in his library.

Other books by Black Mountain people: Ebbe Borregaard presented Olson with his *Sketches for 13 Sonnets* (pseudonym Gerard Boar) (Berkeley: Oyez, 1969); Lou Harrison, of the music faculty, gave him *About Carl Ruggles* (Yonkers: Baradinsky, 1946); Russell Edson's *Appearances* (New York: Thing Press, 1961) was in Olson's library.

24. As Melville's great-grandson, Paul Metcalf was bound to interest Olson, who wrote a long statement for the dust jacket of Metcalf's Melville book, *Genoa* (Jargon 1965). The other of Metcalf's books in Olson's library was *Will West* (Jargon 1956).

25. Olson owned this classic anthology from Grove Press (1960), and the one Donald Allen did with Robert Creeley, *New American Story* (New York: Grove Press, 1965). As a founding editor of *Evergreen Review*, and later as an independent publisher, Donald Allen was in a position to give Olson some eye-catching publications. Olson considered him one of his two "contemporaries"; they had a respectful literary relationship over many years. The following were either gifts or probable gifts from Allen while he was with Grove Press:

Gay Wilson Allen, *The Solitary Singer: A Critical Biography of Walt Whitman* (New York: Grove Press, 1955)—acknowledged in a letter to Allen of 18 March 1960.
James Broughton, *True and False Unicorn* (New York: Grove Press, 1957).
*Evergreen Review Reader*, ed. Barney Rossett (New York: Grove Press, 1968).
Eugene Ionesco, *Four Plays* (New York: Grove Press Evergreen, 1958).
Kenneth Koch, *Ko: or A Season on Earth* (New York: Grove Press, 1959).
Laurette Séjourné, *Burning Water: Thought and Religion in Ancient Mexico* (New York: Grove Press Evergreen, 1960).

26. Olson had one book of poems by Denise Levertov (cited later). Larry Eigner lived not far from Gloucester, but kept in touch mainly by sending his poems: *From the Sustaining Air* (Divers Press, 1953), *Look at the Park* (privately printed, 1958), *The Music, the Poems* (Albuquerque: Desert Review Press, n.d.), *Towards Autumn* (Los Angeles: Black Sparrow Press, 1967), *Air the Trees* (Black Sparrow, 1948), and *The Breath of Once Live Things in the Field with Poe* (Black Sparrow, 1968). Olson's library contained no books by Paul Carroll; he kept *Big Table* 4, where Carroll as editor printed a *Maximus* poem.

27. Olson had William Bronk's *Light and Dark* (Ashland: Origin Press, 1956). He undoubtedly had *The World, the Worldless* (New Directions-San Francisco Review, 1964)—the publisher used one of his comments on Bronk in publicity—though the book was not in his library later. He was sent *The Empty Hands* (New Rochelle: Elizabeth Press, 1969) by the publisher. In an interview of 1969, Olson said he thought that Bronk wrote "a very very marvelous, quiet, distinctive verse" (*Muthologos* 2, p. 97).

Gael Turnbull edited *Migrant* from Malvern, England, and Ventura, California, and kept in touch with Olson on poetry matters. Olson had two of his volumes, *Bjarni Spike-Helgi's Son* (Ashland: Origin Press, 1956), and *With a Hey Ho* (Migrant, 1961).

Olson owned no Niedecker. Snyder is cited later. As publisher, Corman sent Olson Zukofsky's *"A" 1–12* (Ashland: Origin Press, 1959); Robert Kelly sent *I's (pronounced eyes)* (Trobar, 1963); and Jonathan Williams sent *A Test of Poetry* (New York: Jargon/Corinth, 1964).

28. We find in Olson's library that harsh antiphon to the hippy movement, Gershon Legman, *The Fake Revolt* (New York: Breaking Point, 1967).

## 15. Maximus, Away from Gloucester

1. *Guide* (pp. 52–54) quotes from the Olson manuscripts of the two sketches of Gloucester ex-fishermen, "Al Gorman," and "Mason," i.e., Charles Mason Andrews, concerning whom Olson had saved a clipping from the *Boston Post* (18 January 1932), "Insists Upon Right to Live in Hogshead." Barbara Denny seems to have had foreknowledge of the direction the young Olson was to take in giving him as a gift in 1928 Basil Lubbock, *Adventures by Sea from Art of Old Time* (London: The Studio, 1925).

2. "The Peoples of America" series (Lippincott publishers) had been inaugurated in 1943 by Louis Adamic, associated with the Common Council for American Unity, where Olson got his first job on coming to New York City in November 1941. Olson did not retain any of Adamic's books, but we know he thought enough of *Dynamite: The Story of Class Violence in America* (New York: Viking, 1931) to recommend it to Harvey Brown for reprinting by Frontier Press (this was not done). Olson undoubtedly knew of Adamic's widely quoted article, "Education on a Mountain: The Story of Black Mountain College," *Harper's* 172 (April 1936): 516–30, which was included in his *My America* (1938).

Of the Duell, Sloan & Pearce "American Folkways" series, Olson owned Edwin Corle, *Desert Country* (New York, 1941)—flyleaf: "C Olson."

3. Clearly, Olson was reading James B. Connolly from an early age, long before he started collecting his volumes in earnest. The following were in his library:

*The Book of the Gloucester Fisherman* (New York: John Day, 1927)—flyleaf: "Olson this book (I found Jewett Dec 20 59) 59? was pub. by Faber as something like 'Fishermen of the North Atlantic' same year."
*Coaster Captain: A Tale of the Boston Waterfront* (New York: Macy-Masius, 1927).
*The Crested Seas* (New York: Scribner, 1907)—flyleaf: "bought Brown's depart-

ment store Gloucester October 29th, 1965 & read Thursday night November 4th 1965"; notes and markings.

*The Deep Sea's Toll* (New York: Scribner, 1905)—flyleaf: "Olson 59"; includes "The Wicked Celestine" and "The Truth About Oliver Cromwell."

*Gloucestermen: Stories of the Fishing Fleet* (New York: Scribner, 1944)—flyleaf: "Olson Jewett $1."

*Out of Gloucester* (New York: Scribner, 1905)—flyleaf: "Olson (Jewett Dec 20/59 $1"; notes and markings. Includes "From Reykjavik to Gloucester."

*The Port of Gloucester* (New York: Doubleday, Doran, 1940)—occasional notes and markings.

*Sea-Borne: Thirty Years Avoyaging* (Garden City: Doubleday, Doran, 1944)—signed by Mary Shore; Olson's notes inside front cover.

*The Seiners* (New York: Scribner, 1910)—flyleaf: "Charles Olson."

*Tide Rips* (New York: Scribner, 1922)—notes on flyleaf and inside back cover.

Olson also had the issue of *Collier's* 102 (15 October 1938) where Connolly's "Pride of Vessel" appeared, pp. 48–52. It is presumably for the text by Connolly that Olson acquired the photographic book by Albert Cook Church, *American Fishermen* (New York: Norton, 1961).

4. The true tale of Howard Blackburn's endurance in the open sea is told in Charles Boardman Hawes, *Gloucester By Land and Sea* (Boston: Little, Brown, 1923), again an insightful gift from Barbara Denny, for Christmas 1933.

5. Olson owned Percy MacKay, *Dogtown Common* (New York: Macmillan, 1921), a book-length poem on the upper part of Gloucester, of later significance in the *Maximus*.

6. Although Olson did not later own Rudyard Kipling's *Captains Courageous*, it was, according to a letter to Gael Turnbull of 12 November 1958, "the companion of youth." He also saw the film version, made in Gloucester, in an audience made up of Gloucester fishermen.

7. Joseph Berger, under the pseudonym Jeremiah Digges, wrote *In Great Waters: The Story of the Portuguese Fishermen* (New York, 1941). Olson did not own the book.

8. The bibliography of Samuel Eliot Morison, *The Maritime History of Massachusetts* (previously cited as on Harvard list) begins with "Manuscript Sources." Olson also owned Morison's other "Maritime" story, *Admiral of the Ocean Sea: A Life of Christopher Columbus* (Boston: Little, Brown, 1942)—flyleaf: "Olson 1st used April 2/59 as of tit & North Star not true: note my notes, fr some previous date, p. 229 on." But see *Guide*, p. 122.

9. Of the many contributions of Alfred Mansfield Brooks to the *Essex Institute Historical Collections*, Olson owned two dated prior to this time: "The Gloucester Model," 76 (January 1940): 43–45, and "The Pearce-Parrot Garden

in Gloucester," 80 (July 1944): 283–85. He later acquired, in the same series, "Gloucester and the Surinam Trade," 89 (July 1953) 287–91.

Besides Babson's *History of Gloucester*—heavily marked, much used— Olson bought on this occasion *The Fishermen's Own Book* (Gloucester: Procter Brothers, 1882), and *The Fishermen's Memorial and Record Book* by George H. Procter (Gloucester: Procter Brothers, 1973). Other basics of this order that Olson acquired then or soon after were *The Fisheries of Gloucester, from 1623 to 1876* (Gloucester: Procter Brothers, 1876), believed to be by John J. Babson; *Official Year Book of the Fishermen's Union of the Atlantic* (Boston: Fishermen's Union of the Atlantic, 1905).

More important than books, perhaps, was Olson's conversation on this same visit with Frank Miles and Louis Douglas about their ship somersaulting, a story going back to 1905, which led him to look up the *Boston Post* for 7 January 1905, p. 2: "Big Wave Swept Men Overboard" (*Guide*, pp. 195–98). This is the moment when the *Maximus* was conceived, in one of its dimensions.

10. Olson received most of Ferrini's books of verse, then, almost as a family member might (*Muthologos* 1, p. 182):

*The Plow in the Ruins* (Prairie City, Ill.: James A. Decker Press, 1946).
*Sea Sprung* (Gloucester: Cape Ann Press, 1949).
*Injunction* (Lynn: Sand Piper, 1949).
*The Infinite People* (New York: Great Concord Publishers, 1950).
*In the Arriving* (Gloucester: Heron Press, 1954).
*Timeo Hominem Unius Mulieris* Liverpool and Gloucester: Heron Press, 1954).
*Mindscapes* (Mount Vernon, N.Y.: Peter Pauper Press, 1955).
*The Square Root of In* (Gloucester: Heuretic Press, 1957).
*The House of Time* (London: Fortune Press, 1952).
*The Garden* (Gloucester: Heuretic Press, 1958)—passed on to Jean Kaiser.
*Five Plays* (London: Fortune Press, 1959).
*Book of One* (Gloucester: Heuretic Press, 1960).
*Mirandum* (Gloucester: Heuretic Press, 1963).
*I Have the World* (London: Fortune Press, 1967).

In his autobiography *Hermit of the Clouds* (Gloucester: Ten Pound Island Book Co., 1988), Ferrini recalls, among many memories, that Olson "read all my earlier works in the Library and the first book," i.e., *No Smoke* (Portland: Falmouth Publishing House, 1941). Olson, in fact, had a copy of that also.

11. Olson made marginalia to Smith's "The present state of New England" and Prince's "Chronological History of New England" in his copy of vol. 2 of Edward Arber's *An English Garner: Ingatherings from our History and Literature* (London: Constable 1882, 1897)—Olson had all but vol. 6 of the 7 vol-

umes. Did Olson consult the BMC copy of *The Dictionary of National Biography* (Oxford University Press, 1921–22) for John Smith? He is known to have done so for Richard Hawkins (*Guide*, p. 95).

12. In *OLSON* 6, Butterick has revealed that a number of poems were written for the *Maximus* during the period 1953–57 but were discarded as proving to be tangential. David Ingram was one offshoot; Olson saw his story in Brebner (cited elsewhere), and sought background in Frank Aydelotte, "Elizabethan Seamen in Mexico and Ports of the Spanish Main," *American Historical Review* 48 (October 1942): 1–19, which he owned. Olson indicated his interest by marking the heading "West Indies" in his copy of *American Historical Review: General Index to Volumes 21–30, October 1915 to July 1925* (New York: Macmillan, 1926).

13. *History of the Town of Rockport*, compiled by John W. Marshall and others (Rockport: Printed at the Rockport Review Office, 1888)—flyleaf: "Olson Jan '57 fr bookseller Pleasant St (near St Ann's $2"; notes and markings. In a letter to Cid Corman of 24 September 1953, Olson asks him to look out for "any stuff on settlement of yr town," i.e., Dorchester, Mass. Olson specifically mentions *Memoirs of Roger Clap* (Boston, 1844), one of the first settlers there.

14. According to "Clarke's list," Olson also purchased Gaster's *Thespis: Ritual, Myth and Drama in the Ancient Near East* (New York: Schuman, 1950). This concern with the "cradle of civilization" in the eastern Mediterranean proved, of course, not to be tangential, but central to the *Maximus Poems*. Conceivably it was in this splurge Olson acquired the four volumes of *The Pyramid Texts*, ed. Samuel A. B. Mercer (New York: Longmans, Green, 1952).

15. It is not known when Olson acquired his offprint from Driver, *Studies in Cappadocian Tablets* (Paris: Librairie Orientaliste Paul Geuthner, 1927), from *Babyloniaca* 10, fascicle 2–3. He was passionately into these matters in October 1958, when he borrowed John Garstand, *The Land of the Hittites* (New York: Dutton, 1910) from a library, and never returned it.

### 16. April Today Main Street

1. Olson acquired all eight volumes eventually. Vol. 1 "Olson (bot by release fr Essex Inst fr EI Oct/57"; vol. 2 "Olson, Salem, Saturday Sept 19/59"; vol. 3 "Olson (bot Salem Sept 19/59 with C P"; vol. 6 "bought Apr. 1, 1961"; vols. 4, 7, 8 invoiced from Essex Institute, 11 December 1965. Notes and markings on Gloucester matters in all volumes.

2. On the cover of this Government Document Olson wrote: "by usurpation from R. H. Marchant so long ago (note acknowledging my arrogation Sunday Sept 2nd 'LXVIII'"—probably at the same time that he wrote the *Maximus* poem, "A Letter, on FISHING GROUNDS (of, THE GULF OF MAINE) by

Walter H. Rich," ending the poem "with my thanks to R. H. Marchant for letting me keep his copy of Walter H. Rich, to do this" (*Maximus* pp. 345–46). About this time, after correspondence with the Assistant Director of the U.S. Coast and Geodetic Survey, Olson acquired the *Bulletin of the Geographical Society of America* 58 (February 1947) for Harold W. Murray, "Topography of the Gulf of Maine: Field Session of 1940," pp. 153–96. Olson also owned U.S. Senate, Committee on Foreign Relations *Compilation of Reports*, vol. 5: Trade and Commerce with Foreign Nations; Foreign Tariffs; Boundary and Fishery Disputes (Washington: Senate Document 231, part 5, 1901). According to *Guide*, p. 179 Olson referred to the map, "Ships Wrecked on Sable Island" by George T. Bates, in writing the poem "Some Good News."

3. The note is written inside the front cover of Whitehead's *Process and Reality*: "Stiffening in the Master Founders' Will (fr Brooks Adams' The Emancipation—of Massachusetts—ignorance of *greed*." Olson had just acquired from Goodspeed's (19 February 1958) his copy of the two-volume *Three Episodes in Massachusetts History* by Charles Francis Adams (Boston: Houghton Mifflin, 1893). As a further source on the Salem witchcraft trials he had Cotton Mather's *The Wonders of the Invisible World* (London: John Russell Smith, 1862).

4. Olson also owned Shurtlett's *A Topographical and Historical Description of Boston* (Boston: A. Williams & Co., Old Corner Bookstore, 1871)—occasional notes and markings. He later picked up the *Boston Inner Harbor Nautical Chart* put out by the U.S. Department of Commerce Coast and Geodetic Survey, March 1965.

5. He later acquired the James Savage edition of Winthrop's *The History of New England from 1630 to 1649*, 2d ed. (Boston: Little, Brown, 1853), vol. 2 only. Notes from around August 1959 indicate he consulted Savage's *A Genealogical Dictionary of the First Settlers of New England*, 4 vols. (Boston: Little, Brown, 1860–62).

6. Olson consulted the *Proceedings* 42 (March 1909) for Albert Matthews, "Family Tradition and History," pp. 193–95 (*Guide*, p. 137). A notebook of spring 1959 shows that he also consulted the seven volumes of *Colonial Families of the United States of America*, ed. George Norbury MacKenzie (Baltimore: Seaforth Press 1915), and used his notes in a *Maximus* poem in 1961 (*Guide* p. 336). A notebook entry around August 1959 indicates he consulted for a *Maximus* poem James Savage's *A Genealogical Dictionary of the First Settlers of New England* 4 vols. (Boston: Little, Brown, 1860–62) (see *Guide* pp. 333–34).

7. On that same visit Olson acquired Raymond Frederick Allen, *The Allens* (Walton, N.Y.: Reporter Company, 1958)—cover: "Olson via Mrs Connors, June 4, '59"; notes and markings. And presumably also *Town Records of Manchester, From 1718 to 1769*, vol. 2 (Salem: Salem Press, 1891).

8. Butterick has identified, from notes and markings, other articles of the

*Essex Institute Historical Collections* which were used by Olson: Thomas E. Babson, "Evolution of Cape Ann Roads and Transportation, 1623–1955," 91 (October 1955): 302–28; George F. Chever, "Some Remarks on the Commerce of Salem from 1626 to 1740," 1 (July 1859): 77–91; Robert L. Grayce, "Cape Ann Forests: A Review," 88 (July 1952): 207–18; Russell Leigh Jackson, "Kent's Island," 80 (July 1944): 197–207; Hervey Putnam Prentiss, "Pickering and the Embargo," 69 (April 1933): 97–136.

9. Olson owned Townsend's Supplement to *The Birds of Essex County, Massachusetts* (Cambridge: Nuttall Ornithological Club, 1920)—flyleaf: "Charles Olson 1961"—and his *Sand Dunes and Salt Marshes* (Boston: Dana Estes, 1913).

Other bird books that Olson owned were: Allan D. Cruickshank, *A Pocket Guide to Birds* (New York: Washington Square Press, 1960)—flyleaf: "Olson oct 61"; Allan D. Cruickshank and Helen G. Cruickshank, *1001 Questions Answered about Birds* (New York: Grossett & Dunlap, 1958); A. Landsborough Thomson, *A New Dictionary of Birds* (New York: McGraw-Hill, 1964); *Field List of the Birds of Essex County, Massachusetts,* 4th ed. (Salem: Peabody Museum, April 1952); and a specific interest, Frederic Lucas, "The Expedition to the Funk Island, with Observations Upon the History and Anatomy of the Great Auk," reprinted from *Report of the National Museum, 1887–88* (Washington: Smithsonian Institution, 1890). Olson knew, of course, John James Audubon and *The Birds of America*; he mentions him in the *Maximus*, though he did not own the work (*Guide*, p. 692).

10. Morgan was in one of the issues of *New England Quarterly* in which Olson had reviews with a short but significant piece, marked by Olson, "Provisions for the Great Migration," 12 (March 1939): 98–99.

11. Olson had many maps. We have record of the following: *Cape Ann* (Gloucester: Gerald S. Curhan); John Mason's map (*Guide*, pp. 432–33); *Atlas of the City of Gloucester and Town of Rockport* (Philadelphia: G. M. Hopkins, 1884)—gift of Jean Kaiser, summer 1964; *The Macmillan Marine Atlas: New England, 1968/69 edition*, compiled by William B. Matthews.

12. The following books and magazines of a more general nature were probably obtained in this period:

Robert G. Athearn, *The American Heritage New Illustrated Dictionary of the United States*, vol. 1 (New York: Dell, 1963).

Elise Boulding, *Children of Solitude*, Pendle Hill Pamphlet 125 (Wallingford, Pa: Society of Friends, 1962).

G. S. Brindley, "Afterimages," *Scientific American* 209 (October 1963): 84–93—used in a poem (OLSON 1, p. 48).

Roger Casement, *The Crime Against Europe* (Philadelphia: Celtic Press, 1915)—gift of Mary Shore about 1962.

Charles Chaplin, *My Autobiography* (New York: Pocket Books, 1966).

Alexis de Tocqueville, *Democracy in America* (New York: New American Library, Mentor, 1960).

Leon A. Harris, *The Fine Art of Political Wit* (New York: Dutton, 1964).

Billie Holiday, with William Duffy, *Lady Sings the Blues* (New York: Popular Library, 1958).

Richard von Krafft-Ebbing, *Psychopathia-Sexualis* (New York: Paperback Library, 1965)—occasional notes and markings.

D. B. Wyndham Lewis, *François Villon: A Documentary Survey* (Garden City: Doubleday, 1958)—Olson was trying his hand at translating Villon in May 1950.

A. J. Liebling, *The Sweet Science* (New York: Viking, 1956).

Vladimir Mayakovsky, *The Bedbug and Selected Poetry* (New York: Meridian Books, 1960).

Wilfrid Mellers, *Music in a New Found Land: Themes and Developments in the History of American Music* (London: Barrie and Rockliff, 1964)—gift of Eli Wilentz, received 22 September 1964.

Burgo Partridge, *A History of Orgies* (New York: Avon Books, 1960).

H. F. Peters, *My Sister, My Spouse: A Biography of Jan Andreas-Salomé* (New York: Norton, 1962)—see *Collected Poems*, p. 571.

Stuart A. Queen and John B. Adams, *The Family in Various Cultures* (Philadelphia: J. B. Lippincott, 1952)—notes pp. 108–27.

Rose Quong, *Chinese Wit, Wisdom, and Written Characters* (New York: Pantheon Books, 1944).

Ed Reid and Ovid Demaris, *The Green Felt Jungle* (New York: Pocket Cardinal, 1964)—notes and markings.

Karl Shapiro, *In Defense of Ignorance* (New York: Vintage Books, 1965)—Olson also kept Shapiro's *Essay on Rhyme* (New York: Reynal and Hitchcock, 1945).

C. P. Snow, *The Two Cultures and the Scientific Revolution* (Cambridge University Press, 1961).

Freyda Stark, *Alexander's Path, From Caria to Cilicia* (New York: Harcourt, Brace, 1958)—"Clarke's list."

*Tama, The Diary of a Japanese School Girl*, ed. Florence Wells (New York: Woman's Press, 1919).

Albert Payson Terhune, *Famous Hussies of History* (Cleveland: World, 1943).

Henry David Thoreau, *A Week on the Concord and Merrimack Rivers* (New York: New American Library, Signet, 1961).

Morton White, *The Age of Analysis: 20th Century Philosophers* (New York: New American Library, Mentor, 1961).

13. Neville Williams, *The London Port Books* reprinted from *Transactions of the London and Middlesex Archaeological Society*, vol. 18, part 1—cover: "fr.

Prynne air mail Oct 1962"; notes and markings. In a letter of 3 October 1962 Prynne sent extracts from N. J. Williams's edition of *Descriptive List of Exchequer, Queen's Remembrancer Port Book: Part I, 1569 to 1700* (London, 1960).

14. *A Symposium on the Continental Drift*, organized for the Royal Society by P. M. S. Blackett, Sir Edward Bullard and S. K. Runcorn, (London: The Royal Society, 1965)—inscription in the form of poems from Jeremy Prynne and Ed Dorn (visiting Prynne) 14 February 1966.

15. J. H. Prynne, review of *Maximus IV, V, ,VI* in *The Park* 4–5 (Summer 1969): 64–66 (quotation on p. 65), reprinted in *Io* 16 (1973): 89–92. This review is the subject of much comment in *"Paris Review* Interview" *Muthologos* 2.

Other gifts from Prynne (besides those mentioned elsewhere):

Edward Bullard et al., "A Symposium on Continental Drift, IV: The fit of the continents around the Atlantic," *Transactions of the Royal Philosophical Society* 258 (1965): 41–45—an offprint.

*Hittite Art and the Antiquities of Anatolia* (London: Diploma Gallery, Arts Council of Great Britain, 1964)—letter from Prynne, 24 July 1964, laid in.

Alexander von Humboldt, *Cosmos* (London: Bohn, 1848)—xerox copy of the Introduction sent.

Ronald J. Mason, "The Paleo-Indian Tradition in Eastern North America," *Current Anthropology* 3 (June 1962): 227–78—xerox sent.


## 17. Under the Mushroom

Albert Glover has recently told me that the substance used in the Leary sessions was not peyote but manufactured psilocybin. This might make the connection with North American Indian religion rather specious, except that it does not appear so in Olson's expression of it.

1. "Bullfight on Cape Ann" in Edgar Rowe Snow, *Mysteries and Adventures Along the Atlantic Coast* (New York: Dodd, Mead, 1948), pp. 146–56 is Olson's source, though he did not own the volume. A note in Erich Neumann, *The Great Mother: An Analysis of the Archetype* (New York Pantheon Books, Bollingen Series, 1955) indicates "using Nov 1959"; extensive notes and markings throughout, not all complimentary, however.

2. This is apparently the first use of a much annotated volume, Hugh G. Evelyn-White's edition of *Hesiod, The Homeric Hymns and Homerica* in the Loeb Classical Library (New York: Putnam, 1926). Olson later acquired Norman O. Brown's translation of the *Theogony* in the Library of the Liberal Arts (New York: Bobbs-Merrill, 1953).

3. Olson and his wife were frequent guests at the Castle, the home of John

Hays Hammond, Jr. (see *Guide*, pp. 249 and 470–71), where they exchanged book gifts, receiving:

*The Autobiography of John Hays Hammond*, 2 vols. (New York: Farrar & Rinehart, 1935).

Natalie Hammond, *A Woman's Part in a Revolution* (London and New York: Longmans, Green, 1897)—flyleaf: "To Charles and Bet recently adopted into the Hammond Clan (Jack."

*Jack Hays, The Intrepid Texas Ranger* (Bandera, Texas: Frontier Times, 1927)—cover: "To Charles with best regards of 'Jack' Hays Hammond Jr."

*Investigating the Works of John Hays Hammond, Jr. in Remote and Automatic Controls*, Franklin Institute of the State of Pennsylvania for the Promotion of the Mechanic Arts Report No. 3333 (Philadelphia: Hall of the Institute, 1959)—a letter from Hammond and a poem to Olson laid in; notes and markings throughout.

A. C. B. Lovell, *The Individual and the Universe* (New York: Harper, 1959)—flyleaf: To Charles, Improver of the universe Jack Hammond October 1961."

4. The first dated annotation in *Psychology and Alchemy* is 27 November 1959; there are many more: February 1960, 16 November 1960, 11 July 1961, 1 December 1964, 1–2 May 1965, 18 May 1965, 30 January 1966, 10 February 1966, 25 August 1966, 4 February 1967 (London), 21 January 1968, 15 June 1969. Jung's *Aion*, Collected Works 9.2 (New York: Pantheon Bollingen Series, 1959)—flyleaf: "Olson april 60"—has dated annotations in the period September 1960 to 31 December 1965. *The Archetypes and the Collective Unconscious*, Collected Works 9.1 (New York: Pantheon Bollingen Series, 1959) was apparently first read 30 December 1965 and read for the second and last time 11–12 January 1969. *Symbols of Transformation* (previously cited)—flyleaf: "Olson Black Mt winter 56–7," has dated annotations 10 January 1959, 20 January 1959, 13 February 1959, December 1961, and 24 October 1962. Olson bought *Psyche and Symbol: A Selection from the Writings of C. G. Jung*, ed. Violet S. de Laszlo (Garden City: Doubleday Anchor, 1958) when on vacation—flyleaf: "Olson bot P-town Aug 19, 1958"; there are no annotations. *Two Essays on Analytical Psychology*, trans. R. F. C. Hull (New York: Meridian, 1956)—cover: "Olson fr John Grady" has occasional notes and markings, not dated.

5. Hans Jonas, *The Gnostic Religion* (Boston: Beacon Press, 1958)—flyleaf: "Olson—fr Gerrit Lansing Xmas 1959 ok 1st looked into Feb 5, 1960." Also notes dated 17 March 1960, 8 November 1960, and 27 April 1965 "reread." A year later there was another like gift: *Man and Time*, ed. Joseph Campbell (New York: Pantheon Bollingen Series, 1957)—cover: "Charles Olson December 3,

1960 via Garrit at Brown's." Lansing, who had come to Gloucester to live, became an important intellectual companion, as we shall see. Olson owned Lansing's poems, *The Heavenly Tree Grows Downward* (Matter, 1966), and the two issues of his magazine *Set*: Winter 1961/1962 and Winter 1963/1964, the first of which he contributed poems to.

6. Moulavi S. A. Q. Husaini, *Ibn al 'Arabi* (Lahore: Muhammed Ashraf, n.d.)—flyleaf: "Olson fr nick feb 60"; occasional notes and markings. And then: G. Contenau, *La Civilisation Phenicienne* (Paris: Payot, 1949)—flyleaf: "Olson via Nick July 5, 1960"; some notes.

7. *Muthologos* 1, p. 37. Timothy Leary wrote about these sessions in *High Priest*, which Olson received on publication in 1968 (cited later). Koestler's account appeared in the *Sunday Telegraph* on 12 March 1961 under the title "Return Trip to Nirvana"—Olson was sent the clipping. Olson was familiar with *Darkness at Noon* and Koestler's recent *The Lotus and the Robot* (1961), but did not own them.

8. *Muthologos* 1, p. 39. After seeing a photographic piece in *Life*, Olson wrote to the Portland Art Museum, Oregon, for the brochure of their exhibition, Paul S. Wingert, *Prehistoric Stone Sculpture of the Pacific Northwest* (Portland: Portland Art Museum, 1952), and acknowledged receipt in a letter of 10 June 1952: "It is very exciting, both to myself and the men who work directly with me on the American past" (carbon Storrs). He suggests that the Northwest Indian pieces have "important relationships to Mayan and/or Mexican art." As further indications of Olson's longstanding interest, we note in his library Erna Gunther, *Indians of the Northwest Coast* (Taylor Museum of the Colorado Springs Fine Arts Center, and Seattle Art Museum, 1951).

9. Olson apparently knew of Schultes' "In the Land of the Intoxicating Trees," *Illustrated London News* (31 December 1955): 1124–26, and used, but did not own, Nina L. Marshall, *The Mushroom Book: A Popular Guide to the Identification and Study of Our Commoner Fungi* (New York: Doubleday, Page, 1901). Found in the same issue of *Main Currents in Modern Thought* as the Harman article is U. A. Asrani's "A Modern Approach to Mystical Experience," pp. 15–20, which Olson refers to on the tape as Tantric: "I wouldn't touch the drugs because I'm a Tantrist" (*Muthologos* 1, p. 46).

10. Olson did not own Puharich's books, *The Sacred Mushroom: Key to the Door of Eternity* (1959) or *Beyond Telepathy* (1962); nor John C. Lilly's *Man and Dolphin* (1961). He had one book by Alan Watts, *Myth and Ritual in Christianity* (New York: Vanguard Press, n.d.), again via Gerrit Lansing. Watts's *The Joyous Cosmology* (New York: Vintage, 1962) is mentioned on the tape (it had a foreword by Timothy Leary and Richard Alpert) but Olson did not own a copy.

11. The following are mentioned on the tape (*Muthologos* 1, pp. 21–48):

"Instant Mysticism," *Time* 82 (25 October 1963): 86–87.

John Kobler, "The Dangerous Magic of LSD," *Saturday Evening Post* 236 (2 November 1963): 31–40.

"LSD Drug Found to Aid Children," *New York Times* (10 November 1963): 46.

"The pros and cons, history and future possibilities of vision-inducing psychochemicals"—three views by Dan Wakefield, Alan Harrington, and Aldous Huxley in *Playboy* 19 (November 1963): 84–88, 175–79.

12. Gerald Heard, " 'Can This Drug Enlarge Man's Mind?' " *Psychedelic Review* 1 (June 1963). Olson also referred to an article there by Gottfried Benn, "Provoked Life," pp. 47–54. He saved in his library the first four issues of the magazine. Leary kept in touch, sending Olson a couple of publications: "How to Change Behavior" in *Clinical Psychology: Proceedings of the XIVth International Congress of Applied Psychology*, vol. 4 (Copenhagen: Munksgaard, 1962), pp. 50–68; and a mimeographed report written with George Litwin and Ralph Metzner, "Americans and Mushrooms in a Naturalistic Environment" (Cambridge, n.d.). In a letter to Mary Shore of January 1962 Olson mentioned Isaac Asimov on LSD, but the only book by Issac Asimov found in his library was the general paperback, *The Wellsprings of Life* (New York, 1962). Olson later picked up Wayne Barker, *Brain Storms: A Study of Human Spontaneity* (New York: Grove Press, 1968).

13. Butterick thinks that Olson may have had the volume itself in Buffalo, 1964–65, but it was not in his library later. It is not unlikely that he was satisfied with the quotations supplied to him by Richard Sassoon in a letter of November 1963. One might mention here that Olson did not, as far as we know, read Martin Heidegger. In July 1965 he was given a copy of *What is Philosophy?* by Heidegger (New Haven: College and University Press, 1956), but the annotations in the book are by the giver, William Harris.

In this connection (*Muthologos* 1, p. 46) Olson refers to the work of Arthur Young, which was only in manuscript at the time but was later published as *The Reflexive Universe*.

14. A receipt from the Student Book Shop shows these books were purchased on 15 May 1965. *Spiritual Disciplines* is another of the papers from the *Eranos Yearbooks*, edited by Joseph Campbell (New York: Pantheon Books, 1960)—flyleaf: "(bot Buffalo! spring 1965?) read 1966"; notes and markings throughout. Besides *Spiritual Disciplines* and *Man and Time* (previously cited), Olson also had in the *Eranos Yearbook* series, *The Mysteries* (New York: Pantheon Books, 1955), bought at Black Mountain in February 1957, in which he marked especially C. Kerenyi's "The Mysteries of the Kabeiroi" and Fritz Meier's "The Mysteries of the Ka'ba: Symbol and Reality in Islamic Mysticism." It is hard to imagine that Olson did not consult the other three titles in the series: *Spirit and Nature* (1954), *Man and Transformation* (1964), and *The Mystic Vision* (1968), even though he didn't own them.

15. Castaneda's *The Teachings of Don Juan: A Yaqui Way of Knowledge* (Berkeley: University of California Press, 1968) was, according to a letter of 13 November 1968, a gift from Don Allen. Boer reports that Olson was "very fond of the book, and had recommended it to many people in recent months" (p. 103). He must have given his copy to someone before his death.

16. John Philip Cohane, *The Key* (New York: Crown, 1969)—introduction by Cyrus Gordon. Much on this book later. There were actually four copies of Graves's *The White Goddess* among Olson's books. One (New York: Vintage, 1958) was bought when Olson was on vacation in Provincetown—flyleaf: "Olson bought P.town Wed Aug 6 '58 . . . beginning again Dec 58"; notes up to p. 19. Another Vintage (1960) had markings throughout, dated 3 April 1966, 24 July 1966, and 18 July 1969. The other two will be dealt with later.

17. *Muthologos* 1, p. 46. Olson almost bought W. Y. Evans-Wentz, *Tibetan Book of the Dead*, 3d ed. with introduction by C. J. Jung (New York: Oxford University Press, 1957)—he asked the publisher about it on 22 November 1958, but never went through with the ordering. He also wondered about buying Evans-Wentz, *Tibetan Yoga and Secret Doctrines* 2d ed. (Oxford University Press, 1958)—letter to Alan Marlowe, 39 August 1966—but apparently did not get that one either.

The speculative strain was strong, but, for instance, the *I Ching* never had the place that the Tarot had had. Paul Blackburn gave him on publication *The I Ching, or Book of Changes* (New York: Pantheon Bollingen Series, 1961), the Richard Wilhelm edition, translated by Cary F. Baynes, with a foreword by C. J. Jung. His other copy, the 1967 edition, was also a gift—from Charlotte Hussey with "Love & Peace." Although he later bought Hellmut Wilhelm's *Change: Eight Lectures on the I Ching* (New York: Harper Torchbooks, 1964), Olson is not known to have used the *I Ching* or *Kenkusha*, never mind palmistry, though Nellie Simmons Meier, *Lion's Paws: The Story of Famous Hands* (New York: Barrows Mussey, 1937) was one of his books. He also kept Josef Ranald, *How to Know People by their Hands* (New York: Modern Age Books, 1938). His copy of P. D. Ouspensky's *In Search of the Miraculous: Fragments of an Unknown Teaching* (New York: Harcourt, Brace, 1949) contained no reading marks, neither did his copy of Grillot De Givry, *Witchcraft, Magic and Alchemy* (New York: Frederick Publications, 1954).

18. Olson's first copy of Zimmer (New York: Pantheon Bollingen Series, 1947) was passed on by Connie to friends, Elizabeth and John Hamilton of Sanford, North Carolina (still in their possession, according to Butterick's note in *OLSON* 9, p. 88). Olson had to get another copy (New York: Pantheon Bollingen Series, 1953)—flyleaf: "Olson's"; notes and markings throughout, some dated 18 February 1966, 20 August 1966, 28 August 1966, 30 August 1966, 14 December 1967, and 8 May 1969.

19. Henry George Liddell and Robert Scott, *A Greek-English Lexicon*, 8th ed., revised (New York: American Book Co., 1897)—notes and markings throughout. H. J. Rose, *A Handbook of Greek Mythology*, 6th ed. (New York: Dutton Paperback, 1959)—flyleaf "Olson bot G1 May 27 1962 *after* having written Short Guide to Present Advantages"; extensive notes and markings. Olson received as a gift a later edition of Lewis's *An Elementary Latin Dictionary* (Oxford: Clarendon Press, 1963)—"from Harvey Saturday February 25th 1967 17 Hanover Terrace day before his & Polly's departure." Olson also owned *Harper's Latin Dictionary* (New York: American Book Co., 1907); *Allen and Greenough's New Latin Grammar for Schools and Colleges* (Boston: Ginn, 1916—from Boston Girls' Latin School, Constance Wilcock's copy); and Karl Pomeroy Harrington, *Medieval Latin* (Boston: Allyn and Bacon, 1925).

20. *Muthologos* 2, pp. 10 and 26, from the lecture at Beloit College on 25 March 1968 entitled "Poetry and Truth." Goethe's autobiography, *Dichtung und Wahrheit*, was on Olson's mind in all this, the words "poetry" and "truth" of Goethe's title, if not the contents of the book itself. He did not own the book.

21. *Additional Prose*, p. 17. "The Laws of Orientation Among Animals," G. Reynaud's contribution to *Annual Report of the Board of Regents of the Smithsonian Institution . . . for 1898* (Washington 1899), pp. 481–98 has notes and markings throughout.

22. A book he had received more recently as a gift from M. C. Richards, formerly of BMC, is pertinent: Arnold D. Wadler, *One Language—Source of All Tongues* (New York: American Press for Art and Science, 1948)—flyleaf: "Olson (fr MC, spring 1959)." In a letter to Robin Blaser of May 1959 Olson referred to this book: "I love it; and there's *some* truth in it." He was asking Blaser if he knew of any recent dictionary of roots. He knows Lancelot Hogben's edition of Frederick Bodmer's *The Loom of Language* (New York: Norton, 1944)—though he did not own it; "but," he says, "that's discursive: I mean a TOOL, to add to my present dictionary EQUIPMENT"—which includes, we may add, *Webster's New International Dictionary of the English Language*, 2d ed. unabridged (Springfield: G. & C. Merriam, 1927). He goes on to mention to Blaser "the English translation of Curtius' Grundsage on Greek Etymology: 1875"—this must be Georg Curtius, *Principles of Greek Etymology*, trans. A. S. Wilkins and E. B. England, 2 vols. (London: John Murray, 1875) (not owned); but he wants something that "would include Hittite at least" (*Selected Writings*, "Letter to Elaine Feinstein," p. 27). Perhaps it was at this time that he was making his notes and markings in Frank M. Cross, Jr., "The Evolution of the Proto-Canaanite Alphabet," *Bulletin of the American Schools of Oriental* Research No. 134 (April 1954): 15–24.

23. *Addional Prose*, Butterick's note p. 87. Sapir had been used for a *Maximus* poem of January 1959 (*Guide*, p. 201). Annotations in Olson's copy are

dated April 1962 and April 1969. He also owned Edward D. Myers, *The Foundation of English* (New York: Macmillan, 1960), but it contains no markings.

24. Eileen Garrett was someone Olson would have met at Hammond's Castle. He did not have anything by her but would have seen her magazine, *Tomorrow*, over the years. He had nothing by Edward Carpenter.

25. Olson used this quotation as an epigraph to the bibliography of the *Mayan Letters* (*Selected Writings*, p. 125). He later acquired Hyams's *Dionysus: A Social History of Wine* (New York: Macmillan, 1965)—the date 16 March 1968 is written on the back flap of the dust jacket.

26. Noah Gordon, "Hebrew, Greek Link Established," *Boston Herald* (4 April 1962): 1, 10. Another clipping was "Ties Greek, Hebrew to One Culture," *Boston Globe* (4 April 1962).

27. Olson also had Ruth Witt-Diamant's copy of the two-volume *Greek Myths* (1955 printing), presumably from his February 1957 visit to San Francisco. He also had an extra copy of vol. 2. All these volumes contain markings.

28. Frances Densmore, *Teton Sioux Music* (previously cited), p. 205—see *OLSON* 10, p. 35. Olson was still thinking of this image during the "Causal Mythology" lecture at Berkeley in 1965 when he referred to the Sioux belief that "the stone is the truest condition of creation, that it is silence and it is solidity" (*Muthologos* 1, p. 73).

## 18. From Gloucester Out

1. From a tape transcription entitled "On History," *Muthologos* 1, pp. 1–19, see notes pp. 201–2 for topical references to *Time* and *New York Times*.

2. Olson did not actually acquire until later his copy of *The Apocrypha of the Old Testament: Revised Standard Version*, ed. Bruce M. Metzger (New York: Oxford University Press, 1965).

*The Enchanted Pony* in the Classics Illustrated Junior series (October 1959), presumably bought for Charles Peter, stuck in Olson's mind, and he retold the story at length to Ed Dorn at Berkeley (*Muthologos* 1, p. 159). According to Butterick's note there (p. 224), his son Adam Butterick received the copy as a gift from Olson in August 1969.

Olson gave Kenneth Clark, *The Nude: A Study in Ideal Form* (Garden City: Doubleday Anchor, 1959) to his wife in October 1959—flyleaf: "to Bet." On a somewhat less lofty level, we find in Olson's books Peter Lacey, *History of the Nude in Photography* (New York: Bantam, 1964).

As for Frederico Garcia Lorca, Olson had written to Pound 13 July 1946: "Have no Lorca, know none"; and there was none in his library at his death. But prior to this Vancouver session he certainly read most carefully Lorca's essay "The Duende," presumably in the appendix to Ben Belitt's edition of *Poet in New York* (New York: Grove Press, 1955).

3. Fred Wah and Robert Hogg went to Buffalo to do graduate work with Olson 1964–65. Wah's *Lardeau* (Toronto: Island, 1965) and Hogg's *The Connexions* (Berkeley: Oyez, 1966) were in Olson's library. Olson received, and contributed to, George Bowering's magazine, *Imago*. Dan McLeod founded Vancouver's alternative newspaper, *Georgia Straight*, which Olson received regularly, and read. A year after the conference, Earle Birney, Head of the Department of Writing at the University of British Columbia, sent Olson his poems: *Near False Creek Mouth* (Toronto: McClellan & Stewart, 1964). He also acquired Gwendolyn MacEwan, *The Drunken Clock* (Aleph Press, 1961), David McFadden *The Poem Poem* (Toronto: Weed/Flower Press, 1967), and Victor Coleman *One Eye Love* (Toronto: Coach House Press, 1967).

4. David Schaff went to Yale and edited a special issue of *The Yale Literary Magazine* (April 1965), including a *Maximus*. Olson said of Drummond Hadley, as quoted on the jacket of his *Strands of Rawhide* (Goliard 1972): "You're the water table, and when they want it they're gonna have to come to you to get it." Olson owned the one book of Hadley's published before 1970, *The Webbing* (San Francisco: Four Seasons Foundation, 1967). Edward Van Aelstyn went back to the University of Oregon to edit the *Northwest Review* 6, no. 4 (Fall 1963), which was banned by the authorities. Olson, among others, came to his rescue; out of it came *Coyote's Journal*, which Olson received regularly. Van Aelstyn's manuscript-like book of poems, *Migration at Newport Beach* (Eugene, 1965), contained references to Olson, and was presented to him on 12 July 1965. Linda Wagner inscribed to Olson a copy of her *Poems of William Carlos Williams* (previously cited). A letter to Creeley on 14 December 1967 indicates Olson read her "Interview with Robert Creeley, 1955," *Minnesota Review* 5 (October–December 1965): 309–21. Olson had most issues of Larry Goodell's magazine *Duende*, and his *Ode*, published in *Duende Broadside* no. 1 (October 1964).

5. We discover in Olson's library another act of preparation for academia, David M. Zesmer, *Guide to English Literature: From Beowulf through Chaucer and Medieval Drama* (New York: Barnes & Noble College Outline Series, 1963).

Harriet Monroe, *The New Poetry* (New York: Macmillan, 1917) contained Stevens but not Hulme. He did not own this anthology; but he did acquire at some point, probably early, Harriet Monroe and Morton Dauwen Zabel, *A Book of Poetry for Every Mood* (Racine, Wisconsin: Whitman Publishing Co., 1933).

6. *Niagara Frontier Review* 1 (Summer 1964), the review reprinted in *Additional Prose*, pp. 52–55. Later Olson got a xerox copy of James A. Notopoulos, "Parataxis in Homer: A New Approach to Homeric Literary Criticism," *Transactions of the American Philological Association* 80 (1949): 1–23. He had had, presumably for some time, the *Harvard Studies in Classical Philology*, vol. 43 (1932)

containing Milman Parry's crucial article, "Studies in the Epic Technique of Oral Verse-making," pp. 1–47. He acquired Albert Lord's *Singer of Tales* (New York: Atheneum, 1965) upon publication.

Thaddeus Zielinski had previously come to Olson's attention when he received from Melbourne the Poundian magazine *Edge*, whose issue 2 (November 1956) was devoted to Zielinski's "The Sybil: Three Essays on Ancient Religion and Christianity." Olson recommended it to his class in Buffalo on 30 September 1964. He presumably also had at hand Kathleen Freeman's *Greek City-States* (New York: Norton, 1963), just out in paperback.

7. Poem printed in *Editing Maximus*, Appendix 2. Olson dates the poem from Wyoming, New York, a rural community, an hour from Buffalo, where patrons had found him and Betty and Charles Peter suitable accommodation. He got his bearings by buying the *Geologic Map of New York, Niagara Sheet* (Washington, D.C., William and Heintz Map Corporation, 1961).

Mac Hammond responded with a mimeographed article, "The Metonymic Poem," which Olson commented on in a letter, but passed on to somebody along with the original piece, "Poetic Syntax" in *Style in Language*, ed. Thomas A. Sebeok (New York: Technology Press, John Wiley, 1960), pp. 475–82. He kept, however, the presentation copy of Mac Hammond's *The Horse Opera and Other Poems* (Columbus: Ohio State University Press, 1966). Olson also kept the copy of Roman Jakobson and Morris Halle, *Fundamentals of Language* (The Hague: Mouton, 1956) that Hammond loaned him.

8. Olson was not unaffected by the issue, as letters and other writing indicate (see *Muthologos* 1, p. 212). George Starbuck, then working at the University as a librarian, was one of the leaders of the fight against the Feinberg Certificate. Olson received from him later a copy of his *White Paper* (Boston: Little, Brown, 1966).

9. Olson owned the Dorn titles mentioned, including almost a complete run of *Wild Dog*. Presentation copies followed: *Hands Up!* (New York: Totem Corinth, 1964), *Geography* (London: Fulcrum, 1965), *Idaho Out* (London: Fulcrum, 1965)—though this latter title was not in his library later. Frontier Press published *The Rites of Passage* in Buffalo in 1965; Olson had two copies. Found in Olson's library is a copy of Katherine H. Capes, *Contributions to the Prehistory of Vancouver Island*, Occasional Papers of the Museum, no. 15 (Pocatello: Idaho State University, 1964); perhaps Dorn brought this pamphlet to Buffalo in the summer of 1964 as a gift.

10. Olson owned the titles mentioned, plus *The Dead Lecturer* (New York: Grove Press, 1964). In his last letter to Jones, he spoke of seeing an article by him in *Midstream* (1964). He later spoke of seeing *Black Music* (New York: Morrow, 1967), but that was in a letter to someone else. Communication had ceased in 1965, with Jones's change to Amiri Baraka.

11. Besides the titles mentioned, Olson had of Robert Kelly's earlier publications *Round Dances* (Trobar, 1964), *The Scorpions* (New York: Doubleday, 1967), and *Christmas Hymn* (n.d.).

12. George F. Butterick, "Notes from Class," *Magazine of Further Studies* 2 (1966) covers the period from September 1964 to May 1965. Olson did not own any of Henry Fielding's novels, but did consider him a watershed (letter to Creeley, 14 November 1953). Jack Kerouac's "Essentials of Spontaneous Prose" had been published in *Black Mountain Review* 7 (Autumn 1957): 226–28. Olson expressed himself not interested in the "subjective tragedy" of *On the Road* (letter to Creeley, 25 May 1965); but he finally read it on holiday in Provincetown summer 1958 (letter to Creeley, 18 November 1958). Olson felt toward Kerouac as a neighbor, but owned none of his novels.

Butterick's notes also indicate that Olson mentioned in his classes S. N. Kramer's anthology, *Mythologies of the Ancient World* (Garden City: Doubleday Anchor, 1961), which he had read and marked up, and Norman O. Brown, *Hermes the Thief* (Madison: University of Wisconsin Press, 1947), which he may have owned at the time, though not later. Presumably he would have mentioned N. K. Sandars's translation of *The Epic of Gilgamesh* (Baltimore: Penguin, 1964); he bought his copy later.

Stephen Rodefer also took notes, which enable us to add E. R. Dodds, *The Greeks and the Irrational* (Berkeley: University of California Press, 1956); the book was owned by Olson. He also owned Rodefer's poems, *The Knife* (Toronto: Island Press, 1965).

13. Olson bought *William Blake: A Selection of Poems and Letters*, ed. J. Bronowski (Harmondsworth: Penguin, 1961) from the Student Book Shop in Buffalo on 16 May 1964 very soon after the first meeting with Clarke. It was possibly *The Portable Blake* (New York: Viking, 1946) that he had used as a working copy through the years, but it was not found in his library. He came to own *The Marriage of Heaven and Hell*, ed. Clark Emery (Coral Gables: University of Miami Press, 1963), and *William Blake: Water-Color Drawings*, ed. Peter A. Wick (Boston: Museum of Fine Arts, 1957).

Clarke gave Olson others besides Blake, including Richard Maurice Bucke, *Cosmic Consciousness: A Study in the Evolution of the Human Mind*, 19th ed. (New York: Dutton, 1959)—inscribed to Olson on 24 December 1964; Lancelot Law Whyte, *The Unconscious Before Freud* (Garden City: Doubleday Anchor, 1962)—flyleaf: "Charles—Descartes' Dream: 80–84—J C 6/29/65"; other gifts are mentioned elsewhere. It is on record that Clarke called to Olson's attention Alexander Gode-von Aesch, *Natural Science in German Romanticism* (New York: Columbia University Press, 1941), extending Olson's knowledge of Novalis.

14. Olson did not own Kenner's books. When Kenner's *Wyndham Lewis*

arrived for the *Black Mountain Review*, Olson passed it on to Creeley without comment (letter, 23 August 1954).

Olson owned Corso's *Gasoline* (San Francisco: City Lights). Corso heckled him at his Greensleave Coffee House reading on 20 November 1964. Olson was reminded of this on the platform at Berkeley (*Muthologos* 1, p. 133), and of the interview with Corso in Lawrence Lipton's *The Holy Barbarians* (New York: Julian Messner, 1959), which he owned.

Olson was down to introduce McLuhan's talk at Buffalo on 4 March 1965. He owned *Counterblast 1954* (Toronto 1954); he did not own, but presumably looked at McLuhan's *Understanding Media* (New York: McGraw-Hill, 1964), which mentions Olson (see *Muthologos*, pp. 97 and 191).

At this time, Olson owned Gary Synder's *Riprap* (Ashland: Origin Press, 1960) and *Myths and Texts* (New York: Totem, 1960). He would later receive, with the compliments of the publishers, *Regarding Wave* (San Francisco: Grabhorn-Hoyem, 1967) and *The Back Country* (New York: New Directions, 1968).

In a letter to Ed Dorn of 19 March 1965, Olson mentions visits to Buffalo by Robert Graves, "who was swell," and W. D. Snodgrass, "who also is something: the post-Teen Cub Scout Poet." He did not own any of their verse.

Olson picked up a copy of the newly published photography book, *Found Objects*, by Oscar Bailey and Charles Swedlund (Buffalo: State College, 1965).

15. *Peace Eye* (Buffalo: Frontier Press, 1965) stayed in Olson's library. He also had from Sanders his *Fuck God in the Ass* (New York: Fuck You Press, 1965) and *A Description of a Meeting of the Regal Society of Sooey Semen* (New York: Fuck You Press, 1969). Though it was not later in his library, Olson had had *Poem From Jail* (San Francisco: City Lights, 1963): "I think it's one of the essential poems that exists. I lived with it for a year on my kitchen table" (*Muthologos* 2, p. 5).

Ed Sanders also assumed the function of "teacher" of Classics. A sign of his influence is the existence in Olson's library of Hesiod in French, *Théogonie, Les Travaux et les Jours, Le Bouclier* (Paris, 1960), a gift from Sanders.

16. While still at Cambridge, Crozier had edited an Olson-biased "American Supplement" in the student magazine *Granta* 68 (7 March 1964), for which a contribution from Olson was solicited. On arrival Crozier "stuffed into my hand," as Olson put it in a letter to Dorn on 19 March 1965, Donald Davie's *Ezra Pound: Poet as Sculptor* (New York: Oxford University Press, 1964), with its last ten pages on Olson (the result of a conversation between Davie and Prynne, one understands). The book slipped out of Olson's hand, apparently: "I couldn't tell which way he was taking either Pound or myself."

On returning to England, Crozier edited *The English Intelligencer*, a newsletter Olson received but didn't hang on to; and started Ferry Press, publishing, for instance, *Romney Marsh*, two poems by Peter Riley and Andrew Crozier (May 1967). Olson also had Crozier's *Loved Litter of Time Spent* (Buffalo: Sumbooks, 1967) and *4 Poems* (London: Nothing Doing in London, 1968).

17. Olson did not own a Beowulf. Klaeber would have been the standard edition at Harvard. As for recent Celtic interests, we can cite Tom Peet Cross, "The Celtic Elements in the Lays of *Lanval* and *Graelent*," *Modern Philology* 12 (April 1915): 1–60, which Olson apparently saw and used for his Enyalion figure (*Guide*, p. 763); and Ludwig Bieler, *Ireland, Harbinger of the Middle Ages* (London: Oxford University Press, 1963), which he took out from the Lockwood Library of the University of Buffalo, and returned (overdue notices exist for 7 and 13 January 1965).

18. Emmett L. Bennett, Jr., ed., *Mycenaean Studies*, Proceedings of the Third International Colloquium for Mycenaean Studies, September 1961 (Madison: University of Wisconsin Press, 1964)—from a library, due date 21 March 1965, not returned; Denys L. Page, *History and the Homeric Iliad* (Berkeley: University of California Press, 1959)—flyleaf: "bot Cambridge Wed Feb 24, 1965—Tufts?"; Leonard R. Palmer, *Mycenaeans and Minoans: Aegean Prehistory in the Light of the Linear B Tablets* (New York: Knopf, 1963)—flyleaf: "Olson Cambridge Feb 24 65"; Alan J. B. Wace and Frank H. Stubbings, eds., *A Companion to Homer* (London: Macmillan; New York: St. Martin's Press, 1962)—a gift of John Wieners, 21 February 1965. Olson also owned Wace's *Mycenae: An Archaeological History and Guide* (New York: Biblo & Tannen, 1964). All these books show signs of careful reading.

19. Olson was aware of Snorri Sturlson's *Prose Edda*, but no edition survived in his library. Possibly he was depending on reference materials such as his copy of *Everyman's Dictionary of Non-Classical Mythology* compiled by Egerton Sykes (London: Dent; New York: Dutton, 1961). We do find in his library Lee M. Hollander's translation of *The Sagas of Kormak and the Sworn Brothers*, published for the American-Scandanavian Foundation by the Princeton University Press, 1949.

20. Olson later picked up J. Kr. Tornöe, *Columbus in the Arctic? and the Vineland Literature* (Oslo: A. W. Brøggers Boktrykkeri, 1965).

21. In the photographic section of the *Guide* is a snapshot of Ezra Pound at Spoleto signing a book for Charles Olson. No such signed book appeared in Olson's library at his death; it could have been the 1948 *Cantos*, since that title is lacking in the Olson collection.

For a list of poets attending the Spoleto Festival, see *Muthologos* 1, p. 213, Butterick's note to p. 112. Items that Olson received from participants include a mimeographed handout from Pier Paolo Pasolini, a poem "A Desperate Vitality"; Desmond O'Grady presented him with his *Separazioni* (Rome: Edizioni Rapporti, 1965). Afterwards John Ashbery sent *Three Madrigals* (New York: Poets Press, 1968) and Barbara Guest her poems, *The Blue Stairs* (New York:

Corinth, 1968). One notes in Olson's library Franco Migliora, *Figure della Terra (Principi di Effigientica)* (Toronto: "Francesco Petrarca," 1969), inscribed.

Olson later owned Pablo Neruda's *We Are Many* (London: Cape Goliard, 1967), presumably a gift of the publisher. In a letter of 1 March 1960, Olson tells Creeley of reading Neruda poems in the current *Folio* magazine, with the comment: "that vibration of Neruda's ok." He does not seem to have taken much account of Neruda otherwise.

22. The P.E.N. Conference was attended by Robbie MacCauley, Susan Sontag, Keith Botsford, Roger Shattuck, and Arthur Miller, in addition to seven Russians. Olson apparently did not come away with the feeling that he should purchase any of their books.

23. Olson owned James Koller's *Two Hands: Poems 1959–1961* (Seattle: James B. Smith, 1965) and *Brainard and Washington Street Poems* (Eugene: Toad Press, 1965).

He had Jack Spicer's *After Lorca* (San Francisco: White Rabbit, 1957) and *Billy the Kid* (Stinson Beach: Enkidu Surrogate, 1959). Robin Blaser has said that he sent Olson Spicer's *The Heads of the Town up to the Aether* (San Francisco: Auerhahn, 1962), but it was not in his library later. Blaser sent presentation copies of his own *The Moth Poem* and *Les Chimeres* (San Francisco: Open Space, 1964 and 1965 respectively).

Olson owned Ted Berrigan's *The Sonnets* (New York: Lorenz & Ellen Gude, 1964), and *Many Happy Returns to Dick Gallup* (San Francisco: Grabhorn-Hoyen, 1967).

John Sinclair published his work under the Detroit Artists' Workshop imprint. Olson had *A Song for the New Year* (1965), *This Is Our Music* (1965), *Firemusic: A Record* (1966), and *The Poem for Warner Stringfellow* (1966). Among the Detroit contingent at the Berkeley Conference, Robin Eichele was notable for his article-diary, "A Personal Re-cognizance," *Work* 2 (1965): 73–79. (Olson received a set of *Work* plus *Whe're*, from Detroit.) Olson had Robin Eichele's *Four Poems* (published by Victor Coleman, n.d.). Also from Detroit Artist's Workshop: Buzz Klingenberger, *Your Sweet All* (1967), in combination with Ed Rudolph, *Alice in You* (1967), J. D. Whitney, *Hello* (1967), and a John Wieners broadside, *Hart Crane Harry Crosby I see You Going Over the Edge* (1965).

24. Olson received a presentation copy of Loewinsohn's *Against the Silences to Come* (San Francisco: Four Seasons, 1965). He also owned *Watermelons* (New York: Totem, 1959).

Olson had received Lew Welch's *Wobbly Rock* (San Francisco: Auerhahn, 1960) from the publisher on publication. He also came to own *On Out* (Berkeley: Oyez, 1965), *Hermit Poems* (San Francisco: Four Seasons, 1965), and *Graffiti*, a broadside (1965).

The works of all the other poets named as present at Berkeley are dealt with elsewhere, if indeed he owned copies.

25. Notes and markings indicate Olson's interest in Ernst Zander's "War as a Way Out?," *Contemporary Issues* 2 (Autumn 1950): 155–75, and especially his unsigned piece in the same issue, "Documents of 'The Great Business Partnership,'" pp. 177, 180. Butterick lists other marked articles under the names of Harry Ludd, Wilhelm Lunen, Nathan Davidson, and Alan Dutscher. The literary anthology, *Confucius to Cummings*, edited by Ezra Pound with Marcella Spann (New York: New Directions, 1964), which Olson sees as a lesser thing than the econometric and political concerns of Sanders and Zander, was not in his library.

26. Olson owned no Franz Kafka. He wrote in a letter of 15 July 1951 that Kafka divides "art from reality," and compared his work with George B. McCutcheon's fantasy novel, *Graustark* (1901), which he also did not own (*Creeley Correspondence* 6, p. 148).

27. "Still haven't been cool enough to sit down and read that guy"— letter to Dorn. Olson had no Burroughs in his library, but he did acquire a Burroughs-like collage book, Akbar del Piombo, *Fuzz Against Junk* (Paris: Olympia Press, 1959). Olson knew Hubert Selby, also presumably his *Last Exit to Brooklyn*, but he did not own it.

28. Olson is referring to the following:

Douglas S. Byers, *Ipswich B.C.*, offprint from *Essex Institute Historical Collections* 92 (July 1956): 252–64—title page: "bot fr Jewett for 50¢ March 18, 1960."

James Mellaart, "A Neolithic City in Turkey," *Scientific American* 210 (April 1964): 94–104—notes and markings; and his *Earliest Civilizations of the Near East* (London: Thames and Hudson, 1965)—flyleaf: "from Jeremy."

Stuart Piggott, ed., *The Dawn of Civilization* (New York: McGraw-Hill, 1962)—borrowed from Gerrit Lansing. He owned Piggott's *Prehistoric India to 1000 B.C.* (Harmondsworth: Penguin Books, 1950)—occasional notes and markings.

Carl O. Sauer, "Time and Place in Ancient America," *Landscape* 6 (Winter 1956–57): 8–13. Olson owned this, but had passed on his copy of *Land and Life: Selections from the Writings of Carl Ortwin Sauer* (Berkeley: University of California Press, 1963) to Jack Clarke.

Heinrich Zimmer, *Myths and Symbols in Indian Art* (previously cited), edited by Joseph Campbell. Olson did not own Campbell's popular *Hero with a Thousand Faces* nor any of Coomaraswamy's.

A reference in *Pleistocene Man*, p. 13 indicates Olson had been reading a life of Michelangelo; presumably he had obtained by this time his copy of *The Letters of Michelangelo*, ed. E. H. Ramsden, 2 vols. (Stanford: Stanford University Press, 1963). He spoke movingly of Michelangelo's sonnets from the platform at Berkeley (*Muthologos* 1, p. 150), referring to J. H. V. Davies, "The Sonnets of Michelangelo," *Nine* 7 (Autumn 1951): 125–28 as his source.

29. "The Vinland Map Review," reprinted in *Additional Prose*, p. 60. Olson quotes Veblen from Dowd; he owned no Veblen. Olson took the opportunity to go back to an offprint given him years before, Daniel Aaron "The Unusable Man: An Essay on the Mind of Brooks Adams," *New England Quarterly* 21 (March 1948): 3–33—heavily marked and annotated.

30. Sonia Chadwick Hawkes, H. R. Ellis Davidson, and Christopher Hawkes, "The Finglesham Man," *Antiquity* 39 (March 1965): 17–32. Olson is also thinking of a note by Christopher Hawkes later in the issue. *Antiquity* was presumably sent to Olson by Prynne, who around this time sent some xerox pages of W. K. C. Guthrie's *A History of Greek Philosophy*, vol. 1, *The Earlier Presocratics and the Pythagoreans* (Cambridge University Press, 1962), pp. 205–12, which Olson draws on in the review (*Additional Prose*, p. 63), and also a xerox of J. A. Walker "Gothic-leik and Germanic *lic," *Philological Quarterly* 28 (April 1949): 292–93, used likewise (*Additional Prose*, p. 65). Olson turned to his copy of Milton Haight Turk, *An Anglo-Saxon Reader* (New York: Scribner, 1930) for a reference to Bishop Ulfilas. Nor should we neglect to mention the input from John Temple, a young English poet who had been at Buffalo: "Temple, by the way, yesterday sent me wonderful *gripe* poem on Eastward inclines dealing with Cambridgeshire *FENS*" (letter to Andrew Crozier, 18 October 1965)—hence the inclusion of the phrase on p. 63 of *Additional Prose*. The poem, "Meditation on a Landscape," was included in John Temple, *Rothschild's Lapwing* (London: Ferry Press, 1968), which Olson must have received, though it is not found in his library.

31. Cyrus Gordon had sent Olson a hectographed abstract he had prepared for the Mediterranean Studies Colloquium at Brandeis Univeristy on 5 March 1964, "The Phaistos Disk," which Olson used for a *Maximus* poem (*Guide*, p. 557). He also had received and used the *Journal of Near Eastern Studies* 31 (July 1962), containing two pieces by Gordon: "Minoica," pp. 207–10 and "Eteocretan," pp. 211–14. Olson ordered *Before the Bible* in a postcard to the Grolier Bookshop on 1 September 1964. The George Huxley study had been recommended to Olson by Hans Güterbock, and according to a flyleaf note had been bought in the spring of 1964 through Stechert. Charles Boer tussled with Olson over this book in class at Buffalo (Boer, pp. 66–67).

32. In Buffalo, Olson had undoubtedly seen *The Giant's Ladder: David H. Moffat and his Railroad* (Milwaukee: Kalmbach Publishing Co., 1962), the result of University of Buffalo English Professor Harold A. Boner's lifelong passion, with Boner's comment on the dust jacket that trains on the prairies did "what clippers and whalers did to kids in Gloucester and New Bedford."

33. "I sent it over from Brown's. And being the kind of people they

are—his wife is the daughter of a Swedish captain—Ethel made me a cake, and Lou came to the Fort to bring it to me" (*Muthologos* 2, p. 166). A letter to Crozier on 18 November 1965 mentions acquiring his own copy of *Westviking*, which he called in a later letter of 29 November 1965 "a crock of SHIT," but added, "does cool some matters." Olson received from Crozier (or elsewhere) a photocopy of John Lear, "What Did the Norsemen Discover?," *Saturday Review* 48 (6 November 1965): 49–56.

34. Olson also acquired *Eldridge Tide and Pilot Book, 1966* (Boston: Robert Eldridge White, 1965)—some notes and markings: and Dana Story *Frame-Up! The Story of Essex, Its Shipyards, and Its People* (Barre: Barre Publishers, 1964)—flyleaf: "bot abt date—1965? (and given to Creeley—& to Duncan??"; occasional notes and markings. On 13 September 1965 Olson had written to the U.S. Government Printing Office for the Smithsonian *Catalogue of Ship Drawings and Photographs* (Washington: U. S. National Museum, 1937); his request was returned "o.p." From the evidence of a *Maximus* poem (*Guide*, p. 597), it is likely Olson had Howard I. Chapelle's *The History of American Sailing Ships* (New York: Bonanza Books, n.d.) by this time.

35. Olson had studied V. Gordon Childe's two paperbacks, probably gifts from John P. Grady: *What Happened in History* (Harmondsworth: Penguin, 1950) and *Man Makes Himself* (New York: New American Library Mentor, 1951).

36. Preserved in Olson's papers are the excerpts from Velikovsky's *Worlds in Collision* which were published in *Collier's*: "The Heavens Burst" (25 February 1950) and "World on Fire" (25 March 1950). When Boer asked Olson if he had read Velikovsky's *Oedipus and Akhnaten* (Garden City: Doubleday, 1960), he replied, "Yeah, science fiction" (Boer, p. 108).

37. Olson picked up from the Essex Institute vols. 2 and 3 of *Vital Records of Gloucester* (Salem: Essex Institute, 1923 and 1924) in December 1965, and vol. 1 not until July 1969 (cited then). There is no further reference to the Marblehead Records. Olson bought around this time Sumner Chilton Powell's popular *Puritan Village: The Formation of a New England Town* (Garden City: Doubleday Anchor, 1965).

38. Olson had out from a library at the time H. R. Hall and C. Leonard Woolley, *Ur Excavations: Vol. I, Al-'Ubaid: A Report on the Work Carried Out at Al-'Ubaid for the British Museum in 1919 and for the Joint Expedition in 1922–3* (London: Published for the Trustees of the British Museum and of the Museum of the University of Pennsylvania by Oxford University Press, 1927). It was due back 9 January 1966, but he never returned it.

39. Olson had two copies, one apparently a gift from his mother—she wrote "Mr. Charles J. Olson" on the flyleaf. Olson wrote in the margin of p. 21: "What a quiet and exact man this Mr. Walton is."

Olson owned the following books on animals and natural history:

Eugene Burns, *The Sex Life of Wild Animals: A North American Study* (New York: Fawcett Premier Book, 1956).

J. Henri Fabre, *The Life of the Spider* (London: Hodder & Stoughton, n.d.).

Joseph B. Holder, *History of the American Fauna* (New York: Virtue & Yorston, 1877)—"rec'd fr. Con in an exchange 1969 (known for itself 1949, first)."

David Starr Jordan, *A Manual of the Vertebrate Animals of the Northern United States* 5th ed. (Chicago: A. C. McGlurg, 1890).

Percy A. Morris, *A Field Guide to Shells of our Atlantic Coast* (Boston: Houghton Mifflin, 1947).

Walter Needham and Barrows Mussey, *A Book of Country Things* (Brattleboro: Stephen Greene Press, 1965).

Charles G. D. Roberts, *The Kindred of the Wild* (Boston: Page Co., 1919).

40. Mary Shore sent for Charles Peter in August 1960 Irma C. Kierman, *The Sea Serpent of Cape Ann: An Exciting and Authentic Narrative of the Visits of the Sea Serpent to Cape Ann in the Years 1817 and 1886* (Rockport: by the author, 1950).

Olson wrote to the editor of *The Old Farmer's Almanac* on 12 March 1966 (copy at Storrs) about the phrase "Beware of Old Colins" in the "current Almanac." We find the *Almanacs* for 1958 and 1959 in his library.

41. His presentation copy of Dorn's *Geography* (London: Fulcrum, 1965) had turned up damaged (letter to Dorn, 18 January 1966). Dorn sent another inscribed copy 26 April 1966. This letter of 7 February 1966 includes Olson's statement that he hasn't read Robert Lowell, "to whom these Englishmen are *always* referring, as though they had somebody in court, or a friend." Possibly it was Dorn, then, who sent Robert Lowell, *Selected Poems* (London: Faber, 1965), which remained in Olson's library.

42. Olson had Mircea Eliade, *Myths, Dreams and Mysteries* (New York: Harper, 1960)—flyleaf: "Charles bot April-May 1964 alone with Charles Peter read 1st week June 1964 Wyoming read at Saturday April 17th, 1965." On the endpapers is an exasperated opinion; a toned down version appears on the title page: "Gallimard 1957, shame on them except that Eliade must be allowed to have done one job good (cf. *Ancient Religions*," i.e., Eliade's contribution, "Shamanism," to Vergilius Ferm's anthology (previously cited).

Olson had acquired C. Kerenyi's *Asklepios: Archetypal Image of the Physician's Existence* (New York: Pantheon Bollingen Series, 1959)—flyleaf: "Feb 1.," i.e., 1963; and his *The Gods of the Greeks* (New York: Grove Evergreen, 1960). Kerenyi's "The Mysteries of the Kabeiroi" in *The Mysteries* (previously cited) is heavily marked.

The two items by Hallam L. Movius owned by Olson were not exactly recent: "Old World Prehistoric Archaeology: 1948," Preliminary Report for Committee on Interrelations of Pleistocene Research (Washington: National Research Council, n.d.)—cover of this mimeographed booklet: "Olson's copie"; notes and markings. And *El arte mobiliar del Perigordiense Superior de la Colombiere (Ain)* (Barcelona: Comision Internacional para el Estudio del Arte Prehistorico, 1952).

Olson's library did not in the end contain a copy of *Wah'Kon-tah: The Osage and the White Man's Road* by John Joseph Mathews (Norman: University of Oklahoma Press, 1932).

Since Olson's library later contained no work by Dell Hymes, we can only guess that the title mentioned was *Language in Culture and Society* (1964).

43. Olson did not own Schmid, nor Gerald F. Else, *Aristotle's Poetics: The Argument* (Cambridge: Harvard University Press, 1957). He may have had in mind the offprint he had received and read thoroughly, Else's "Aristotle on the Beauty of Tragedy," *Harvard Studies in Classical Philology* 49 (1938): 179–204.

44. *Idaho Out* (London: Fulcrum, 1965) was inscribed by Dorn to Olson on 22 February 1966.

45. "Olson in Gloucester, 1966," *Muthologos* 1, p. 193. Olson is referring to Jonathan Bayliss, a long-time Gloucester resident, and his novel, *Prologos*. Olson also saw Bayliss's article, "Ritual and Dramatic Poetry" in *Audience* 7 (Autumn 1960): 43–53. Bayliss's novel *Gloucesterbook* (1992) contains a character based on Olson.

What provoked Olson to write the essay entitled "A House Built by Capt. John Somes 1763" (*Additional Prose*, pp. 43–44) was Gino Clays' "Omnia Mea Mecum Porto" in *A Pamphlet* (19 March 1962), which Olson received and kept (*Muthologos* 1, p. 187). Olson also retained ten issues of *Wild Dog*, which Gino Clays and others edited from Pocatello 1963–66.

46. Olson wanted the annotated volume back and enclosed $20 for the Boston Public Library, whose book it was. It was not returned to Olson, and is now preserved in their Special Collections Library.

47. "I'm so delighted to have that book on the gulls. (Actually, I had known some of his results from a peel-off from it in a *Scientific American* a few years ago" (letter to Dorn, 31 August 1965). Olson had kept the issue of *Scientific American* 203 (December 1960) for Tinbergen's article "The Evolution of Behavior in Gulls," pp. 118–30.

48. Hoping Olson might review it for the first issue of *Pacific Nation*, Robin Blaser sent him Carl O. Sauer, *The Early Spanish Main* (Berkeley: University of California Press, 1966); Olson couldn't do a review, but kept the book. In the curious conjunction of names listed in this letter we have reference to Ammon Hennacy, *The Book of Ammon* (Salt Lake City, 1965), which Olson may have

heard of from Ed Dorn; he did not own it. Olson was aware of Charles Ives, if only from Jonathan Williams's review in *BMR* 5 of Henry and Sidney Cowell, *Charles Ives and His Music* (New York: Oxford University Press, 1955). Ives himself wrote *Essays Before a Sonata* (New York: Norton, 1916; reissued 1962), but Olson did not own it.

Olson retained three of Wallace Stevens's poetry volumes from Black Mountain College Library (see that listing). He later bought *The Necessary Angel* when it came out in Vintage paperback in 1965. "I don't of course believe at all what Stevens proposes, that the poems of heaven and of hell have been written, and it is the poem of Earth which now is ours to write" (letter to Frank Davey, not sent, at Storrs, dated 6 May [1966]).

Olson owned Isadora Duncan, *My Life* (Garden City: Garden City Publishing Co., 1927).

49. In this letter Olson speaks of reading a book of his son's, *Mountain Man*, presumably the children's book by Rutherford G. Montgomery (Cleveland: World Publishers, 1957), though this was not later found in Olson's library. Of Henry Nash Smith's *Virgin Land* (New York: Vintage, 1957), Olson admitted, in this letter, "I've never had my hands on it."

Around this time Olson bought James Duncan Phillips, *Salem in the Seventeenth Century* (Boston: Houghton Mifflin, 1933) and used it in a *Maximus* (*Guide*, p. 659), having previously used the Sawyer Free Library copy. The poem indicates he was using Perry Miller's *Orthodoxy in Massachusetts* (previously cited); there is a note in the volume: "read Sunday to Monday May 29th to 30th 1966."

50. "I wonder if he *does* know how much I enjoyed his novel last year in my motel in Buffalo? It was one of the *few* or about *unique* comforts I had"—letter to Zoe Brown 17 May 1966, regarding the first printing of extracts from the novel under the title "In Honeytown," as *Coyote's Journal* 3 (1965).

51. Similarly, the flyleaf of a duplicate copy of Graves's *The White Goddess* (New York: Vintage, 1960)—"bot. Berlin Wednesday December 28th (by porter)—& read at beginning Tuesday night January 3rd, 1967." Günter Grass gave a reading two nights after Olson's; possibly Olson bought his copy of *The Tin Drum* (New York: Crest, 1964) for the occasion.

It seems likely that while in Germany he acquired Rolf Krusche, ed., *Die Maya-Handschrift Codex Dresdensis* (Frankfurt am Main, 1962), in which he wrote a note in February 1967 (*Editing Maximus*, p. 65); and Richard Graul, *Grüenwalds Handzeichnungen* (Leipzig: Im Infed-Verlag, n.d.).

52. Butterick's *Guide* illustrates with a page facsimile Olson's heavy use of this book, and indicates (p. 704) that he read it with the assistance of his *Langenscheidt's Pocket-Dictionary of the English and German Languages*, 5th ed. (Berlin, 1956).

53. Also from Renate, the widow of Rainer Gerhardt, came Olson's sec-

ond copy of Turville-Petre's *Myths and Religion of the North* (cited previously), inscribed on 2 January 1967; Arthur Brown and Peter Foote, eds., *Early English and Norse Studies Presented to Hugh Smith in Honour of his Sixtieth Birthday* (London: Metheun, 1963)—flyleaf: "rec'vd fr Renate Gerhardt via Creeley Friday night Jan 13th 1967"; and P. H. Sawyer, *The Age of the Vikings* (London: Edward Arnold, 1962)—flyleaf: "fr Renate, February 20th (1967)—London & begun to read same night."

54. Johannes Brøndsted, *The Vikings* (Harmondsworth: Penguin, 1960) was acknowledged in a letter to Tom Raworth on 4 January 1967: "A dull book in fact. Too bad." Olson tore out and retained the few pages that interested him—including pp. 195–96, used in a *Maximus* (*Guide*, p. 750).

Olson owned Tom Raworth's *The Big Green Day* (London: Trigram Press, 1968) and *Relationship* (London: Goliard, 1969), and a broadside, *Continuation*.

55. Among many notes in his copy of *The Concise Oxford Dictionary of Current English*, 4th ed., eds. H. W. and F. G. Fowler, revised by E. McIntosh (Oxford: Clarendon Press, 1954). We also find in Olson's library *The Pocket Oxford Dictionary of Current English*, 4th ed. (Oxford, 1965).

56. Paul Kenyon and Donna Smith, "Death of a Poet," *North Shore '70* (24 January 1970): 5. Since the back packs were not catalogued separately, the list is a conjecture as to the contents. Others that might well have been acquired in England are:

Edward Atiyah, *The Arabs* (Harmondsworth: Penguin, 1955).
John Boardman, *The Greeks Overseas* (Harmondsworth: Penguin, 1964).
Dora Broome, *Fairy Tales from the Isle of Man* (Harmondsworth: Penguin Puffin Story Books, 1951).
Alistair MacLean, *Night Without End* (London: Fontana, 1959).
Edward Lucie-Smith, ed., *The Penguin Book of Elizabethan Verse* (Harmondsworth: Penguin, 1965).
A. E. Trueman, *Geology and Scenery in England and Wales* (Harmondsworth: Penguin, 1961).
T. B. L. Webster, *Greek Terracottas* (Harmondsworth: King Penguin, 1950).

57. Olson picked up the Great Britain Ordnance Survey Catalogue for 1967, and acquired their *Map of Roman Britain* (1956) and *Map of Britain in the Dark Ages* (2d ed. 1966). The Esso Road Map of Ireland and Esso Map of France suggest other roads not taken. We do not know if he used *Cruising Guide: River Thames from Richmond to Lechlade* (Esso Ltd.). In September 1966 he had been given J. Pringle and T. Neville George, *British Regional Geology: South Wales*, 2d ed. (London: HMSO, 1964), which he kept.

58. Dorn had prepared him earlier with the gift of C. F. C. Hawkes and M. R. Hull, *Camulodunum: First Report on the Excavations at Colchester 1930–1939*

(Oxford University Press for The Society of Antiquaries of London, 1947). Olson prepared himself with the Ordnance Survey, *Colchester Area* (1961), and presumably picked up at the site *Camulodunum and the Temple of Claudius* (Colchester Museum & Muniment Committee, 1966).

It is not at the present time clear what poets sought him out. Perhaps Andrew Crozier brought him the newly published Sam Abrams *Barbara* from his Ferry Press 1966. Perhaps Michael Horovitz brought his *Poetry for the People* (London: Latimer Press, 1966). Olson also had later from him his *Bank Holiday* from the same press (1967). Perhaps Elaine Feinstein brought him her *For the Baiting* (London: Goliard, 1966). Perhaps he saw Nathaniel Tarn, who had sent his *Old Savage/Young City* (London: Cape, 1964) inscribed 7 July 1965.

59. Olson armed himself for the expedition with the Esso, *Map of South and West England*, the Bartholomew 1/2" *Map of Dorset*, and Ordnance Survey *Map of Dorchester* and *Weymouth Harbour*. He also acquired in Dorchester:

*Dorchester, Dorset: Official Guide* (Dorchester: Friary Press, n.d.).

*The Dorset County Museum* (Dorchester: The Dorset Natural History & Archaeological Society, n.d.).

Barbara Kerr, *Dorset Cottages* (Dorchester: Dorset Natural History & Archaeological Society, 1963).

V. L. Oliver, *Tudor Buildings in Weymouth*—an address given on 14 December 1938.

G. M. Robertson, *More Dorset Walks (With a Car)* (Sherborne, Dorset: Abbey Press, 1966).

*Short Notes on the Roman House, Colliton Park, Dorchester* (Dorchester: Dorset Natural History & Archaeological Society and the Dorset County Council, n.d.).

J. M. C. Toynbee, *The Christian Roman Mosaic, Hinton St. Mary, Dorset* (Dorchester: Dorset Natural History & Archaeological Society, 1964).

Notes indicate that Olson had with him in Dorchester T. S. Willan, ed., *A Tudor Book of Rates* (Manchester University Press, 1962). A clipping found in Olson's papers refers to a neighboring part of England: Victor Bonham-Carter, "What Is the Future of Exmoor?," *The Sphere* (15 March 1938): 431–33.

60. Olson was not strong on Hardy owning only *The Return of the Native* (London: Macmillan's Pocket Hardy, 1923) and *Far From the Madding Crowd* (London: Macmillan; New York: St. Martin's Press, 1965). In his last days in Connecticut, Olson was reminded of Thomas Hardy's landscape, and he recited at dinner table Hardy's poem "Going and Staying."

61. Besides *Company of Heroes*, he had the following, all from William Morrow, N.Y.:

*Ark of Empire: The American Frontier, 1784–1803* (1965);
*Disinherited: The Lost Birthright of the American Indian* (1966);
*The Final Challenge: The American Frontier, 1804–1845* (1966);
*Forth to the Wilderness: The First American Frontier, 1754–1774* (1965).

Olson purchased about this time, too, Alden T. Vaughan, *New England Frontier: Puritans and Indians 1620–1675* (Boston: Little, Brown, 1965)—with a rather disparaging note on the flyleaf; John F. A. Taylor, *Masks of Society: An Inquiry into the Covenants of Civilization* (New York: Appleton-Century-Crofts, 1966); and Marie Svoboda, *Plants That the American Indians Used* (Chicago: Field Museum of Natural History Museum Storybook, 1967).

62. Chad Walsh, "The Sound of Poetry in the Age of McLuhan," *Washington Post Book World* (15 October 1967): 6. Walsh sent Olson copies of the *Beloit Poetry Journal* (Olson kept five issues), and his own book, *End of Nature* (Chicago: Swallow, 1969).

63. This book was called to Olson's attention by Robert Gorham Davis's review in the *New York Times* (3 September 1967) of Allegra Stewart, *Gertrude Stein and the Present* (Cambridge: Harvard University Press, 1967), a book for which he wrote to the publishers. He received an invoice, but perhaps not the book—it was not in his library later. He quotes from the review in his lecture at Cortland (*Muthologos* 2, pp. 3–4). He also had in his library Gertrude Stein's *Four in America* (New Haven: Yale University Press, 1947)—"Ex Libris The Metcalfs"; in Paul Metcalf's possession until at least February 1957.

64. It appears that Olson had received a typescript of Creeley's introduction to Louis Zukofsky's *"A" 1–12* (Garden City: Doubleday, 1967). Olson did not have this volume, nor Zukofsky's collected Catullus translations.

65. Olson's copy of Pierre Teilhard de Chardin's *The Phenomenon of Man* (New York: Harper Torchbook, 1961) was presented to him by Tom McDonnell on 27 September 1961.

Olson told Charles Boer (p. 84) that Ungaretti "stole the show" at the International Poetry Festival, Queen Elizabeth Hall, London, 12 July 1967. Olson owned his *A Portir du Désert: Journal de Voyage* (Paris: Editions du Seuil, 1965). Olson had asked Grolier Bookshop for Patrick Kavanagh's "whole output" on 6 October 1967. He ended up with *Tarry Flynn* (New York: Devin-Adair, 1949), *Self Portrait* (Dublin: Dolmen Press, 1964), and *Collected Poems* (New York: Devin-Adair, 1964).

66. Donald Sutherland inscribed a copy of his *The Bacchae of Euripides* (Lincoln: University of Nebraska Press, 1968) to Olson on publication.

67. Olson owned and read Fred Hoyle, "Speculations on Stonehenge," *Antiquity* 40 (December 1966): 262–76. He also had Hoyle's *The Nature of the Universe* (New York: New American Library Mentor Book, 1960).

68. Subsequent presentation volumes from Ed Dorn were: *Our Word:*

*Guerilla Poems from Latin America* with Gordon Brotherson (London: Cape Go-
liard, 1968); *Gunslinger Book I* (Black Sparrow Press, 1968)—apparently an ad-
vance copy, received 11 November 1967: *Gunslinger Book II* (Black Sparrow
Press, 1969)—a signed copy dated 14 June 1969 San Cristobal; and *Twenty-four
Love Songs* (San Francisco: Frontier Press 1969), presumably from the publisher.

69. A note by George Butterick at Storrs indicates that this bound volume
was purchased originally through Jean Kaiser on 22 February 1966 along with
a bound volume of the *Gloucester Daily Times* for 1889, and possibly also a
bound volume of *Cape Ann Weekly Advertiser* 1878–1879.

70. Olson must have acquired a copy of H. W. Parke, *The Oracles of Zeus:
Dodona, Olympia, Ammon* (Cambridge: Harvard University Press, 1967) about
this time; Butterick, visiting Gloucester in June 1968, saw Olson's written notes
in the volume. It was not in his library later, however.

71. There is a note dated 19 December 1967 in the copy of *Black Elk Speaks:
Being the Life Story of a Holy Man of the Oglala Sioux* as told through John G.
Neihardt (Lincoln: University of Nebraska Press Bison Book, 1961) in Olson's
library, presumably the one taken from Harvey Brown, for a letter to Grolier
Bookshop 8 January 1968 tells Gordon Cairnie to send a replacement direct to
Harvey Brown.

72. According to the *Guide*, p. 710, it was Brian Shore, son of Mary Shore,
who gave Olson pages torn from *National Fisherman combined with Maine Coast
Fisherman* (August 1966) containing John Gardner's "New Theory Offered On
Beothuk Canoe Origin," pp. 8A and 31A, in which a further article on the sub-
ject was referred to: E. F. Greenman's "The Upper Palaeolithic and the New
World," *Current Anthropology* 4 (February 1963): 41–66. On request, George
Butterick sent a xerox of this latter article, in which Olson saw a reference to "a
woman in Gloucester" by Frank Speck, and wrote it into a *Maximus* poem.·
Butterick also notes (Storrs manuscript) that he sent a xerox of Speck's *Beothuk
and Micmac* (New York: Museum of the American Indian, Heye Foundation,
1922), which Olson read and marked.

73. A note on the copyright page: "I received 32 (& 31) from him after
January 7th 1968." The collection at Storrs contains the typescript of "Passages
32," heavily annotated by Olson.

Besides the volumes listed under Oyez Press and elsewhere, Olson had
the following Duncan items:

*Fragments of a Disordered Devotion* (San Francisco: privately published,
1952)—one of 50 copies, not for sale.
*The Song of the Border-Guard* (Black Mountain College Graphics Workshop,
1952)—Olson organized the printing of this broadside; not in his library
later.

*Faust Foutu* (1953, previously cited) and (Stinson Beach: Enkidu Surrogate, 1959)

*Opening of the Field* (New York: Grove Press, 1960)—letter to Duncan 10 March 1961: "I think yr book (Opening of the Field) is so beautiful and I haven't *yet* got beyond *one poem* I read St. Valentine's Day, the wondrous big steady song in Capitals (in sixers, and a wondrous couplet burden?) I read it to Gerrit in his kitch while he and Bet were making supper and was still going on abt it last night at Brandeis"; the volume is missing from Olson's library.

*From The Mabinogion*, reprint of the printing in *Quarterly Review of Literature* 12 (1963).

*Writing Writing* (Albuquerque: Sumbooks 1964)

*Roots and Branches* (New York: Scribner, 1964)

Olson also received as a gift *The Dioskuroi*, a reprint of the collages Jess Collins published in the Fall 1963 edition of *Northwest Review*.

74. Olson possibly also acquired at this time his copy of Nilsson's *The Mycenaean Origin of Greek Mythology* (New York: The Norton Library, 1963)—notes and markings throughout.

75. The review was not printed. Olson retained the issue of *Harper's*, and did not acquire the novel, *Armies of the Night*, which it became, though he refers to the novel later (*Muthologos* 2, p. 72): "we were talking last night about that new novel of Mailer's. It's like Dunkie the Fairy, suddenly—like Mailer the All-American Male—suddenly both these stand forth like American men. It's as beautiful as that."

Olson spoke to Charles Boer about Norman Mailer's article "Fire on the Moon" in *Life* (29 August and 14 November 1969), which Olson said "were not only the finest things Mailer ever wrote, but the prose itself was of a new order—talking of devils and gods and with a cosmological awe" (Boer, p. 46). In the spring of 1968, Harvey Brown gave Olson Clancy Sigal's *Going Away* (Boston: Houghton, Mifflin, 1962), which he kept.

## 19. Terrestrial Paradise

1. Review cited previously. There seems to be no doubt that Olson would have received the issue of *Prospect* edited by Jeremy Prynne, issue 6 (Spring 1964), which included a *Maximus* poem, as well as poems by Prynne, Crozier, Dorn, Creeley and others; but it did not remain in his library. Neither did Prynne's own books published while Olson was alive: *Kitchen Poems* (London: Cape Goliard, 1968) and *Aristeas* (London: Ferry Press, 1968).

Late books by English poets that are found in Olson's library are: Jeff Nuttall, *Love Poems* and Bill Butler, *White Skin*, published in Brighton by Unicorm Press, 1969 and 1968 respectively.

2. A letter of 4 November 1967 to Gordon Cairnie requests the following, none of which were obtainable:

George Calder, *Auraicept na n-esces: The Scholars' Primer, Being the texts of the Ogham tract from the Book of Ballymote* (Edinburgh: J. Grant, 1917).

R.A. S. Macalister, *The Secret Languages of Ireland* (Cambridge University Press, 1937) and his *Tara: A Pagan Sanctuary of Ancient Ireland* (New York: Scribner, 1931).

Thomas F. O'Rahilly, *Early Irish History and Mythology* (Dublin Institute for Advanced Studies, 1946).

Books that he managed to get in this area were:

Myles Dillon and Nora K. Chadwick, *The Celtic Realms* (New York: New American Library, 1967).

Joseph McGarrity, *Celtic Moods and Memories* (New York: Devin-Adair, 1942)—perhaps acquired early.

Richard Murphy, *The Last Galway Hooker* (Dublin: Dolmen Press, 1962).

Brian O'Cuiv, *Literary Creation and Irish Historical Tradition* reprinted from Proceedings of the British Academy, vol. 49 (London: Oxford University Press, 1963).

Diarmuid Russell, ed., *The Portable Irish Reader* (New York: Viking Press, 1960).

3. Flyleaf of the presentation copy: "The first copy to Charles who placed me *beside* Melville too. With gratitude and love, Ann Charters 1/6/69." Charters also gave Olson her *Melville in the Berkshires* (Brooklyn, 1969), and a copy of Jack Kerouac's *Book of Dreams* (San Francisco: City Lights, 1966).

4. "On Black Mountain (II)" *OLSON* 8, p. 73; Olson reads the Dorn passage for the NET film (*Muthologos* 1, p. 175). David Ossman sent his *The Sullen Art* (New York: Corinth, 1963) inscribed "for Charles Olson regretting that we have not met or talked . . . 4/8/63." In January 1967 Ossman sent Olson his *The Crescent Journals* (1966).

5. Gerard Malanga brought a book gift, possibly Madeline Gins, *Word Rain: or, A Discursive Introduction to the Intimate Philosophical Investigation of GRETA GARBO It Says* (New York: Grossman, 1969).

The conflations and inaccuracies of transcription in the published "The Art of Poetry XII—Charles Olson," *Paris Review* 49 (Summer 1970): 176–205 made the recently deceased poet turn over in his grave. (Compare *"Paris Review* Interview," *Muthologos* 2, pp. 105–53.)

6. Olson's copy of *Numbers* (Stuttgart, 1968), inscribed by Creeley, is in private hands (*Muthologos* 2, p. 193).

7. The last of Olson's Jung purchases, *Memories, Dreams, Reflections*, ed. Aniela Jaffé (New York: Vintage, 1965), was "bought in California, either Sunday in Carmel Valley or Monday in Santa Cruz(?) on trip to Carmel one week after end of Berkeley Poetry conference summer 1965" (flyleaf).

8. *Guide*, pp. 570–72. Olson was using his copy of Otto Rank, *The Myth of the Birth of the Hero and Other Writings*, ed. Philip Freund (New York: Vintage, 1959). He had also borrowed for a period from Mary Shore (and returned) her copy of Rank's *Art and Artist* (New York: Tudor, 1932)—Olson's notes on pp. 59, 379, 382–83, 391.

Olson owned no Reich, but he seems to be referring in *Muthologos* 2, p. 113 to *Character Analysis* (1933). He paid an elegiac tribute to Reich in a letter to the *Gloucester Times*, 29 January 1969; and in a letter to Jerry Suls on 20 October 1968 stated: "how more *valuable* every day the life of Wilhelm Reich strikes one."

9. *Muthologos* 2, p. 115. Oppen reviewed Olson in *Poetry* (August 1962), and Olson wrote to William Bronk about it 21 December 1962: "I do know Oppen, and though some of my friends thought his review of *The Distances* . . . was the old Business of measuring me by Pound, and I thought myself he raced his motor on *Maximus from Dogtown*, I thought his picking 'The Satyrs' for a voice which was peculiarly my own, true enough. (I haven't yet seen his poems at all . . ." (quoted in *Guide*, pp. 495–96). Olson had been roused by Oppen's article, "The Mind's Own Place," *Kulchur* 10 (Summer 1963): 2–8 (Guide, pp. 494–95). Oppen's *This in Which* (New York: New Directions, 1965) was "sent for review," though there is no evidence Olson had undertaken to do such a thing.

10. Presumably this indicates his Folger Library General Reader's Shakespeare, *Henry IV Part I* (New York: Washington Square Press, 1961).

11. Amended and enlarged ed. (New York: Farrar, Straus, and Giroux, 1966). The salmon motif also has its source for Olson in Jessie L. Weston *From Ritual to Romance* (Garden City: Doubleday Anchor, 1957)—flyleaf: "purchased P.Town Sat Aug 2, 1958; read P-Town Mon & Tues Aug 4 & 5th, 1958"; notes and markings throughout, including on p. 135 the note, "Maximus is a Fisher Man." (See *Guide*, p. 576.)

12. The clipping of this anonymous piece is with the Barry Hall letters at Simon Fraser University Library. Apparently Olson did not have access to a copy of Alfred Wegener, *The Origin of Continents and Oceans* (London: Methuen, 1924). He had been introduced to J. Tuzo Wilson's work by being given a xerox by Dan McLeod in Vancouver of Wilson's "Cabot Fault: An Appalachian Equivalent of the San Andreas and Great Glen Faults and Some Implications

for Continental Displacement," *Nature* 195 (14 July 1962): 135–38; and then noticed Wilson's "Continental Drift" in an issue he owned of *Scientific American* (previously cited).

13. *Guide*, pp. 686–88. Olson owned Otto Jespersen, *Growth and Structure of the English Language* (Garden City: Doubleday Anchor, 1956)—title page: "Olson feb 1/58," and Eva Matthews Sanford, *The Mediterranean World in Ancient Times* (New York: Ronald Press, 1938)—dated on p. 67: "21 Jan 1962."

14. There is no sign that Olson had Eliade's *Yoga*, or turned to Norman Cohn, *The Pursuit of the Millennium* (New York: Oxford University Press, 1957). The Scholem and Guthrie were returned to Lansing; the Sabatino Moscati, *The Face of the Ancient Orient* (New York: Doubleday, 1962), was not. The Garma C. C. Chang, *Teachings of Tibetan Yoga* (New Hyde Park: University Books, 1963) in Olson's library was presumably Lansing's; likewise, his Vergilius Ferm, ed., *Ancient Religions* (New York: Philosophical Library, 1950)—"originally published as *Forgotten Religions*"—which he had been using since 1963. Lansing's note also mentions that Olson has a "Nerval" volume; it has not at present been identified.

15. *Guide*, pp. 718–20. Olson's James Phinney Baxter, ed., *The Trelawny Papers*, Documentary History of the State of Maine, vol. 3 (Portland: Maine Historical Society, 1884) was a gift from a student at Black Mountain—flyleaf: "Olson fr John Grady 1954–5," with added comment: "most obliged (1960!")"; notes and markings throughout. John Pike Grady in later years became the publisher and editor of the Border History Fathom Series, and sent Olson no. 1: C. Donald Brown, *Eastport: A Maritime History* (1968), a reprint from *The American Neptune* 27 (1968)—"For Charles—this is just a wee craft, but with a Fast Wind who can say what may follow in her wake, with all best wishes—John." Grady is on record as having given Olson several gift volumes, including (not noted elsewhere): H. D. F. Kitto, *The Greeks* (Harmondsworth: Penguin, 1951); Alfred Korzybski, *Manhood of Humanity: The Science and Art of Human Engineering* (New York: Dutton, 1921); C. G. Jung, *Two Essays on Analytical Psychology* (New York: Meridian, 1956); Simone Weil, *The Iliad; or, The Poem of Force*, Political Pamphlet no. 1 (Wallingford: Pendle Hill, 1956); *The Catholic Historical Review* 21 (April 1935)—Olson had notes and markings in William Stetson Merrill's article, "The Vinland Problem Through Four Centuries," pp. 21–48; and *Atlantic Monthly* 170 (August 1962)—MacKinley Helm's article, "Angel Mo' Had Her Son: Roland Hayes," pp. 3–10 was used in an unpublished *Maximus* poem.

16. Carl O. Sauer, *Northern Mists* (Berkeley: University of California Press, 1968)—flyleaf: "acquired July—26th, 1968: as a present (from Don Allen? Shipped direct, with bill of lading (enclosed showing a publisher's discount: read, 1st (starting with the Greenlanders' Saga) Sunday July 28th"; notes and

markings throughout. In a letter to Gordon Cairnie of Grolier Bookshop on 29 June 1968 he had asked for it to be ordered "air mail *both ways*"; apparently this, or a second discarded copy, was acquired from Grolier.

17. *Guide*, pp. 720–26. Olson may also have referred to his two other books by Nasr, *Three Muslim Sages: Avicenna—Suhrawardi—Ibn 'Arabi* (Cambridge: Harvard University Press, 1964), and *An Introduction to Islamic Cosmological Doctrines* (Cambridge: Harvard University Press, 1964)—flyleaf: "Given to me by Harvey Saturday night February 25th 1967 10 Hanover Terrace London (after having loaned it to me since his arrival January 25th, approximately."

18. Olson spent time at the Lane show at De Cordova Museum, Lincoln, Massachusetts on 15 and 17 April 1966; the catalogue he acquired, *Fitz Hugh Lane: the First Major Exhibition* (1966) is extensively marked. At an unknown date, Olson picked up another brochure from the De Cordova Museum, *A Decade in Review: Painting-Sculpture, England-France-Italy-U.S.*

At a previous Lane exhibition at the Boston Museum of Fine Arts, Olson had picked up and annotated the catalogue, *Fitz Hugh Lane* (1956) edited by Richard B. K. McLanathan, who also edited another catalogue Olson owned, *Ship Models* (Boston: Museum of Fine Arts, 1957).

19. Olson also had Samuel Gottscho, *A Pocket Guide to Wild Flowers* (New York: Pocket Books, 1951), and Herbert S. Zim and Alexander C. Martin's Golden Nature Guide, *Flowers: A Guide to Familiar American Wildflowers* (New York: Golden Press, 1962). In the Golden Nature Guide series, he also had Herbert S. Zim and Robert H. Baker, *Stars: A Guide to the Constellations, Sun, Moon, Planets, and Other Features of the Heavens* (New York: Simon & Schuster, 1956).

20. This letter exists at Storrs, which suggests that it was never sent. Olson did not live to see the proposed volume published as the "350th Anniversary Edition" of John J. Babson, *History of the Town of Gloucester* (Peter Smith, 1972), with an introduction and a "Historical Review since 1860" by Joseph E. Garland, who does not mention Olson in the edition and, moreover, talks about "the rich economic nourishment offered by Route 128" (p. xxxxvii).

Peter Smith Publishers is a reprint house in Gloucester, of some note. Peter Smith passed on to Olson an M.A. thesis written about him at Florida State University, Frances Ohmes, *Scarce and Desirable* (June 1961). Olson had from him *The Diary of William Bentley* (previously cited), Anne Bradstreet, *Works* (1962), *The Fugitive* (bound collection, 1967), and Theodore Spencer, *A Garland for John Donne: 1631–1931* (1958).

21. Olson owned an inscribed copy of Garland's *That Great Pattillo* (Boston: Little, Brown, 1966); also Garland's *Lone Voyager* (Boston: Little, Brown, 1963). He did not live to see the finished *Eastern Point* (Peterborough: Noone

House, 1971), or *Boston's North Shore: Being an Account of Life among the Note-worthy, Fashionable, Wealthy, Eccentric and Ordinary 1823–1890.*

22. Charles Edward Mann, *In the Heart of Cape Ann* (1906, previously cited) was heavily marked from repeated use—flyleaf: "Olson—given to me by Jean 1957/8—3 yrs ago (as I now write)." Some of the notes are dated 20 November 1960. Olson adds in 1968: "—now *8 years* ago."

23. In a letter of 4 December 1968 to Richard Grossinger, Olson recommends plate 14, "The Zodiacal Giants of Somerset," adding that Michell included the map in an article in *International Times* (London) "just about a year ago." (Olson received and kept *IT*, nos. 43, 46, and 67.) Olson acquired a second book by John Michell, *The View Over Atlantis* (London: Sago Press, 1969).

24. Olson apparently wrote to Rosenthal, and received from him his *The New Poets: American and British Poetry Since World War II* (New York: Oxford University Press Galaxy Book, 1967), *100 Postwar Poems* (New York: Macmillan, 1968), and *William Carlos Williams Reader* (New York: New Directions, 1966).

25. *Additional Prose*, p. 78. Charles Doria's translation of the Paros Chronicles with an introduction by Charles Olson was announced by Frontier Press in 1965, but was not published. Dated 9 December 1963, Olson wrote an introductory note to "A Bibliography on the State of Knowledge for Charles Doria," was entitled "The Advantage of Literacy Is That Words Can Be On The Page." It was published in *Coyote's Journal* 1 (1964) and reprinted in *Additional Prose*, pp. 50–51. The "Bibliography" itself—if done—has not been made available. Nothing of Richard Grossinger's, except for some of the *Io* magazines he edited, was found in Olson's library.

26. Olson's library contained a second copy of *Fisheries of Cape Ann*, formerly belonging to Otis Riggs, Jr. (name on flyleaf). He acquired around this time W. Raymond McClure, *They That Go Down to the Sea in Ships* (privately printed, 1968).

27. Descendents of Epes Sargent of Gloucester include John Singer Sargent, the artist, and Charles Sprague Sargent, who produced the 14 volumes, *The Silva of North America* (1893–1902), mentioned in the *Maximus* poems (*Guide*, p. 691).

28. This volume of poems is dedicated to Olson, using a phrase from a letter of 31 October 1960 to the author, which letter indicates that Olson has read Hollo's poems in *Satis* (issues 1–5 are found in Olson's library), where he also read Matthew Mead, " . . . Alun Lewis, Poet," *Satis* 1 (Autumn 1960): 15–24, from which he writes a poem (*Collected Poems*, p. 525). Olson's library contained two other poetry volumes by Anselm Hollo: *Buffalo-Isle of Wight Power Cable* (State University of New York at Buffalo, 1967), and *3* (Toronto, 1967).

29. Boer, p. 85. James Laughlin also sent, at Olson's request, Pound's

*Thrones 96–109 de los Cantares* (New York: New Directions, 1959), "the one missing piece of the Cantos I don't have" (letter, 26 July 1969).

30. Within the year, Robert Kelly was able to send Olson *Finding the Measure* (Black Sparrow, 1968), *The Common Shore* (Black Sparrow, 1969), and *The Well Wherein a Deer's Head Bleeds* (Black Sparrow, 1968).

31. Olson owned only one of Frank O'Hara's books, *Meditation in an Emergency* (New York: Grove Press, 1957), but spoke of him with affection. Olson's statement was eventually printed in Berkson's magazine *Big Sky* 11/12 (1978).

32. Olson went deeply into the Santorin question—on p. 30, he writes: "2 AM of Thurs Jl 24th 1969 just struck." He keeps on through the book, and on the night of 10 September 1969 makes a telephone call to Mavor about certain details. Olson's interest in Atlantis goes back a long way to an early reading of H. Rider Haggard's *She*, though he did not keep the book; to Ignatius Donnelly's *Atlantis: The Antediluvian World* (1st published 1882), though again he did not hang on to the book. He owned James Churchward, *The Lost Continent of Mu* (New York: Ives Washburn, 1931)—notes on it are found in a journal of 1939. All these are mentioned in the bibliography of *Mayan Letters* (*Selected Writings*, p. 129). A book which sites the volcanic explosion in Heligoland caught Olson's eye; we find in his library Jurgen Spanuth *Atlantis—The Mystery Unravelled* (New York: Citadel, 1956).

33. Not in Olson's library. The title came up in a conversation with John R. Butterick on 31 December 1968, and Olson said he had read it in the Boston Athenaeum. Thorpe Feidt bought R. Gordon Wasson's *Soma: Divine Mushroom of Immortality* (New York: Harcourt, Brace, 1968) for Olson on 13 July 1969.

34. He did not own this volume, but one illustration of an Algonquin mother and child in limestone so impressed Olson that the next time he was in Cambridge he arranged for the Peabody Museum to make him a plaster cast of it (*OLSON* 1 pp. 38–39; *Muthologos* 2, p. 201). Olson picked up around this time a pamphlet by Leo Bonfanti, *Biographies and Legends of the New England Indians* (Wakefield: Bonnell Publishing Co., 1968).

35. The books mentioned were Geoffrey Ashe, *Land to the West* (London: Collins, 1962), Rhys Carpenter, *Discontinuity in Greek Civilization* (Cambridge University Press; Norton Library, 1968), and Ezra Asher Cook, *Secret Societies Illustrated* (Chicago, 1887). These books of course did not form part of his Gloucester library; they were presumably Boer's. One book of Boer's is found in Olson's books, Boer's own verse *The Odes* (Chicago: Swallow, 1969), a presentation copy.

36. *Last Lectures* as heard by John Cech, Oliver Ford, and Peter Rittner (Iowa City: The Windhover Press, 1974), pp. 4 and 6. Olson acquired a copy of Louis E. Roy, *Quaboag Plantation alias Brookefield* (West Brookfield, Mass.: by the

author, 1965)—flyleaf: "Sunday November 2nd 1969," with two bibliographical items written inside the front cover: John W. DeForest, *History of the Indians of Connecticut from the Earliest Known Period to 1850* (Hartford, 1851), and Levi Badger Chase, *The Bay Path and Along the Way* (Norwood, Mass: by the author, 1919). He probably hunted for these in local bookshops; he found Roger N. Parks, *Roads and Travel in New England, 1790–1840* (Sturbridge, Mass.: Old Sturbridge Village, 1967). He was working the Connecticut border of Massachusetts down. In the Olson Collection at Storrs there is John Milton Niles, *The Connecticut Civil Officer*, 3 vols. (Hartford: Huntington & Hopkins, 1823).

37. "Clarke's list" of Olson's library includes Leo Tolstoy, *The Death of Ivan Ilyitch and Other Stories* (New York: Modern Library, n.d.)

38. Facsimiles, transcriptions, and notes, edited by George F. Butterick for *OLSON* 3 (Spring 1975): 64–92, the whole reprinted in Charles Stein, *The Secret of the Black Chrysanthemum* (Barrytown: Station Hill Press, 1987) as Appendix 1.

# Index

Ralph Maud was born in Yorkshire, England. He received his A.B. degree from Harvard College in 1953, and his Ph.D. degree from Harvard University in 1958. His seven years of teaching at Buffalo culminated in Dylan Thomas's *Notebooks* (New Directions), edited from the manuscripts in the Poetry Room of the University. He met the Gloucester poet Charles Olson when they were colleagues at SUNY at Buffalo. He has taught Olson's *Selected Writings* consistently in classes at Simon Fraser University during his thirty-year career in Vancouver, B.C. He is now emeritus professor of English and associate of the Institute for the Humanities, Simon Fraser University. His immediate project is an edition of *The Selected Letters of Charles Olson* for the University of California Press.